EXCAVATING THE MIND

EXCAVATING THE MIND

Cross-sections through culture, cognition and materiality

Edited by Niels Johannsen, Mads D. Jessen
& Helle Juel Jensen

Aarhus University Press

Excavating the Mind

Cover design and type setting: Grafisk SIGNS
Type: Arno Pro
Printed by Narayana Press, Gylling
Printed in Denmark 2012

ISBN 978 87 7934 217 0

Aarhus University Press
Langelandsgade 177
DK-8200 Aarhus N
www.unipress.dk

International distributors:
Gazelle Book Services Ltd.
White Cross Mills
Hightown, Lancaster, LA1 4XS
United Kingdom

IS Distribution
70 Enterprise Drive
Bristol, CT 06010
USA

Published in collaboration with
The Jutland Archaeological Society

Published with financial support by
The Aarhus University Research Foundation
The Humanities Research Focus Area 'Cognition, Communication and Culture'
Queen Margrethe II's Archaeological Foundation

CONTENT

List of contributors 7

Editors' acknowledgements 9

Introduction 11
Mads D. Jessen & Helle J. Jensen

Debating the mind

Imitation, Mirror Neurons and Material Culture 25
Svend Østergaard

Boxes or Creepers? Containments and entanglements of mind and matter 39
Tim Ingold

On Being More-Than-One and Doubts About Mind 57
Chris Gosden

Linear B as Distributed Cognition: Excavating a mind not limited by the skin 69
Lambros Malafouris

Cultural practice, material reference and the generation of meaning

Meaning in Miniature: Semiotic networks in material culture 87
Carl Knappett

Of God Stones and Dance Plazas: The material mediation of historical consciousness 111
Robert W. Preucel

The Hall and the Church during Christianization: Building ideologies and material concepts 133
Mads D. Jessen

In Small Things Remembered: Pottery decoration in Neolithic Southern Italy 161
John Robb & Kostalena Michelaki

Colourful Meaning: Terminology, abstraction and the Near Eastern Bronze Age 183
David A. Warburton

Agency, technology and society

Making Daggers and Scouting for Talents: Situated learning in Late Neolithic Scandinavia 211
Deborah Olausson

Decision-making and Structuration: A study of the minds behind private statues in New Kingdom Egyptian temples 233
Annette Kjølby

Combined Efforts: The cooperation and coordination of barrow-building in the Bronze Age 255
Mads Kähler Holst & Marianne Rasmussen

Literacy: A tool of modernity and community in Vanuatu 281
Janet Dixon Keller

Archaeology and the Inanimate Agency Proposition: a critique and a suggestion 305
Niels Johannsen

List of contributors

Chris Gosden
Institute of Archaeology
University of Oxford
Institute of Archaeology
36 Beaumont Street
Oxford, OX1 2PG
England, UK
chris.gosden@arch.ox.ac.uk

Mads K. Holst
Section for Archaeology
University of Aarhus, Moesgaard
Moesgaard Allé 20
DK-8270 Højbjerg
Denmark
mads.holst@hum.au.dk

Tim Ingold
Department of Anthropology
School of Social Science
University of Aberdeen
Aberdeen AB24 3QY
Scotland, UK
tim.ingold@abdn.ac.uk

Helle Juel Jensen
Section for Archaeology
University of Aarhus, Moesgaard
Moesgaard Allé 20
DK-8270 Højbjerg
Denmark
farkhjj@hum.au.dk

Mads D. Jessen
Department of Prehistory
National Museum of Denmark
Frederikholms Kanal 12,
DK-1220 København K
Denmark
mads.dengsoe.jessen@natmus.dk

Niels Johannsen
Section for Archaeology
& Velux Core Research Group
Technologies of the Mind
University of Aarhus
Building 1453
Jens Chr. Skous Vej 3
DK-8000 Aarhus C
Denmark
niels.johannsen@hum.au.dk

Janet D. Keller
Department of Anthropology
University of Illinois
607 S Mathews Ave.
M/C 148
Urbana, IL 61801
USA
jdkeller@illinois.edu

Annette Kjølby
Editorial Board
Samfundslitteratur, SL Publishers
Rosenørns Allé 9
DK-1970 Frederiksberg C
Denmark
ak@samfundslitteratur.dk

Carl Knappett
Art History
University of Toronto,
19 Russell Street,
Toronto, ON, M5S 2S2
Canada
carl.knappett@utoronto.ca

Lambros Malafouris
Keble College
University of Oxford
Oxford, OX1 3PG
England, UK
lambros.malafouris@keble.ox.ac.uk

Kostalena Michelaki
School of Human Evolution and Social Change
Arizona State University
P.O. Box 872402
Tempe, AZ 85287-2402
USA
kmichela@asu.edu

Deborah Olausson
Department of Archaeology and Ancient History
University of Lund
Sandgatan 1
Box 117, 221 00 Lund
Sweden
Deborah.Olausson@ark.lu.se

Robert W. Preucel
Department of Anthropology
University of Pennsylvania
3260 South Street Philadelphia,
PA 19104-6398
USA
rpreucel@sas.upenn.edu

Marianne Rasmussen
Department of Heritage
Danish Agency of Culture
H.C. Andersens Boulevard 2
DK-1553 København K
Denmark
marali@kulturarv.dk

John Robb
Department of Archaeology
University of Cambridge
Downing Street
Cambridge CB2 3DZ
England, UK
jer39@cam.ac.uk

David A. Warburton
Section for the Study of Religion
University of Aarhus
Building 1442
Tåsingegade 3
DK-8000 Aarhus C
Denmark
dw@teo.au.dk

Svend Østergaard
Center for Semiotics
University of Aarhus
Building 1467
Jens Chr. Skous Vej 7
DK-8000 Aarhus C
Denmark
semsvend@hum.au.dk

Editors' acknowledgements

This book has been in the making for a very long time. The process towards its publication started with the symposium *Excavating the Mind: cross-sections through culture, cognition and materiality*, organized by the Department of Prehistoric Archaeology in cooperation with the Centre for Cultural Research at the University of Aarhus in October 2004. During 2005 we received contributions from most of the symposium speakers for the edited volume that we had decided to produce in continuation of the stimulating talks and discussions at the meeting. The contributions went through peer reviews and, after some delays in that process, we received the revised contributions from the authors in 2007 and early 2008. By late 2008 we had completed final content revisions of the individual chapters, but then several cases of serious illness in the editorial group and our families brought our work on the book to a halt. We are extremely grateful to Aarhus University Press and to the contributors of this volume for their immense patience as well as their encouragement as various deadlines slipped away.

The publication of this volume has been made possible by generous donations from the Aarhus University Research Foundation, the Humanities Research Focus Area 'Cognition, Communication and Culture', the Jutland Archaeological Society and Queen Margrethe II's Archaeological Foundation. The symposium in 2004 was sponsored by the Danish Research Council for the Humanities (SHF), Knud Højgaard's Foundation and the Niels Bohr Foundation.

Finally, there are several people whose support has been decisive for the completion of this book. In particular, we would like to thank Sanne Lind Hansen at Aarhus University Press, Jesper Laursen at the Jutland Archaeological Society, Ulla Rasmussen Billings at the Faculty of Arts, Aarhus, and not least the six reviewers who provided competent critique of individual chapters and thus aided their authors in forming and improving the arguments that constitute the contents of this book.

Introduction

Mads D. Jessen & Helle J. Jensen

Science has started to change its mind about the relationship between humans and the material world, and has begun to recognize material culture and technology as important factors in human mental life. This renewed interest in materiality and the mind has raised a series of central questions concerning their relation and dependency. What is the position of material culture in the construction of meaning? How does the existing material culture influence human development, learning and cooperation? Does the cultural environment form part of the human cognitive architecture? These are not just central topics in the growing debate concerned with such cross-sections through culture, cognition and materiality, but are highly relevant for the understanding of human ontology in general.

However, from an archaeological perspective, it is interesting to observe the growing interest in material culture in the academic world. In most branches of learning which study the intersection of human culture and cognition, the material world has usually been of secondary importance. With some notable exceptions to the mainstream, this secondary position has only recently started to be modified (Lave 1988; Merleau-Ponty 1945; Modée 2005).

Nevertheless, the study of material culture has always been the primary domain of archaeology, but the discipline has gone through considerable problems trying to define the significance of material culture for human ontology. This has at least two reasons: Firstly, the discipline itself does not have access to the empirical richness of specific thoughts and actions of individual agents, and this has made it difficult to come to terms with the details of human-artefact interactions. Secondly, the limited interest of neighbouring disciplines in the material domain has reduced the possibility of importing relevant theory into archaeology. These shortcomings can often find a rather straightforward remedy in the establishment of cross-disciplinary studies, and a more open-source attitude towards the sharing of information between different research traditions. A multidisciplinary approach will be especially fertile when it comes to such weighty and fundamental questions as the faculties of human (material) culture and human ontology – subject matters which cannot be embraced by any separate perspective. The different analysis and cross-disciplinary discussions presented in the book are therefore meant to provoke new ideas about mind and matter.

However, archaeology is not only in a position to receive theoretical input, it equally has something important to add to the debate. The uniquely diachronic perspective of archaeology may sometimes be able to supplement or even correct the account of human ontology that is derived from the more synchronic focus of other disciplines. Therefore, supplementing the prevailing research in cognitive studies, which tend to focus on modern, predominantly Western societies and individuals with studies of different cultural contexts and processes in the evolutionary and historical past as well as the ethnographic present, should give rise to a deeper insight into the long-term, recursive relationship between the material culture of humans and our mental worlds. Such processes as how cultural information is transferred from one generation to the next can only be explained through diachronic studies, and as the material side of many human activities persist for several centuries, the study of materiality generates a tangible and enduring platform for understanding the continuity as well as transformation of cultures.

Furthermore, the growing emphasis of material culture and of cognition in a range of subject matters now creates a favourable environment for the exchange of ideas between disciplines (see DeMarrais, Gosden & Renfrew 2004; Renfrew *et al.* 2009; Renfrew & Malafouris 2010; Renfrew & Zubrow 1994), which formerly had limited contact. Our initiative to this anthology is an attempt to contribute to this momentum, and further exchange between disciplines.

Taking a look at the titles of the papers presented in this volume, it is clear that the authors are inspired by research in a wide range of disciplines. These include at least anthropology, archaeology, cognitive science, philosophy, psychology, semiotics and the study of religion. But despite this diversity of inspiration, the articles also suggest a commonality of purpose. This commonality concerns the interest in developing integrative ideas about the interaction of human beings and their material surroundings. And it is linked to a general reorientation of the way in which the human mind is conceived in a number of disciplines. To put it simply, this is the recognition that we can no longer claim to be studying the human being as an organic computer or a Cartesian subject. On the contrary, the importance and complexity of cross-sections through culture, cognition and materiality are becoming increasingly clear. In other words, it is no longer sustainable for disciplines concerned with human beings to study one without the others. Furthermore, it carries the implication that the traditional distinction between idiographic and nomothetic approaches must be moderated, because the relationship between the specific and the general constitutes one of the main questions.

Another and related way in which the study of mind and matter cross-cuts traditional boundaries has to do with its wide chronological relevance. The exploration of certain important questions concerning the future of humankind may require us to study not only the present, but also the past. Considering the speed with which modern societies change their material culture, one cannot help wondering what will happen to the human mind in the coming decades and centuries. Is there a limit to the degree of complexity we can handle in our interactions with the material world, or can we keep on pushing the boundaries? In other words, is there a finite maximum capacity of the human mind – are we going to hit the ceiling? Perhaps there can be no *pre factum* answers to such questions, but the study of long term developments in the history of human thought may at least point us in the right direction.

For these reasons, it seems that a point has been reached, at which our attempts to come to terms with our own materiality are changing fundamentally. All of the authors of *Excavating the Mind* – in one way or another – contribute to the growing multidisciplinary debate on the uniquely human entanglement of complex material cultures and mental worlds, and we believe that some of the potential that lies in the current situation is exposed in the following articles.

Setting up the cross-sections

The book has been organized into three sections each focusing on different cross-sections through culture, cognition and materiality. In each of these groups, the texts have an overall thematic commonality, or share a range of viewpoints and follow similar lines of argumentation. At the same time, the divisions are by no means mutually exclusive, and the contributions often expose the same layers as are investigated in the other sections.

Debating the mind

This first section takes up the fundamental problem of trying to define the mind. In doing so, the basic premises for describing the mind, and its relation to material culture, figures prominently. First and foremost, the writers contest the classical notion of the Cartesian mind, where mind is regarded as having a completely immaterial character. Instead, the mind is described as an inherently composite apparatus, which consist of an intricate interface between brain, body and socio-material environment. This standpoint leads to the direct acceptance of a distinct interdependency between concepts and practices, and the contemporary technological environment. The considerable interchange of knowledge taking place between technological domains and social domains, often creates a cultural situation where human thinking become distributed across several domains, which so-called ontological reasoning cannot keep separate. In effect, the writers advocate a distributed notion of the human mind, where the mind assimilates extra-somatic materials with constructs inside the human skull. Physical engagement with the (technological) world therefore seems to play centre stage when people enter into complex social formations such as economic exchange, the image of nature or the understanding of time and space, or even when unfolding the origin of cultural diversity itself. As a result of this standpoint it is consequently argued that the cognitive architecture behind the construction of multifaceted and complex cultural objects (and objects in general) is best understood as an amalgamation of individual and group-based actions, which originates in the physical interaction with the object under construction. Accordingly, the 'things' which are involved in human acting and thinking should not be regarded as decoupled objects which require special types of mental computations, but rather be understood as active components in the overall cognitive organization, just as much as the naked brain is an active element. For this reason, one of the main arguments in this section is that the particular type of material environment with which humans engage inevitably will influence the way we think, and the notion of mind thus cannot be secluded from the notion of materiality.

Svend Østergaard takes an evolutionary look at the preconditions for the human use and development of material culture. Inspired by neuro-cognitive studies of 'mirror-neurons' and by primate research by Michael Tomasello, Østergaard outlines a possible explanation behind the advance of meta-cognition, artefact use and symbolic representations. Central to his idea is the universal inclination for individuals and local groups to imitate each other. Because imitation is also a principal component in children's development, Østergaard regards imitation as a decisive factor in cultural learning *per se*. The neural grounding of such imitation might be presented by the function of mirror-neurons. In combination, imitation and mirror-neurons entail a local adaptation and streamlining of behavioural strategies and goals. Tools are, both with regards to production and function, intrinsically goal-oriented, and effective tools will, for that reason, be imitated within the local group. A side-effect is that each local group often equips its tools with particular symbolic expressions and therefore the dynamics of local imitation will generate a large scale emergent structure, i.e. cultural diversity.

Lambros Malafouris's examination of the Mycenaean Linear B tablets focuses on human cognitive architecture and how external materialities influences cognitive processes. He identifies the Linear B system as a cognitive artefact which forms part of a distributed system of Mycenaean thinking, in which internal as well as external components constitute the overall cognitive configuration. In doing so, Malafouris breaks down the classic division of brain, body and culture in favour of a notion on human thinking which essentially is an extended functional system integrating all three elements. For this reason, Linear B tablets can no longer be seen solely as inscribed abstract codes, but as engaged in a distributed cognitive system that unfolds in time and space, between human and material actors. By replacing the image of the isolated scribe who externalizes information on clay with that of a dynamically coupled network of agents that form a coalition and complement each other, the physical features of the Linear B tablets can be directly linked with human cognitive operations.

Chris Gosden follows a similar line of reasoning as he investigates the mutual dependency between abstract ideas and their expression in material culture. He advocates an understanding of the human involvement with material culture which underlines the non-isolatory nature of human tool-use and concept building. In essence, human thought is distributed over a variety of different media which include words, artefacts or particular types of behaviour. It is argued that even a complex concept such as time can be intimately related to and recognized in certain artefacts. Gosden uses the Iron Age Celtic torcs in Britain as point of reference for describing the relationship between mental and material entities. The torcs have an elaborate decoration and the ornamental elements tend to, over time, exhibit an accumulative and referential style, thus incorporating and mixing former elements with novel ones. This combinatory approach indicates that (former) times and (other) places where condensed into a single object, the torc, and that Iron Age Britain had an ambiguous conception of time with a multiplicity of possible readings.

Also **Tim Ingold** has explored the way in which different technologies interfere with our original way of conceptualizing the world. Ingold especially draws attention to how fundamental assumptions about mind and nature are grounded in the pervasive aspects of everyday life, and in this case movement and wayfaring. By exemplifying how the use of rigid footwear, the paving of roads and the introduction of vehicular transport have occasioned the nomination of the foot as deprived of any significant intellectual relevance for the perception of the environment, he parallels this development to the problematic conceptualization of the mind as being carried around in a container, the body, without any direct contact with the surrounding milieu. Instead Ingold promotes (i.e. moves forward) an understanding of mind and matter which emphasizes the obvious interdependence of the two, and in that sense, the human involvement with the environment is therefore best indentified as a domain of entanglement.

Cultural practice, material reference and the generation of meaning

In section 2, *Cultural practice, material reference and the generation of meaning*, the central problem of ascribing meaning to material objects is debated. This problem is only touched upon occasionally in most philosophical writing, and in these writings materiality is regularly described as having only a secondary function. Objects have therefore been regarded as mere representations that one should think *of* and not active elements that one should think *through*. In order to broaden the understanding of the diverse range of meanings embedded in and generated by material objects, examination of the various connections between cultural practices and materiality figure prominently in all of the articles in this section. In their examinations, as well as in their general theoretical debate, the writers tie together works from a diverse range of disciplines, with linguistic theory as a recurring field of reference. In particular, the works of C.S. Peirce, Lakoff & Johnson and Berlin & Kay loom large and point towards the dominant position that the study of language has had in the description of meaning. Most importantly, however, the case studies give evidence to the significant influences that materiality has on human meaning construction and to the point that language cannot stand alone. In fact, the articles underline material culture as a generative factor in the construction of meaning, and criticize former theoretical frameworks for being overly linguistic when focussing on meaning. Furthermore, a combination of the group's articles provides the identification of what could be termed a triple grounding of meaning. Firstly, the possibilities of describing certain universal human traits which persist across cultures, such as the perceptual system or body format, and assert meaningful and comparable exchange between humans and their environment. Secondly, that the cultural context and practices often generate a particular version of a meaningful concept, and are, over time, susceptible to change. Thirdly, that such concepts present themselves across a wide variety of media, ranging from performances to words to objects. This triple grounding is to be understood as the recognition of the distributed quality which characterizes the cognitive processes generating meaning in human thinking – a recognition that, unlike most former theories on meaning, positions the material centrally in the dissipated network of cultural meanings.

The first paper in this section, by **Carl Knappett**, examines the effects of small-scale artefacts. He does so by focussing on 'situated semiotics', which is a collocation of ecological psychology and Peircean semiotics. In advocating such a coupling Knappett outlines a methodological stance which highlights direct as well as indirect perception as part of any meaning-constructing process related to artefacts. With regard to miniatures and small-scale artefacts, this approach makes possible the description of the elaborate network of 'inter-artefactual' relations in which the small artefacts take part. In the Aegean Bronze Age the different types of models and miniatures seemingly follow an abstracted form of meaning construction which exhibits a sort of selective concretisation, where certain elements are scaled down while others dissolve. This process of alteration and selection grants an improved access to the abstract relation the artefacts represent, because redundant meanings and functions are left out. In other words, minimising maximises the semiotic effect of the artefact design.

Archaeological semiotics is also forefronted by **Robert W. Preucel** in his interpretation of the position of material culture in the mediation of historical consciousness. Based on the works of Charles S. Peirce, Preucel seeks to promote an inclusive definition of the representational position that material culture takes in meaning construction, which encompasses the many diverse ways in which meanings are constituted. By analyzing the materiality of revitalization during the Pueblo Revolt of 1680 in New Spain, he points out the different historical connotations which are embedded and emphasized in the material culture of the revolt (such as a 'proper' way of material life). The result is an archaeological semiotics which focuses on the historical dynamism of material culture, in which the material sign is in constant flux; material culture is simultaneously resting on the understanding of previous signs as well as pointing towards new signs. Therefore, the representational position of material culture is intrinsically historical, as well as characterized by advancement and transformation.

Mads Dengsø Jessen analyses the conceptual correspondence between architectural features and the way in which humans describe social position. More concretely, he points out the recursive use of verticality and size when expressing importance and power in both architecture as well as social classification. For example, in the principal houses of the Scandinavian Viking Age, the halls, there is a pronounced tendency to build them large and lofty, and to situate them in conspicuous settings where they dominate the landscape. Similarly, in the written records the proprietors are described as tall and stoutly built, thus underlining their influential social position. Evidently, there is no obvious way of separating the conceptual understanding of the physical setting that the hall provides and the social significance of the owner, which attest to a distributed notion of concept formation. Furthermore, the understanding of these simple concepts – height and dimension – is identified as having a common universal grounding in our bodily experience of acting and moving in space, but concretized in a variety of abstractions across time and space.

The small things of every-day life in the Italian Neolithic are under scrutiny in the article by **John Robb** and **Kostalena Michelaki**. The delicate ornaments and decorations on Neolithic pottery, as well as the creation of ceramics, cannot be ascribed any simple practical necessity but must, nevertheless, be indicative of meaningful behaviour. With this in mind, Robb and Michelaki have examined the Neolithic pottery assemblages as instances of 'creative action', which mixes tradition and innovation into an important exercise of intentional agency. This way, the context of the potters becomes a significant feature when studying their exercise of skill and their manipulation of difference in creating decoration. The authors therefore advocate a local and contextualized understanding of pottery and decoration, which highlight the contribution pottery makes with regard to forming the identity of the community. The potters were important actors in mediating between their own personal role as innovative craftsmen and the wish to maintain a meaningful pottery style which was appreciated and understood by their contemporaries.

David A. Warburton investigates the development of particular cultural expressions, which show universal features but are grounded in a limited point of origin. The development of colour domains and concepts is explained by Warburton as tightly connected to the use and distribution of specific materials and their social function. In fact, he argues that without the human involvement with certain materials the development of a distinct colour terminology could not have been established. For example, the generation of the word *blue* in Greek is derived from Near Eastern words for the semi-precious stone Lapis Lazuli. Importantly, these Lapis Lazuli were central to the oldest systematized exchange network known, and as the demand for such stones increased, the linguistic designation for the actual stone expanded into referring to 'anything blue'. This progression suggests that in the domain of colours, archaeological and philological sources offer a unique insight into the cognitive development of abstract entities such as colour terminology, exchange systems and economics.

Agency, technology and society

The third section entitled *Agency, technology and society* explores the impact of technological practice, innovation and change on human ways of acting and thinking. The articles examine how new ways of perceiving and organising the world are constitutive of technological innovation and, correspondingly, how the operation of new technologies can change the way in which the world is perceived and organised. Obviously, these two processes are hard to tell apart, and all of the articles in this section advocate a dialectic and dynamic relationship between cultural change and cultural continuity. Consequently, it is argued, on the one hand, that the established techno-social platform has a tendency to generate a sort of self-reinforcing stability across generations and between social groups in favour of traditional practices. On the other hand, it is exemplified how novel technological arrangements and practices are prone to generate a revaluation of existing cultural constellations. Only rarely, though, will the introduction of new technology initiate a complete upheaval of established technological knowledge or occasion an all-encompassing reorganization of traditional practices. Another returning theme in the articles is the unspoken scepticism towards technological determinism: because human history has provided ample evidence for the fact that the intricate relationship between human techno-complexes and the human mind always generate complex social systems (including the showcases in the section), a convincing anti-reductionist viewpoint characterizes the articles. Naturally, the writers recognize that certain materialities provide certain affordances, but also, that the specific cultural application of these *a priori* functions cannot be forecasted or described by any simple terminology or theory. Instead, deep descriptions based on the particular cultural contexts of technological change and/or continuity characterizes the majority of the contributions in the section. Another targeted feature refers to the instances where the production of material culture is a type of social event which requires cognitive coordination at a group level, as well as resting on individual ingenuity or prowess. In particular the everyday activities taking place between groups of people who have had previous and regular contact, are described in the group's writings. It is convincingly argued that during such situations material culture will perform as a constitutive element in the exchange of 'social knowledge', and that it makes little sense to view materiality as a separate fraction of human life. Instead, the creation of material culture can be viewed as internal to the formation of a group identity, as well as to define the position of the individual in and between groups.

Development and learning figure prominently in the article by **Deborah Olausson**. She investigates the establishment of elaborate technologies, in this case the Late Neolithic dagger production in Scandinavia, and how such intricate procedures can be transferred from one generation to the next. The reason for producing such exceptional and prestigious artefacts as the daggers could be economic as well as social, but will, in any case, necessitate a limited number of producers. Olausson therefore focuses on how, for example, the transfer of knowledge and know-how, as well as the nursing of talented individuals, affect the production of daggers, and argue that control of each of the production facets will increase the appreciation and value of the artefacts. Therefore, the transfer of knowledge and hands-on learning processes play centre stage in retaining the status of the daggers, and underline the importance of cognitive development in tool production and use.

Annette Kjølby investigates the creation process behind the production of private statues in New Kingdom Egypt. In particular the differences and relations between individuals and groups of individuals and how their interdependent decision-making courses of action are affecting the design choices and types of representations the statues expose, figure prominently in her article. Also how these intricate processes are modified over time in a long-term perspective is taken into consideration. By careful examination of the discrete stages which are necessary in the production of the statues – the day-to-day agency of the producers and their intimate involvement with the materiality of the statue – the various steps in the conceptual formation of the statue design can be discerned. Furthermore, within the production practices the social position of the producers is clearly recognizable, and provides a frame for understanding the social negotiations that influence each decision-making stage. The interdependency of hierarchical structure and individual, artistical agency is therefore imperative for understanding New Kingdom statue production.

Mads Kähler Holst and **Marianne Rasmussen** are describing the various fundamental challenges which arise when people are required to cooperate and work together in larger groups. Often cooperation is accompanied by competitive strategies which can be both internal to the group, but also dominate the social relations at an intergroup level. Organising the large and numerous South Scandinavian Bronze Age barrows necessitates a constructing programme in which cooperative as well as competitive features materialize. By a meticulous archaeological investigation of the architecture of a single Bronze Age barrow Holst and Rasmussen decipher the individual construction phases, technical solutions and building routines, which all bear an impression of the cooperative principles behind the building of the barrow. Furthermore, these principles refer to the contemporaneous social structures, such as norms, ethics, institutions, technology and the existing social networks. Thereby the specific form of barrow-cooperation provides a means to model the general composition of the social institutions dominating the period.

Janet D. Keller takes a closer look at the boundaries of technology and examines the way in which different use patterns emerge as a consequence of the introduction of new technologies. The advent of literacy in Vanuatu in the southwest

Pacific shows features of unique practices regarding reading and writing, which, on the one hand, are grounded in structural continuities and socio-historical trends, while, on the other hand, are highly sensitive to subjective and individual initiatives. Via extensive ethnographic fieldwork Keller has, for example, demonstrated that narrative performances and recitation are tightly connected to certain families, places or expertise, and therefore difficult to transfer to an open-access medium such as the written word and writing. These problems have resulted in a combinatory way of reading and writing which integrate the traditional performative features with modern literacy. Consequently, in Vanuatu, the technology of reading and writing is contextually adapted to the traditional narrative milieu, while at the same time being subjected to the global standards of literacy.

The concept of *agency*, which has traditionally been synonymous with human action, is discussed by **Niels Johannsen**. Recently, a number of authors have suggested that a useful way of giving things due causal significance is to acknowledge that inanimate entities exhibit an active *agency* of their own. Johannsen, who refers to this as the 'Inanimate Agency Proposition' (IAP), agrees with the need to revise strictly 'human-bound' notions of agency, and he acknowledges that variants of the IAP represent different attempts to better our understanding of the immense causal role that non-human entities play in the ways that human lives are lived. Johannsen is concerned, however, that the ontological premises and implications of this very inclusive notion of agency do not provide for a concept that is analytically attractive to archaeology. Johannsen presents a comprehensive critique of the IAP and then proposes an alternative revision of the concept where *agency* is regarded as the basic capacity which living organisms (including humans) have for instantiating changes in their environments. As such, he argues that agency is not something dependent on 'intentionality', 'consciousness' or other mental features, but rather a much more basic feature of organic life. Drawing inspiration from niche construction theory, Johannsen emphasizes the historicity of all human action and argues that the concept of agency in archaeology should be attuned to this temporal situatedness.

References

DeMarrais, E., C. Gosden & C. Renfrew (eds.) 2004. *Rethinking Materiality – the Engagement of Mind with the Material World*. Cambridge: McDonald Institute for Archaeological Research.

Lave, J. 1988. *Cognition in practice: Mind, mathematics, and culture in everyday life*. New York: Cambridge University Press.

Leroi-Gourhan, A. 1993. *Gesture and speech*. Cambridge: MIT Press.

Merleau-Ponty, M. 1945. *Phénoménologie de la Perception*. Paris: Gallimard.

Modée, J. 2005. *Artifacts and Supraphysical Worlds. A Conceptual Analysis of Religion*, Lund: Centre for Theology and Religious Studies.

Renfrew, C. & E. B.W. Zubrow (eds.) 1994. *The Ancient Mind. Elements of Cognitive Archaeology*. Cambridge: Cambridge University Press.

Renfrew, C., C. Frith & L. Malafouris 2009. 'Introduction.' In: C. Renfrew, C. Frith, L. Malafouris (eds.), *The sapient mind: archaeology meets neuroscience*. Oxford: Oxford University Press, ix-xiv.

Renfrew, C. & L. Malafouris (eds.) 2010. *The Cognitive Life of Things: Recasting the Boundaries of the Mind*. Cambridge: McDonald Institute for Archaeological Research.

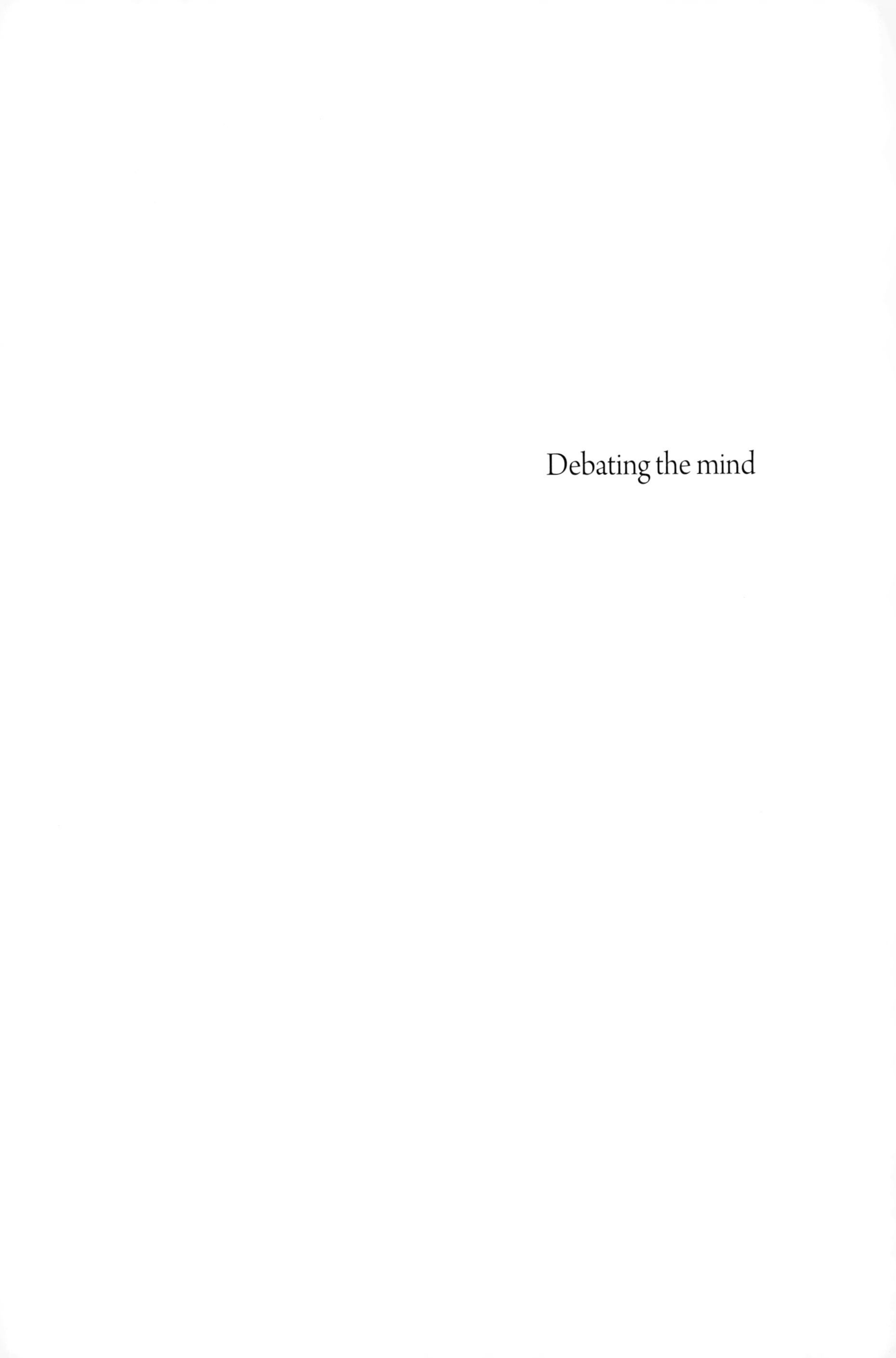

Debating the mind

Imitation, Mirror Neurons and Material Culture

Svend Østergaard

Introduction

This paper is about the neuro-cognitive precondition for the development of material culture. Following Tomasello (1999), I present a set of minimal changes in the behaviour the individual displays when meeting other individuals; changes which occurred in the evolution from non-human primates to humans, and which probably are necessary conditions for the development of meta-cognition, material culture, and symbolic representations. It is generally the case for all species that when two individuals meet they modify each others behaviour. If the community is large, then this local dynamics between two individuals can spread and have a rather large effect on the global structure, this is what is normally called the emergence of structure in a dynamic system.[1] It also follows from this property of dynamic systems that a minimal change in the dynamics of local interaction might have a significant and unexpected global effect. Tomasello's theory deals with the minimal local interactions that can lead to the emergence of culture, and by reference to neuro-science I will in the following also present a hypothesis about what minimal changes in brain structure might bring about the type of behaviour that Tomasello points out.

If we then consider the complexity of human society and culture as emergent phenomena, the task is to find the properties of the local dynamics that might cause the emergence. Tomasello calls attention to *imitation* as a decisive factor. Humans have a tendency to imitate other humans' motor as well as expressive behaviour. Already neonates reproduce the movements of the mouth and the head of adults; see Meltzoff and Moore (1977). Several studies point to imitative learning as a decisive factor in children's development. See for instance Tomasello (1999) for an extensive reference to literature that points in that direction. Imitation seems to be linked to what adults would qualify as intentional behaviour; for instance, if an adult turns on a light by bending over and touching a button with her head, most fourteen-month-old children who have observed this will perform the task more or less in the same way, even though it would be easier to press the button with their hand (Meltzoff 1988). However, if the adult has a blanket wrapped around her body so she cannot use her hands freely, the children will use their hands. Presumably, the children assume that in the first condition the adult uses her head intentionally and so there must be a reason for that behaviour, whereas in the second condition the children assume the adult would use her hand if she had the opportunity. Imitation thus only occurs in situations where there is alternative behaviour possible. We tend to say that this is because the child has an understanding of intentionality; however, this is an explanation that refers to higher order concepts. From a dynamic systems point of view we have an organism that imitates the behavioural strategy of another organism, but only if there is not a more likely strategy available. This mechanism can easily be automatic and bypass any conceptual representation, but it is likely that this mechanism is the base for the development of adults' understanding of choice-making and intentional behaviour.

We thus have two types of imitation. On the one hand we have the general contagious effect of expressive behaviour. This also works in adults: we tend to attune to each others' vocalization, face expressions, emotions etc. It is possible that this attunement reflects an identification process as suggested by Stern (1985) in relation to infants' matching of adult emotional states. On the other hand, we have the instrumental imitation that mainly works when contrasted with a more likely behavioural strategy. It is possible that this mechanism is automatic in young children, whereas for older children and adults it is modulated by a conscious evaluation of the most appropriate strategy. In both cases we have a description of the dynamics at work when two individuals are interacting. In the theory of dynamic systems this is called 'local' dynamics, and in some cases the global features of the system emerge from this. Although Tomasello does not refer to dynamic systems, he is in fact – in Tomasello (1999) – describing how the global phenomenon of culture emerges from the local dynamics of imitation. I will argue that certain meta-cognitive abilities of the individual are also emergent properties of this local imitation dynamics. As for the minimal changes of brain structure supporting the disposition to imitate, it is tempting to connect them to the newly found mirror system in the brain. However, there are two problems in that. Firstly, although the mirror neurons are supposed to deal with the recognition and/or prediction of an observed act, this does not necessarily imply that the observer will imitate what has been observed. Secondly, the mirror system is not special for humans, in fact, it was discovered in the macaque monkeys, therefore if imitation is connected to mirror neurons this has to be because of a new exploitation of this system, not found in non-human primates. One could argue that this is linked to the development of the frontal lobes of the human brain with the extended ability to make comparisons and choices.

Force Dynamics

One important aspect of human cognition is the ability to act in a situation according to an abstract schematic representation, which is independent of the specific material manifestations and therefore in a flexible way can be used in apparently very different scenarios. For instance, humans do not simply act according to an experientially based correlation between cause and effect, but instead according to some abstract understanding of the force dynamic possibilities in the situation (cf. Talmy 2000). Talmy argues for our cognitive representation of force being Aristotelian. This implies that a moving object has an inherent tendency to move based on an inherent force that can be transferred to another object on interacting with it. Conversely, an object that is not moving has an inherent tendency to rest and will, if subjected to an external force, 'offer' resistance; cf. an expression like: 'The window withstood my pressure'. In other words, in their interaction with the physical world humans are guided by abstract schematic models of force dynamics. We thus have the following cognitive models of force dynamic interactions:

1. An object that is at rest – i.e. with an inherent tendency to 'resist' force actions – can only be put into motion if another object exerting a 'greater force' is impinging on it.
2. An object with an inherent tendency to motion – i.e. with an inherent force dynamic potential; for instance, an object on a hill side – can be prevented from motion if it is blocked by another object with a greater inherent force potential. On removal of the blocking object the first one can be set in motion.

Apparently, the two models described above are actively used by the human mind in conceptualizing a dynamic scenario. Although very simple, they are also very powerful, since they do not specify anything about the object, the situation, and the type of impingement in question. Moreover, they are based on the concept of 'force' as something inherent in an object, depending on its position in a specific scenario. Humans are therefore able to understand the dynamic possibilities in a specific situation based on a notion that is not visually or otherwise accessible to our senses. 'Force' is an abstract invisible entity that is used by the human mind in order to construct models of the world with a view to manipulating the dynamic possibilities in specific scenarios.

There is evidence that humans differ from other primates in that regard. In an experiment described by Tomasello (1999, 22), subjects catch hold of some food placed in a tube by using a stick. In the tube there is a trap so if the subjects try to pull the food towards the end where they are standing, the food disappears through a hole. However, if you know about gravity and the force dynamics of sticks pushing objects, you should know how to avoid the trap and instead push the food out through the opposite opening of the tube. If this experiment is performed with chimps, they have about 70 trials where they push and pull by chance before they learn the correct strategy. Moreover, if you turn the tube around so the trap becomes harmless, they still use the learned behaviour even if an easier strategy could have been adopted. If 2-year-old children are used in this experiment they immediately use the most optimal strategy in both cases.

The conclusion Tomasello draws from this experiment is that chimps do not have a mental representation of 'hidden forces' that either have to be overcome or that can be used strategically. That does not prevent chimps from developing sophisticated strategies useful for acquiring food, but they are – according to Tomasello – developed on a trial and error basis whereby the chimps can learn important correlations between cause and effect. A study by Horner & Whiten (2005) seems to cast light on the difference between humans and chimps in terms of causal understanding. In the study, wild-born chimpanzees and 3- to 4-year-old children observed a demonstrator use a tool to retrieve a reward from a box. The experimenter both showed relevant and irrelevant actions in two conditions: one in which the box was opaque and therefore not all causal information was available for the observers, and one in which the box was transparent and therefore the causal information was available. The result of the study is that in the opaque case the chimps use imitation as an overall strategy to retrieve the reward, i.e. they reproduced the irrelevant actions as well as the relevant ones. In the transparent case the chimps used emulation as strategy, i.e. they did not reproduce the irrelevant actions, but apparently learned about the causality of the situation by watching the demonstrator, and then retrieved the reward by using their own efficacious actions. The children, however, used imitation to solve the task in both conditions. This fits well into Tomasello's suggestion that imitation is the behavioural strategy that distinguishes humans from non-human primates. In the study the chimps do imitate, but only in the situation where causal information was not available. The children imitate in all cases, which shows that their imitation is independent of the perceptually accessible causal information. This is probably because imitation in the case of the children is a consequence of a dynamics of interaction as much as it is a strategy for retrieving the reward. Also, the apparently stupid behaviour of the children fits into the idea of a more abstract representation of causality. If force-dynamic relations are invisible as claimed above, then the irrelevant actions are performed even in the transparent case, because they might hit upon some dynamic aspects of the situation that are not accessible through perception.

As for the chimps, the study shows that they do imitate as a strategy, if the causal relations are opaque, and if not, they emulate. This shows that chimps have sophisticated causal knowledge, but of course, we do not know what format this knowledge has; is it an experiential-based learning of causal correlations – for instance, that contact between the tool and the reward is needed in order to acquire the reward, that a barrier prevents contact with the reward etc. – or is it based on a conceptual representation[2] of force? And if the latter is the case, what kind of representation do we have? Is it possible to manipulate with the force-dynamic potentials independently of what is perceptually accessible? The last ability distinguishes between humans and chimps according to Tomasello (1999). However, one has to admit that there are cases of animal use of tools that are so complicated that it seems inconceivable that they do not have some conceptual representation of force; see in that regard Weir *et al.* (2002).

In all cases, without some abstract representation of a force independent of on-going perception, it is not possible to find new ways of representing the same force. Given an antecedent-consequent relation, it is therefore likely that non-human primates do not have the ability, independently of ongoing perception, to represent different antecedents with the same consequent. If this is the case it is not possible to develop tools that are not already part of the environment in which the tool is supposed to be used. In other words, in the cases where animals do use tools this is probably dependent on an experientially developed correlation, where the animal exploits the dynamic possibilities that are directly available through sensory-motor experience.

Humans, on the other hand, seem to have an abstract representation of 'force'. When humans manipulate with the visually accessible physical world they probably do that on the basis of an underlying force dynamic model which is not visible itself. There is therefore a crucial distinction between the overt behavioral strategy, on the one hand, and the invisible dynamic schema on the other, meaning that different strategies might fit into the same schema. Humans can therefore change strategy according to their understanding of the forces needed to accomplish the task. For instance, if you want to lift an object you might try to use your hands. If that doesn't work you might get the idea to use your hands on a lever instead, thereby exploiting the fact that a small force at a greater distance to the pivot point can neutralize a greater force at a smaller distance. In other words, an understanding of abstract force dynamic schemas, as those analysed in Talmy (2000), is a necessary condition for an extensive and systematic development of tools.

Imitation and the mirror system

One of the cornerstones in Tomasello's theory of culture is the human disposition to imitate at all levels of human interaction, starting with neonates' tendency to imitate facial expressions and later shown in 2-year-old children's imitation of observed behavioural strategy relative to a goal. In this context imitation is considered as part of the dynamics at work when individuals meet each other; it is, so to speak, part of a local dynamics. Children's tendency to imitate any observed behaviour continues until about four years of age; from then on the propensity for imitating is counterbalanced by a propensity for doing things on one's own. The local dynamics is then a dialectic tension between imitation and non-imitation. It is this local dynamics that is a precondition for the development of culture because the imitation secures stability and the transfer of behaviour from generation to generation. However, if imitation becomes too strong there would be no innovation and the society would perish. This is counteracted by non-imitative behaviour, which is the source for new ideas and new behavioural strategies.

The development of an inclination to imitate might then be one of the changes in the local dynamics of interaction between two individuals which has a large-scale effect on the social structure of the community. In a phylogenetic perspective, this change has to be correlated with changes in brain structure and it is likely that a sophisticated exploitation of the so-called system of mirror neurons in the brain has led to the sophisticated forms of social interaction that we find amongst humans.

The mirror neurons are located in the ventral premotor area of the macaque monkey's brain and in the inferior parietal cortex, see Rizzolati et al. (1996). Most of them discharge when the monkey executes specific hand actions – for instance, pinching a small object – and they are also activated when the monkey observes another individual perform similar actions. But there are other neurons that respond to more schematic types of motor activity – for instance, taking an object with the hands – irrespective of how this is done. The mirror neurons constitute a complex neural system and there is no doubt that a similar system can be found in humans. Using brain imaging, Jeannerod (2003) found areas in the brain being active both when the subject observes another person perform an activity and when the same activity is self-generated. Moreover, the same areas are active when the subject imagines the activity and when it intends to perform the activity. These areas, which include parts of motor cortex, are likely to contain networks of cells that perform some of the same functions as the mirror neurons found in monkeys.

The precise function of the mirror neurons is not known. One possibility is that they have a goal-understanding function; by activating the neurons that discharge if the observer himself were to execute the observed action, they help the observer to understand the meaning of the action (Rizzolati *et al.* 2001). For example, if the monkey observes someone reach for an object, it will experience the anticipation of grasping and thereby understand the goal of the observed action. Csibra (2005) mentions however a list of empirical evidence that is in conflict with this interpretation: the most important is that there seems to be no activation of the mirror neurons without a goal. Thus mirror neurons do not respond to mimicked actions; for instance, when the monkey observes someone pretend to grasp – in the absence of any object – there is no activation (Gallese *et al.* 1996). It seems therefore unlikely that the mirror neurons serve goal understanding. Csibra suggests instead that they serve an action-prediction function in a situation where the goal is already known, i.e., by mirroring the action of an observed individual in its own motor system, it should be possible for the monkey to anticipate the behaviour of conspecifics.

Explaining imitation by means of mirror neurons has already been suggested, for instance in Iacoboni *et al.* (1999) where they present evidence for a direct matching between the observed action and an internal motor representation of that action ('direct matching hypothesis'). Since mirror neurons are active in observation of another's action and imitation is a self-generated motor activity following observation, a possible link between mirror neurons and imitation has to go further than predicting the outcome of an observed action. It might well be that action prediction is the basic function of mirror neurons which has developed further in humans to yield the specific human version of imitative behaviour. A speculative hypothesis in that regard is that in the context of a known goal the matching hypothesis is working, i.e. there is an encoding at the neural level of a motor representation of an observed action leading to that goal. When the individual later is confronted with the same goal, the neural representation of the correlated action discharges and the individual 'imitates' the observed action. In any case, the observation that mirror neurons do not serve goal understanding is consistent with the kind of imitation we find in humans, since it is basically an imitation of strategy in the context of a known goal.

Gallese & Goldman (1998) have proposed a theory according to which the mirror neurons form a much more extended system in the human brain. They are not just activated by observation of motor activity, but also on perceiving all sorts of expressive behaviour: speech, facial expressions, emotional expressions etc. It is well known that humans automatically imitate subtle face movements. If we see someone smile we tend to smile a little too and thereby feel happier. In other words: other people are contagious. If this is due to mirror neurons then they serve another function than those activated in observing goal directed action. They do not just mirror the observed expression but they automatically activate the relevant muscles for imitating it. The purpose of this is probably to create a group feeling and to increase the general positive feeling among the group members; for instance, it has been shown that a waitress gets a higher tip if she imitates the customer's behaviour (van Baaren 2005). This is an example where you consciously 'trick' someone into having a more empathic feeling towards you, but in general the mechanism supporting the contagious imitation of expressive behaviour is unconscious as opposed to the imitation of instrumental behaviour.

In any case, for instrumental behaviour the mirror neurons secure a fast, non-conceptual motor representation of the observed activity. That is, at a very basic level humans have an immediate embodied representation of the other's activity, where by *embodied* I refer to the fact that the observation of a motor action will activate parts of the motor system that are activated if I myself had to carry out the observed activity.

Consider now the following situation: a child observes on two different occasions an adult using two different behavioural strategies for the same task. Due to the attention paid to the behaviour and, accordingly, the neural mirroring of it, the child will then have two different motor representations of the behaviour necessary to achieve the same goal. This distinction might in itself enhance a development through which the child becomes able to distinguish between behavioural strategies, on the one hand, and the goal on the other. Experiments devised by Piaget (1954) seem to confirm that this distinction develops from eight months old and onwards, because the infants of that age used different behavioural means for the same goal and were able to use intermediate behavioural strategies to pursue a goal, whereas the infants younger than 8 months did not display this type of behaviour. Since the child observes that an adult can achieve a certain goal in two different ways on two different occasions, this might lead to an understanding of the adult as one who makes behavioral choices relative to a given goal. Likewise, if there are two different sensory-motor representations for how to act relative to a given task that the child is going to perform, she will experience herself as making a behavioural choice. In both cases, the experience of the other as well as of the self as making behavioural choices is almost equivalent to experiencing the other and the self as intentional agents. I am not claiming that there is a direct link between mirror neurons and the understanding of intentionality, but it is possible that the mirror system plays a part in the conceptual distinction between the behavioural strategy and the goal, which then leads to the experience and thereby the representation of the other as an intentional agent. But to understand the other as intentional is the same as to have a representation of the other as one who acts according to a mental representation, which is not visible itself and which is selected amongst many possible representations. This connects to the discussion on force presented above. Humans not only understand that other people are acting according to an invisible mental state selected amongst others, but also that the choice is determined in view of how to optimize the use of invisible forces.

The use of the word *choice* above does not necessarily refer to the ordinary meaning of that word. I am referring rather to basic experiences that lay the foundation for what we understand as "making a choice". We can imagine that these experiences enhance the development of brain structure being used for changing strategy. If a person is using a bad strategy relative to a goal, if she 'knows' that different manipulations of forces might lead to the desired goal, and if she 'knows' that the strategy used is one selected amongst many others, all this might motivate a change of behaviour, and thereby the development of procedures for changing strategy. As evident from Horner *et al.* (2003), monkeys use imitation when the dynamic affordances of the objects are opaque, in other words they don't use imitation as a means to learn a new strategy in a situation where one strategy is already evident from the causal information available. Monkeys are good at learning the dynamic affordances if they are transparent and they can use this information to achieve the desired change of state in the environment – this is called emulative learning – but it seems as if they are focused on the change of state and therefore indifferent to the possibility of new strategies. This correlates well with the knowledge we have that strategy change is processed in the frontal part of the brain and that the main differences in brain structure between monkeys and humans are in the frontal part, which is much bigger in humans. It is clear that this development towards the ability of choosing among different force dynamic manipulations, connected with an understanding of the force dynamic affordances of the object world, is likely to lead to the manipulation of tools with the aim of obtaining the desired goals.

The described mechanisms based on mirror neurons and imitation also entail the ability to have meta-cognitive representations. If a person has two different embodied representations of how to achieve a goal, she has to compare and choose the one that is most appropriate. We can consider this as a meta-cognitive process involving more than just an automatic execution of an entrenched motor scheme. This process is part of a dynamic flow of representations, cf. footnote 2. In Jeannerod & Gallagher (2002), the authors propose that there is a hierarchy of such representations in relation to goal oriented behaviour. At the bottom of the hierarchy we have motor schemes. This is a neural mechanism securing that I 'know' how to grasp a glass of water. It is probably at this level we find the mirror neurons. At least – as mentioned above – there are single neurons in the primates that are only active when the animal performs this kind of motor activity, with some neurons only responding to very specific motor activity and some having a more schematic response-field. The activation of the motor schemes at this level is automatic and unconscious and there is also an automatic and unconscious adjustment to small changes in the target object (cf. Jeannerod 2003).

The motor schemes are embedded in neural networks that represent behavioural strategies relative to goals. This level includes what in cognitive linguistics is known as experiential schemes (cf. Lakoff & Johnson 1999). For instance, if I am thirsty, my goal is to get some water. A strategy for achieving this is to go to the kitchen, take a glass from the shelf, turn the tap on, and fill the glass with water, etc. This is an experiential scheme which is also in general activated automatically and unconsciously. The experiential schema is build up by means of a series of specific motor actions. On observing the behaviour of a con-specific, a motor action is simulated by the mirror system to the extent that the observer can embed it in a larger experiential scheme, which describes the goal of the action. As for material objects, they can be understood to the extent that we can simulate an interaction with them relative to an experiential scheme. In other words, this is an embodied theory of the meaning of material objects.

The structures of the brain responsible for making choices can be considered as part of a meta-cognitive system, but in ongoing behaviour this system is only activated if something fails. As mentioned above, the experiential schemes are executed more or less automatically without any specific awareness, but they are accessible to consciousness if something goes wrong or if an unexpected obstacle suddenly appears. The main occupation of the brain is to predict the outcome of either perceived action or self-generated action. As long as the sensory-motor feed-back information does not deviate too much from the predicted outcome, everything works on an automatic mode. But if the predictions fail, then consciousness intervenes to assess the failed strategy relative to the goal – possibly comparing it to alternative strategies. In that regard, it is important that for humans the prediction is related to an awareness of the strategy, because other primates are also occupied with predicting, but if there is no conscious awareness of the strategy, their attention is oriented towards the changes in the environment and therefore a failed prediction does not necessarily lead to a change in strategy.

What has all of this to do with culture and the use of tools? Well, it seems reasonable to assume that the development of tools is dependent on three basic skills: 1) an ability to take a meta-cognitive stance towards a task that fails or is difficult to carry out. 2) In the meta-cognitive reflections, the attention is directed towards details of the behavioural strategy. 3) An abstract understanding of the force-dynamic requirements to perform the task and thereby an ability to manipulate with the dynamics of the situation. On the other hand, tool making is a fundamental aspect of human culture.

Culture

The main idea in Tomasello (1999) is to explain cultural diversity as a result of a general cognitive disposition rather than as a result of the development of specific modules in the brain: tool making, symbolic expressions, paintings, decorations, language, mathematics, etc. are thus seen as developing from minimal changes in human interaction. One of these changes is the disposition to imitate. In experiments with chimps and eighteen-month-old infants where the experimenter shows good or bad strategies for achieving a goal, the chimps do not imitate the strategy of the experimenter. They are goal-oriented and try to solve the problem according to their own understanding of the dynamic affordances. The children, on the other hand, imitate what they observe, irrespective of whether it is a good or a bad strategy for obtaining the goal (Tomasello 1999, 83). Apparently the children are not as clever as the chimps, but the advantage of the behaviour they display is evident when an individual in the human society begins to solve a problem in a new and more efficient way; this new behaviour will then quickly spread in the community and even be transmitted to the next generation. In the chimp community the new invention is likely to die out with the inventor, so it is clear that imitation is a necessary condition for the developing of cultural diversity.

Imitation is not only related to an experimental manipulation of the object world. There is also an extended imitation of all sorts of expressive gestures (cf. Gallese & Goldman 1998). This is connected with an emergent understanding of the expression as something that refers to a mental state. In some cases this reference is also intended; for instance, a sound pattern might be interpreted as the expression of an intention concerning the attention of the hearer: the sound maker has a mental representation that she wants the hearer to attend to. Due to the imitation mechanism (the mirror system), the perceiver of the expressive behaviour will imitate it for expressing a similar mental state of her own. The dynamics of this interaction might lead to a stable sign system. It seems in any case that imitation and the development of sophisticated expressive behaviour lead to a situation where the individuals in the community try to share their mental states. Any expression is interpreted as information about a mental state and likewise the interpreter imitates this by expressing her own mental state in a similar manner. This mechanism might be transferred to tools. Decoration of tools is an aspect of expressive behaviour. When people of the same tribe meet they exchange expressive signs just to mark that they are part of the same community and share the same fate. Likewise, the decoration of tools might mark that this is not just a functional thing but also a symbolic entity that serves the expression of a mind, which is also a part of the community.

In this paper I have tried to relate imitation to an extended use of the mirror system in the brain. This modification of the mirror system is then a minimal change in the brain that at the phenomenological level changes the mutual behavioural modification that takes place whenever two individuals of the same species meet. This local dynamics of mutual imitations constitutes a dynamic system with large-scale emergent phenomena, i.e. cultural diversity. As argued above, imitation reinforces and is connected to an emergent understanding of the difference between the behavioural strategy and the goal, which enforces the development of a system for making behavioural choices, essentially in the frontal parts of the brain. This system already implies some meta-cognitive abilities whereby the subject can choose the most appropriate strategy, especially in cases where a given strategy does not come up to the expected result. This development of meta-cognitive strategies further enhances of course the tool making process and thereby the development of a material culture.

Notes

1 For instance, the global structure of an ant hill emerges from the local exchange of the chemical pheromone between the individual ants. Similarly, it is likely that what we know as syntactic structure is an emergent property of the dynamics of individuals exchanging signifying sound patterns.

2 When I use the word *representation* I am referring to a pattern of neural activation. The most basic form of representation is when the neural pattern is correlated with some specific form of motor behaviour. By *conceptual representation* I refer to a pattern of neural activity that exists independently of the sensory motor activity, i.e. the agent has some understanding of the situation, independently of its motor activity, cf. Jeannerod & Gallagher (2002).

Literature

Csibra, G. 2005. Mirror neurons or emulator neurons? *International workshop 2005: Contribution of mirroring processes to human mindreading*. www.mirrorneurons.free.fr

Gallese, V., L. Fadiga, L. Fogassi & G. Rizzolatti 1996. 'Action recognition in the premotor cortex.' *Brain*, 119, 593-609.

Gallese, V. & A. Goldman 1998. 'Mirror neurons and the simulation theory of mind-reading.' *Trends in Cognitive Science*, 2, 493-501.

Horner, V. & A. Whiten 2005. 'Causal knowledge and imitation/emulation switching in chimpanzees and children.' *Animal Cognition*, 8, 164-81.

Iacoboni, M., R.P.Woods, M. Brass, H. Bekkering, J.C. Mazziotta & G. Rizzolatti 1999. 'Cortical mechanisms of human interaction.' *Science*, 286, 2526-28.

Jeannerod, M. & S. Gallagher 2002. 'From action to interaction.' *Journal of Consciousness Studies*, 9(1), 3-26.

Jeannerod, M. 2003. 'Consciousness of action and self-consciousness – a cognitive neuroscience approach.' In: J. Roessler, N. Eilan (eds.), *Agency and self awareness: issues in philosophy and psychology*. Oxford: Oxford University Press, 128-49.

Lakoff, G. & M. Johnson 1999. *Philosophy in the Flesh*. New York: Basic Books.

Meltzoff, A. 1988. 'Infant imitation after a one-week delay: Long-term memory for novel acts and multiple stimuli.' *Developmental Psychology*, 24, 470-76.

Meltzoff, A. & K. Moore 1977. 'Imitation of facial and manual gestures by newborn infants.' *Science*, 198, 75-78.

Piaget, J. 1954. *The construction of reality in the child*. New York: Basic Books.

Rizzolatti, G., L. Fadiga, V. Gallese, & L. Fogassi 1996. 'Premotor cortex and the recognition of motor actions.' *Cognitive Brain Research*, 3, 131-41.

Rizzolatti, G., L. Fogassi & V. Gallese 2001. 'Neurophysiological mechanisms underlying the understanding and imitation of action.' *Nature Neuroscience Reviews*, 2, 661-70.

Stern, D. 1985. *The interpersonal world of the infant*. New York: Basic Books.

Talmy, L. 2000. 'Force Dynamics in Language and Cognition.' In: L. Talmy, K. Allen (eds.), *Toward a Cognitive Semantics*. Cambridge, MA: MIT Press.

Tomasello, M. 1999. *The cultural origins of human cognition*. Cambridge, MA: Harvard University Press.

Van Baaren, R.B. 2005. 'The parrot effect: How to increase tip size.' *Cornell Hotel and Restaurant Administration Quarterly*, 46, 79-84.

Weir, A.A.S., J. Chappell & A. Kacelnik 2002. 'Shaping of Hooks in New Caledonian Crows.' *Science*, 297, 981.

Boxes or Creepers? Containments and entanglements of mind and matter

Tim Ingold

The anthropologist Gregory Bateson, in a lecture delivered in 1970, declared that 'the mental world – the mind – the world of information processing – is not limited by the skin' (Bateson 1973, 429). His point was that the processing loops involved in perception and action are not interior to the creature whose mind we are talking about, whether human or non-human, nor can that creature's activity be understood as mere behaviour – that is, as the mechanical output of one or more cognitive devices located in the head. Rather, such activity has to be understood as one aspect of the unfolding of a total system of relations comprised by the creature's embodied presence in a specific environment. Bateson's example was the blind man, finding his way along the street by means of a cane. Does the cane serve simply to conduct impulses from the physical world 'out there' to the interiority of the organism where, turned over to the mind and registered as sensations, they become the raw material from which the mind constructs a provisional picture or representation of what the external world might be like? This is what Descartes thought. In his *Optics* of 1637, Descartes had also resorted to the example of the blind man. The cane, he reasoned, functions for the blind just as do rays of light for the sighted. Both canes and rays transmit stimuli across a boundary between outside and inside (Descartes 1988, 67). But for Bateson the very idea of such a boundary, dividing the mind 'in here' from the world 'out there', appeared absurd. Do we draw the boundary around the blind man's head, at the handle of the cane, at its tip, or halfway down the pavement? If we ask where the mind is, the answer would not be 'in the head rather than out in the world'. It would be more appropriate to envisage mind as extending outwards into the environment along multiple sensory pathways of which the cane, in the hands of the blind man, is just one. Much more recently, in his book *Being There*, Andy Clark has made the same point. The mind, Clark tells us, is a 'leaky organ' that refuses to be confined within the skull but mingles shamelessly with the body and the world in the conduct of its operations (Clark 1997, 53). More strictly, he should have said that the skull is leaky, whereas the mind is what leaks!

My question is this. If mind is not an intrinsic property of the organism as a thing-in-itself, but rather immanent in the organism's relations within its environment, then in what sense can mind be said to evolve? And how might that evolution be explained? My argument is arranged in three parts. The first part is a negative one. It is to show that an evolutionary psychology that equates mind with an invariant and universal cognitive architecture, boxed inside the head of each and every individual, will not do the job. In the second part I explore the reasons why the science of the mind has come to 'think about thinking' in the way it predominantly does. I show that these have to do with a growing separation, in the constitution of modern metropolitan societies, of knowledge from movement. Finally, I suggest an alternative approach, according to which it is precisely through their movements along ways of life that organisms or persons grow into a knowledge of the world around them. Mind, then, extends along these very ways, traced out in processes of movement and growth, and evolves even as persons and organisms go about their lives.

The mind as architecture

The account of the evolution of mind proposed by evolutionary psychology is explicitly couched within a paradigm that appeals to Darwin for its scientific authority. Yet what has come to be known as 'neo-Darwinism' bears little resemblance to anything that Darwin ever wrote. Harnessed to the rhetoric of geneticism, the mechanism of natural selection has served as a back door through which the principle of intelligent design has been reintroduced into science, not as a manifestation of divine inspiration but as a reflection of scientific reason itself in the mirror of nature.[1] In evolutionary biology the argument by design is propped up by means of a conceptual distinction – first enunciated in 1911 by the Danish biologist Wilhelm Johannsen – between genotype and phenotype. The phenotype is the form or behaviour of an organism as manifested at any particular moment in its development; the genotype is a design specification or algorithm for building an organism of a certain kind that could, depending on the environmental conditions it encounters, take on the range of forms or exhibit the range of behaviours that we actually observe. Johannsen's key contribution was to insist that the manifest traits or characters comprising the phenotype could not be transmitted directly from parents to offspring. Rather, they are separately developed, in each successive generation, from the underlying genotype. The fundamental principle that only the characteristics of the genotype, and not those of the phenotype, are passed across generations has since become part of the central dogma of Darwinism.[2] Thus if we ask what evolves, the answer must be the genotype – that is, the organism not in its real observable form but in the 'virtual' guise of a yet-to-be-realised design. And this evolution comes about, it is supposed, because of changes, compounded over many generations, in the frequency of the genotype's information-bearing elements, namely genes.

A neo-Darwinian account of the evolution of mind therefore presupposes, first, that the mind is constructed according to a set of design specifications that are given in the genotype, independently and in advance of the organism's growth and development within an environment, and secondly, that the mind evolves as these genotypic specifications change. Evolutionary psychologists are inclined to speak of the mind as though it had an 'architecture' of cognitive devices for processing the data of sensory experience (Tooby & Cosmides 1992, 45-6). While these data are bound to vary from one environment to another, the architecture is said to be irrevocably fixed as a legacy from the evolutionary past, bestowed upon the organism with its genes at the very point of inauguration of its life-cycle. There are two problems with this account, one common to Darwinian evolutionary explanations in general, the other more specific to the project of evolutionary psychology. The first problem is that genes, on their own, encode nothing at all.[3] To put it another way, there is no 'reading' of the genetic 'script' that is not part and parcel of the developmental process itself (Ingold 2001, 121-2). Thus the genotype, conceived as a programme or specification that can be read off from the DNA of the genome in advance of development, and independently of its environmental context, does not exist – save as a construct in the imagination of the observing scientist. That is why, as noted above, the ultimate source of the design that natural selection is alleged to explain lies within science itself.

Evolutionary psychology, however, calls for more than the existence of the genotype – and this is the second problem. It requires that the cognitive devices needed for processing sensory data are already in place, not just in the virtual form of a design, but in the concrete hard-wiring of the brain. Somehow or other, strands of DNA have to turn themselves into neural circuitry, even before the organism embarks upon its life in an environment. How this happens remains a mystery.[4] Neo-Darwinism, in short, offers us an account of the evolution not of real organisms, alive to the world and active within it, but of virtual organisms in a continuum of abstract time and space. And evolutionary psychology offers an account of the mind as if it belonged to this virtual reality, and as if the real world were engineered in accordance with it. In this virtual world, minds are transported about within the bodies to which they belong. Carried across like pieces of portable architecture from point to point, they are supposed to assemble the data collected at each point into an overall representation of the world. Thus the mechanical, point-to-point displacement of the body is entirely detached from the intellectual processing of sensory inputs by the mind. Locomotion is one thing, cognition quite another. Only because of this imagined separation is evolutionary psychology able to envisage the mind as having an architecture that is 'hard', immune to the ebb and flow of life into which real organisms, indissolubly body and mind, are cast and destined to make their way around.

Thinking on one's feet

The idea that thinking involves the operation of a mind at rest, encased within a body in motion, holds a powerful sway over the modern imagination. How else can we explain the widespread credence accorded to the manifestly implausible accounts offered by evolutionary psychology? That it does not seem strange or counter-intuitive to separate knowledge from movement stems, I argue, from three areas of technological development, all of which are characteristic of modern metropolitan life. The first lies in the use of rigid footwear, the second in the paving of roads and streets, and the third in destination-oriented, vehicular transport.[5] To suggest that such mundane matters as the shoes we wear, the streets we walk on and the means of transport we use should have any bearing at all on the great philosophical questions of the day might seem outrageous. I would contend, however, that the strength, resilience and appeal of fundamental assumptions about mind and nature lie precisely in their grounding in pervasive aspects of everyday life generally considered so trivial as to escape critical attention. The revelation and acknowledgement of this grounding may then help us to find alternative ways of thinking more in tune with the experience and conditions of pre-modern – and especially of prehistoric – life.

Let me begin with the question of footwear. When Darwin, in presenting his theory of human evolution in *The Descent of Man*, compared the anatomy of human beings and the great apes, he placed much emphasis on the pronounced division of function, in humans, between hands and feet. The hands, he claimed, are servants of the intellect, put to work to implement the designs of the mind. The feet, by contrast, serve simply as mechanical supports for the body, making possible the achievement of upright posture, which in turn frees up the hands for their superior role.[6] In apes this division is much less developed – not only are the hands regularly used alongside the feet, for support, but also the feet retain a certain dexterity in the performance, alongside the hands, of complex manipulative operations (Darwin 1874, 77). This same theme of the division between hands and feet was also taken up in the works of T.H. Huxley and Edward Tylor, but it was significantly accompanied by an admission that the prototypical human foot, taken to exemplify the contrast, actually came from the modern European whose feet had been clad since childhood in stiff leather boots. Indeed Tylor owns that the contrast would have been far less striking, had the prototype of the human foot been taken from a 'savage' accustomed to going unshod (Huxley 1894, 119; Tylor 1881, 43-4).

The shoe was not, of course, a modern invention. People in the American Southwest were already wearing sandals some 9,000 years ago (Geib 2000), and it is likely that the use of moccasins made of woven fibre or animal skins dates back much further, to the Upper Palaeolithic of Eurasia, providing necessary thermal insulation against the rigours of winter in a glacial environment (Trinkaus 2005). Moreover, even the simplest footwear can affect the bone development of its habitual users (Tenner 2003, 58). Unlike the hard-soled sandal or the softer and more flexible moccasin, however, the leather boot encases the foot to a degree and with a rigidity unmatched by any previous shoe type. When such boots are worn from an early age they constrict the bones of developing feet, significantly reducing the splay and room for manoeuvre of the toes. Thus, if there is such a thing as the 'natural', evolved human foot, it is certainly not that of the boot-clad European. The effect of the boot is to amplify the support function, while at the same time greatly restricting dexterity. Picking things up or manipulating them with the toes becomes practically impossible. The boot moreover eliminates direct tactile contact with the ground surface, leaving the hands as the primary organs of touch.[7] Deprived of sensory contact and with its prehensile powers drastically curtailed, the foot was effectively reduced, in Tylor's own words, to a 'stepping machine' (1881, 43). The result was to divorce the mechanics of locomotion from the sphere of operation of human intelligence, delivered through the hands. Yet however much this separation may be obvious to the booted citizens of modern cities, it would have seemed strange to their predominantly barefoot, sandal-wearing or moccasin-clad rural predecessors.

Let me now turn to the question of paving. There is of course a connection between the impetus to pave the streets and the adoption of the boot. The hard pavement provides the ideal surface on which boot-clad pedestrians can exercise their feet as pedals of a stepping machine. On unpaved roads walkers have to pick their way, nimbly and with caution, avoiding ruts and potholes, as well as the accumulated filth deposited by people and animals whose lives are lived along the route. This calls for a degree of dexterity that is difficult to achieve with rigid boots. Indeed we know this only too well from the frequency with which we trip and fall when walking on poorly maintained pavements, where slabs have been lifted by tree-roots or other underground movements to leave dangerous exposed edges, or where the proverbial banana skin has been left ready for us to slip on. The ideal pavement offers no obstacles of this kind: it is perfectly smooth, and regularly swept of dirt. But by the same token it should afford nothing of interest to travellers who are free to look around, exercising to the full their powers of visual perception while leaving their feet, as it were, to look after themselves. Ideally the paved street should be open and straight, and properly lit at night, creating a fitting environment for the exercise of vision (Ogborn 1998, 91-104). Here again, we see how the work of the feet was excluded from the process of environmental perception, which became increasingly ocular rather than tactile. It is as though the traveller, in moving about, skims across the surface of the world, renewing total sensory contact only at the points where he or she comes to a halt.

This relates to a further and quite critical impact of paving. When you walk along an unpaved path or track, even though it may have been trodden by many feet before, your own movement contributes to its ongoing formation. You leave a trail, whether in the form of footprints or of other traces in the ground or vegetation cover. Each such trail is, quite literally, a way of life. Every person advances through life along the way, much like the tip of a growing root, laying a trail as they go.[8] The person, then, is instantiated in the landscape as the sum of their trails (Wagner 1986, 21). Paved surfaces, however, remain unmarked by the passage of human life. People, as they walk the paved streets, leave no trace of their movements, no record of their having passed by. It is as if they had never been. Thus, far from being instantiated in the world as a path of travel, each person appears as a self-contained module, propelled from point to point in a world that is already mapped out and constructed for them to occupy.

This brings me to the issue of transport. Literally, transport means the carrying across of people and/or goods from one location to another. As such, I suggest it should be distinguished from what I shall call wayfaring (Ingold 2007, 75-84). Throughout history and prehistory, the vast majority of human beings have been wayfarers. They have travelled along customary paths to and from places, from and to places elsewhere. Of course from time to time they have paused to rest, and have even returned repeatedly to the same place to do so. But these rests are just pauses in a life of movement, which continues for as long as life goes on.[9] Thus wayfaring always overshoots its destinations: wherever you are (and you are always somewhere) there is somewhere further you can go. Transport, by contrast, is destination-oriented. That is, it figures simply as a means to get from A to B. All movement is confined within these destinations; thus what for wayfarers are places of rest are – for transported passengers – sites of occupation. They are where all the activity is. In between, encased and relatively immobile within their vehicles, and deprived of direct sensory contact with the environment, passengers are nowhere. In effect, they no longer move but are moved. Whereas the wayfarer's movement is one of becoming, in that it is as much a process of growth or self-renewal as it is one of travel, the movement in transport is one of an already completed being from point to point. And whereas the wayfarer travels *along* paths *through* the world, the transported passenger routes from point to point *across* the surface of the world.

To this distinction between wayfaring and transport, as modalities of movement, there corresponds an equally crucial difference in our understanding of the growth and integration of knowledge (Ingold 2007, 87-90). In transport, the traveller moves *across* in order to build *up*, assembling the observations or materials collected at each successive destination into overarching structures of ever-increasing scope and generality. The lateral movements, here, are entirely ancillary to the vertical assembly of knowledge, in rather the same way that the movements of a conveyor belt, on an industrial production line, are ancillary to the assembly of the components added at successive stations. Herein lies the practical source of the distinction, which I have already shown to be deeply ingrained in evolutionary psychology, between locomotion and cognition. The mind is imagined as though it were carried about in the body, like a passenger in a vehicle, collecting data from successive points *en route* and piecing them together into map-like representations, without leaving any trace on the ground or being in any way marked by the experience of movement itself. The movement, here, simply serves to relocate the body from one point of observation to the next, and plays no part in the integration of the data so obtained.

Of course there *are* forms of movement, even on foot, that approximate to the model of pure transport. One such is the so-called 'striding gait', a rigidly mechanical, straight-legged oscillation from the hips, with the eyes gazing steadfastly ahead rather than downcast, that only really works with booted feet on a paved, level surface such as a parade ground.[10] On any other surface one would be liable to trip up. Evolutionary theorists, modelling the walking of ancestral humans as transport, have long considered the striding gait to be the quintessential human locomotor achievement (for example, Napier 1967). But the stride enacts a bodily image of colonial occupation, straddling the distance between points of departure and arrival as though one could have a foot in each simultaneously, encompassing both – and all points in between – in a single appropriative movement. Our earliest ancestors, however, were inhabitants, not occupants. Far from striding out in heavy boots across the paved surfaces of the world, they made their way for the most part lightly, dextrously and often barefoot (or in soft-soled shoes). Nor were the feet used exclusively for walking.

They could be used, in conjunction with the hands, for creeping, crawling, climbing and a host of other purposes.[11]

It is in this dextrous wayfaring along paths of life and travel, I contend, and not in the processing of data collected from multiple points of observation, that inhabitants' knowledge is developed. This knowledge is not so much built *up* as forged *along* paths of movement, in the passage from place to place and the changing horizons along the way (Ingold 2000, 227). For inhabitants, moving *is* knowing. It is through the practices of wayfaring, then, that knowledge is integrated. Inhabitants do not so much construct or assemble their knowledge as grow into it, in their movements along ways of life. Or in short, inhabitant knowledge is not vertically but *alongly* integrated. Locomotion and cognition are inseparable: thought, in the words of dance philosopher Maxine Sheets-Johnstone, 'is motional through and through' (1999, 486). It follows that an account of mind must be as much concerned with the work of the feet as with that of the head and hands.

The mind as meshwork

How, then, should we imagine the mind? Not, I suggest, as a fixed architectural structure, whose box-like compartments or capacities are to be filled with appropriate cultural content. The mind is not a container for knowledge, nor will it be contained. We should rather think of it as comprising ever so many paths, trails or creepers, threading their way through the environment, along which a person lives and moves, and thereby grows into knowledge. To adopt this image entails a fundamental shift of perspective, of precisely the kind that Bateson called for in the lecture to which I referred at the outset. We are so used to thinking of mind as 'in here' rather than 'out there', invoking a frontier between the inside and the outside of a person or organism where none exists. I believe that this habit stems from a certain logic, deeply sedimented in the canons of modern thought, which seems bent on converting the paths along which life is lived and knowledge is grown into boundaries within which it is contained. I call this the logic of inversion. Through inversion, beings originally open to the world are closed in upon themselves, sealed by an outer shell that protects their inner constitution from the traffic of interaction with their surroundings, much as transported passengers are sealed within their vehicles. Thus in the distinction between phenotype and genotype, which as we have already seen is foundational to the entire neo-Darwinian paradigm, the organism – living and growing along lines that bind it into the web of life – is reconfigured as the outward expression of an inner design. Likewise the person, acting and perceiving within a nexus of intertwined relationships, is presumed to behave according to the directions of cultural models or cognitive schemata installed inside his or her head.

My aim in this final section is to reverse this logic.[12] The mind having been turned, as it were, 'outside in', I shall endeavour to turn it inside out again in order to recover that original openness to the world in which inhabitants dwell. To explain what I mean, let me present a simple illustration. Imagine an organism or a person. We might depict it like this:

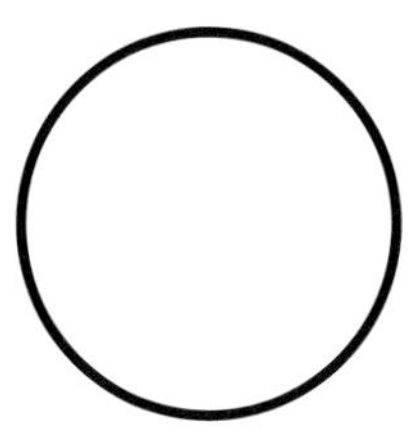

But in this apparently innocent depiction I have already effected an inversion. I have folded the being in on itself such that it is delineated and contained within a perimeter boundary, set off against a surrounding world – an environment – with which it is destined to interact according to its nature. The organism or person is 'inside', the environment 'outside'. But instead of drawing a circle, I might just as well have drawn a line. So let us start again. Here is an organism-person:

In this depiction there is no inside or outside, and no boundary separating the two domains. Rather there is a trail of movement or growth.

Every such trail traces a relation. But the relation is not *between* one thing and another – between the organism-person 'here' and the environment 'there'. It is rather a trail *along* which life is lived. Neither beginning here and ending there nor vice versa, the trail winds through, or *amidst*, without beginning or end, as do the waters of a river whose line of flow is orthogonal to the transverse connection across its banks. It is in coursing along and amidst, as the philosophers Gilles Deleuze and Félix Guattari put it, that 'things take on speed' (1983, 58). The trail, in short, is a 'line of becoming' which, as Keith Ansell Pearson explains, 'is not defined in terms of connectable points, or by the points which compose it, since it has only a "middle"' (Pearson 1999, 169). Becoming is not a connection between this and that but follows a 'line of flight' that pulls away from both. Each such line, however, is but one strand in a tissue of lines that together make up the texture of the lifeworld. This texture is what I mean when I speak of organisms or persons being constituted within a relational field. It is a field not of interconnected points but of interwoven lines, not a network but a *meshwork*.

The distinction is critical. Yet it has been persistently obscured, above all in the elaboration of what has come to be known, rather unfortunately, as 'actor-network theory'. For many, the appeal of the theory lies in its offer of a way to describe interactions among persons and things that does not concentrate mind or agency in human hands, but rather takes it to be distributed around all the interconnected elements of an assemblage, whether human or non-human, animate or inanimate. The term 'actor-network', however, first entered the literature as a translation from the French *acteur réseau*. And as one of its leading proponents – Bruno Latour – has observed in hindsight, the translation gave it a significance that was never intended. In popular usage, inflected by innovations in information and communications technology, the defining attribute of the network is connectivity: 'transport *without* deformation, an instantaneous, unmediated access to every piece of information' (Latour 1999, 15). But *réseau* can refer just as well to netting as to network – to woven fabric, the tracery of lace, the plexus of the nervous system or the web of the spider. The lines of the spider's web, for example, quite unlike those of the communications network, do not connect points or join things up. They are rather spun from materials exuded from the spider's body and are laid down as it moves about. In that sense they are extensions of the spider's very being as it trails into the environment. They are the lines *along* which it lives, and conduct its perception and action in the world.

The *acteur réseau* was intended by its originators (if not by those who have been beguiled by its translation as 'network') to be comprised of just such lines of becoming. Like the web, it is – in our terms – not a network but a meshwork. Of course to depict the organism or person within the meshwork as a single line, as we have done above, is a gross over-simplification. As with the spider, lives generally extend along not one but multiple lines, knotted together at the centre but trailing innumerable 'loose ends' at the periphery. Thus each should be pictured, as Latour has latterly suggested, in the shape of a star 'with a center surrounded by many radiating lines, with all sorts of tiny conduits leading to and fro' (Latour 2005, 177).[13] It now looks something like this:

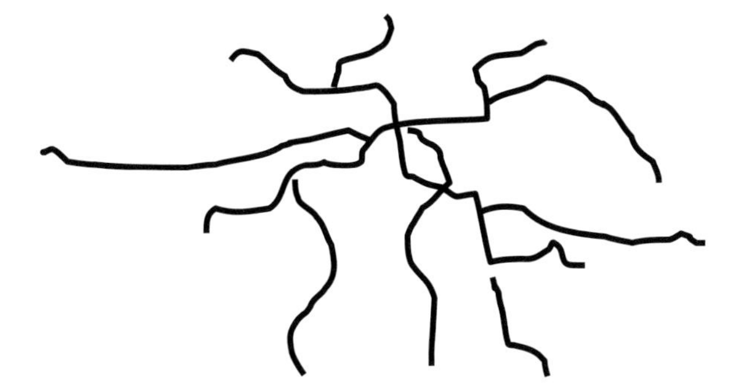

No longer a self-contained object like a ball that can propel itself from place to place, the organism-person now appears as an ever ramifying web of lines of growth. Deleuze and Guattari (1983) famously likened this web to a rhizome, though I prefer the image of the fungal mycelium. As the mycologist Alan Rayner (1997) has suggested, the whole of biology would be different had it taken the mycelium as the prototypical exemplar of a living organism.[14] By starting with the 'mycelial person' (Ingold 2003) as a bundle of lines, I believe our understanding of social life can be similarly transformed.

But what, now, has happened to the environment? It cannot be what literally *surrounds* the organism or person, since you cannot surround a web without drawing a line around it. And that would immediately be to effect an inversion, converting those relations along which the organism-person lives its life in the world into internal properties of which its life is but the outward expression (Ingold 2006, 13). We can imagine, however, that lines of growth issuing from multiple sources become comprehensively entangled with one another, rather like the vines and creepers of a dense patch of tropical forest, or the tangled root systems that you cut through with your spade every time you dig the garden. What we have been accustomed to calling 'the environment' might, then, be better envisaged as a domain of entanglement. It is within such a tangle of interlaced trails, continually ravelling here and unravelling there, that beings grow or 'issue forth' along the lines of their relationships.

This tangle is the texture of the world – the 'big tapestry of Nature', as the geographer Torsten Hägerstrand prophetically put it, 'which history is weaving'.[15] It has no insides or outsides, only openings and 'ways through'. As beings do not simply occupy the world but inhabit it, so – in threading their own paths through the meshwork – they contribute to its ever-evolving weave. Thus we must cease regarding the world as an inert substratum, over which living things propel themselves about like counters on a board. They are not objects that move, undergoing displacement from point to point across the world's surface. Indeed the inhabited world, as such, has no surface. Whatever surfaces one encounters, whether of the ground, water, vegetation or buildings, are *in* the world, not *of* it (Ingold 2000, 241). And woven into their very texture are the lines of growth and movement of its inhabitants. Every such line, in short, is a way *through* rather than *across*. And it is as their lines of movement, not as mobile, self-propelled entities, that beings are instantiated in the world.

I have argued that the knowledge of inhabitants, far from being assembled into received compartments of an architectural structure, is continually forged in the process of moving around. This, in turn gives us an open-ended way of thinking about mind as a flow, current or circulatory movement in which knowledge undergoes perpetual formation. Can we, then, describe this movement as a process of evolution? I think we can, but it means adopting a sense of evolution quite different from that enshrined in neo-Darwinian orthodoxy. According to the latter, as we have seen, every individual is (phylogenetically) endowed with the essential specifications for carrying on a particular form of life, independently and in advance of its (ontogenetic) growth and development in an environment. Each exists to be itself, to fulfil a project coterminous with its own life-span. What is passed on to the future is not its life, but a set of elementary instructions that may be recombined in the formation of other projects for other lives (Ingold 1986, 106-7). This is the founding axiom of what I have elsewhere called the 'genealogical model' (Ingold 2002, 2009), and its effect, as Charles Gillespie rightly notes, is to convert 'the whole range of nature which had been relegated to becoming, as a problem in being, an infinite set of objective situations reaching back through time' (Gillespie 1959, 291). While the life of the organism may be mapped geographically as sequence of point-to-point transports across a plane surface, from a genealogical perspective its entire life is condensed into a single point. It is no wonder that Charles Darwin, in the only illustration in *The Origin of Species*, chose to depict the phyletic line as a series of dots (Darwin 1950 [1859], 90-1).

For an alternative image we can turn to the philosopher Henri Bergson. In his *Creative Evolution* of 1911, Bergson declared that 'the living being is, above all, a thoroughfare'. Though presenting the appearance of a self-contained, bounded entity or module, in reality 'the very permanence of [its] form is only the outline of a movement' (Bergson 1911, 135). Following Bergson's lead, I have suggested that every being is instantiated in the world not as a bounded entity but as a thoroughfare, along the path of its own movement and activity. What we call 'mind', then, is an entwinement of these proliferating trails. This is not, to repeat, the 'adapted mind' of evolutionary psychology, with its suite of pre-programmed computational devices, engineered by natural selection and installed inside the head as a precondition for its possessor's encounter with the environment. Nor however is it equivalent to the 'extended mind' of the network theorist who would have us believe that mental activity enchains heterogeneous devices from a material world beyond the bounds of the organism or person. To the contrary, we hold that the organism-person is no more bounded than the mind is. Mind is neither an internal property of discrete, bounded individuals, nor is it distributed around extended networks of persons and things. It is rather immanent in what Annemarie Mol and John Law (1994) have called 'fluid space' – a field of relations constituted by the flows, circulations and transformations of vital materials that come together in the forms and agencies of the living world.

The evolution of mind has therefore to be understood, topologically rather than statistically, as the temporal unfolding of this relational field. In such a relational conception of the evolutionary process, there can be no distinction between genotype and phenotype or, correspondingly, between phylogenesis and ontogenesis. Mind evolves, as we have seen, along the meshwork of trails that infiltrates the lifeworld and gives it its characteristic texture. If we would excavate the mind, then what we may expect to unearth is not a box of devices but a morass of creepers.

Notes

This chapter is based on a paper originally presented to the conference *Excavating the Mind*, held at the University of Aarhus in October 2004. A year later I revised it for publication in the conference volume. The final revisions were made, in response to the very helpful comments of two anonymous reviewers and the volume's editors, more than two years later – in December 2007. Over the course of these three years my own ideas have moved on considerably, largely thanks to the award by the UK Economic and Social Research Council of a three-year (2005-08) Professorial Fellowship for a programme of research entitled *Comparative Explorations in the Anthropology of the Line*. Inevitably, therefore, this chapter presents something of an amalgam of arguments drawn from different stages in the development of this programme. The chapter, then, should be read as a record of work in progress rather than as a final statement of my current thinking.

1 It is important to distinguish the rhetoric of geneticism from the science of genetics. The science is open to a variety of interpretations as to the nature of the gene and its role in developmental processes. The rhetoric, by contrast, is one that imagines a design specification for the construction of the organism, abstracted from any particular environmental context, pre-installed at the heart of the organism itself, whence it orchestrates the processes of development. Those who voice this rhetoric in the name of Science differ hardly at all from their most bitter opponents – the advocates of 'intelligent design' – who justify their position by appeal to fundamentalisms of a more theological kind. Both sides are equally committed

to the principle of intelligence in nature. The issue is about whose intelligence has the greater authority.

2 On the history of the phenotype/genotype distinction, and its role in twentieth century biological thought, see Gudding (1996).

3 The idea that genes encode 'information' is based on a simple confusion between the specialised, information-theoretic sense of the term and its more conventional, semantic sense (Kay 1998; Ingold 2004a). This confusion is still rampant.

4 I should stress that the problem here is logical rather than empirical. I have no wish to deny the huge advances in the neurophysiology of early ontogenetic development. But at whatever point in the life-cycle of an organism – even before birth – we might identify a particular 'device' or processing circuit, a history of development already lies behind it. Thus the mammalian foetus, even as it inhabits the womb, develops in the uterine environment – an environment that is not constant but susceptible to the surroundings, activities and diet of the mother. Birth, as Catherine Dent (1990, 693) has pointed out, 'is a transition, not a magic starting point before which experience cannot play a role.' The logical fallacy, most succinctly stated by Susan Oyama, is simply to suppose that forms or structures pre-exist the processes that give rise to them (Oyama 1985, 13).

5 I have presented this argument at greater length elsewhere (Ingold 2004b), and merely summarise it here.

6 The idea that bipedal locomotion liberates the hands, and furthermore that the free hand endows human beings with an intellectual superiority over all other creatures, was by no means original to Darwin, and can be traced back to classical Antiquity. It is to be found in the writings of Xenophon, Aristotle, Vitruvius and Gregory of Nyssa, and was already commonplace among naturalists of the eighteenth and early nineteenth centuries (Stoczkowski 2002, 87-8).

7 It could be argued, of course, that the hard calluses that develop on the feet of people who habitually go barefoot have the same effect as the soles of boots, in blocking tactile sensation. I do not believe, however, that this block is nearly so pronounced. Indeed, as Richard Sennett has recently argued, with regard to the calluses developed by people who use their hands professionally, the thickened layer of skin, far from deadening touch, may have the reverse effect: 'the callus both sensitizes the hand to minute physical spaces and stimulates the sensation at the finger tips' (Sennett 2008: 153).

8 Batek women from Pahang, Malaysia, according to Tuck Po Lye (1997, 159), actually say that the roots of the wild tubers they collect for food 'walk' as humans and other animals do. For the Batek, walking is a matter of laying a trail as one goes along. And this is exactly what roots do as they issue forth along lines of growth, threading their ways through the soil. The walker's trail and the trailing root are phenomena of the same kind.

9 I contend that life is lived in movement, regardless of whether the people concerned are regarded, according to a more conventional anthropological classification, as nomadic or sedentary. So-called nomads do not, of course, wander aimlessly but along well-worn paths and through well-established places, the longevity of which often exceeds that of settlements whose more sedentary populations place a greater strain on environmental resources in the vicinity. In their everyday labours, however, sedentary people move no less than nomads: the difference is in the *pattern* of movement, not in its extent. Settlers return more constantly, or with less intermission, to the same places of rest.

10 That the striding gait has been taken as the prototypical instance of human walking owes much, as Mary Flesher (1997) has shown, to the fact that the scientific study of human locomotion has its roots in military discipline. Indeed many of the earliest subjects to be roped into locomotion research were soldiers, already trained in the routines of the drill. It is hardly surprising that when commanded to walk they stepped out as if on parade!

11 For a range of ethnographic and historical examples, see Watanabe (1971) and Devine (1985).

12 I draw here on an argument presented more fully elsewhere (Ingold 2006).

13 In this regard, Latour's position would come close to ours, were it not for his persistent confusion of knots with nodes (for example, see 2005, 44), and hence of the meshwork with the network (Ingold 2007, 98-100). This has led many of his followers, such as the geographer Sarah Whatmore, to confuse connectivity with flow. Whatmore calls for 'hybrid geographies' that would be characterised by 'a shift in analytical emphasis from reiterating fixed surfaces to tracing points of connection and lines of flow' (2007, 343). Tracing connections is one thing, however; following flow-lines is quite another.

14 As Pearson has shown (1999, 166-8), there are indeed clear parallels between Rayner's work and the rhizomatics of Deleuze and Guattari.

15 Hägerstrand imagined every constituent of the environment – including 'humans, plants, animals and things all at once' – as having a continuous trajectory or line of becoming. As they move through time and encounter one another, the trajectories of diverse constituents are bundled together. 'Seen from within one could think of the tips of trajectories as sometimes being pushed forward by forces behind and besides and sometimes having eyes looking around and arms reaching out, at every moment asking "what shall I do next"?' (Hägerstrand 1976, 332).

References

Bateson, G. 1973. *Steps to an Ecology of Mind*. London: Granada.

Bergson, H. 1911. *Creative Evolution*, trans. A. Mitchell. London: Macmillan.

Clark, A. 1997. *Being There: Putting Brain, Body and the World Together Again*. Cambridge, Mass.: MIT Press.

Darwin, C. 1874. *The Descent of Man, and Selection in Relation to Sex* (2nd edn.). London: John Murray.

Darwin, C. 1950(1859). *On the Origin of Species by Means of Natural Selection, or, the Preservation of Favoured Races in the Struggle for Life*. London: Watt.

Deleuze,G. & F. Guattari 1983. *On the Line*, trans. J. Johnston. New York: Semiotext(e).

Dent, C.H. 1990. 'An Ecological Approach to Language Development: An Alternative Functionalism.' *Developmental Psychobiology*, 23, 679-703.

Descartes, R. 1988. *Descartes: Selected Philosophical Writings*, trans. J. Cottingham, R. Stoothoff, D. Murdoch. Cambridge: Cambridge University Press.

Devine, J. 1985. 'The Versatility of Human Locomotion.' *American Anthropologist*, 87, 550-70.

Flesher, M.M. 1997. 'Repetitive Order and the Human Walking Apparatus: Prussian Military Science Versus the Webers' Locomotion Research.' *Annals of Science*, 54(5), 463-87.

Geib, P.R. 2000. 'Sandal Types and Archaic Prehistory on the Colorado Plateau.' *American Antiquity*, 65, 509-24.

Gillespie, C.S. 1959. 'Lamarck and Darwin in the History of Science.' In: B. Glass, O. Temkin, W. L. Straus, Jr. (eds.), *Forerunners of Darwin: 1745-1859*. Baltimore, MD: Johns Hopkins University Press, 265-91.

Gudding, G. 1996. 'The Phenotype/Genotype Distinction and the Disappearance of the Body.' *Journal of the History of Ideas*, 57(3), 525-45.

Hägerstrand, T. 1976. 'Geography and the Study of the Interaction Between Nature and Society.' *Geoforum*, 7, 329-34.

Huxley, T.H. 1894. *Man's Place in Nature, and Other Anthropological Essays*. London: Macmillan.

Ingold, T. 1986. *Evolution and Social Life*. Cambridge: Cambridge University Press.

Ingold, T. 2000. *The Perception of the Environment: Essays on Livelihood, Dwelling and Skill*. London: Routledge.

Ingold, T. 2001. 'From the Transmission of Representations to the Education of Attention.' In: H. Whitehouse (ed.), *The Debated Mind: Evolutionary Psychology Versus Ethnography*. Oxford: Berg, 113-53.

Ingold, T. 2002. 'Between Evolution and History: Biology, Culture, and the Myth of Human Origins.' In: M. Wheeler, J. Ziman, M.A. Boden (eds.), *The Evolution of Cultural Entities*. (Proceedings of the British Academy, 112). Oxford: oxford University Press, 43-66.

Ingold, T. 2003. 'Two Reflections on Ecological Knowledge.' In: G. Sanga, G. Ortalli (eds.), *Nature Knowledge: Ethnoscience, Cognition, Identity*. New York: Berghahn, 301-11.

Ingold, T. 2004a. 'Beyond Biology and Culture: The Meaning of Evolution in a Relational World.' *Social Anthropology*, 12(2), 209-21.

Ingold, T. 2004b. 'Culture on the Ground: The World Perceived Through the Feet.' *Journal of Material Culture*, 9(3), 315-40.

Ingold, T. 2006. 'Rethinking the Animate, Re-animating Thought.' *Ethnos*, 71(1), 1-12.

Ingold, T. 2007. *Lines: A Brief History*. London: Routledge.

Ingold, T. 2009. 'Stories Against Classification: Transport, Wayfaring and the Integration of Knowledge.' In: S. Bamford, J. Leach (eds.), *Kinship and Beyond: The Genealogical Model Reconsidered*. New York: Berghahn, 193-213.

Kay, L.E. 1998. 'A Book of Life? How the Genome Became an Information System and DNA a Language.' *Perspectives in Biology and Medicine*, 41, 504-28.

Latour, B. 1999. 'On Recalling ANT.' In: J. Law, J. Hassard (eds.), *Actor Network Theory and After*. Oxford: Blackwell, 15-25.

Latour, B. 2005. *Reassembling the Social: An Introduction to Actor-Network Theory*. Oxford: Oxford University Press.

Lye, T.-P. 1997. *Knowledge, Forest, and Hunter-Gatherer Movement: The Batek of Pahang, Malaysia*. Unpublished doctoral dissertation, University of Hawai'i at Manoa.

Mol, A. & J. Law 1994. 'Regions, Networks and Fluids: Anaemia and Social Topology.' *Social Studies of Science*, 24, 641-71.

Napier, J. 1967. 'The Antiquity of Human Walking.' In: *Human Variations and Origins: Readings from the Scientific American*. San Francisco: Freeman, 116-26.

Ogborn, M. 1998. *Spaces of Modernity: London's Geographies, 1680-1780*. London: Guildford Press.

Oyama, S. 1985. *The Ontogeny of Information: Developmental Systems and Evolution*. Cambridge: Cambridge University Press.

Pearson, K.A. 1999. *Germinal Life: The Difference and Repetition of Deleuze*. London: Routledge.

Rayner, A. 1997. *Degrees of Freedom: Living in Dynamic Boundaries*. London: Imperial College Press.

Sennett, R. 2008. *The Craftsman*. London: Allen Lane.

Sheets-Johnstone, M. 1999. *The Primacy of Movement*. Amsterdam: John Benjamins.

Stoczkowski, W. 2002. *Explaining Human Origins: Myth, Imagination and Conjecture*, trans. M. Turton. Cambridge: Cambridge University Press.

Tenner, E. 2003. *Our Own Devices: The Past and Future of Body Technology*. New York: Alfred A. Knopf.

Tooby, J. & L. Cosmides 1992. 'The Psychological Foundations of Culture.' In: J.H. Barkow, L. Cosmides, J. Tooby (eds.), *The Adapted Mind: Evolutionary Psychology and the Generation of Culture*. New York: Oxford University Press, 19-136.

Trinkaus, E. 2005. 'Anatomical Evidence for the Antiquity of Human Footwear Use.' *Journal of Archaeological Science*, 32, 1515-26.

Tylor, E.B. 1881. *Anthropology: An Introduction to the Study of Man and Civilization*. London: Macmillan.

Wagner, R. 1986. *Symbols That Stand for Themselves*. Chicago: University of Chicago Press.

Watanabe, H. 1971. 'Running, Creeping and Climbing: A New Ecological and Evolutionary Perspective on Human Evolution.' *Mankind*, 8, 1-13.

Whatmore, S. 2007. 'Hybrid Geographies: Rethinking the "Human" in Human Geography.' In: L. Kalof, A. Fitzgerald (eds.), *The Animals Reader*. Oxford: Berg, 337-48.

On Being More-Than-One and Doubts About Mind

Chris Gosden

The key question I shall address in this chapter is: what makes us more-than-one? And, more pertinently for the subject of this book, how does the fundamentally relational character of human being influence the usefulness of the concept of mind?

Human beings are sensate, skilled, discriminating and desiring. Each of these human attributes requires a relationship – one cannot be sensate without something to sense; skills are exercised with people or things and commonly with both; discrimination requires choice between alternatives and desire turns a person outward as much as in. Our relations with the world are multiple and derive from stances and attitudes stemming from our history as cultural beings. The state of being more-than-one encompasses human relations with objects, with other species and with humans. Being more-than-one is not a state someone can control straightforwardly but derives from the influences from all parts of their relationships. It is constant in the fact that we are always combined with others, but changing as these relationships move and shift. Skills are not learned alone, but as members of a group. Most activities are carried out by a collective and although an individual organism feels desire, such feelings have broader resonance and social sanction.

The fact that we are all more-than-one calls into question the importance of mind. I have a brain made up of neurons and synaptic connections, linked in complicated ways to the rest of my body through the central nervous system, influenced by the limbic system and other elements of my biochemistry. The conjoined nature of brain and body mean that the brain spends a lot of time monitoring the states of the body, so that it is profoundly influenced by these. In Western thought we often conflate the mind and the brain. If the former has a location anywhere it is in our heads, linked to the location and the workings of the brain. The mind is crucially immaterial; an abstract mental space where imagination unfolds and ideas are born. An immaterial mind makes for a massive disjuncture between the physicality of the body and our mental processes. The location of the mind in the head has acted somewhat to dematerialise the brain, the electrical, synaptic aspects of which sit most happily with a notion of mind. But now that the material nature of the brain is being re-emphasised by some, as well as the intimacy of its connection with the rest of the body, the connection with an immaterial mind is called into doubt (Damasio 2000). Furthermore, many social sciences are keen to connect the human body with the material world as a whole. Here thinkers like Latour (2005) are key in sketching out the entangled nature of things and people, whereby the capacities of people are only activated and developed through objects of particular types and these objects are brought into being by people. There is a strong recursive element, in that as people shape the world it then shapes them, and so on, in an infinite spiral. Two points emerge here: the radical connectedness of all aspects of the human body, including the brain, and their consequent mutual influences; the embeddedness and entanglement of humans in a broader material world which helps to link people together in complicated ways. But a third element of the argument is possible and for me most important – that we can and should doubt the discontinuity between an abstract mind and a material body in its world. Setting up such a bi-partite model of humanity makes it hard to understand how material forces in the musculature or biochemistry of the body in conjunction with wood or stone or metal can be transformed into virtual thoughts, images or verbal constructs.

One way of dealing with this division is through notions of extended mind or embodied cognition which see cognitive processes that happen in our minds as being due to interactions with the material world through the medium of the body. Andy Clark (1997), Mark Rowlands (2003) and Mike Wheeler (2005) have built on longer philosophical traditions going back to Heidegger and Marx to develop concepts of extended mind or externalism. Extended mind keeps the concept of mind and the inside::outside distinction, but looks for greater parity in the causal efficacy of what is happening outside the body with what is taking place in the mind. Thus in this argument physical things can act as mnemonics, so that streets we have not walked down for years can prompt us from one street corner to the next and the route gradually unfolds as we walk, even though we were not able to construct the whole route in our memories before we started our walk. In this instance, memory does not just reside in the mind but in the prompts to action the world provides through the processes of that action.

I have been greatly influenced by these notions of extended mind or externalism, but have come to see them as not going far enough. The major metaphors used are spatial – those of extension and embodiedness – but these leave intact a crucial element of older ideas of mind which lies in the differences between the material and the immaterial, with the consequent problem of how to connect them. The concentration on the cognitive too has a tendency to see information retrieval and processing (as in the case of remembering a route) as the fundamental human attributes. If we start instead with a greater emphasis on desire and emotion as animators of action the body comes to the fore. Remembering a route is not an isolated act. We are retracing our steps, nervous perhaps of the interview we are going to attend, or excited about seeing an old friend. The nervousness felt in our stomachs or the light-headedness of excitement are profoundly bodily and derive from a particular condition of relatedness, of being more-than-one. Such sensations are temporal, so that they unfold over time and such unfolding gives them much of their quality and force. The nature of temporality in human action needs emphasis so as to complement spatial metaphors which tend to start with the idea of an interior mind and work outwards from that. A counter picture of a distributed system in which the sequence or frequency of connections gives value and force to cultural processes is one which needs exploring.

Two key changes are necessary to develop productive approaches to intelligence and mind. The first is a concentration on time and temporality, rather than space or extension. The second is to erase the idea of mind, taking with it the discontinuity between the material and the immaterial. Rather than develop these points in the abstract, as I have done so far, I would like to dwell on an example before coming back to more general points at the end. This will involve an initial move away from issues of mind, so as to introduce the archaeology of interest, which in this case is so-called Celtic art in Britain from the third century BC to the period after the Roman invasion in AD 43.

'... an art with no genesis...' (Jacobsthal 1944, 157)

The material known as Celtic art in Britain represents an odd collective of objects which owes as much to archaeologists' categories as it does to any mode of grouping or using the material in the Iron Age. Generally included under this label are personal ornaments (such as arm rings and torcs), weapons or armour (daggers, helmets, shields and swords), horse and chariot gear and varied items including fire dogs, mirrors, spoons and tankards. This material is decorated variously with fine incised lines forming linear and circular forms, relief decoration upstanding from the general body of the object and through the use of coral or glasses to provide colour contrasts. Brooches and coins are generally excluded, except on those occasions where details of form or iconography make it relevant to draw them into a discussion. These items are first found in Britain around 300 BC (although dating is a problem) and they continue until well after the Roman invasion of AD 43. A variety of decoration is seen ranging from human or animal forms to the three-dimensional nature of some objects, for instance terrets or massive armlets, with enamelling a prominent feature of the British material. The majority of objects are made from bronze, brass or iron, but are also found in silver, electrum or gold, or, very rarely pottery, wood and bone. The forms and decoration of the British objects are often linked to continental types and seen by many to have continental origins ultimately. The lack of graves in Britain for much of the Iron Age means that the majority of the finds counted as Celtic art are from dry land hoards or wet contexts, with a minority from settlements or burials, so that they lack the sorts of contextual details that can link them to other aspects of the archaeological record. The British metalwork is part of a larger distribution from Ireland to Romania and north Germany to northern Italy. Human bodies in Britain were linked into a widespread pattern of aesthetics and sensibility which gained some power from being so widely shared. The effectiveness of these material forms is demonstrated by the rapidity of its spread. As the Jacobsthal quote above indicates, there is no slow coming into being of Celtic art. It starts suddenly in the decades before 400 BC and carries on in most of Europe for about three centuries, except for Britain where objects within the general style are produced through the Roman period and beyond. Although fine metalwork is widespread individual forms and modes of decoration are localized, so that in Britain complex curvilinear decoration is found to a greater extent than elsewhere (apart from Ireland) as is the use of colour through glass inlays. The phenomenon known as Celtic art encompasses both widespread forms with highly localized manifestations helping to create local aesthetic conditions and effects, but also maintaining connections to a wider world.

In looking at such aesthetic effects I am interested in investigating what objects of particular forms and types of decoration could do in terms of creating and shaping human experience and social relations between people. In making such a move I am following recent trends within anthropology which focus not on what objects mean, but on what they do in shaping relationships between people (see Gell 1998 for a polemical rehearsal of this position). There has also been a drawn out and sometimes productive debate in anthropology as to whether art or aesthetics is a more conducive conceptual starting point for productive analysis (see Gell 1998 again, also Ingold 1996; Banks & Morphy 1997). The argument against either term is that they are too culturally loaded, freighted down with western preconceptions concerning material and visual culture. This is undoubtedly true (as it is of all terms) but I feel that the idea of aesthetics can be freed from notions of refinement and beauty to look at the sensory appeal that objects have, and through the senses the emotional impacts they are likely to create (see Gosden 2005 for a longer rehearsal of this argument). The key link is between the formal characteristics of objects (their morphology and decoration) and their impact on people, which then gives content to social relations. In archaeology, we may never know the specific impacts that individual objects had, but can discuss this in general terms looking at the objects themselves, the materials from which they are made and their occurrences in archaeological contexts (Garrow & Gosden in prep. will follow through these approaches in more detail). An approach which focuses on the impact that objects have on people is likely also to explore the active role of objects in shaping and channelling human relationships.

Materials matter and their characteristics influence the ways in which they are both used and categorized. We need to be aware that substances we group together may not have been categorized in the same manner in the Iron Age. Here, our category of metal might be suspect, making us wonder whether bronze and iron were seen as equivalent substances. Bronze needed trade links to bring together the various components of the alloy and consequently had particular social as well as chemical requirements. Bronze could also turn from solid to liquid and back to a solid state, something not possible with iron in Europe until the early modern period. Neither did bronze decay in the same manner as iron once in the ground. Its lack of decay and the possibility of becoming liquid was something that bronze shared with silver and gold, both of which see a resurgence of use in the late Iron Age after some centuries of absence. Iron is a reluctant technology, being found in Britain from at least 1000 BC, but not becoming common until 200 years later. Even then, however, iron did not so much replace bronze as complement it and the relationship between the two materials would bear much more study (both Bradley 2007 and Hingley 2006 have started to explore the possible differences between iron and bronze, but much more could still be done). If it is true that iron and bronze did not naturally fit within a single category of metal, then objects containing both substances might well have been of great and multiple importance. We need also to be aware of the possible temporal differences of varying substances – in late prehistory bronze could be melted and hence recycled, so that old bronze could be incorporated into new objects. But this was not true of iron, which could not be melted, so that although older material might be forged together with new, this was an arduous process not likely to have been undertaken regularly. Once buried, iron and bronze enjoyed different life cycles, with iron rusting and decaying rapidly as archaeologists know to their cost, but bronze behaving more like gold in that it resisted decay more vigorously, so that it could be re-used once it had been buried.

Temporal complexity is also found in the matter of decorative styles. Jacobsthal (1944) developed a four-stage style sequence for the art which has remained the basis for most subsequent schemes. In his Early style there are palmette and other vegetal forms of ornament, ultimately derived from Greek art by way of the Etruscans, mixed with older geometric Hallstatt motifs. These date from around 420 BC until around 350 BC, when they are superseded by the so-called Waldalgesheim style, named after a site in Germany. Here rounded triangular shapes have a tendril emanating from one corner to form a wave-like frieze of considerable complexity. From around 250 BC in Jacobstahl's scheme are two parallel styles, the Plastic and Sword styles. In the former, relief is common either through complex repousse work (where metal is beaten out from the back to form a raised front surface) or added metal or coral to give a three-dimensional effect. The Sword style encompasses figurative forms sometimes seen as dragon-pairs and also complex curvilinear incised ornament. For Continental Europe the three sequential styles (Early, Waldalgesheim, Plastic/Sword) describe the whole of Celtic art from the early fifth to the second centuries BC. British art has greater longevity with much of importance starting in the second century, and here Style IV or the Insular style are used to designate much of this art, by now characterized by complex curvilinear ornament amongst other things. There are considerable differences of opinion over British chronologies. Stead (1985) has stuck most clearly to the Jacobsthal scheme with the addition of Insular style IV which he has done much to define. I feel that the scheme has some validity in that palmette-based motifs and Waldalgesheim tendrils clearly occur early in the British sequence, but these do not drop out, but are added to by newer forms of decoration. Celtic art in Britain does not work so much by the battle-ship curve model of style, where new forms of ornament are found initially sporadically, grow in popularity to then eventually die away. Rather this is an accumulative and referential set of styles where new motifs join old, giving them novel significances whilst they retain connections to older people and places. Some objects, such as a scabbard from Standlake on the Thames, have at least two different styles on the same piece. Furthermore, some items were old when they were deposited, keeping alive older forms and modes of decoration.

Objects acted as complex referential pieces, making present other times and places, which were to some degree condensed into a single object, to be physically appreciated, talked or sung about, to be displayed and used. Far away and long ago were brought into direct connection with the present and this may have been a more general aspect of Iron Age material culture, whereby the stones and earth used to make hillfort ramparts helped link that one site to other places (Lock *et al.* 2005) or the temper used in pottery was chosen not just for its functional quali-

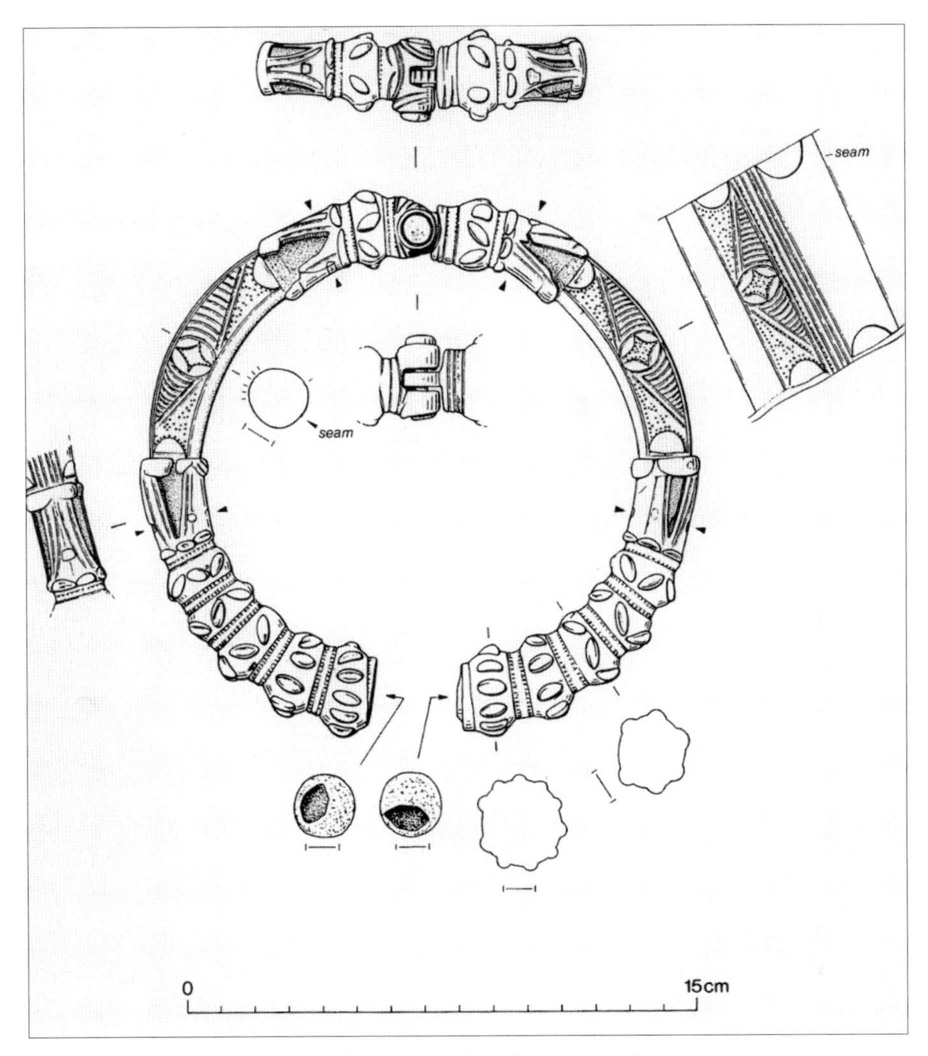

Fig. 1. The torc from Dinnington (after Beswick *et al.* 1990, Fig. 2).

ties but due to its cultural associations. In the latter two cases references could be rather direct, but with Celtic art transformation is key, so that plants, animals and birds may well be present in decorations but in a manner which is transformed, leading to an ambiguity and a multiplicity of readings. It is this multiple nature that might be key to the cultural power of Celtic art.

To pursue the referential nature of metalwork a little more, let us take a single object, a torc from Dinnington, although we will raise the question as to how far this was a single object at all. This neckring was found by a metal detectorist in 1984 in a wood near Dinnington in Yorkshire in the north of England (Beswick *et al.* 1990). It probably came from within the area of a sub-rectangular enclosure which has produced other finds dating to between the first and fourth centuries AD, which fits the date of the piece which is probably second century AD. This is one of over 100 torcs found in Britain, many from hoards in the east of the country. They are generally of gold, bronze or brass (as this one is), only rarely being of iron.

The torc is small (Fig. 1) being 375 mm in inner diameter and 480 mm on the outside. It has a hinge at the back, allowing it to open out and when fully extended has a gap at the front of 160 mm. The piece is heavy, being 758 gm, but marks of polish and damage shows that it was worn regularly unlike some similar objects, which might have been mainly for display. The torc is made from six sections, four of which are cast tubes. Two of these tubes are at the front with cast-on beads as decoration. Two shorter tubes are at the back with similar decoration and are joined by a hinge. Between the front and back cast tubes are two tubular sheets, which were made as flat sheets of metal and then rolled. These were inserted into the ends of the cast tubes, which had v-shapes cut into them to facilitate this insertion. These rolled sheets were around lead cores, which helps account for the weight of the torc (Beswick *et al.* 1990).

This complex object creates a series of associations linking it to other items. The bead decorations on the cast sections connects this item to a broader class of beaded torcs, some of which have beads cast into their shape, as here, and others have beads as additions (Beswick *et al.* 1990). In general they fit within the emphasis on plastic decoration found in many British pieces. Beaded torcs have a northern British distribution, being found north of line between the Humber and Mersey and south of one joining the Forth and the Clyde, so that the Dinnington torc is just to the south of its main distribution. Temporally it fits well into the main period of use of beaded torcs within the first and second centuries AD.

The hinge on the Dinnington piece links it with the so-called Wraxall torcs with a predominant distribution in the southwest of Britain from Somerset to Cornwall far to the south of the Dinnington findspot. The most mysterious link is that provided by the rolled tubular sheets, which are mainly found in gold, such as that from Hoard A at Snettisham or from Dorchester, Devon (Beswick *et al.* 1990). These are also generally much earlier than the Dinnington torc, being first or second centuries BC. The hatched triangular decoration on these tubes have their best parallels early, such as the scabbards from Fovant in Wiltshire which dates to the third or second centuries BC (Beswick *et al.* 1990, 28).

The complexities of the Dinnington torc are increased by the results of metallurgical analysis. The various aspects of the torc are made generally of brass and gun metal, due to the addition of zinc, metals which probably only come into

Britain after the Roman conquest in AD 43, although a small number of imported fibulae in brass may be found before that (Beswick *et al.* 1990, 22). Interestingly, each of the components of the torc were of different compositions, so that the two pieces of tubular sheet varied in composition (Beswick *et al.* 1990, 22). However, they were different also from the cast sections of the torc and may have been tinned on their surface, giving them a much whiter colour than the deeper brown of the cast tubes. Play with colour was an important aspect of this piece, important to its overall effects, and variability of visual effect was added to in a minor way by the fact that the triangular decoration on one side was infilled with dots, while the other was left empty.

In all this was a most complex piece which referenced objects thought to have a different spatial distribution such as the Wraxall-type torcs of the west country or from much earlier times in the form of the tubular torcs mainly found three to four hundred years before the Dinnington torc. The fragmentary nature of our evidence of fine metal work probably reduces our ability to understand the range of references contained in any one object, so that many more connections might have been perceptible to people in the second century AD.

Discussion

In discussing the transactions taking place in the kula ring in Papua New Guinea, Nancy Munn (1986; 1990) makes the point that time and space are not abstract dimensions within which human life is played out, but that notions of near and far, recent or long past, propitious or dangerous are all values created and given shape through human action. A map of the islands taking part in kula will only allow us a partial understanding of distance which is not only to be measured in kilometres or days of canoe travel, but rather through perceptions of how far away things and people are, in which kinship, desire for proximity or fear of danger all play a vital part. Similarly, some events are assigned to the distant past, but others still have a great effect on actions in the present – causal immediacy and efficacy have little to do with any absolute distance in time and more with the vital impact of the past in the present.

People do not just perceive time and space, but help create them. This creation takes place in considerable part through objects, so that for Munn particular kula objects (arm-shells or necklaces) which have names and histories of transactions attached are key nodes in connecting up places and periods or, indeed, in making them distant. For late prehistoric objects, we do not know whether they had names or what they were, nor do we know in any detail the histories and human connections that streamed out from them. All we can do is work from the formal characteristics of the objects themselves to see some of the network of associations they helped create. In such complex networks there are no prime relations, such as ideas in the mind of the makers or the users of objects. Nor does it make any sense to see webs of connection, which are ultimately ego-centred, as are modelled by the idea of the extended mind. We are looking rather at more radically distributed effects. A single human body is not singular, but rather contains a bundle of impulses and affects. The fizz of neuronal activity is counter-balanced by the steadier beat of the human heart, the mingled operation of the senses and the muscles acting in concert with varying materials. Similarly a single object is not singular, but a bundle of projects allowing for a variety of modes of making, using and discarding, as a shifting support for stories and songs which might accumulate over time around one object. A single object or a person's body is never isolated, but enjoys implicit and explicit links to other things and people.

The Dinnington torc was deposited for almost two thousand years in one spot in what we now call Yorkshire. Before that it was mobile on the necks of its wearers and maybe through relations of exchange. Since its re-discovery in 1984 it has been on the move again, active in the creation of new relationships including the one we are both party to now. Its most recent relationships were almost certainly not foreseen by its original makers, but are powerful and important for all that. During its use in the early Roman period, the torc was a condensation of connections through time and space, with places distant to it and with people long-dead or objects that had been destroyed or hidden through deposition. The manner in which these connections were actualized or activated, were from the point of view of individuals infinite and inexhaustible. Many connections could not be put into words or summed up in a succinct thought, but evoked through the colour, texture and weight of the torc, judged implicitly or explicitly against a mass of other objects, all of which were complex entities.

In looking at the creation of time and space by objects and humans, we are dealing with lots of different scales. The quick-silver reactions of the human body derive from the speed and malleability of synaptic connections from which derive the peculiar sensitivity of the human organism to the human and material world. When people are joined as groups the reaction of the whole is slower, building and shifting in subtle ways as a joint sense of joy, anger, belonging or isolation emerges. Objects represent more durable energies, so that a single item of so-called Celtic art is connected to many others across Europe, which gives that individual thing vast connectedness and potential valences. Most importantly, objects endure through time. The sensitivity of our organisms can be linked to those 2000 years ago through the medium of metalwork. We have come to see our reactions as internal and concentrated in our minds, but probably those of the Iron Age and Roman periods did not. In order to understand the breadth and depth of connections through objects a notion like mind is not at all helpful, as it separates people and their objects. Connections through space and across time are more productive to contemplate, reminding us of the infinite ways in which we are always more-than-one.

Acknowledgements

I am very grateful to the Excavating the Mind team for inviting me to a most stimulating conference and for being so patient as my paper came in. The comments of an anonymous reviewer were extremely useful.

References

Banks, M. & H. Morphy (eds) 1997. *Rethinking Visual Anthropology*. New Haven and London: Yale University Press.

Beswick, P., M.R. Megaw, J.V.S. Megaw, P. Northover 1990. 'A decorated late Iron Age torc from Dinnington, South Yorkshire.' *Antiquaries Journal*, 70, 16-33.

Bradley, R. 2007. *The Prehistory of Britain and Ireland*. Cambridge: Cambridge University Press.

Clark, A. 1997. *Being there. Putting brain, body and world together again*. Cambridge, Mass.: MIT Press.

Damasio, A. 2000. *The Feeling of What Happens. Body, emotion and the making of consciousness*. London: Vintage.

Garrow, D. & C. Gosden in prep. *Technologies of Enchantment? Celtic Art in Britain in the late Iron Age and Roman periods*. Oxford: Oxford University Press.

Gell, A. 1998. *Art and Agency. An anthropological Theory*. Oxford: Clarendon Press.

Gosden, C. 2005. 'What do objects want?' *Journal of Archaeological Method and Theory*, 12, 193-211.

Hingley, R. 2006. 'The Deposition of Iron Objects in Britain during the Later Prehistoric and Roman Periods: Contextual Analysis and the Significance of Iron.' *Britannia*, 37, 213-57.

Ingold, T. (ed.) 1996. *Key Debates in Anthropology*. London: Routledge.

Jacobsthal, P. 1944. *Early Celtic Art*. Oxford: Clarendon Press.

Latour, B. 2005. *Reassembling the Social. An Introduction to Actor-Network Theory*. Oxford: Oxford University Press.

Lock, G., C. Gosden, P. Daley 2005. *Segsbury Camp: Excavations in 1996 and 1997 at an Iron Age Hillfort on the Oxfordshire Ridgeway*. (OU School of Archaeology Monograph 61). Oxford: Oxford University.

Munn, N. 1986. *The Fame of Gawa*. Cambridge: Cambridge University Press.

Munn, N. 1990. 'Constructing regional worlds in experience: kula exchange, witchcraft and Gawan local events.' *Man*, 25, 1-17.

Rowlands, M. 2003. *Externalism*. McGill: Queen's University Press.

Stead, I.M. 1985. *Celtic Art in Britain before the Roman Conquest*. London: British Museum Press.

Wheeler, M. 2005. *Reconstructing the Cognitive World: the next step*. Cambridge, Mass.: MIT Press.

Linear B as Distributed Cognition: Excavating a mind not limited by the skin

Lambros Malafouris

Introduction: Mind 'just ain't in the head'

The title of this volume, 'excavating the mind', can be understood in many different senses, and one feature that all those different senses share in common is a metaphoric meaning. The reason is simple enough. Archaeologists, most people would agree, do not excavate minds but the material remains of the past. What the archaeology of mind as a method refers to is the use of the latter for gaining information about the former. If we ask, 'where precisely is this ancient mind located?', the obvious answer would be: Inside the head of the prehistoric individual. And if we ask, 'how is this ancient mind actually manifest and related to the material remains that archaeologists excavate?', the most common reply would be: Through some form of internally driven action or symbolic representation. Simply put, according to the dominant view in contemporary cognitive science and archaeology, although material culture can be seen to operate as prompt input or output of the cognitive system, it remains 'external' and thus cannot be seen as a part of the cognitive system proper. Thinking is what the brain does.

Given this deeply entrenched assumption about the intracranial ontological boundaries of human cognition, what archaeologists can be said to excavate are the residues of past intelligent behaviour and assemblages of material signs. Our knowledge about those signs, although fragmentary and lacking in detail, nonetheless carries with it the promise of interpretation. Those cognitive traces, in other words, embody the possibility, and thus reiterate the archaeological aspiration, that if they are properly processed and analysed they may give us a glimpse of what went on inside the head of the prehistoric individual; that is, where true cognitive states and processes are supposedly instantiated. No doubt then, when archaeology recovers a corpus of artefacts, like the Mycenaean Linear

B tablets that I will be using as my case study in this paper, where the previously mentioned vague interpretive promise becomes an explicit message, inscribed on clay, the obvious thing to do would be, very simply, to read it. And indeed, whatever methodological objections one may entertain about the possibility of 'reading the past' (Hodder 1986), the case of the Linear B tablets presents – thanks to the efforts of Ventris & Chadwick (1973) who managed to break the code of the Mycenaean script – one of those rare examples where this famous and much contested archaeological phrase actually works.

Be all that as it may, for my purposes in this paper I shall resist the temptation to read the Mycenaean mind as a message inscribed on the tablets. I do this not so much because – as someone familiar with the corpus of Linear B might think – on the basis of present archaeological evidence, in following this avenue one will end up finding out about numbers and commodities rather than about Mycenaean thought and beliefs. In fact, a great deal of information about the latter can be, and indeed has been, deduced over the last decades through the systematic efforts of many scholars specializing in the study of Mycenaean documents (e.g. Chadwick 1976; Palaima 1988a; 1988b; 2004; Shelmerdine 1997; Bennet 2001). The reason I am shifting my focus away from text is rather because in this paper I want to ask a different sort of question. More specifically, I want to use the example of Linear B tablets for raising the question of *how*, rather than *what*, was Mycenaeans thinking? I am interested in other words, not in the *content* of Mycenaean thought but in the *process* of Mycenaean thought and more specifically in the possible ways this process relates and interacts with the Linear B system. To this end, it is necessary first to understand the Linear B system as a cognitive artefact, and this is not simply a matter of decoding the meaning of the Linear B signs but primarily of penetrating the gray zone 'where brain, body and culture conflate', mutually catalyzing and constituting each other (Malafouris 2004; Malafouris & Renfrew 2010). However, entering into this realm of material engagement the classic question of 'where does the mind stop and the material world begins?' becomes meaningless. The categorical Cartesian division between the 'internal' mind and the 'external' world gives way to a more subtle image of human cognition along the lines of what I call the hypothesis of the constitutive intertwining of cognition with the material world (Malafouris 2004). As such, in what follows, instead of using the Linear B tablets as a medium for getting inside the Mycenaean head, I intend to show that a great deal of Mycenaean cognition lies out there in the world and it is enacted *through*, rather than written *upon*, the Mycenaean tablets.

The distributed cognition approach (Dcog)

Beginning to delineate a map of the cognitive territory that the Mycenaean tablets shape and inhabit, I suggest that a new model of human cognition needs to be adopted. Such a model must be able to provide us, on the one hand, with a more dynamic and extended view of the human mind, and on the other, enable us to expose those conventional and to a large extent problematic assumptions about the nature of human cognition that I suggest archaeology needs to overcome. To this end, in this paper, I shall be focusing on the so-called theory of distributed cognition (Dcog). The Dcog approach to the study of mind is a theoretical framework developed primarily by the anthropologist Ed Hutchins (1995a,b; 2005; Hollan *et al.* 2000). What distinguishes this framework from the so-called 'Classical' cognitive science can be nicely expressed by way of two basic theoretical commitments, which also constitute the crux of the Material Engagement approach (Malafouris 2004; 2008; 2010; Malafouris & Renfrew 2010; Renfrew 2006; 2007).

The first theoretical commitment pertains to the boundaries of the unit of analysis for the study of human cognition. It relates, in other words, to the crucial methodological question of *where do we look for the mind*? As already discussed, the standard reply to this question according to the traditional 'all in the head' view of human cognition, is basically the following: *what is outside the head is outside the mind*. However, for the Dcog approach a cognitive process is not simply what happens inside the brain of the individual; a cognitive process can also be what happens in the interactions among many individuals or, even more importantly, in the interactions among persons and things (see also Clark 1997; 2003; Knappett 2005; Varela *et al.* 1991; Van Gelder 1995). This drastic expansion of the unit of analysis for the study of cognitive phenomena, now pursued 'in the wild', leads us directly to the second and correlated theoretical commitment of Dcog which now pertains to the range of mechanisms that can be assumed to characterize the nature of our mental machinery. In particular, once you expand the territory of the human mind beyond the skin and skull of the individual, as the Dcog approach proposes, the traditional computational image of the mind as a storehouse of internal representational structures and computational procedures is no longer sufficient. From the perspective of Dcog our mental machinery is essentially an extended functional system that does not simply involve internal representational states but, most importantly, the transformation and propagation of such states across external media. This means more simply, that although mental states can be 'internal' in the traditional intracranial representational sense, they can also be outside the individual (e.g. maps, charts, tools etc.) and thus 'external' to the biological confines of the individual. In other words, for Dcog "a cognitive process is delimited by the functional relationships among the elements that participate in it, rather than by the spatial co-location of the elements" (Hollan *et al.* 2000, 176). No proper understanding of our mental machinery can be accomplished either by leaving those 'external' cognitive events outside the cognitive equation proper, or by reducing them altogether to some 'internal' neuronal activity or brain process. For example, rather than asking who is responsible for steering the ship into the harbour, we should ask how the necessary knowledge is enacted and propagated across people, artefacts and time (Hutchins 1995a,b).

Linear B as a cognitive artefact

Let us now turn to the Linear B system. By way of basic background let me start my discussion in this section with a few broad remarks concerning the archaeology of the tablets. The system of writing, which we call the Mycenaean Linear B script, originates around the 15th century BC to serve the administrative (record-keeping and accounting) demands of the gradually emerging Mycenaean palatial system (Chadwick 1987; Palaima 1988a; Shelmerdine 1997). The script, which comprises some 89 syllabic signs and over one hundred ideograms, was adapted from the earlier Linear A Minoan writing system. Up to the present two major textual forms have been recovered and come exclusively from the major palatial centers of the Greek Mainland and Minoan Crete. The first, and dominant one, consists of tablets of unbaked clay. The second consists of painted inscriptions on large stirrup jars. Perhaps a third recording format might have consisted of less-permanent, and thus archaeologically non-recoverable, materials.

The use of the Mycenaean script was strictly confined to record keeping in the context of palatial administration. Unlike the situation in the Near East there are no historical documents like annals, diplomatic correspondence, treaties or religious texts proper. There are no actual names of kings – besides the title of 'the king' (wa-na-ka) – or specific dates – besides the use of 'last year' or 'this year' accompanying the listings of various commodities. The content of the written material so far available consists mainly of inventories and catalogues. Thus it is primarily in the economic and administrative field that the Mycenaean script offered the most valuable information. Careful records of raw material distribution and circulation, detail listings of weaponry and other military equipment, lists of animals, agricultural products and various other commodities, offer unique information about the economic and social system of this period. Moreover, the 'lists of personnel', as classified by Ventris and Chadwick, speak of a high degree of specialised craftsmanship in the Mycenaean world. In addition, it was primarily on the basis of the Linear B evidence that the well developed perfumed oil industry at Pylos (Shelmerdine 1985) was revealed showing that the interests of the Mycenaean palatial system went far beyond the production and control of agricultural and livestock resources. However, with only a few exceptions, outside the sphere of economy and administration the Linear B has little information to offer. For example in the context of Mycenaean religion a unique example can be seen in the case of the Pylos Tn 316 tablet (Chadwick 1973, 284-9). The tablet records offerings of three different types of precious gold vases *i.e.* *213 VAS [handless cup/bowl], *215 VAS [handled cup/goblet] and *216 VAS [chalice] to a variety of divinities and, according to Palaima, represent a major calendar religious festival of Pylos with the particular vessels associated on a traditional ritual basis with particular deities (1996, 403).

There can be no doubt that the decipherment of the script in 1952 by Ventris and Chadwick constitutes a major turning point in the history of Mycenaean studies opening a wide range of new possibilities for studying Mycenaean prehistory. However, an unfortunate consequence of those new possibilities was that the focus of Mycenaean archaeology shifted away from the materiality of the script. With a few notable exceptions (e.g. Palaima 1988a; Bennet 2001) the study of Linear B tablets as a unique aspect of Mycenaean material culture was subsumed under the text. Gradually, and as a consequence of the above, a common implicit agreement seems to have arisen that, as far as the Linear B is concerned, what really matters in the study of Mycenaean culture and by extension of the Mycenaean mind is the internal structure, origin and development of the script rather than the nature and affordances of the medium that carried this script. The assumption, in other words, is that if there is anything that the Mycenaean writing system can tell us about the Mycenaean mind, this has to be found behind the signs inscribed on the clay tablets.

In what follows, I want to challenge this assumption. My argument is that if we seek to understand the Linear B system as a cognitive artefact focusing only on what is written on the surface of the Mycenaean tablets, or the internal structure of the script, we will inevitably only see part of the picture. Consider the obvious example of Mycenaean memory. If one attempts to examine Mycenaean mnemonic practices adopting the conventional distinction between "inscribed" and "incorporated" memory practices (Rowlands 1993) it would certainly be the former rather than the latter that can be seen to characterize the Linear B system. No doubt it is primarily through inscription that the Mycenaean scribe remembers, and it is because of this feature that we can count in the present the precise number of figs stored in the palace of Pylos. As Chadwick correctly observes:

> It cannot be too strongly emphasized that what mattered most to the users of these documents was the numerals. The numbers and quantities are important details which cannot be confided to the memory; the remainder of the text is simply a brief note of what the numerals refer to, heading to enable the reader to identify the person or place associated with the quantity recorded (Chadwick 1976, 27).

However, can inscription by itself account for the mnemonic properties of the Linear B system? Can we really ever understand how the Mycenaean palatial administration system remembers without taking into account some basic considerations about the physical properties of the script such as the fact that, unlike what we know from Anatolia, the Mycenaean tablets were never deliberately baked?

Keeping this basic point in mind let us now proceed to explore what a Dcog approach to the Linear B system amounts to. The first thing to note in this respect is the change in perspective. Linear B is no longer seen as an abstract code but as a constitutive part of a densely coupled distributed cognitive system that unfolds in time and space. This change in perspective also involves a change of analytic unit, and as such of analytic scale, from the micro-level of semantics to the macro-level of practice. In other words, it necessitates adopting a level of description capable of revealing to us the cognitive properties and processes that characterize Linear B as a functional cognitive system. To this end, the obvious point of departure would be focusing on the interactions between human and material actors and to discern their properties, emergent or other, relevant to the working space and social setting. Focusing, for example, on the distribution of labor or on the factors that determine the size of a clay tablet, or even on the various communicative pathways that define the flow of information across the different representational states and modes of the system (e.g. verbal to inscribed) may be more important for understanding the cognitive operations involved than any isolated observation about the representational content of the tablets. To illustrate better how such an analysis can be understood let us use Chadwick's description of some elementary technical processes that may have taken place in the main Archive room at the Mycenaean palace at Pylos:

> The scribe sits on a stool (*thranus* on the tablets) in the Main Archive Room; through the door at the back we can see through into the Annex, where most of the tablets were found. The written tablets are tidily filed in their labeled baskets; a few lie exposed drying before being put away. The scribe holds the tablet he is working on in his left hand; it is quite often possible to see the fingerprints on the reverse where the tablet was held, and large tablets have sometimes here depressions corresponding to the positions of the thumb and fingers. Next to him

> stands an official who has returned from a tour of inspection and is dictating the details he wishes to record; he has brought with him a tally-stick to remind him of the correct figures – a gratuitous invention, but it is certain that some form of temporary mnemonic would have been needed to ensure that the official got his figure right. In the foreground a small boy is kneading clay ready to make the next tablet for the scribe (Chadwick 1976, 20).

Certainly the above description gives us only a small part of the complex interactions that characterize the usage and processing of the tablets. The operational sequence can be easily extended further to incorporate elements ranging from the construction of inscribed labels – small blobs of wet clay pressed onto the outside of the baskets used for the storage of thc tablets (Chadwick 1976, 18-9) – to facilitate the identification of the tablets after their storage, to the spatial position and architecture of the Archive room at Pylos.

Yet I believe the above image sufficiently brings about and illustrates the basic point of our present discussion: That is, that speaking about the Mycenaean Linear B script in the context of cognitive archaeology we are not simply speaking about disembodied signs and brains. We are speaking, instead, about a temporally unfolding process, or sequence of related processes, encompassing both interaction between humans, situated tool use, and intelligent use of space, bodies and things.

It is important to note at this point that, when from the perspective of Dcog we are speaking about interaction, we do not simply refer to the process where several individuals are bringing together their isolated bits of knowledge. The focus is rather on how those bits of knowledge are acquired, coordinated and distributed in action, keeping in mind that the interactions that define a distributed cognitive system do not simply occur between individual human agents but also between human and material agents. The crucial assumption, in other words, is that a cognitive system that involves more than one individual has cognitive properties that differ from those of the individuals who participate in the system taken in isolation. This also means that no matter how detailed the knowledge of the cognitive properties of those individuals in isolation might be, it is not in itself sufficient to account for the operations of the system as a whole (Hutchins 1995b, 265). The mnemonic properties of the Linear B system are not the sum of the biological capacities of the Mycenaean scribe plus the mnemonic affordances and storage capacity of a Linear B tablet. It is instead a new *hybrid historical synergy* that brings about a mnemonic function that neither persons nor things can develop in isolation. Contrary to what many people seem to believe, a cognitive artefact does not simply amplify the cognitive system but often brings about radical changes in the nature of the cognitive operations involved and the functional structure of the system as a whole (Norman 1991; 1993). Indeed, what really happens in the case of Linear B is that a different set of functional skills and affordances is introduced into the extended system. The individual using the tablets now engages in a different sort of cognitive behaviour. A different cognitive operation i.e. reading, now emerges and becomes available in the system. As Donald correctly remarks:

> The external memory field is not just another sector of working memory. It taps directly into the neural networks of literacy, located in brain regions that are distinct from those of working memory. Working memory and the external memory field thus complement each other, and this allows the brain to exploit their distinct storage and retrieval properties (Donald 2001, 314).

For example, the numerals and iconographic signs that as mentioned constitute the mnemonic component par excellence of the Linear B system did not simply help Mycenaeans to remember the precise quantities of the recorded commodities; rather, they were part of the process by which the Linear B system remembers. From the system's view-point it is not the individual scribe that remembers but the Linear B tablet. The individual simply reads what the Linear B tablet remembers. The Linear B tablets by 'being there' in the 'outside' world enable the Mycenaean scribe to substitute recognition for recall thus transforming a difficult 'internal' memory problem to an easier 'external' perceptual one. Information once inscribed on the clay tablet transcends the limitations of the individual person and its biology and becomes available 'out there'.

Moreover, once an internal problem is transformed into an external perceptual one a number of new possibilities become available which, if actualised, can further enhance the efficacy of the cognitive system. This is so because the spatial physical properties of the tablet can now be manipulated to further simplify the mnemonic task. As I will discuss in more detail in the following section, the common idea about the environment as a static external recourse devoid of agency comes under question (Knappett & Malafouris 2008).

Trying to understand the nature of the cognitive operations involved as isolated, atemporal, and disembodied mental states in the mind of the Mycenaean scribe, is like trying to account for the shape, size and proportions of a given Linear B tablet without giving any consideration to the actual length and nature of the information recorded on it. There are no fixed mental templates that shape the mental world of the Mycenaean scribe as there are no fixed material templates upon which the scribe shaped the size and proportions of the Mycenaean tablets.

Cognition and action dialectically shape each other. The numerous examples of words or even complete lines of writing subsequently added over the main text – an annotation or continuation of the text for which there was not enough space (Chadwick 1987, 16) – clearly indicate that in the case of Linear B, as with many other activity contexts, Suchman's law – i.e., internal plans and models are always too vague to accommodate in advance the manifold contingencies of real-world activity (Suchman 1987) – is confirmed.

In other words, in the case of Linear B, understanding the mind behind the artefact is not simply a matter of postulating the representational states being created inside the head of the Mycenaean person when he/she is reading or writing a tablet. It is also a matter of postulating the dynamic interaction between that person and the physical properties of the medium of representation as a material thing *i.e.* a clay tablet.

The intelligent use of clay

It follows from the above discussion, that even in the cases of inscriptive technologies and artefacts, such as the Linear B system, which seem to fall under the category of 'external symbolic storage' and which as such allow an approach from a representational stance, the nature of the relationship between cognition and material culture cannot be accounted for solely on the basis of some representational mechanism. Even in those cases, an important type of cognitive event should not be neglected, and that is the following: a cognitive system does not make use of external representations simply for what *they stand for* but also for what *they are*. More simply, in the case of Linear B, thinking is not simply a matter of reading a series of meaningful linguistic signs inscribed on the surface of a tablet but also of meaningfully engaging with the tablet itself as a material sign. Let us explore that issue at a more concrete level.

There are two major types of Linear B tablet as far as their physical morphology is concerned. These are the 'leaf-shaped' tablet, so-called because of their small and elongated shape, and the large 'page-shaped' tablets. Concerning their function, the main difference is that 'leaf-shaped' tablets are usually parts of a larger set, whereas the 'page-shaped' ones are usually complete documents in themselves. This functional differentiation, far from trivial, embodies the solution to a very important problem imposed on the writing process and the memory of the Mycenaean scribe by the very materiality of the tablets. This is the following: Once something is written on the surface of the wet clay it dries rapidly (a few hours, perhaps a day at most). That means that no further additions or corrections could have been possible after the clay of a tablet became dry. An implication of that would have been that if a tablet were to contain a large number of entries, all the relevant information about those entries should have been available within the mentioned time limits. If this was not possible and the information required came in pieces at different times or even from different persons, then the use of small individual tablets for each piece would have been necessary for storing the incoming information. These small tablets could then be filed in order like a card index. And once the file was complete it could if required be subsequently recopied onto large tablets. Archaeologically it is not always easy to recover those files and the sets or groups of tablets that were intended to be read as a single document. However, in a few cases direct evidence about this practice has been preserved in the archaeological record. An excellent example can be seen in the case of the Pp. series recovered *in situ* by Evans in the course of his excavation at the palace at Knossos, showing not "merely the set but the order in which the tablets were filed" (Chadwick 1976, 22) (Fig. 1). Another concrete example of this process can be seen in the case of "the 'land-tenure' tablets from Pylos, where a large set of small, individual tablets (as the Eb series) have been recopied in groups on large tablets (Ep) to form a long continuous document" (Chadwick 1976, 26).

If we attempt to characterize the cognitive processes involved in the use and manipulation of those files, they could be certainly classified as an instance of

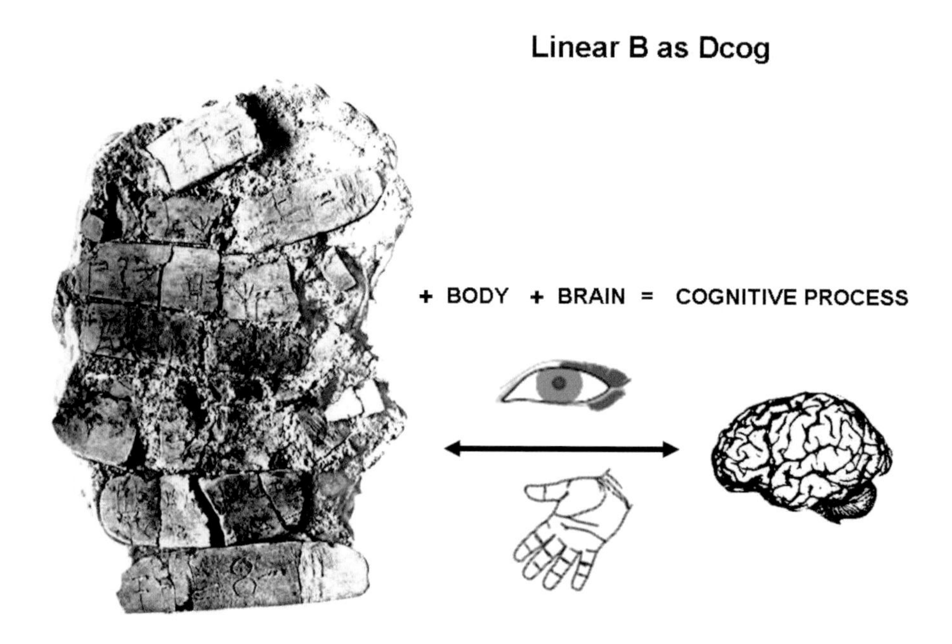

Fig. 1. Linear B as Dcog (the Pp. series file redrawn after Evans 1935, fig. 655).

memory and information processing. But an argument can be made that if we were to locate precisely where these cognitive processes were enacted, it would be very difficult to draw the boundary between the internal and external parts of the cognitive system involved.

Clearly in this case, the cognitive strategy does not simply involve the internal representation of symbols via the Linear B code in order to produce the outcome that we see inscribed in the tablets. The cognitive strategy also involves the physical manipulation of the properties of the representational medium as a material object in real time and space in order to produce the file. And the file seen as a material spatial arrangement, is not simply amplifying the problem-solving process by reducing the complexity of the cognitive task – for example, directing attention so as to reduce the cost of visual search and to make it easier to notice, identify and remember the items. The file, I want to suggest, is also transforming the physical boundaries of the problem's space and as such restructures the actual nature of the problem solving process. Indeed, any given task space or context affords only certain possibilities of action. That means that by changing the physical properties of activity space one can restrict the freedom of the agent. However, the fewer degrees of freedom in a given context that an agent has, the simpler is the cognitive task. As such, by exploiting the properties of activity space one can simplify and reduce the computational load of a given problem.

It should be emphasized that, for distributed cognition, space is not simply the passive background against which the activity unfolds but something that can be used itself as a cognitive artefact. Indeed, according to David Kirsh (1995; 1996), spatial arrangements form an important part of the functional architecture of any distributed cognitive system, in at least three important and correlated respects: That is, by supporting *choice, perception* and *problem solving*. For example, space can be used to simplify choices either by constraining what is feasible in a given situation – hiding affordances – or by cueing attention to what is feasible – highlighting affordances. Moreover, spatial properties can be used to facilitate perception by directing attention and offering visual cues for action. Two obvious examples are size and colour which can be used as such attention-getting features as when we highlight or underline a text as an attention-focusing feature. Such elementary 'epistemic actions' (Kirsh & Maglio 1994; Knappett 2004) have a long history and may well be traced to when our Palaeolithic ancestors mark the spot on a rock face to ease the flaking of a tool. However, their cognitive significance has been rather downplayed in human cognitive evolution. Indeed, a number of such epistemic features can be traced in the case of the Linear B script. To mention some of the most salient examples, several transverse lines running the full width of the tablets are usually drawn by hand before the text was written to facilitate the identification and perception of the information inscribed on the tablets. Another nice example can be seen when, especially in the case of elongated tablets, the first word of the text is written in large signs, or when the document is split up into paragraphs by inserting one or two blank lines (Chadwick 1987, 16).

Recognisably, those 'epistemic features' of the Linear B system mentioned above, together with many others such as the repetition of standard formulae within set spatial formats, the careful spatial separation of individual entries, the stoichedon formatting of lexical and ideographic items within successive entries, and in general the systematic use of ideograms as an information reference and retrieval tool (Palaima 1988a, 330-32), may seem trivial from the perspective of the contemporary and fully literate Western individual. Yet in the context of Mycenaean prehistory they reflect, as Palaima observes, "a noticeable development of what we may call the information recording and retrieval techniques and capabilities on clay records" moving from Cretan Hieroglyphic and Linear A to the Mycenaean Linear B (Palaima 1988a, 331), that demands our attention. Moreover, it can be argued that these 'epistemic features' exemplify an important class of events that I want to suggest constitute the crux of the relationship between cognition and material culture. More specifically they exemplify that the engagement between cognition and material culture is not simply a matter of representation but most importantly of dense structural coupling between internal and external cognitive domains. Where this class of cognitive events differs from those we traditionally associate with the idea of external symbolic storage, is that in this case it is not simply information that is externalized but also the actual processing of this information.

Conclusion: Excavating the mind?

As the cognitive psychologist Don Norman suggests (1991; 1993): it might be that the hallmark of human cognition lies in our ability to construct external cognitive artefacts and to use these artefacts to compensate for the limitations of our biological memory. Indeed, if no more than half a minute is the amount of time that we can retain new information in our working memory without the need of rehearsal, and if five to nine items is the maximum amount of information digits that the human mind can process at any one time (Miller 1956), then the construction of some sort of mnemonic device or external scaffolding is a matter of increased evolutionary significance. It is precisely this premise for the gradual externalization and materialization of memory that has been placed in its evolutionary dimension by Merlin Donald (1991; 1998; 2001). His suggestions about the implications of external symbolic systems for the structuring and organization of biological memory have been undeniably very influential in this respect. Each of the three major stages in the evolution of human cognition that he proposes, i.e. mimetic, mythic and theoretical, is defined by the nature of the available technologies for the preservation and usage of information stored outside the human brain and body. According to Donald, external symbolic devices and technologies such as the Mycenaean Linear B script provide what he calls "external memory field" that transforms the mental architecture of the unaided brain and thus expands "the range of mental operations available to a conscious mind" (2001, 315).

Of course it should be emphasised that no cognitive artefact in isolation can do much. What matters is not the cognitive potential that a given cognitive artefact can be argued to embody but how this potential becomes actualised in a given social matrix. This is something that the Mycenaean case, in particular, proves beyond doubt. Despite having developed a technology able to set free the Mycenaean society from the constrains of oral tradition and biological memory, there is no scribal interest in, or awareness of, the important cognitive and social capabilities of such a technology. One might blame the internal structure of the script for that, but the situation is far more complicated. Indeed, there are good indications that script itself did not pose an obstacle to a more advanced use of literacy. In fact even if someone prefers to think the opposite he or she would still have to account for the "perfectly astounding" fact, as Palaima refers to it (1987, 503), "that no Mycenaean ever had the impulse to scratch a full inscription on the surface of a sherd". Obviously the answer to the question of 'why did the Mycenaeans fail to realize the full potential of their script?' should be rather sought in the social life of this cognitive artefact; and the thing to note about this social life is that it never moved beyond the administrative sphere of the Mycenaean palaces.

By making this point however, I do not mean to imply that the social and cognitive lives of things belong in two different and separate planes of existence and as such that they should be treated separately. To the contrary, what I mean is that the cognitive and the social are inseparable often to such an extent that from the perspective of distributed cognition one may see the social organization of the Linear B system as a *form of cognitive architecture in itself*.

This last premise carries with it major implications for the study of human cognition especially from an archaeological perspective. As I discuss in more detail elsewhere (Malafouris 2004), grounding the challenging task of cognitive archaeology upon a model that conspicuously mistakes "the properties of the socio-cultural system for the properties of the person" (Hutchins 1995, 366), and for which material culture has a place in the mind only as a disembodied digit of information written somehow on the neural tissue, is not simply to undermine the whole project from the very start, but to deprive it of the possibility of making any significant contribution to the understanding of the human mind.

In this paper I have sought to explore the cognitive efficacy of the Linear B system not by reading what a Linear B tablet *tells* us about the Mycenaean mind as a message, but instead by exploring what a Linear B tablet *does* for the Mycenaean mind as a distributed cognitive system and situated practice. To this end, I have replaced the image of the isolated scribe who externalizes information on clay with that of a dynamically coupled network of agents that form a coalition and complement each other. I have argued that some basic aspects of the cognitive life of this artefact can only be understood if one conceives the tablets as being at the same time mental and physical. An important general implication for cognitive archaeology thus follows: Collapsing the equation of the cognitive with the symbolic and recognizing the ability of things to operate as their own best representation (Brooks 1991) gives to the phrase 'excavating the mind' a whole new meaning. Archaeology need no longer look for the mind behind the artefact, thus reducing the complexity of an extended cognitive system to the isolated brain of a delimited human agent: "the mental characteristics of the system are immanent, not in some part, but in the system as a whole" (Bateson 1973, 316). Evans, in the case of the Pp. series file from Knossos discussed previously, did not simply uncover a series of artefacts but a concrete and constitutive part of the thinking process itself. From the perspective of Material Engagement theory and Distributed cognition he has excavated a part of the ancient mind.

Acknowledgements

I want to thank the organizers M.D. Jessen, N.N. Johannsen and H.J. Jensen for inviting me to participate in this stimulating conference. I want to thank also the two anonymous reviewers and Carl Knappett for their most valuable comments. The research presented in this paper was funded by the Balzan Foundation.

References

Bateson, G. 1973. *Steps to an Ecology of Mind*. London: Granada.
Bennet, J. 2001. 'Agency and bureaucracy: thoughts on the nature and extent of administration in Bronze Age Pylos.' In: S. Voutsaki, J. Killen (eds.), *Economy and politics in the Mycenaean palace*

states. (Cambridge Philological Society, Supp. Vol. 27). Cambridge: Cambridge Philological Society, 25-35.

Brooks, R. 1991. Intelligence without representation. *Artificial Intelligence*, 47, 139-59.

Chadwick, J. 1976. *The Mycenaean World*. Cambridge: Cambridge University Press.

Chadwick, J. 1987. *Linear B and related scripts*. Berkeley, CA: University of California Press.

Clark, A. 1997. *Being There: Putting Brain, Body and World Together Again*. Cambridge (MA): MIT Press.

Clark, A. & D. Chalmers 1998. 'The Extended Mind.' *Analysis*, 58(1), 10-23.

Donald, M. 1991. *Origins of the Modern Mind: Three Stages in the Evolution of Culture and Cognition*. Cambridge, MA: Harvard University Press.

Donald, M. 1998. 'Material culture and cognition: Concluding thoughts.' In: C. Renfrew, C. Scarre (eds.), *Cognition and Material Culture: the Archaeology of Symbolic Storage*. Cambridge: The McDonald Institute Monographs, 181-87.

Donald, M. 2001. *A Mind So Rare: The evolution of human consciousness*. New York: W.W. Norton.

Evans, A. 1935. *The Palace of Minos*, 4. London: MacMillan.

Hodder, I. 1986. *Reading the Past*. Cambridge: Cambridge University Press.

Hutchins, E. 1995a. *Cognition in the Wild*. Cambridge, MA: MIT Press.

Hutchins, E. 1995b. 'How a cockpit remembers its speeds.' *Cognitive Science*, 19, 265-88.

Hutchins, E. 2005. 'Material anchors for conceptual blends.' *Journal of Pragmatics*, 37, 1555-77.

Hollan, J. D., E. Hutchins & D. Kirsh 2000. 'Distributed Cognition: a new foundation for human-computer interaction research.' *ACM Transactions on Human-Computer Interaction*, 7(2), 174-96.

Kirsh, D & P. Maglio 1994. 'On Distinguishing Epistemic From Pragmatic Action.' *Cognitive Science*, 18, 513-49.

Kirsh, D. 1995. 'The intelligent use of space.' *Artificial Intelligence*, 73(1-2), 31-68.

Kirsh, D. 1996. 'Adapting the Environment instead of Oneself.' *Adaptive Behavior*, 4(3-4), 415-52.

Knappet, C. 2004. 'The Affordances of Things.' In: E. DeMarrais, C. Gosden, C. Renfrew (eds.), *Rethinking Materiality: The Engagement of Mind with the Material World*. Cambridge: The McDonald Institute Monographs, 43-51.

Knappett, C. 2005. *Thinking Through Material Culture: An Interdisciplinary Perspective*. Philadelphia, PA: University of Pennsylvania Press.

Knappett, C. & L. Malafouris 2008. *Material Agency: Towards a non-anthropocentric perspective*. New York: Springer.

Malafouris, L. 2004. 'The Cognitive Basis of Material Engagement: Where Brain, Body and Culture Conflate.' In: E. DeMarrais, C. Gosden, C. Renfrew (eds.), *Rethinking Materiality: The Engagement of Mind with the Material World*. Cambridge: The McDonald Institute Monographs, 53-62.

Malafouris, L. 2008. 'At the Potter's Wheel: An argument for Material Agency.' In: Knappett C., L. Malafouris (eds.), *Material Agency: Towards a non-anthropocentric perspective*. New York: Springer, 19-36.

Malafouris L, 2010. '*Metaplasticity* and the human becoming: principles of neuroarchaeology.' *Journal of Anthropological Sciences*, 88, 49-72.

Malafouris L. & C. Renfrew (eds.) 2010. *The Cognitive Life of Things: Recasting the Boundaries of the Mind*. Cambridge: The McDonald Institute Monographs.

Miller, G.A. 1956. 'The magical number seven, plus or minus two.' *Psychological Review*, 63, 81-97.

Norman, D. 1988. *The Psychology of Everyday Things*. New York: Basic Books.

Norman, D. 1991. 'Cognitive artefacts.' In: J.M. Carroll (ed.), *Designing interaction: Psychology at the human-computer interface*. Cambridge: Cambridge University Press, 17-38.

Norman, D. 1993. 'Cognition in the head and in the world.' *Cognitive Science*, 17(1), 1-6.

Palaima, T.G. 1988a. 'The Development of the Mycenaean Writing System.' *MINOS*, Supp.10, 269-342.

Palaima, T.G. 1988b. 'The Scribes of Pylos.' *Incunabula Graeca*, 87, Rome: Edizioni dell' Ateneo.

Palaima, T.G. 1992. 'Mycenaean scribal aesthetics.' In: R. Laffineur & J.L. Crowley (eds.), *EIKON Aegean Bronze Age Iconography: Shaping a Methodology*. (Aegaeum 8). Liège: Université de Liège, 63-75.

Palaima, T.G. 1996. 'Pylos Tn 316 and the relationship between vase offerings and divinities in Linear B documents.' *American Journal of Archaeology*, 100, 403.

Palaima T.G. 2004. 'Mycenaean Accounting Methods and Systems and Their Place Within Mycenaean Palatial Civilization.' In: C. Wunsch, M. Hudson (eds.), *Creating Economic Order: Record-Keeping, Standardization and the Development of Accounting in the Ancient Near East*. (International Scholars Conference on Ancient Near Eastern Economies, 4). Baltimore: CDL Press, 269-301.

Palaima, T.G. 2003. 'Archaeology and text: Decipherment, translation and interpretation.' In: J.K. Papadopoulos, R.M. Leventhal (eds.), *Theory and practice in Mediterranean archaeology: Old world and new world perspectives*. (Cotsen Advanced Seminars, 1). Los Angeles: The Cotsen Institute of Archaeology, 45-73.

Renfrew C. 2006. 'Becoming human: the archaeological challenge.' *Proceedings of the British Academy*, 139, 217-38.

Renfrew, C. 2007. *Prehistory, the Making of the Human Mind*. London: Weidenfeld & Nicolson.

Rowlands, M. 1993. 'The Role of Memory in the Transmission of Culture.' *World Archaeology*, 25(2), 141-51.

Shelmerdine, C.W. 1997. 'Review of Aegean prehistory VI: The palatial Bronze Age of the southern and central Greek mainland.' *American Journal of Archaeology*, 101, 537-85.

Shelmerdine, C.W. 1985. *The perfume industry of Mycenaean Pylos*. Göteborg: Åström.

Suchman, L.A. 1987. *Plans and Situated Action*. New York: Cambridge University Press.

Varela, F., E. Thompson & E. Rosch 1991. *The Embodied Mind*. Cambridge, MA: MIT Press.

Van Gelder, T. 1995. 'What might cognition be, if not computation?' *Journal of Philosophy*, 91, 345-81.

Ventris, M. & J. Chadwick 1973. *Documents in Mycenean Greek*. Cambridge: Cambridge University Press.

Cultural practice, material reference and the generation of meaning

Meaning in Miniature: Semiotic networks in material culture

Carl Knappett

Introduction

This paper addresses the dynamics of material culture meaning. Its principal assumption is that such meaning is contingent upon both direct and indirect perception, or what we might also call 'firsthand' and 'secondhand' experience respectively (Reed 1996, 94; see also Windsor 2004, 180). This dual process is here explored through one particular category of material culture: miniaturized or small-scale artefacts. Such objects can, on the one hand, be apprehended 'firsthand', directly understood in relation to the scale of the human body (see Costall 2006); on the other hand, they may be versions of larger vases not immediately co-present, thereby demanding 'secondhand' experience of the wider assemblage to be more fully comprehended. By taking these two processes together, in what might be termed a 'situated semiotic' perspective, this paper seeks to shed a little light on the effects of scale reduction on artefact meaning. In so doing it aims to go beyond the standard archaeological interpretation of miniatures as toys, ritual items or burial offerings, and to consider scaling issues in material culture more broadly.

Situated semiotics

What do I mean by a 'situated semiotic' perspective? While at first it might appear self-contradictory, the idea is to marry insights from two quite different strands of thought: ecological psychology (e.g Gibson 1979; Reed 1996; Costall 2006) and semiotics (Peirce 1931-58; Preucel 2006; Watts 2009). In the former, it is argued that an artefact's affordances are *directly* perceived, apparent from the artefact and its context alone; and Gibson essentially equated an artefact's affordances with its meaning (Gibson 1979). In semiotics, however, a key tenet is that many facets of artefactual meaning are not directly present in a given situation, but are *indirectly* present, perceived or cognised through association (the 'secondhand' experience mentioned above). These semiotic associations can take numerous forms and vary in degree and quality.

These two approaches do not appear to have much in common, and have rarely overlapped in the literature on perception. Indeed, there is a deep-rooted opposition between the two within the psychology of perception (Palmer 1999). And yet in reality these two dimensions, direct affordances and indirect associations, tend to articulate and interact in the generation of material culture meaning: the pragmatic and the significative come together. Some would go so far as to say that a theory of material culture cannot work unless it succeeds in articulating the evident links between the pragmatic and the significative, between the object as sign and as material (Warnier 1999, 28). This may be rendered feasible with the fuller development of what can be termed 'situated semiotics'. One particular approach to semiotics is the key, that of Charles Sanders Peirce, the 'groundedness' of which has recently been explored by scholars across a range of disciplines (Sonesson 1989; Csordas 1994; Riggins 1994; Gottdiener 1995; Parmentier 1997; Nellhaus 1998; Preucel & Bauer 2001; Bauer 2002; Keane 2003; Lele 2006; Preucel 2006; Watts 2009). Such an approach has the capacity to cope with both the direct and indirect dimensions of artefactual meaning.

While I have focussed on affordances and associations elsewhere (Knappett 2004; 2005), a brief recap is in order. One useful example to help convey the main points comes from J. J. Gibson himself, the principal proponent of the 'direct perception' approach in which the concept of affordances plays a key role. Gibson argued that many kinds of objects, indeed perhaps all objects, could have their function directly perceived; a postbox, for example, can be directly seen to afford letter-mailing (Gibson 1979, 139). Certainly, the physical size and shape of the slot would seem to invite the deposit of a letter-sized object. But, Palmer (1999, 409) counters this, stating that some litter bins have similar slots that might be seen to afford letter-mailing. The choice of postboxes rather than litter bins to post letters is not solely contingent upon the physical form of the receptacle; the user possesses cultural information such that he/she knows the letters will be emptied from the box and eventually delivered (Noble 1991, 207-8). This understanding of the function of the postbox is not accessible from its physical form alone, but derives from numerous associations and access to internal representations. Its function is thus in large part *indirectly* perceived, or apprehended through 'secondhand' experience (Windsor 2004). There are further aspects of affordances worth discussion (see Knappett 2004; 2005), but here my aim is to further develop certain ideas concerning indirect associations, and the spatio-temporal configurations that diverse semiotic interconnections may take on.

Inter-artefactual networks

It is useful to take a leaf out of the mathematicians' and physicists' book, and think of associations as 'edges' or 'links', connecting different 'vertices' or 'nodes' (see Newman et al. 2006, and Newman 2010, for recent survey of network analysis). We can then picture networks composed of nodes and links within which meaning may be densely woven, or indeed widely distributed. In some applications of network theory in the social sciences, the heterogeneity of nodes and links is increasingly acknowledged; the idea of 'agent-artefact space', for example, allows for the inclusion of both human agents and material artefacts in complex socio-technical networks (Lane *et al.* 2009). The characteristics of such networks need to be more fully explored if we are to understand the dynamics of material culture meaning. Indeed, many previous investigations of artefact meaning have failed to assign sufficient weight to the generative role of interactive relations. This is perhaps part of a wider tendency within the social sciences to make entities rather than connections our analytical units, although Actor-Network Theory does of course represent a significant move towards relational approaches (e.g. Latour 2005).

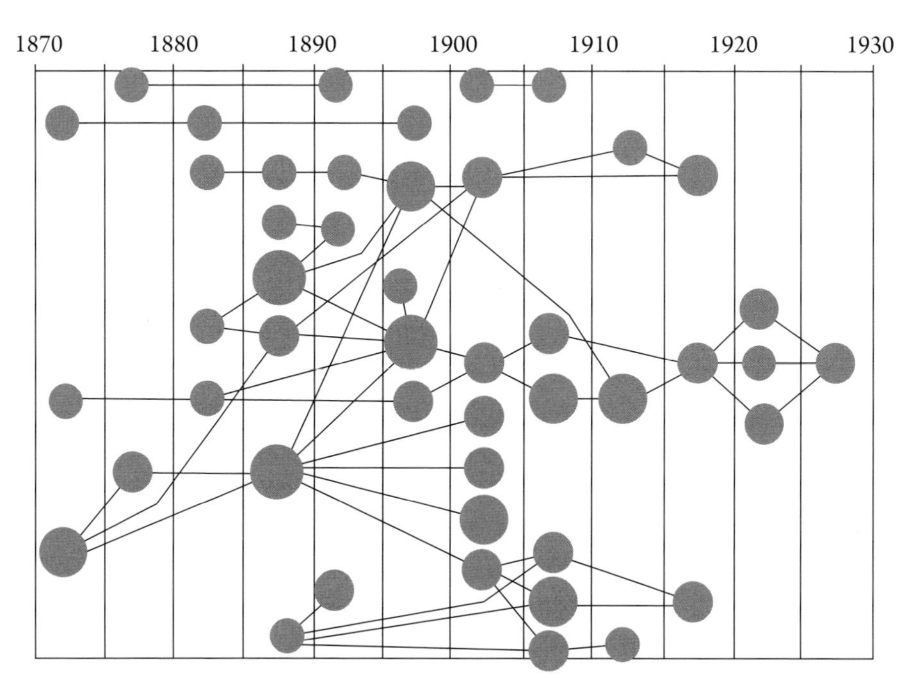

Fig. 1. A diagram of inter-artefactual relations: Maori meeting houses (after Neich 1996/Gell 1998).

The idea that connections may exist between artefacts as well as between human agents has already been explored, notably in the work of anthropologist Alfred Gell (1998). He suggests that individual objects are "holographic fragments of the larger unities to which they are united by stylistic linkages", (Gell 1998, 220). Examples as diverse as Kula valuables, Malangan carvings, Maori meeting houses and the artworks of Marcel Duchamp are used to illustrate this idea of a 'cultural tradition' somehow having a dynamic of its own. The point emerges particularly well through Gell's discussion of Roger Neich's work on Maori meeting houses (Gell 1998, 251-8; Neich 1996). Gell shows a diagram (Fig. 1; Gell 1998, 255, fig. 9.6/3) devised by Neich depicting the distribution over space and time of various kinds of figurative painting traditions (found within and on the meeting houses). It is a kind of inter-artefactual network in which the 'nodes' have quite variable identities, but the links are very simple and of one kind only. Gell does discuss the directionality of such links in a similar diagram he produces to explain the 'protentions' and 'retentions' in Duchamp's oeuvre, but other qualities (of the links) are not considered.

The notion that direct connections can be made between different individual elements within an oeuvre or cultural tradition is perhaps unsurprising to archaeologists, who do something seemingly very similar in constructing artefact typologies within spatio-temporal frameworks. However, these connections are rarely depicted as networks, and tend to be static rather than dynamic (for a dynamic approach, see Gosden 2005). The absence of humans from such constructs is not usually considered problematic with a descriptive tool of this kind, although

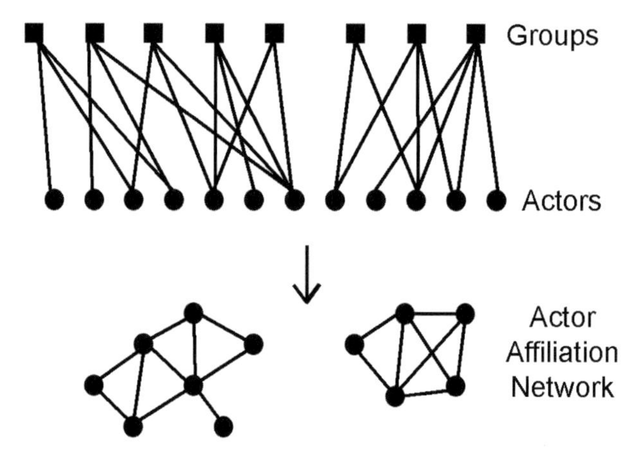

Fig. 2. A two-mode network

it does contribute to an unhelpful decoupling of description from interpretation. The apparent absence of humans from the inter-artefactual networks mapped by Neich and Gell seems rather more problematic. It may appear as if this nonhuman network has some life or dynamic of its own. However, it must be understood that what is depicted is actually a single-mode projection of an underlying two-mode network, so called because the nodes in the network can have one of two identities. That is to say, in this two-mode network, which is only barely implicit in Neich/Gell, both humans and nonhumans (Maori houses) are present as nodes. Moreover, humans do not connect directly to each other, but only indirectly via houses (Fig. 2). But in the diagram shown by Neich/Gell, in which two modes are collapsed into one, the nodes are the houses and the *links* are actually human individuals or groups. One could of course reverse this, showing a map of individuals or groups connected by houses, which have now become the links. Such thinking, drawn from social network analysis (e.g. Wasserman and Faust 1994; Scott 2000; de Nooy *et al.* 2005), offers an important clarification of what is otherwise a problematic representation. In inter-artefactual relations, it is crucial to think about the identity of the *links*: this is where to find the 'hidden' humans.

While Gell's approach appears to be broadly consistent with Peircean semiotics, explicit connections are lacking. A fuller consideration of the kinds of semiotic associations that might contribute to an artefact's meaning within inter-artefactual networks would probably, therefore, be worthwhile. Along with the work of Peirce, the contributions of Sonesson in visual semiotics and art history are also fundamental (Sonesson 1989; 1998). At the risk of oversimplification, semiotic associations can best be understood as based principally on relationships of similarity (often visual, but perhaps also aural, olfactory, sensual), contiguity, factorality, causality and convention (Knappett 2005). A portrait, for example, is a sign that connects to its referent through iconic resemblance or similarity. A shop sign refers to a shop principally through indexical contiguity – the sign hangs over the shop. Factorality refers to the relationship of part to whole, such that a part is taken to represent the whole – the rolling gait of a sailor, or the crown of a king. A causal index is when the sign is caused by the referent, as for example when fire causes smoke, or the wind causes a weathervane to point in a particular direction. Finally, conventional symbols may be artefacts such as 'stop' signs, or indeed words. This is a rather curtailed semiotic perspective; a much fuller development of Peirce's ideas for archaeological application can be found in the work of Preucel (2006) and Watts (2009).

These different forms of semiotic relationship can be characterised further still in terms of their degree and quality. We can assess their frequency, fidelity, distance and directionality. It is perhaps best to explore what these terms may mean through examples, namely those that will form the main focus of this paper: small-scale ceramic vessels from the Aegean Bronze Age.

Miniaturising meaning

We may analyse the 'inter-artefactual' properties of small-scale or 'miniature' vessels in terms of frequency, fidelity, distance and directionality. First, the *frequency* with which a 'canonical' form is reproduced at small scale, for example, may vary considerably – certain vessels may be very frequently scaled down, such as jugs, while others only occur in miniature form but rarely, such as cooking pots. Secondly, the *fidelity* of the small-scale version may also be different from one case to another. In some instances there may only be the merest gesture made towards the full scale form, with much detail sacrificed. Alternatively, the ceramic miniature may reproduce the original with incredible accuracy. Thirdly, an association may be maintained over short or long *distances*. On the one hand, a link based on similarity can, in some sense, transcend time and space, recognisable over almost any scale (thus miniatures from peak sanctuaries may recapitulate forms more commonly found at relatively distant settlement locations). On the other hand, a link based on contiguity is much more dependent upon a spatial relationship between sign and referent (for example when miniatures are found next to their full scale equivalents). Fourthly and finally, there may be *directionality* in the associations observed: full scale ceramics may be imitated in small-scale, but some vessels which are designed to be small may not be recapitulated at a larger scale.

By taking such relationships into account, one should be able to put together a diagram of connections that displays the complex reticular relations that can emerge (although this is a larger project, beyond the scope of this short paper). There is a kind of three-dimensional topology constituted of many different nodes tied together by a range of links. One can also see that in these interlinkages between artefacts and people, some links will be human-to-human, others human-to-nonhuman, and nonhuman-to-nonhuman. Let us consider some of these possibilities further, and their implications for material culture meaning.

However, as far as miniature artefacts are concerned, the interpretations usually offered in archaeology are more specific, and thus not readily integrated into broader understandings of material culture meaning. Miniatures are usually seen as toys, burial offerings or ritual objects. All three of these roles are, for example, seen in Inuit society (Park 1998). Children use miniature sledges, kayaks, cooking pots, harpoons and dolls with which to play; miniaturised versions of a deceased's possessions are buried with the individual; and miniature items are part of a shaman's paraphernalia (Park 1998, 275). Occasionally, some of these functions may be combined. In Early Anglo-Saxon England, miniature grave goods are found in association with child burials (Crawford 2000, 176-7). In the Andes today, miniatures used by children in play can also be used as offerings in household rituals; indeed, it has been argued that the ritual significance of miniatures derives from their very association with children and play (Sillar 1994, 54-5; Sillar 2004, 161). When it comes to the Aegean Bronze Age, miniatures are most often interpreted in ritual terms as votive offerings. This is not without reason, as they are most commonly found on peak sanctuaries or in caves (Girella 2002; Tournavitou 2009), sites which clearly performed a ritual role. The notion that miniatures might also be toys is only rarely advanced, in large part because they are not commonly found in settlement contexts. It may also be in part due to the lack of thought devoted to children as a social category in archaeological theory, a position which has recently begun to change (e.g. Moore & Scott 1997; Derevenski 2000).

What I wish to do here, then, is look specifically at some examples of miniature and small-scale ceramic vessels from the Aegean Bronze Age, with a view to understanding their meanings in much broader terms. I examine a range of such vessels from settlement contexts on Crete, in which they are not obviously used as either votives or toys. This will then lead onto a more general interpretation of the meaningfulness of miniature and small-scale vessels, drawing on very different strands, archaeology, cognitive science and contemporary art respectively: work on figurines by Douglass Bailey (2005), on models and surrogate situations by Andy Clark (2010), and sculptural works by Charles LeDray.

Minoan miniature and small-scale vessels

Let us begin by taking one kind of vessel common through much of the Bronze Age of Crete – the 'pithos', a type of large storage jar (Fig. 3). They are known from many different sites and periods, but let us just focus on examples from one time and place – Malia in the Protopalatial period (c. 1900-1700 BC). At this site many complete pithoi have been excavated from a set of town buildings called 'Quartier Mu' (Poursat 1992, 1996; Poursat & Knappett 2005). These vessels are generally between 70-100 cm tall, with a capacity around 100 litres, but up to c. 340 litres in some cases (example M67/1, 126cm tall: Poursat & Knappett 2005, 205, pl. 7). The affordances of these large vessels can be understood quite directly. Their volume and weight render them cumbersome and difficult to move. They have particular shape features that are suggestive: multiple sturdy handles, presumably adapted to lifting such a heavy object, perhaps with the help of ropes; and a thickened, everted rim that would afford the fitting of a lid or cover. There are also features of their context that are directly perceptible: sometimes such vessels are placed in particular rooms with installations for collecting liquid run-off. In such cases it is thus the vessels and the setting combined that have affordances (cf. Knappett 2004, 46, on the affordances of *situations*). This moves us into the question of associations – clearly pithoi have spatial connections, in being contiguous with particular installations, not to mention other vessels (e.g. Chamaizi pots – see below).

In this regard, we should note that, visually, these large storage jars do actually look incredibly similar to some vessels – notably miniature versions of themselves that have been found in the same complex. At a height of only 14 cm, and a capacity of just 0.7 litre, one example, M67/102 (Fig. 4), could hardly be said to fulfil the same storage function – it has none of the same affordances (Poursat

Fig. 3. Canonical pithos from Quartier Mu, Malia (after Poursat 1992, 35, fig. 26)

Fig. 4. Miniature pithos from Quartier Mu, Malia (photograph by the author)

Fig. 5. Miniature carinated cups from Quartier Mu, Malia (photograph by the author)

Fig. 6. Miniature tumblers and conical cups from Quartier Mu, Malia (photograph by the author)

Fig. 7. Miniature bowl-ladle from Quartier Mu, Malia (photograph by the author)

Fig. 8. Miniature jugs from Quartier Mu, Malia (photograph by the author)

& Knappett 2005, 236, pl. 33). And yet it has precisely the same characteristics of shape, handle attachment, and decoration – it is *iconically* very close in terms of its shape, although in terms of decoration it does not share the same trickle pattern. We may also briefly consider these inter-artefactual relations in terms of frequency, fidelity, distance and directionality. These connections do not appear to be made with any great frequency: in the very large ceramic assemblages of Quartier Mu, miniature pithoi are relatively rare. The connections do, however, display fidelity, with the full-size pithoi faithfully reproduced in miniature form. In terms of distance, this phenomenon does seem to be confined largely to Malia; although the archaeological record is of course patchy, there is little sign of this being a practice closely followed at other sites. As for directionality, we can be fairly confident in stating that the miniature forms are clearly mimicking the larger ones, rather than vice versa. That said, the existence of these miniature pithoi would presumably in some way have impinged upon the meaningfulness of the full-scale versions.

Other examples from Quartier Mu, which with circa 200 miniatures has one of the largest such assemblages from Bronze Age Crete, also involve a 'scaling down' of canonical, functioning forms, such as carinated cups (Fig. 5), tumblers, conical cups (Fig. 6), bowl-ladles (Fig. 7), jugs (Fig. 8) and amphorae (Poursat & Knappett 2005). The miniaturised versions of these are also too small to be functional. They can be characterised in a similar way to the pithoi in terms of frequency, fidelity, distance and directionality, although some of the cups shown in the lower row of figure 6 seem to be somewhat more schematic and abstracted than the others.

By no means are all of the 200 or so ceramic types of Protopalatial Malia rendered in miniature – choice has been exercised in the process of miniaturisation. For example, hardly any miniature cooking pots are known. Sometimes the miniaturisation process does not scale down all the way to the point where functionality is lost – some miniature amphorae, for example are not 'true' miniatures in that they could conceivably still hold a certain amount of liquid, close to 1 litre in some cases. And some very small vessels like Chamaizi pots are not miniaturised versions of anything 'canonical' – they only exist at this small scale, generally about 5.5 cm tall (Poursat & Knappett 2005, 83-4, pl. 36). Note too that there are some rare examples bearing writing in the Cretan Hieroglyphic script, another unique feature for Protopalatial pottery at Malia (Fig. 9).

In the assemblages from Quartier Mu the only other miniatures not to have been scaled down are the so-called 'cupules' (Poursat 1994). These are extremely small, with a diameter of just 1.5 cm and only 1 cm high, and so flat as to barely be describable as vessels at all (Fig. 10). Most of them were found in groups, notably

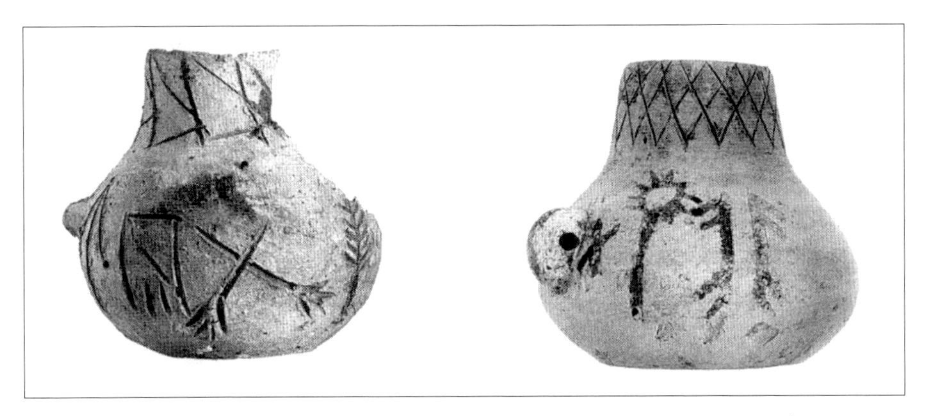

Fig. 9. Chamaizi pots, with Cretan Hieroglyphic script; from Quartier Mu, Malia (after Poursat 1992, 29, figs.19-20)

in room IV 4 (Poursat 1994, 250-1), and in areas where archival documents have also been recovered. This has led to their interpretation as 'tokens', used in some way to represent units of commodities. What processes of meaning are at work here, if small-scale vessels are being used to signify commodities in some indexical fashion? If they are connected through relations of similarity or contiguity to other artefacts, then those artefacts are not so much ceramic vessels as archival documents. And if we seek to characterise these in terms of frequency, fidelity, distance and directionality, they have quite different traits to those miniaturised vessels such as pithoi and cups described above.

This interpretation of miniatures as tokens, taken from the Near East in the main (Schmandt-Besserat 1996), also arises with one particular assemblage from Knossos. A deposit of c. 200 complete vessels from the area of Early Magazine A (D.VII 14 & 16), and dating to the beginning of the Protopalatial period (MM IB), contains 22 miniature vessels (Macdonald & Knappett 2007, see Fig. 11). The goblets, tumblers, cups, bowls and juglets are all scaled down versions of canonical forms, many of which are present alongside them in the same deposit. In terms of inter-artefactual relations, the close spatial proximity (i.e. 'distance') between

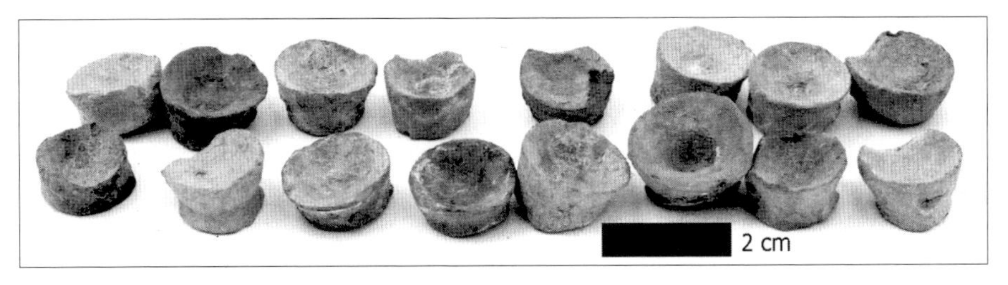

Fig. 10. 'Cupules' or tokens from Quartier Mu, Malia (photograph by the author)

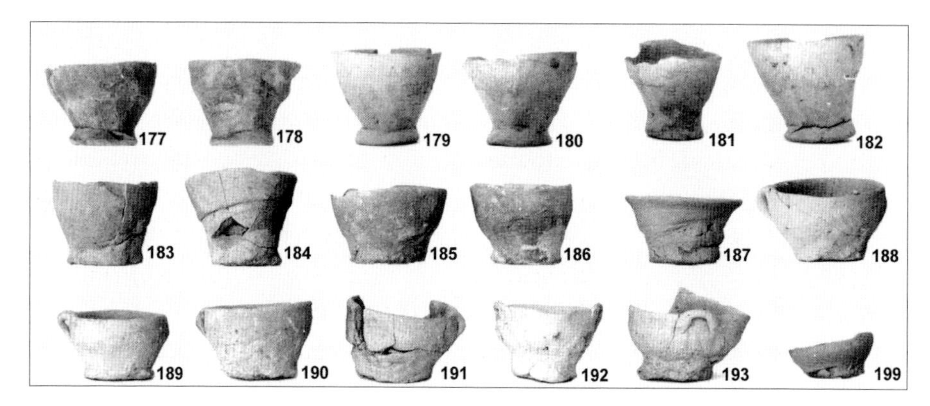

Fig. 11. Miniature vases from Knossos (after Macdonald & Knappett 2007, plate 17; courtesy of the British School at Athens)

miniaturised and canonical forms is striking, and there is a clear directionality in this relationship. The links are perhaps only infrequently made, but perhaps most interesting is their 'fidelity' – they do visually resemble one another, but the miniaturised versions have had little care taken in their forming – hardly a process of 'faithful' distillation designed to accentuate form (Fig. 11). Indeed, Weingarten (2007) has interpreted them as tokens, each one representing a unit of some commodity; interpreted in this way, they do not need to be 'faithful' iconically, as they are functioning indexically. But what would they have stood for? Does it really make much sense to manufacture a miniature goblet to function as a token for a normal goblet? A one-to-one correspondence seems unlikely; much more probable is a scenario in which one miniature denotes a large batch, perhaps fifty or one hundred.

The juxtaposition of the canonical and the miniaturised in this deposit is

Fig. 12. Ceramic kantharos containing miniaturised versions of itself; from Myrtos Pyrgos (after Cadogan 1977-78, 75, fig. 12; courtesy of the British School at Athens)

seen elsewhere, albeit in different form. One striking example is a kantharos from Myrtos Pyrgos, also of Protopalatial date (Cadogan 1977-8; Knappett 2002, fig. 2; see Fig. 12). The standard size kantharos, strongly imitative of a metallic prototype, contains within it a number of miniaturised versions of itself. If we assess the relations between them, we can note the multiplication of miniatures (frequency); the faithful reproduction of form in the miniaturised versions (fidelity); the concerted effort to create a spatial concentration (distance); and the clear directionality from 'standard' kantharos to the miniaturised (directionality). Together these features create a greater intensity of meaning by accentuating form over function. Furthermore, the skeuomorphic form of these kantharoi would have held great resonance, given the high value of the silver originals on which they were modelled.

Interpreting miniatures

In the above examples from Bronze Age Crete, we see different kinds of 'small-scale' vessels. Some are indeed miniaturised versions of canonical forms. Others only exist at their own small scale. Their semiotic connections with other parts of the overall material culture assemblage in Bronze Age Crete are thus likely to have been quite different.

But what is perhaps the most striking pattern is that those small-scale vessels which are linked iconically to canonical forms do actually replicate them quite faithfully; while those that seem to be operating as indexes or tokens are much less carefully produced. With the former, it is difficult to assess the scale of the vessel from the form alone; while with the latter the lack of attention to detail makes the small scale much more apparent. Expressed in terms borrowed from complexity theory, it could be said that the iconic miniatures are 'scale invariant', displaying 'fractality' (e.g. Barabási 2002; Bentley & Maschner 2003; Lehner 2000; Brown *et al.* 2005). A change in scale may not affect their fundamental form, but it does affect their function: miniature pithoi clearly cannot function in the same way as the full-size versions. This loss of function with reduced scale only serves to throw the fidelity of form into even sharper relief.

However, there appears to be uncertainty in the literature as to the extent to which scaled-down artefacts should be expected to maintain faithful connections with their full-scale counterparts. Douglass Bailey comments on this relationship in his work on prehistoric figurines, and in particular in his observations on miniaturism and dimensionality (Bailey 2005, 26-44). He draws a strong distinction between models and miniatures. For the former he has in mind accurate scale models as created by architects. He seems to imply that such models are not selective, but keep all detail. The latter, on the other hand, i.e. miniatures, do involve a process of abstraction, such that some details are deliberately excluded. If we follow Bailey's argument, our Cretan Bronze Age examples include both models and miniatures: the faithfully miniaturised vessels such as pithoi and carinated cups would count as models, whereas the rather abstracted tokens (e.g. the Quartier Mu 'cupules') would qualify as miniatures. However, there are surely grounds for questioning this distinction: surely any model, however precise, is an abstraction of sorts, given the evident loss of functionality?

Certainly, in the work of Clark (2010), to which we might now usefully turn, his discussion of models/toys in relation to surrogate situations does not make such a distinction between models and miniatures (while not dealing explicitly with miniatures). Clark argues that the reason models are efficient forms of 'offline' reasoning is that they present surrogate situations through which we can think more effectively about the real world; and in so doing they deliberately suppress some information, through what he calls 'selective concretisation' and 'temporal relaxation'. We will come back to the latter in the section below on narrative. But this idea of selective concretisation is very pertinent here, and parallels most usefully the observations made by Bailey on abstraction and compression. Following Markman & Gentner (1993), Clark stresses that the grasp of abstract relations improves when the richness of the representation of the related objects is decreased. This, though, must surely also apply to both 'models' and 'miniatures' in Bailey's terms?

While we should probably hesitate before forcing the Cretan Bronze Age examples into either the 'model' or 'miniature' boxes suggested by Bailey, it is evident that these small-scale vessels do suppress detail in different ways. On the one hand, the tokens from both Malia and Knossos are lacking in detail and thus do seem to show 'selective concretisation'. On the other hand, the iconic miniatures do not really suppress any formal details, yet they are nonetheless 'selective' in that their functional qualities have been sacrificed (as too, you would assume, is the case with architectural models). The Chamaizi vessels are of course different by being at their own scale (and perhaps the Hieroglyphic writing emphasises this – it does not appear itself to be miniaturised).

The small scale and miniature in art: Charles LeDray

Let us now take another angle on this question of the meaningfulness of the small-scale. Modern and contemporary art can offer many insights into artefactual meaning (Renfrew 2003; Renfrew *et al.* 2004; Knappett 2006). Artists such as René Magritte and Claes Oldenburg have changed the scale of objects, either in

Fig. 13. Charles LeDray, Oasis, 1996-2003 (detail). Glazed ceramic, glass, steel, 96 x 36 x 36 inches (243.8 x 91.4 x 91.4 cm.) overall. Collection of the Museum of Modern Art, Courtesy Sperone Westwater, New York

painting or sculpture, to challenge our encounters with everyday objects; however, they tend to scale objects up rather than down. Here, I focus on the work of contemporary artist Charles LeDray, in which the retention rather than the suppression of detail in the very small-scale leads to some interesting tensions. In one of his works, 'Oasis, 1996-2003', hundreds of miniature ceramic vessels fill a large glass display case (Fig. 13). Although 'miniature' versions of forms more commonly encountered at a large scale, forms which should 'function' at full scale, they nonetheless retain high levels of detail. LeDray's miniatures seem not to involve any kind of suppression of detail. If one were to follow Bailey's logic, outlined above, these would then count as models and not as miniatures at all. This is perhaps what makes them real, the fact that nothing is 'missing'; and it is thus that "LeDray resists the connotations of the miniature: the cute, the whimsical, and – perhaps worst of all – the collectible" (Ferguson 2002, 14).

Reviewing similar works by LeDray, Susan Hagen suggests that "the subject is distilled through a reduction in scale into a more emotionally intense version of its source." (Hagen 2002). This idea of distilling form to create greater intensity is very persuasive; it should be added that in the distillation process functionality is lost, further adding to the focus on form.

Interesting observations on the phenomenon of miniaturisation are also found in the more literary approach of Stewart (1993), focussing primarily on miniature books and minute writing (micrographia). Stewart notes that "a reduction in dimensions does not produce a corresponding reduction in significance" (1993, 43). Indeed, quite the opposite: reduction could be said to result in "a multiplication of ideological properties" (Stewart 1993, 48). And perhaps, as Stewart implies, this process could be performed quite deliberately, with the real world "miniaturised or giganticized to test the relation between materiality and meaning" (1993, 57).

Miniatures as icons and indexes

Iconic miniatures do not only create an intensification of meaning. They allow a distance to open up between the canonical form and the miniature, because iconicity as a sign relation does not have a spatial boundedness in the way that contiguity does; indeed, Gell makes a similar point about 'stylistic linkages' not being spatially limited (Gell 1998, 221-58). The visual associations between the iconic miniature and the canonical form can transcend space, existing in a kind of virtual space or relational network (cf. Amin & Cohendet 2004, on relational communities). Iconicity thus has a very different spatial (and presumably temporal) 'pattern' when compared to those forms of indexicality based on contiguity; and this property must surely have an effect upon how meaning is generated. However, other forms of index *can* transcend physical space, unlimited by contiguity, as we will see in the examples from voodoo magic below.

Miniaturised forms can indeed transcend physical space, as their size facilitates transport. This property can be further explored through an unlikely source: the realm of voodoo and magic. Two forms of voodoo magic can be distinguished, sympathetic and contagious (Gell 1998). The former essentially works through iconicity – the target is evoked through connections of similarity, often in the form of a visual likeness such as a doll. There need not have ever been any physical contact between the target and its visual likeness. Contagious magic, on the other hand, operates through indexicality – some physical component of the target is needed, usually exuviae such as hair, nails etc. In each case the target is intensified through reduction – either through a miniature likeness, or a small fragment of the whole. And interestingly, even though contagious magic does require some prior bodily contact to acquire the exuviae, both forms of voodoo can be carried out remotely, thanks largely to the size and transportability of the icon or index.

To summarise, miniatures have certain physical and semiotic properties (or, in other words, affordances and associations) that enable them to bear meaning in an intensified fashion, while paradoxically being physically remote from those forms of which they are iconic or indexical. It is, of course, interesting to note that these properties are not fully exploited with the miniatures from Quartier Mu Malia, Knossos and Myrtos Pyrgos, which are found close to their canonical equivalents. However, these examples are atypical of Cretan Bronze Age miniatures in being from settlement sites. Most miniatures are associated with ritual locations, such as burials, peak sanctuaries and caves (Girella 2002; Simandaraki forthcoming). More than one hundred years ago, miniature vessels were found on the peak sanctuary of Petsophas, above the site of Palaikastro in east Crete (Myres 1902-3; Rutkowski 1991). Miniatures have also been discovered on the 'Minoan' peak sanctuary of Ayios Georgios on the island of Kythera (Sakellarakis 1996; Tournavitou 2009). In the light of the previous discussion, we can perhaps begin to understand more clearly the processes which led to this association of miniatures with ritual places. Peak sanctuaries are often distant from settlements on high peaks and difficult of access. Their 'condensed' physical and semiotic form meant they could retain their power and intensity, potentially crucial in a ritual setting. Burials tend not to be so far from settlements, but the same logic, of maintaining the intensity of meaning in ritual practice, should hold true.

There is a need to consider the topology of meaning further still. How do miniatures take on meaning by virtue of their complex, spatially *distributed* connections with the canonical, and vice versa, how are canonical forms altered when miniaturised versions are created? If we were to create a network representation of such connections, we would need to be aware, as was stressed earlier in the paper, of the two-mode character of such a network. That is to say, it would be composed of both people and artefacts, humans and nonhumans, even if we may choose to represent two modes as one (see Fig. 2). This can be done by representing the artefacts as the nodes in the network, with the humans as the links connecting them (or vice versa, for that matter). We also noted above that the links in a network can have varying texture, frequency, distance and directionality, which we would then have to consider in terms of the kinds of links people in a given set of contexts might be creating between different groups of miniatures and canonical forms (Fig. 2).

Inter-artefactual relations and narrative

We have not yet made mention of the temporal dimension, and a brief note is in order. In this regard Stewart makes an intriguing comment on the relation between miniaturisation and time:

> The reduction in scale which the miniature presents skews the time and space relations of the everyday lifeworld, and as an object consumed, the miniature finds its "use value" transformed into the infinite time of reverie (1993, 65).

This view is very closely paralleled in Clark's argument (2010) that the use of models in surrogate situations creates a 'temporal relaxation'. Furthermore, Bailey refers us to the psychological experiments of Alton Delong, showing that *spatial* compression (i.e. miniaturisation) can at the same time instill a proportionate *temporal* compression (Bailey 1995, 36-38; Delong 1983). If we follow these views, there is a sense in which miniatures work against narrative, or at least force other kinds of narrative. The same might very well be said of giganticised artefacts, such as the oversize artworks of Claes Oldenburg. Thus various kinds of artefact, or sets of artefacts, that are spatially compressed or expanded, might resist conventional linear narratives. This surely has implications for the ways in which we seek to understand material culture meaning, particularly given the prevailing tendency in material culture studies to give precedence to artefact 'biographies'. The biographical approach has been a rich mode of analysis; yet an artefact's life history is only a partial view in that it takes a vertical rather than a horizontal tranche through inter-artefactual relations, rather than looking horizontally. Examining the 'horizontal' networks of meaning might seem little different from a consideration of 'context'; yet context is often taken to imply some predetermined setting, rather than a more fluid situation determined by active circumstance (Bal & Bryson 1994, 141). The idea of a semiotic network conveys this dynamic quality more effectively, I would argue, allowing us to see how meaning might be dynamically generated, rather than predetermined by a static 'context'. Furthermore, the 'biographical' approach is facilitated by its tendency to focus on individual artefacts rather than selecting assemblages for study. Tackling artefact assemblages might challenge our assumptions about the temporal trajectories of artefacts, particularly when the 'inter-artefactual relations' (Gell 1998; Gosden 2005) are affected by shifting spatial scales.

Conclusions

This paper has considered the spatial scale of artefacts in relational terms. Some small-scale vases are indeed miniaturised versions of canonical forms, while others are only ever found at that scale. It is these relationships between forms in an assemblage – what we might call 'semiotic networks' – that are crucial, then, to the emergence of meaning. However, these semiotic relationships are at the same time grounded in the material properties of the artefacts themselves – in the fidelity of form and the attention afforded to decorative detail. It is in this sense that the perspective adopted here is a 'situated semiotic' one, drawing on both the semiotics of Peirce and the ecological approach of Gibson.

The links and relations that emerge inter-artefactually soon spiral out into complex webs of interconnections in which humans as well as nonhumans are of course entangled. And complex networks can have their own peculiar behaviours or dynamics – complex in terms of the unpredictable relationship between the local and the global (Bentley & Maschner 2003, 1). While many archaeologists, and indeed social scientists more generally, have been very much aware of this, it is hoped that this paper, with its focus on semiotic networks, and the properties of frequency, fidelity, distance and directionality, gives some pointers towards a *methodology* for bridging the gap between the local and the global in the generation of material culture meaning.

Acknowledgements

I am most grateful to the organisers – Mads Jessen, Niels Johannsen and Helle Juel Jensen – both for the invitation to participate in such a stimulating conference, and for the wonderful hospitality shown to us in Aarhus. My thanks also go to Chris Gosden for highlighting the relevance of Gell's work on inter-artefactual relations; and to Jennifer Burbank of Sperone Westwater for facilitating the reproduction of the work by Charles LeDray in figure 13. As this paper was written before 2008, it does not make reference to any of the ideas presented in John Mack's excellent book on miniatures, *The Art of Small Things.*

References

Amin, A. & P. Cohendet 2004. *Architectures of Knowledge: Firms, Capabilities and Communities.* Oxford: Oxford University Press.

Bailey, D.W. 2005. *Prehistoric Figurines: Representation and Corporeality in the Neolithic.* London: Routledge.

Bal, M. & N. Bryson 1994. 'Semiotics and Art History.' In: M. Bal (ed.), *On Meaning-Making: Essays in Semiotics.* Santa Rosa, CA: Polebridge Press, 137-204.

Barabási, A.-L. 2002. *Linked: The New Science of Networks.* Cambridge, MA: Perseus Publishing.

Bauer, A.A. 2002. 'Is What You See All You Get? Recognizing Meaning in Archaeology.' *Journal of Social Archaeology,* 2(1), 37-52.

Bentley, R.A. & H.D.G. Maschner 2003. 'Preface: Considering Complexity Theory in Archaeology.' In: R.A. Bentley, H.D.G. Maschner (eds.), *Complex Systems and Archaeology.* Salt Lake City: University of Utah Press, 1-8.

Brown, C.T., W.R.T. Witschey & L.S. Liebovitch 2005. 'The Broken Past: Fractals in Archaeology.' *Journal of Archaeological Method and Theory,* 12(1), 37-78.

Cadogan, G. 1977-8. 'Pyrgos, Crete 1970-7.' *Archaeological Reports,* 24, 70-84.

Clark, A. 2010. 'Material surrogacy and the supernatural: reflections on the role of artefacts in 'off-line' cognition', in L. Malafouris and C. Renfrew (eds.), *The Cognitive Life of Things: Recasting the Boundaries of the Mind.* Cambridge: McDonald Institute Monographs, 23-28.

Costall, A. 2006. 'On Being the Right Size: Affordances and the Meaning of Scale.' In: G. Lock, B.L. Molyneaux (eds.), *Confronting Scale in Archaeology: Issues of Theory and Practice.* New York: Springer, 15-26.

Crawford, S. 2000. 'Children, Grave Goods and Social Status in Early Anglo-Saxon England.' In J.S. Derevenski (ed.), *Children and Material Culture.* London: Routledge, 169-79.

Csordas, T.J. (ed.) 1994. *Embodiment and Experience: The Existential Ground of Culture and Self.* Cambridge: Cambridge University Press.

Delong, A. 1983. 'Spatial Scale, Temporal Experience and Information Processing: an Empirical Examination of Experiential Reality.' *Man-Environment Systems,* 13, 77-86.

Derevenski, J.S. (ed.) 2000. *Children and Material Culture.* London: Routledge.

Ferguson, R. 2002. 'Attention Level.' In: C. Gould (ed.), *Charles LeDray, Sculpture 1989-2002.* Philadelphia: Institute of Contemporary Art, 13-24.

Gell, A. 1998. *Art and Agency: Towards a New Anthropological Theory.* Oxford: Clarendon Press.

Gibson, J.J. 1979. *The Ecological Approach to Visual Perception.* Boston: Houghton Mifflin.

Girella, L. 2002. 'Vasi Rituali con Elementi Miniaturizzati a Creta, in Egeo e nel Mediterraneo Orientale alla Fine dell'Età del Bronzo. Indicatori Archeologici ed Etnici.' *Creta Antica,* 3, 167-216.

Gosden, C. 2004. 'Making and Display: Our Aesthetic Appreciation of Things and Objects.' In: C. Renfrew, C. Gosden, E. DeMarrais (eds.), *Substance, Memory, Display: Archaeology and Art.* Cambridge: McDonald Institute Monographs, 35-45.

Gosden, C. 2005. 'What Do Objects Want.' *Journal of Archaeological Method and Theory,* 12(3), 193-211.

Gottdiener, M. 1995. *Postmodern Semiotics: Material Culture and the Forms of Postmodern Life.* Oxford: Blackwell.

Hagen, S. 2002. 'The Bone Collector.' Review of Charles LeDray, Sculpture 1989-2002, Institute of Contemporary Art, Philadelphia, May 10-July 14, 2002. *Philadelphia City Paper,* May 30, 2002 edition.

Keane, W. 2003. 'Semiotics and the Social Analysis of Material Things.' *Language and Communication,* 23, 409-25.

Knappett, C. 2002. 'Photographs, Skeuomorphs and Marionettes: Some Thoughts on Mind, Agency and Object.' *Journal of Material Culture,* 7(1), 97-117.

Knappett, C. 2004. 'The Affordances of Things: a Post-Gibsonian Perspective on the Relationality of Mind and Matter.' In: E. DeMarrais, C. Gosden, C. Renfrew (eds.), *Rethinking Materiality: The Engagement of Mind with the Material World.* Cambridge: McDonald Institute Monographs, 43-51.

Knappett, C. 2005. *Thinking Through Material Culture: An Interdisciplinary Perspective.* Philadelphia, PA: University of Pennsylvania Press.

Knappett, C. 2006. 'Beyond Skin: Layering and Networking in Art and Archaeology.' *Cambridge Archaeological Journal,* 16(2), 239-51.

Lane, D., D. Pumain, S.E. van der Leeuw & G. West (eds.) 2009. *Complexity Perspectives on Innovation and Social Change.* New York: Springer Methodos series.

Latour, B. 2005. *Reassembling the Social: An Introduction to Actor-Network-Theory.* Oxford: Oxford University Press.

Lehner, M. 2000. 'Fractal House of Pharaoh: Ancient Egypt as a Complex Adaptive System.' In: T.A. Kohler, G.J. Gumerman (eds.), *Dynamics in Human and Primate Societies: Agent-Based Modeling of Social and Spatial Processes.* Oxford: Oxford University Press, 275-353.

Lele, V.P. 2006. 'Material Habits, Identity, Semeiotic.' *Journal of Social Archaeology,* 6(1), 48-70.

Macdonald, C.F. & C. Knappett 2007. *Knossos: Protopalatial Deposits in Early Magazine A and the South-west Houses.* (British School at Athens, Supp. Vol. 41). London: British School at Athens.

Markman, A. & D. Gentner 1993. 'Structural Alignment During Similarity Comparisons.' *Cognitive Psychology* 25, 431-67.

Merleau-Ponty, M. 1962. *The Phenomenology of Perception.* London: Routledge.

Moore, J. & E. Scott (eds.) 1997. *Invisible People and Processes – Writing Gender and Childhood into European Archaeology.* London: Leicester University Press.

Myres, J.L. 1902-3. 'Excavations at Palaikastro II. The Sanctuary Site of Petsofa.' *Annual of the British School at Athens,* 9, 356-87.

Neich, R. 1996. *Painted Histories: Early Maori Figurative Painting.* Auckland: Auckland University Press.

Nellhaus, T. 1998. 'Signs, Social Ontology, and Critical Realism.' *Journal for the Theory of Social Behaviour,* 28(1), 1-24.

Newman, M., A.-L. Barabási & D.J. Watts (eds.) 2006. *The Structure and Dynamics of Networks.* Princeton, NJ: Princeton University Press.

Newman, M.E.J. 2010. *Networks: An Introduction.* Oxford: Oxford University Press.

Noble, W. 1991. 'Ecological Realism and the Fallacy of Objectification.' In: A. Still, A. Costall (eds.), *Against Cognitivism: Alternative Foundations for Cognitive Psychology.* London: Harvester Wheatsheaf, 199-223.

De Nooy, W., A. Mrvar & V. Batagelj 2005. *Exploratory Social Network Analysis with Pajek*. Cambridge: Cambridge University Press.

Palmer, S.E. 1999. *Vision Science: From Photons to Phenomenology*. Cambridge, MA: MIT Press.

Park, R.W. 1998. 'Size Counts: the Miniature Archaeology of Childhood in Inuit Societies.' *Antiquity*, 72, 269-81.

Parmentier, R.J. 1997. 'The Pragmatic Semiotics of Cultures.' *Semiotica*, 116, 1-115.

Peirce, C.S. 1931-1958. *Collected Papers of Charles Sanders Peirce*. Cambridge, MA: Harvard University Press.

Poursat, J.-C. 1992. *Guide de Malia – Quartier Mu*. Ecole Française d'Athènes, Sites et Monuments VIII.

Poursat, J.-C. 1994. 'Les Systèmes Primitives de Contabilité en Crète Minoenne.' In: P. Ferioli, E. Fiandra, G.G. Fissore, M. Frangipane (eds.), *Archives Before Writing. Proceedings of the International Colloquium, Oriolo Romano, October 23-25 1991*. Rome: Centro Internazionale di Richerche Archeologiche, Anthropologiche e Storiche, 247-54.

Poursat, J.-C. 1996. *Artisans Minoens: Les Maisons-Ateliers du Quartier Mu. Fouilles Executées à Malia: Le Quartier Mu III*. Paris: Etudes Cretoises 32.

Poursat, J.-C., & C. Knappett 2005. *Le Quartier Mu IV. La Poterie du Minoen Moyen II: Production et Utilisation*. Paris: Etudes Crétoises 33.

Preucel, R.W. 2006. *Archaeological Semiotics*. Oxford: Blackwell.

Preucel, R.W. & A.A. Bauer 2001. 'Archaeological Pragmatics.' *Norwegian Archaeological Review*, 34(2), 85-96.

Reed, E. 1996. *The Necessity of Experience*. New Haven: Yale University Press.

Renfrew, C. 2003. *Figuring It Out: The Parallel Visions of Artists and Archaeologists*. London: Thames and Hudson.

Renfrew, C., C. Gosden & E. DeMarrais (eds.) 2004. *Substance, Memory, Display: Archaeology and Art*. Cambridge: McDonald Institute Monographs.

Riggins, S.H. (ed.) 1994. *The Socialness of Things: Essays on the Socio-Semiotics of Objects*. Berlin: Mouton de Gruyter.

Rutkowski, B. 1991. *Petsophas. A Cretan Peak Sanctuary*. Warsaw: Institute of Art and Archaeology.

Sakellarakis, Y. 1996. 'Minoan Religious Influence in the Aegean: the Case of Kythera.' *Annual of the British School at Athens*, 91, 81-99.

Schmandt-Besserat, D. 1996. *How Writing Came About*. Austin: University of Texas Press.

Scott, J. 2000. *Social Network Analysis: A Handbook*. London: Sage.

Sillar, B. 1994. 'Playing with God: Cultural Perceptions of Children, Play and Miniatures in the Andes.' *Archaeological Review from Cambridge*, 13(2), 47-63.

Sillar, B. 2004. 'Acts of God and Active Material Culture: Agency and Commitment in the Andes.' In: A. Gardner (ed.), *Agency Uncovered: Archaeological Perspectives on Social Agency, Power, and Being Human*. London: University College London Press, 153-89.

Simandiraki, A. forthcoming, '*Miniature vessels in Minoan Crete.' Proceedings of the 10th International Cretological Congress*, Chania, Crete, Greece, 1-8 October 2006.

Sonesson, G. 1989. *Pictorial Concepts. Inquiries into the Semiotic Heritage and Its Relevance for the Analysis of the Visual World*. Lund: Lund University Press.

Sonesson, G. 1998. 'Index, Indexicality.' In: P. Bouissac (ed.), *Encyclopedia of Semiotics*. Oxford: Oxford University Press, 306-11.

Stewart, S. 1993. *On Longing: Narratives of the Miniature, the Gigantic, the Souvenir, the Collection.* London: Duke University Press.

Tournavitou, I. 2009. 'Does Size Matter? Miniature Pottery Vessels in Minoan Peak Sanctuaries.' In A.-L. D'Agata and A. Van de Moortel (eds.), *Archaeologies of Cult: Essays on Ritual and Cult in Crete in Honor of Geraldine C. Gesell.* (Hesperia Supplement 42). pp. 213-30.

Warnier, J.-P. 1999. *Construire la Culture Matérielle: L'Homme qui Pensait avec ses Doigts.* Paris: Presses Universitaires de France.

Wasserman, S. & K. Faust 1994. *Social Network Analysis: Methods and Applications.* Cambridge: Cambridge University Press.

Watts, C. 2009. 'On Mediation and Material Agency in the Peircean Semeiotic.' In: C. Knappett, L. Malafouris (eds.), *Material Agency: Towards a Non-Anthropocentric Approach.* New York: Springer, 187-208.

Weingarten, J. 2007. 'Three MM IB Noduli and Other Administrative Material from Deposit A.' In: C.F. Macdonald, C. Knappett (eds.), *Knossos: Protopalatial Deposits in Early Magazine A and the South-west Houses.* (British School at Athens, Supp. Vol. 41). London: British School at Athens.

Windsor, W.L. 2004. 'An Ecological Approach to Semiotics.' *Journal for the Theory of Social Behaviour,* 34(2), 179-98.

Of God Stones and Dance Plazas: The material mediation of historical consciousness

Robert W. Preucel

Material culture occupies a prominent place in the history of Anglo-American anthropology. E.B. Tylor (1871), Lewis Henry Morgan (1877), and Sir James Frazer (1890) all invoked material culture both as a means of differentiating cultures from each another and as a way of evaluating a culture's evolutionary stage. With the emergence of structural-functionalism (Malinowski 1922; Mauss 1924; Radcliffe-Brown 1957), interest shifted to objects in motion and how their circulation established and reinforced social relations, the classic examples being the South Pacific kula ring and the Northwest Coast potlatch. Indigenous art as an expression of universal aesthetics within specific historical contexts developed as a secondary interest (Boas 1927). Material culture, however, fell out of favor with the rise of structural anthropology (Leach 1961; Levi-Strauss 1967) and the emphasis on kinship studies, social organization, and myth. The study of ethnographic objects was relegated to the museum and the creation of didactic exhibits. In the past twenty years, however, material culture has returned to center stage. This development is conveniently marked by the publication of Arjun Appadurai's (1986) influential edited volume, "*The Social Life of Things: Commodities in Cultural Perspective*." This work has inspired new studies of consumption (Miller 1987; Myers 2001), inalienable possessions (Miller 2001; Weiner 1992; Thomas 1991), and object biographies (Hoskins 1998).

By contrast, during this same period, Anglo-American archaeology has maintained a constant focus on material culture even as it has embraced different theories of meaning. The early culture historians regarded material culture as representing past ethnic groups and physical evidence for their migrations and the diffusion of ideas from one group to another (Childe 1925). This relationship was conceived as a "symbolic" relationship (in the Saussurian sense) whereby the association between artifact type and ethnic group was historically configured. Processual archaeologists viewed material culture as human's primary extrasomatic means of adaptation (Binford 1962; Watson, LeBlanc & Redman 1971). Here too the relationship was regarded as symbolic but, in this case, it was seen as the product of evolutionary process. A few processualists did address social or ethnographic variables and used material culture to reconstruct prehistoric social organization (Hill 1970; Longacre 1968). However, postprocessual and some processual archaeologists countered that material culture did more work than symbolically represent the social; it actively constituted it (Hodder 1982; Renfrew 1994). This insight was considered sufficient grounds to reject the representational model of meaning in favor of more practice-based and experiential ones (Hodder 1986; Miller 2005; Olsen 2003; Tilley 1999). These issues are now being explored in archaeological studies of inalienable possessions (Mills 2004) and object biographies (Bradley 2002; Gosden 1994; Meskell 2004) as well as considerations of materialization (DeMarrais *et al.* 1996; DeMarrais 2004) and material engagement (Knappett 2004; Malafouris 2004; Renfrew 2004).

There is today a growing convergence between sociocultural anthropology and anthropological archaeology in their approaches to material culture. In general, this convergence is indicated by the move to conceptualize material culture not only as a form of communication (Schiffer 1999), but also as a process of social constitution. This latter development is marked by the use of the term *materiality* (Meskell 2004; Miller 2005). Materiality can be defined as the social constitution of self and society by means of the object world. As Lynn Meskell (2004, 28) perceptively notes, it "links both to the radical ideas of mimesis, simulacra, and agency and to the more mundane notions of goods, services, and economic structures." At present, there seem to be two main ways in which scholars are approaching the problem of materiality. The first is via the concept of objectification and the second is through the idea of semiotic mediation. In what follows, I review these different approaches and then illustrate the material mediation of historical consciousness with two case studies. The first case study is Richard Parmentier's ethnographic account of the materiality of mythohistory for the Belauans of Micronesia and the second is my own archaeological account of the materiality of revitalization in the context of the Pueblo Revolt in New Spain (the Southwestern United States).[1]

Objectification

The origins of the notion of objectification are intimately associated with the subject-object duality so pervasive in Western thought. This duality refers to the distinction made between actors (the subjects) and what they think about or act upon (the objects). René Descartes considered the subject-object duality to be a fundamental epistemological opposition and held that it underlay the rational foundations of modern science (Sorrell 1987). He privileged the thinking subject because he or she exists first and is, therefore, directly knowable and accessible. Consciousness is thus independent of matter. Similarly, Immanuel Kant placed considerable weight on the subject side of the subject-object relationship (Cassirer 1981). He regarded the rational human subject as the center of the cognitive and moral worlds. But for him, science could never fully account for the world by means of analytic statements. Rather the world must also be understood as the product of synthetic, rule-based activity. His transcendental idealism holds that since objects can only be experienced in space and in time, knowledge of them must come from sensory experiences which are synthesized by the mind.

The modern form of the subject-object relationship is usually traced to Georg Hegel who devised a developmental model (Miller 1987). In the first stage of his model, the subject is unconscious and undifferentiated. It then achieves awareness, knowledge of itself as non-other, which creates the separation between subject and object. It then repeats this process through several different stages in each case becoming more complex and differentiated. With the emergence of reason, the subject gains a broader knowledge of self and other as being embedded in social relations. As the distance between the subject and object increases, the consequences of the subject's realization that the external object is in fact a projection of the subject becomes greater. This point was adopted by Karl Marx who replaced Hegel's idealism with his own view of materialism which acknowledged that the objects of knowledge are constructed.

Ferdinand Saussure challenged the subject-object relation with his famous model of the sign. For him, the sign is a "two-sided psychological entity" linking a concept and a sound pattern" where the concept is the signified (*signifié*) and sound pattern is the signifier (*significant*) (Saussure 1966, 66). The concept is thus not a thing-in-the-world, but rather a mental image of that thing. Similarly, the sound pattern is not a physical sound, rather it is the hearer's cognitive interpretation of a sound. The concept and sound pattern are thus both mental entities and independent of any external object. He then proposed that the language system can be understood as a sequence of linked signs. He writes, "(w)hether we take the signified or the signifier, language has neither ideas nor sounds that existed before the linguistic system, but only conceptual and phonetic differences that have issued from the system" (Saussure 1966, 120). The sign context is more important than the idea or sound since the value of the sign may change without affecting its meaning or sound when a neighboring sign has changed. There is, therefore, nothing that exists outside the semiological system, no pre-existing ideas. This claim is, therefore, a repudiation of Platonic essences and Kantian idealism.

Pierre Bourdieu critiqued both the Kantian view of the priority of the subject and the Saussurian view of language. He wrote, "The construction of the world of objects is clearly not the sovereign operation of consciousness which the neo-Kantian tradition conceives of; the mental structures which construct the world of objects are constructed in the practice of a world of objects constructed according to the same structures" (Bourdieu 1977, 91). He continues, "the mind born of the world of objects does not rise as a subjectivity confronting an objectivity: the object universe is made up of objects which are the product of objectifying operations structured according to the very structures which the mind applies to it. The mind is a metaphor of the world of objects which is itself but an endless circle of mutually reflecting metaphors" (Bourdieu 1977, 91). Similarly, he finds fault with Saussure's objectivism because it is unable to conceive of speech as execution. Saussure thus privileges the structure of signs at the expense of their practical functions, which Bourdieu (1977, 24) says, are "never reducible to the functions of communication or knowledge." From this perspective, all agents are the producers and reproducers of objective meaning. However, because their actions are the product of preexisting actions and unconscious structures, agents are always overtaken by their own intentions.

Inspired by Hegel and Marx, Daniel Miller (1987, 33) has proposed objectification as the foundation for a dialectical theory of culture. For him, it merges the subject/object and individual/society dualities by insisting that both pairs of oppositions are as much constituted by culture as constituting it. Because culture is not merely reflective, Miller does not consider it to be a process of signification. He holds that "objectification is therefore an assertion of the non-reductive nature of culture as process" (Miller 1987, 33). For Hegel, objectification involves externalization and sublation, processes by which self-alienation becomes the instrument of the historical making of culture. Miller holds that more than self-alienation, praxis understood as material strategies based upon objective conditions is central. In our modern society, mass produced goods are the ways in which we create our identities and social affiliations in modern culture. The key issue is the process of alienation by which goods become transmuted through consumption into desires. This approach has influenced numerous anthropological studies, including those dealing with exchange, social biographies, practice theory, symbolic capital and art (see Tilley 2006 for a good review).

Colin Renfrew's material engagement theory, although deriving from a different source than Miller's work, is nonetheless a similar attempt to transcend the subject-object opposition. For Renfrew, material engagement theory refers to an investigation of the cognized or conceptualized dimensions of materiality where "the physical and conceptual aspects merge together" (Renfrew 2004:23).

It thus holds that the subject-object relationship which underlies such dualities – as mind/matter, symbol/reference, signified/signifier – must be understood as only apparent and not real and as masking a deeper underlying relationship. Drawing from the social lives of things approach (Appadurai 1986) as well as cognitive philosophy and evolutionary psychology (Donald 1991; Searle 1995), he argues that material symbols are self-referential with an "indissoluble reality of substance" such that material precedes concept in the sense that the concept is meaningless without the thing it refers to (Renfrew 2004, 25). Malafouris (2004) has offered an important extension to this idea suggesting that material engagement theory must reject the opposition of cognitivism and materialism and embrace the idea of the "extended mind," the idea that the mind is not bounded by the body.

Mediation

These studies of objectification have undoubtedly been very useful, but they leave unexplored the diverse ways in which meanings are constituted and the variety of registers at which cultures deploy them. There is, as yet, limited exploration of the different kinds of material signs used as semiotic resources. Indeed, there is a general tendency to assume that all signs work in the same way, namely that there is a symbolic or arbitrary relationship between signified and signifier, as originally proposed by Saussure, and that since material culture has non-arbitrary references this is sufficient reason to reject semiotics. There is, however, an alternative view of semiotics that is sensitive to different kinds of signs and emphasizes the centrality of semiotic mediation in the cultural production of meaning. This approach is that developed by Charles Sanders Peirce, who is widely regarded, along with Saussure, as one of the fathers of modern semiotics (Misak 2004).

The notion of mediation refers to the process where two elements are brought together by means of a third element and the third element serves as the instrument for the transmission of information (c.f. Parmentier 1985a, 25). The classic example given by Peirce is billiards (CP 1.532).[2] In this case, the action of the cue stick on the white cue ball causes the cue ball to strike the eight-ball and propel it into a pocket in the billiards table. Here the cue ball mediates the action of the cue stick and the eight-ball. Peirce regards this case as an example of "degenerate" rather than "genuine" mediation since the three elements are reducible to dyads – the action of the cue stick on the cue ball and the action of the cue ball on the eight ball – and because no interpretation or representation is transmitted by the action. In order to understand genuine mediation it is necessary to understand Peirce's notion of the sign.

For Peirce, the sign is "something which stands to somebody for something in some respect or capacity" (CP 2.228). It is irreducibly triadic in nature and contains within it the ability to produce another sign in an endless process of semiosis. As Lee (1997, 96) writes, "the sign mediates the relationship between itself and a object in such a way as to cause another sign to relate to it in the same way it relates to the object and so on." This processual definition is a significant improvement over the Stoic philosophers' idea of the sign as "something that stands for something else" and goes well beyond Saussure's dyadic signified-signifier model in accounting for things-in-the-world.

The sign relation can be more productively seen as consisting of three elements – the sign, the object, and the interpretant. Peirce explains that, "a sign endeavors to represent, in part at least, an Object, which is therefore in a sense the cause, or determinant, of the sign even if the sign represents its object falsely. But to say that it represents its Object implies that it affects a mind, and so affects it as, in some respect, to determine in that mind something that is mediately due to the Object. That determination of which the immediate cause, or determinant, is the Sign, and of which the mediate cause is the Object may be termed the Interpretant" (CP 6.347). Significantly, the three elements of the sign relation – the sign, object and interpretant – are not permanently set; rather, they can shift roles as further semiosis takes place.

Peirce developed a series of complex sign typologies. The best known of these is based upon the sign-object component of the sign relation and identifies icons, indices, and symbols. *Icons* are signs that refer to an object by virtue of its characteristics. They are "mimetic," an example being a diagram or a painting. An *Index* is a sign that denotes its object by being affected or modified by that object. It can be thought of as a pointer or indicator- for example, a weathervane is an index that indicates the direction of the wind. A *Symbol* is a sign that obtains its character by virtue of some law, usually an association of general ideas. In this case, meaning is the result of cultural convention. For example, a flag has no inherent meaning, yet it is commonly taken as a symbol of a country. There is a hierarchical relationship between these three kinds of signs. All indices involve icons and all symbols are indexical because they act through tokens or replicas.

Peirce's sign theory has two important implications. The first is that a sign never exists in isolation; it is always connected to other signs. It is part of an infinite series which points back in time toward the Object and simultaneously points forward into the future toward the Interpretant. This view recalls Saussure's notion of semiosis as a chain of signifiers. The second implication is that signs have a life of their own. Signs have the capacity to generate new signs since the Interpretant of one sign relation can become the Object for another sign

Table 1. Comparison of Saussure's semiology and Peirce's semiotic (from Singer 1978, Table 1)

Point of Comparison	*Semiotic (Peirce)*	*Semiology (Saussure)*
1. Aims at a general theory of signs	philosophical, normative but observational	a descriptive generalized linguistics
2. Frequent subject matter	logic, mathematics, sciences, (logic-centered)	natural languages, literature, myth (language-centered)
3. Signs are relations, not "things"	a sign is a triadic relation of sign, object, and interpretant	a sign is a dyadic relation of signifier and signified
4. Linguistic signs are"arbitrary"...	but also include "natural signs" – icons and indexes	but appear "necessary" for speakers of the language
5. Ontology of "objects" of signs	existence presupposed by signs	not given, but determined by sign linguistic relations
6. Epistemology of empirical ego or subject	included in semiotic analysis	presupposed by but not included in semiological analysis

relation and so on, in a process of endless semiosis. In this sense, the sign can be said to have agency. Peirce regards semiosis as the fundamental process by which realty and representation are brought together in living systems. Some scholars have questioned the universal status of these sign types (e.g. Layton 2006). However, as Keane points out, the effectiveness of signs depends upon *how* people take them to signify (1997, 19, his emphasis). That is to say, icon, index and symbol are not simply intrinsic properties of signs as things-in-the-world. Rather they represent a particular culture's understanding of how any given sign works.

Milton Singer is one of the first scholars to have applied Peircian semiotics to cultural anthropology (Singer 1978). Of special interest is his systematic comparison of Peircian and Saussurian semiotics (Table 1). Here, he shows that although they share the similar goals that is, a general theory of signs, they differ significantly with respect to their subject matter, their specific concepts and laws, and their epistemology and ontology. For example, the subject matter of the Saussurian approach is natural language, literature, legends, and myths, while the subject matter of the Peircian approach is logic, mathematics and the sciences. In terms of the sign, the Saussurian approach observes a dyadic relationship (signified-signifier) while the Peircian approach recognizes a triadic one (sign-object-interpretant). For the Saussurian approach, signs are arbitrary, however, for the Peircian approach they include icons and indices, signs that have non-arbitrary relations to their referents. Saussurian approaches regard the existence of objects to be determined by linguistic relations while Peircian approaches argue that signs presuppose prior existence. Finally, the actor/speaker is assumed, but not included, in Saussurian analysis; however, in a Peircian analysis the actor/speaker is an integral part of the process of semiosis.

For Singer, there is a compelling reason to prefer Peircian semiotics over the Saussurian version in the development of anthropological theory. He wrote, "it [the Peircian approach] can deal with some of the difficult problems generated by acceptance of the complementarity of cultural and social systems" and that it has the potential to deal with extra-linguistic relations such as "how the different cultural 'languages' are related to empirical objects and egos, to individual actors and groups" because a *semiotic anthropology is a pragmatic anthropology* (Singer 1978, 50, emphasis in the original). This idea of pragmatic semiotics has been extremely influential in linguistic anthropology (Hanks 1990; Parmentier 1994; Silverstein 1976) and in some quarters of sociocultural anthropology (Daniel 1984; Munn 1986; Parmentier 1994; Singer 1984; Tambiah 1984) and biological anthropology (Deacon 1997; Sebeok 1976).

The materiality of Belauan mythohistory

How do societies deploy material culture as a semiotic resource in the mediation of historical consciousness? The first case study I wish to consider is Richard Parmentier's ethnographic study of myth, history and polity in Belau, Western Micronesia. Parmentier (1985b; 1987) takes as his starting point the fact that all societies exhibit some form of history in which different states of society are expressed by signs across a range of media organized according to local forms of categorization. He is particularly interested in three issues: how history is connected to notions of time, how power is expressed by the control and destruction of historical events, and the variety of media used to code historical consciousness. He seeks to rehabilitate the term "history" and show that "the intentions and intentionality of people who create and interpret their own past is essential, rather than supplementary, to adequate ethnological study" (Parmentier 1987, 7).

Crucial to his analysis is the distinction between two categories of material signs – "signs in history" and "signs of history." The former refers to value-laden objects implicated in social strategies that focus attention on specific historical processes. He regards these signs as the sites of historical intentionality. They can be thought of as pragmatic responses to existing problems. The latter kind

Table 2. Relation of sign class, social order, hierarchy and modalities of time (from Parmentier 1985b, Table 1).

Sign Class	Social Object	Hierarchy	Modality of Time
Village stones	Villages	Capital-satellite	Long duration
Grave pavements	Houses	Principal-affiliate	Social time
Bead money	Persons	Chiefs-commoners	Individual time

of sign describes the particular ways in which a society objectifies its past. It is metapragmatic since it permits the discourses of history, particularly how historical knowledge is recorded and transmitted. He considers the relationships between these two kinds of signs to be complex and observes that in traditional, non-literate societies "signs of history" are often simultaneously "signs in history." What is important then is the study of how different material culture signs come to be implicated in social action, their dynamic and fluid roles in manipulating, contesting, and concealing meanings.

Using ethnographic data from Belau, Parmentier identifies three kinds of material culture as examples of these historicizing signs (Table 2). These are village stones, stone grave pavements and Belau "money." Four named stones are associated with each of the four principal villages that form the "cornerposts" of the political order. These stones are "descendants" of the four stones born of the goddess *Milad* and are part of the discourse about villages and their relationships. For example, *Imiungs,* the capital village of the *Ngeremlengui* district, is associated with *Imiungsdab* (*Imiungs* stone), the oldest son of *Milad. Melekeok,* a satellite village, is linked with the second son, *Olekeokelbad*. Here political hierarchy recapitulates birth order within the family. These stones are "signs of history" in that they mark "long duration" time and code the permanence of the political order, implying that it was preordained by the gods.

A second kind of object, stone pavements, play much the same role for houses as the stones do for the villages. In each village, there are four ranked social groups or lineages around which lesser groups are clustered. At *Imiungs,* for example, these chiefly houses are named *Klang, Ngerturong, Ngerutelchii,* and *Sibong*. Each residence is fronted by a rectangular paved area containing the graves of male and female ancestors. This area thus serves as a physical reminder, an index in Peirce's sign typology, of the house's genealogical history. The mortuary ritual itself marks out important people who are "strong" members of the house and codes marriage alliances, descent ties and chiefly titles. Because these stone pavements exist at each of the four houses, they also permit the differentiation of lineages. Together, they reproduce the village's social structure in "social time," the life of the ranked lineage.

A third kind of object is Belau money. It consists of "names, precious beads, cylinders, and bracelet sections" which originated from the Philippines, Indonesia or neighboring islands in antiquity (Parmentier 1985, 141). There are two broad categories of money. The most valuable are red and yellow ceramic rings called *bachel* that are worn as necklaces by the wives of wealthy men. They are named and used to pay relations at the annulment of marriage or death of a spouse. Because they circulate between high ranking houses, they index descent genealogies, social rank, and appropriate marriage partners as women are encouraged to pursue specific valuables that have been alienated by marrying their owners. The second category is the black spherical bead called *chelebucheb*. These beads are used mainly in transactions between chiefs as they establish political alliances, pay off insults, or purchase head trophies. Unlike the village stones and grave pavements, Belau money functions at the level of individual time as they mediate discourses of marriage, chiefly alliances, and inheritance.

Parmentier (1985b, 146) concludes that in Belau persons, houses, and villages occupy three levels of social order and that each level is hierarchically integrated across this order. This is to say, the actions of chiefly persons determine house rank since they, and not commoners, have genealogies that are marked by stone pavements. Similarly, the social history of chiefly houses, particularly through marriage alliances and the circulation of money, create the dynamic of political relations among villages. It is thus control over these semiotic resources and the temporalities they offer that constitutes Belauan history and self-understanding. The advantages of this study then are that Parmentier locates semiotic power not only in terms of different kinds of signs, but also in terms of social hierarchies that are created by their pragmatic use.

The materiality of the Pueblo revitalization movement

My second case study focuses on the co-deployment of words and things as semiotic resources during the Pueblo Revolt of 1680 and its aftermath (Preucel 2006). The modern view of the revolt is that it was a cultural revitalization movement, led by a charismatic leader known as Popé, which sought to reestablish a way of life that preexisted the coming of the Spaniards (Gutiérrez 1991; Ortiz 1994; Reff 1995). Few studies, however, have examined how the movement took shape and how its discourse circulated among Pueblo people. My research identifies the specific semiotic modalities central to establishing political alliances and forging consensus among rival Indian factions. In particular, I show that Pueblo leaders co-deployed speech acts and architecture as mutually supporting semiotic resources to create and legitimize a new revitalization ideology.

It is possible to gain glimpses into the revitalization rhetoric through a close linguistic analysis of the depositions given by the Pueblo Indians captured by Governor Antonio de Otermín during his failed reconquest attempt in 1680 and 1681. The relevant depositions are from Pedro Namboa, an eighty year old man from Alameda Pueblo, Juan, a twenty-eight year old man from Tesuque Pueblo, Pedro Naranjo, an eighty year old man from San Felipe Pueblo, Juan and Francisco Lorenzo, two brothers, twenty and eighteen years old respectively, also from San Felipe Pueblo, and Lucas, a twenty year old Piro man. The deponents thus include young and old men (but not middle aged men) from four different pueblos (Alameda, Tesuque, San Felipe, and an unnamed Piro village) representing four different language groups (Tewa, Keres, Tiwa, and Piro).

Table 3. References to Time in the Depositions taken from Pueblo Indians during Otermin's Reconquest Expedition of 1681.	
1	they have inherited successively from their old men the things pertaining to their ancient customs (Pedro Namboa, Sept 6, 1680- Hackett & Shelby 1942, 61)
2	which were the crops of the ancestors (Juan, Dec 18, 1681- Hackett & Shelby 1942, 235)
3.1	they were going underground to the lake of Copala (Pedro Naranjo, Dec 19, 1681- Hackett & Shelby 1942, 246)
3.2	now they were as they had been in ancient times (Pedro Naranjo, Dec 19, 1681- Hackett & Shelby 1942, 247)
3.3	they had always desired to live as they had when they came out of the lake of Copala (Pedro Naranjo, Dec 19, 1681- Hackett & Shelby 1942, 247)
3.4	they thereby returned to the state of their antiquity, as when they came out of the lake of Copala (Pedro Naranjo, Dec 19, 1681- Hackett & Shelby 1942, 246-7)
3.5	living thus in accordance with the law of their ancestors (Pedro Naranjo, Dec 19, 1681- Hackett & Shelby 1942, 248)
4	living according to their ancient customs (Juan and Francisco Lorenzo, Dec 29, 1681- Hackett & Shelby 1942, 251)
5	each one was to live according to such law as he wished, forsaking that of the Spaniards (Lucas, Dec 19, 1681- Hackett & Shelby 1942, 244)

The depositions were elicited in the responses to a series of standard questions posed by the Spaniards:[3]

1. Why did the Indians of New Mexico rebel?
2. Why did they obey Popé and hold him in such fear?
3. How did Popé organize the rebellion?
4. What happened after the Spaniards left?
5. Did they think that the Spaniards would return?
6. Who are their leaders?
7. How did they learn of the return of the Spaniards?
8. Did they notice that Spaniards had not harmed anyone at Isleta Pueblo (during their return)?
9. What led them to come among the Spaniards?
10. Why did they not establish peace with the Spaniards after the emergence of Don Luis Tupatu (as leader)?[4]

The depositions are, of course, problematic because they were produced under coercion, translated by Indian interpreters with their respective biases, and recorded by the Spaniards for their own purposes. Nonetheless, these accounts can be fruitfully compared for linguistic patterning to reveal aspects of the temporal dimensions of Pueblo revitalization ideology. I have abstracted the relevant sentences and clauses and organized them by deponent in Table 3.

In each of these cases, time is evoked through the use of temporal nouns and adjectives associated with deceased relatives, traditional laws, and customs. The actual words are translated as follows: "ancestors" (2, 3.5), "antiquity" (3.4), "ancient times" (3.2), "ancient customs" (1, 4). In one case (5), the temporal referent is suppressed and only implied by the notion of law. It is clear that these references to the past do not simply refer to the time prior to the coming of the Spaniards. Rather, they refer to mythic time, the time of origin when the Pueblo people emerged from the underworld to inhabit the world as they know it. In Peirce's sign typology, they are rhematic indexical sinsigns (individual phrases indexing a particular conception of the past) acting to constitute a rhematic symbol (the revitalization discourse).

Pedro Naranjo's deposition provides additional support for this line of argument. Here time is associated with a particular geographical referent, the lake of Copala (3.1, 3.3, 3.4). This lake may refer to the primordeal lake of emergence mentioned in the Tewa origins myth. In this sense, it can be interpreted as a dicent indexical legisign (the mythological lake) embodying a rhematic iconic sinsign (the specific location commonly identified as the place of origin). The lake of emergence was the place were supernatural beings, people, and animals lived together and death was unknown (Ortiz 1969).

Copala also has at least two historically documented place associations, one in Mexico and another in Utah. It is sometimes identified as the ancestral home of the Aztecs and reputed to have been fabulously wealthy (Hammond 1979, 29). In 1565, Francisco de Ibara was commissioned to locate it and he searched the area north and west of Zacatecas, but was unsuccessful.[5] It has also been linked to the Great Salt Lake. In 1626, Fray Gerónino de Zarate Salmeron, while living among the Mohave people, learned that the lake of Copala was located a fourteen day journey to the west-northwest, in the vicinity of the Great Salt Lake (Tyler 1952). It was later identified with the Great Salt Lake by the Domínguez-Escalante expedition of 1776 (Hammond 1979, 30).

There are also a series of Southwestern accounts known as *Montezuma* legends that, although complex and difficult to interpret, are suggestive of close interrelations between Pueblo and Mexican Indians during the colonial period. These legends generally refer to the Southwest as the home of *Montezuma*, the first Aztec king, and describe the southern migration of the Aztec people to the valley of Mexico. As Parmentier (1979, 615) points out, *Montezuma* is closely linked to *Poseyemu*, a Tewa Indian culture hero. Both are ambiguously human and divine, both have the power to visit the supernatural world, both changed their societies in fundamental ways. *Montezuma* and *Poseyemu* are even interlinked in some of the accounts of the revolt. "They had the mandate of an Indian who lives a very long way from this kingdom, toward the north, from which region Montezuma came and who is the lieutenant of Po he yemu" (Hackett & Shelby 1942, 15). Parmentier (1979, 622) concludes that *Poseyemu* became a symbol of pan-Pueblo religious nationalism during the Revolt of 1680.

There is compelling evidence that Pueblo leaders used village architecture to mediate their revitalization movement. Immediately following the Pueblo Revolt of 1680, Popé, Alonzo Catiti, and a number of the other leaders, made an inspection tour of the Pueblos. They preached a form of revivalism involving the renouncement of Spanish beliefs and customs, ritual purification, and the performance of traditional ceremonies. They instructed the pueblos to "break up and burn the images of the holy Christ, the Virgin Mary and the other saints, the crosses, and everything pertaining to Christianity, and that they burn the temples, break up the bells, and separate from the wives whom God had given them in marriage and take those whom they desired" (Declaration of Pedro Naranjo, in Hackett & Shelby 1942b, 247-8). They told them to purify themselves in order to expunge the stain of Catholicism. Finally, they encouraged them to repair their kivas and instructed them "to dance the dance of the cacina"

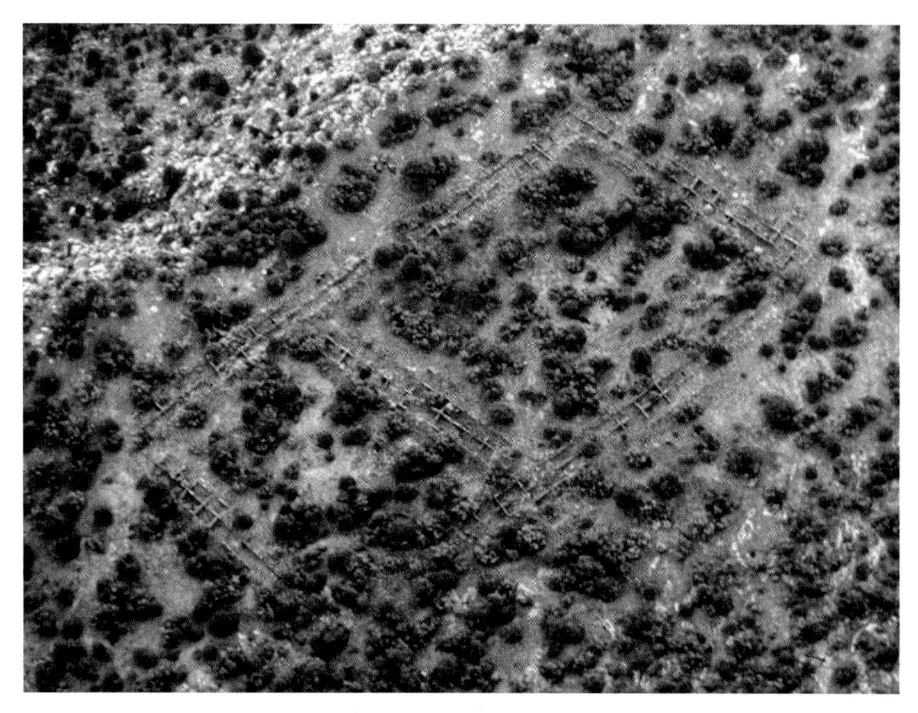

Fig. 1. Aerial view of Kotyiti Pueblo (Kotyiti Research Project photo, Tom Baker, Aerial Archaeology, Albuquerque).

so that they might live "in accordance with the laws of their ancestors." They promised that compliance would assure the "harvest (of) a great deal of maize, many beans, a great abundance of cotton, calabashes, and very large watermelons and cantaloupes; and that they *could erect their houses* and enjoy abundant health and leisure" (Declaration of Pedro Naranjo, in Hackett & Shelby 1942b, 247-8, my emphasis).

Kotyiti Pueblo was one of several new mesatop villages established in the northern Rio Grande in the years following the Revolt (Fig. 1). It was founded by people from Cochiti Pueblo and contained refugees from the neighboring pueblos of San Felipe and San Marcos. The proposition here is that Kotyiti is an example of intentional architecture and was built "in accordance with the laws of the ancestors." In Parmentier's sense, it functions as a "sign of history," objectifying and stabilizing specific aspects of the revitalization discourse preached by Popé and his associates. But what were these aspects? We can interpret some of the meaning of the architectural form of the Kotyiti plaza pueblo through the judicious use of Keresan ethnography (Snead & Preucel 1999). According to Leslie White (1964), the Keres people conceptualize their world as a series of nested, but interrelated, regions containing mountains, lakes, springs, hunting

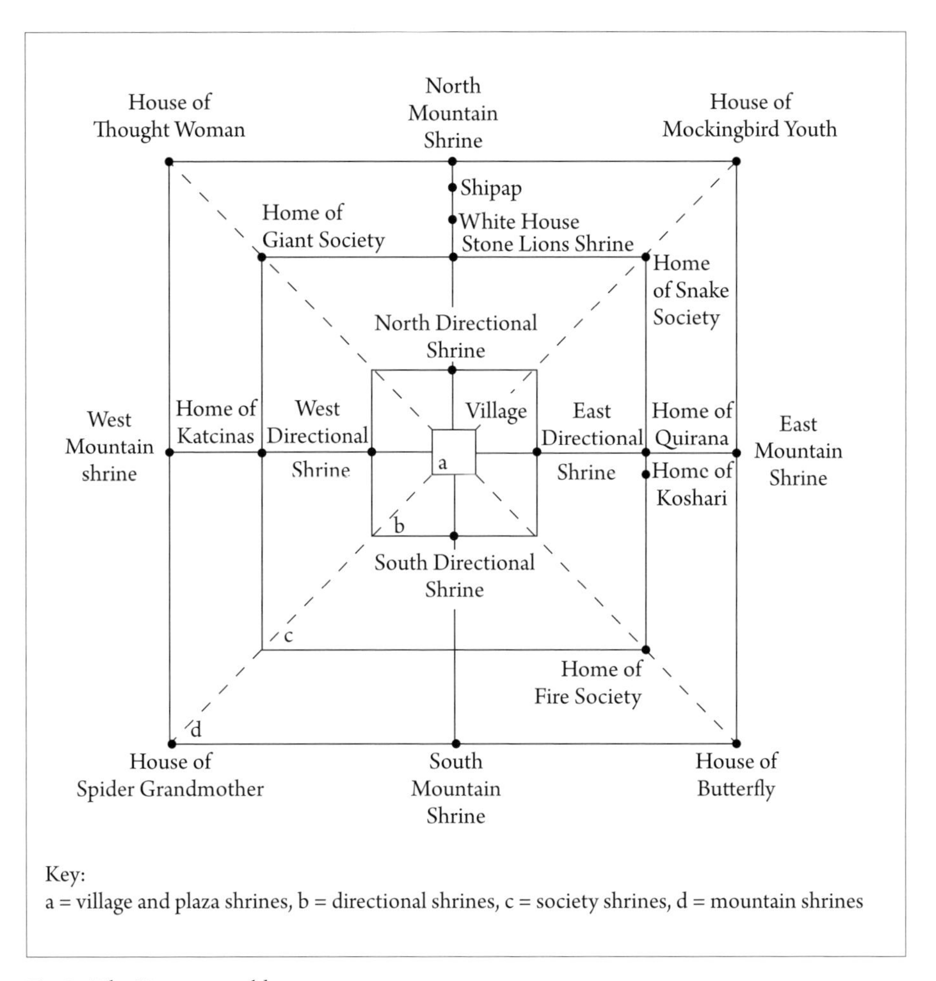

Fig. 2. The Keresan world.

grounds, agricultural fields, and mineral resources, all of which focus on a central village (Fig. 2). The farthest, and most dangerous, region consists of the places at the edge of the world inhabited by powerful supernatural beings. The next region, somewhat closer in, is defined by the homes of the supernatural deities associated with the medicine societies so prominent in Keres ceremonialism. Immediately outside the pueblo are the village directional shrines marking the symbolic boundaries of the village. And finally, there are a series of shrines within each village, the most important being the plaza shrines.

The Keres world is divided in half along gender lines with the deities of the west being female and those of the east male. The female deities are frequently mentioned in oral narratives (e.g. Benedict 1931), and Thought Woman (also called Yellow Woman), is the creator deity who "thought people into being." Her

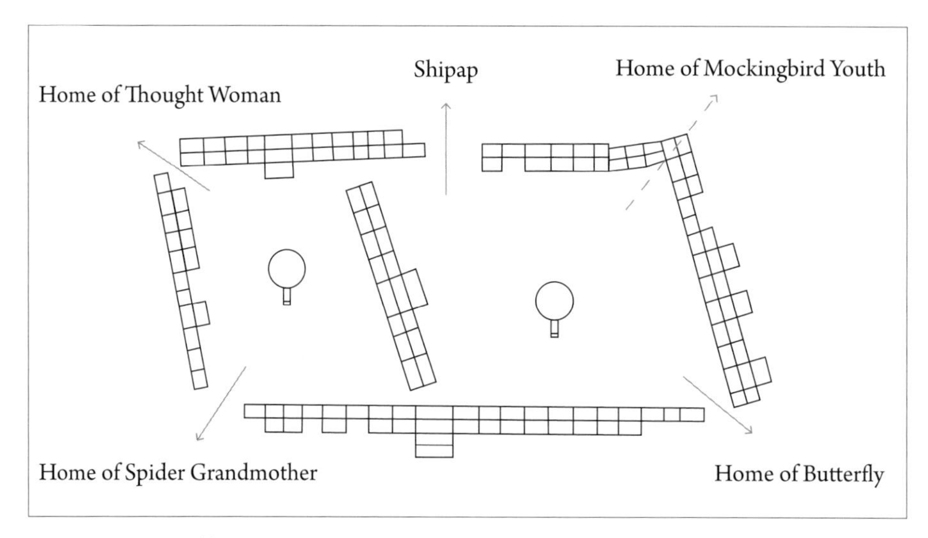

Fig. 3. Kotyiti Pueblo as a cosmogram.

house, known as the House of Leaves, is located in the northwest corner of the world. Spider Grandmother is the constant helper of people in trouble, and her house, called Lumber House, is found in the southwest corner. The male deities appear to be associated with the movements of the sun. Butterfly is the protector of the cacique, the supreme religious leader within Keres communities. His home is at Turquoise House in the southeast corner. Mockingbird Youth lives in his house in the northeast. These latter two corners are associated with the summer and winter solstices respectively.

In the six cardinal directions (the four directions plus the zenith and nadir) are the sacred mountains and lakes. At each of these places live pairs of male and female deities who bear special responsibility for the weather and the seasons. Each of these mountains is also associated with its own color, animal, and tree. The names of these mountains appear to be shared by most of the Keres pueblos, although their physical referents vary depending upon the location of the pueblo. For example, Mt. Taylor is the West Mountain for the Laguna people, but it is the North Mountain for the Acoma people (White 1935, 32). These natural features are further sacralized by the construction of shrines. Ritual practitioners visit these shrines at specific times of the year in order to pray for good crops and success in hunting.

The Kotyiti plaza pueblo can be interpreted as an "indexical icon" that entextualized certain aspects of the Keres worldview in order to legitimize the political agenda favored by the leaders of the Pueblo Revolt (Fig. 3). Three of the four corner gateways likely point to the corners of the world and refer to the deities dwelling there. The fourth gateway, once present, appears to have been walled up to create additional residential space. The fifth gateway positioned between the two north roomblocks likely gave access to Shipap, the mythological place of emergence from the underworld. Also evoking Shipap is a plaza shrine located in the center of the west plaza. Thus we can see that the plaza pueblo materializes a particular view of tradition by referring to the corners of the world, the north direction, and the center. It appears less obviously to refer to the other cardinal directions. By analogy with the modern Pueblo of Cochiti, the western dance plaza and kiva likely represents the Pumpkin moiety and the eastern the Turquoise moiety. These dance plazas would have functioned in the renewal of katcina ceremonies and thus physically embodied the semiotic ideology of living in accordance with the laws of the ancestors. Because of this high degree of semiotic coding, it is plausible that the new pueblo was conceptualized as White House, the "original village" occupied by the Keres people after their emergence and the place where katcinas and people lived together in harmony.

This idea finds indirect support in a story gathered by Matilda Cox Stevenson which recounts the founding of an ancestral Zia village in the image of White House.[6] According to this account, the cacique wished "to build a village… after our white-house of the north," but he could not "remember clearly the construction of the house," so he instructed Swallow to "study the structure of the white-house in the north; learn all about it, and bring… all the details of the buildings; how one house joins another" (Stevenson 1894, 57-8). The Zia people, in fact, built a double-plaza mesatop village at Cerro Colorado after the revolt. It is obviously impossible to demonstrate that this account dates to the Revolt period and describes Cerro Colorado, but it does suggest close relationships between an ideology of the ancestors and architecture at some Keres villages.

These linguistic and architectural analyses provide preliminary support for the thesis that the leaders of the revolt constructed a new form of temporality that circulated widely among Indian people to create a new semiotic ideology. It underwrote a rhetoric which advocated the renouncement of Spanish beliefs and customs, ritual purification, and the reinstatement of traditional ceremonies. The ideological frame for this discourse was provided by the belief that these practices would allow people to live like their ancestors and enjoy future health and prosperity. The citation of Poseyemu, Montezuma, and the lake of Copala as indexical icons of a primordeal spacetime drew different Indian peoples together in a shared genealogy that transcended long-standing ethnic distinctions and village rivalries, giving them a common historical destiny. As Parmentier (1979, 622) puts it, the Montezuma discourse is "the signpost for Pueblos' encounter with historical consciousness."

Conclusions

In the last twenty years or so, material culture studies have emerged as a distinctive research focus uniting several disparate strands of sociocultural anthropology and anthropological archaeology. Yet, within this convergence remains a diversity of approaches. The two broad theories currently in use are those that are associated with objectification and those that advocate semiotic mediation. Many post-processualists have critiqued Cartesian dualisms, particularly the subject-object opposition, and championed a Hegelian form of objectification as a means of exploring how objects are embedded in lifeworlds. Similarly, many processualists have also sought to go beyond these same dualities and identify the underlying cognitive process of material engagement. Significantly, some processualist and postprocessualists joined together in the rejection of semiotics and meaning.

This rejection of semiotics, however, should be understood as a rejection of a particular kind of semiotics, namely the version developed by Saussure and his followers. Even poststructuralists in their critiques of structuralism have adhered to some version of the arbitrary sign. Material culture, however, is not fully encompassed by the notion of the symbol and arbitrary meanings. As Elizabeth Mertz (1985, 1) points out, "the symbol is only one kind of sign, and the collapsing of 'semiotic' into symbolic fails to do justice to the complicated system by which signs carry and constitute sociocultural meanings." In fact, it can be argued that culture primarily engages with motivated signs and indexical meanings. This means that material culture is pragmatically grounded in the real world in ways that much of language is not. It also implies that the ambiguity celebrated by some postprocessualists (e.g Tilley 1991) is overdrawn since meanings are not inherently ambiguous, but become so as interpreters engage with the sign over time and in different contexts.

In order to demonstrate the utility of a Peircian semiotics for material culture studies, I have provided two case studies as examples of how two different cultures exploit the multimodality of signs in pragmatic discourse on historical consciousness. The Belauan case identifies three kinds of material resources that are used to create different temporalities. The named village stones are "signs of history" which mark long duration and mythic time. The stone mortuary pavements are "signs in history" and mark social or genealogical time. Belau money are "signs in history" that index individual time and mediate marriages, alliances, and inheritance. Parmentier emphasizes that knowledge of the past is mediated by how ranked titleholders deploy these historical markers for their political benefit. This knowledge is in turn reinterpreted by the historicizing practices of successive generations.

In the Pueblo Revolt case, Pueblo leaders conjoined a popular revitalization discourse with a specific material expression of proper living. They chose village architecture as one of the sites for this discourse because of its preexisting cosmological significance and the potential of dwellings and dance plazas to generate habitual action. The village form, a double plaza shape, is simultaneously a "sign of history," since it indexes balance and harmony, values articulated in the revitalization discourse, and a "sign in history" because it indexes the political alliance between Cochiti people and the San Marcos Pueblo and San Felipe Pueblo refugees. Both these case studies demonstrate that historical consciousness is the product of preexisting signs incorporated into historicizing actions appropriate to specific political contexts.

Notes

1 Both of these examples are discussed in more detail in my book *Archaeological Semiotics* (2006).

2 The standard way of citing quotes from the eight volume set of Peirce's writings published by Charles Hartshorne, Paul Weiss, and Arthur Burks (1931-1958) is for the number to the left of the decimal point to refer to the volume and the number to the right to refer to the numbered section of the text.

3 This is a composite list compiled from the questions used during Otermín's reconquest attempt in 1681 (Hackett & Shelby 1942).

4 Luis Tupatu from Picuris Pueblo succeeded Popé, as the leader of the Pueblo people.

5 There is a town of San Juan Copala located in the Sierra Madre Mountains in the state of Oaxaca, Mexico.

6 Zia Pueblo is a Keresan speaking community located 23 miles southwest of Cochiti Pueblo.

References

Appadurai, A. (ed.) 1986. *The Social Life of Things: Commodities in Cultural Perspective*. Cambridge: Cambridge University Press.

Benedict, R. 1931. *Tales of the Cochiti Indians*. (Bureau of American Ethnology, Bulletin 98). Washington D.C.: Bureau of American Ethnology.

Binford, L.R. 1962. 'Archaeology as Anthropology.' *American Antiquity*, 28, 217-25.

Bourdieu, P. 1977. *Outline of a Theory of Practice*. Cambridge: Cambridge University Press.

Bradley, R. 2002. *The Past in Prehistoric Societies*. London: Routledge.

Cassirer, E. 1983. *Kant's Life and Thought*. New Haven: Yale University Press.

Childe, V.G. 1925. *The Dawn of European Civilization*. London: Kegan Paul.

Daniel, E.V. 1984. *Fluid Signs: Being a Person the Tamil Way*. Berkeley: University of California Press.

Deacon, T.W. 1997. *The Symbolic Species: The Co-evolution of Language and the Brain*. New York: Norton.

DeMarrais, E. 2004. 'The Materialization of Culture.' In: E. DeMarrais, C. Gosden, C. Renfrew (eds.), *Rethinking Materiality: The Engagement of Mind with the Material World*. Cambridge: The McDonald Institute Monograhs, 11-22.

DeMarrais, E., L.J. Castillo & T. Earle 1996. 'Ideology, Materialization, and Power Strategies.' *Current Anthropology*, 37, 15-31.

Frazier, J. 1890. *The Golden Bough: A Study in Magic and Religion*. London: Macmillan.

Gosden, C. 1994. *Social Being and Time*. Oxford: Blackwell.

Gutiérrez, R.A. 1991. *When Jesus Came, the Corn Mothers Went Away: Marriage, Sexuality and Power in New Mexico, 1500-1846*. Stanford: Stanford University Press.

Hackett, C.W. & C.C. Shelby (eds. and trans.) 1942. *Revolt of the Pueblo Indians of New Mexico, and Otermín's Attempted Reconquest, 1680-1682, vol.1-2*. Albuquerque: University of New Mexico Press.

Hammond, G.P. 1979. 'In Search of the Fabulous in the Settlement of the Southwest.' In: D.J. Weber (ed.), *New Spain's Far Northern Frontier: Essays on Spain in the American West, 1540-1821*. Albuquerque: University of New Mexico Press, 17-33.

Hanks, W. 1990. *Referential Practice: Language and Lived Space among the Maya*. Chicago: University of Chicago Press.

Hartshorne, C., P. Weiss & A.W. Burks (eds.) 1931-1958: *Collected Papers of Charles Sanders Peirce, vol.1-8*. Cambridge: Harvard University Press.

Hill, J.N. 1970. *Broken K Pueblo: Prehistoric Social Organization in the American Southwest*. (University of Arizona Anthropological Papers, 18). Tucson: University of Arizona Press.

Hodder, I. 1982. *Symbols in Action*. Cambridge: Cambridge University Press.

Hodder, I. 1986. *Reading the Past: Current Approaches to Interpretation in Archaeology*. Cambridge: Cambridge University Press.

Hoskins, J. 1998. *Biographical Objects*. London: Routledge.

Keane, W. 1997. *Signs of Recognition: Powers and Hazards of Representation in an Indonesian Society*. Berkeley: University of California Press.

Keane, W. 2003. 'Semiotics and the Social Analysis of Material Things.' *Language and Communication*, 23, 409-25.

Knappett, C. 2004. 'The Affordances of Things: A Post-Gibsonian Perspective on the Relationality of Mind and Matter.' In: E. DeMarrais, C. Gosden, C. Renfrew (eds.), *Rethinking Materiality: The Engagement of Mind with the Material World*. Cambridge: The McDonald Institute Monographs, 43-52.

Kopytoff, I. 1986. 'The Cultural Biography of Things.' In: A. Appadurai (ed.), *The Social Life of Things: Commodities in Cultural Perspective*. Cambridge: Cambridge University Press.

Layton, R. 2006. 'Structuralism and Semiotics.' In: C. Tilley, W. Keane, S. Küchler, M. Rowlands, P. Spyer (eds.), *Handbook of Material Culture*. London: Sage Publications, 29-42.

Leach, E.R. 1961. *Rethinking Anthropology*. London: The Althlone Press.

Lee, B. 1997. *Talking Heads: Language, Metalanguage and the Semiotics of Subjectivity*. Durham: Duke University Press.

Levi-Strauss, C. 1967. *Structural Anthropology*. Garden City: Anchor Books.

Longacre, W.A. 1968. 'Some Aspects of Prehistoric Society in East-Central Arizona.' In: S.R. Binford, L.R. Binford (eds.), *New Perspectives in Archeology*. Chicago: Aldine, 89-102.

Malafouris, L. 2004. 'The Cognitive Basis of Material Engagement: Where Brain, Body and Culture Conflate.' In: E. DeMarrais, C. Gosden, C. Renfrew (eds.), *Rethinking Materiality: The Engagement of Mind with the Material World*. Cambridge: The McDonald Institute Monographs, 53-62.

Malinowski, B. 1922. *Argonauts of the Western Pacific*. London: Routledge.

Mauss, M. 1924. *The Gift.* London: Cohen & West.
Mertz, E. 1985. 'Beyond Symbolic Anthropology: Introducing Semiotic Mediation.' In: E. Mertz, R.J. Parmentier (eds.), *Semiotic Mediation: Sociocultural and Psychological Perspectives.* New York: Academic Press, 1-19.
Meskell, L. 2004. *Object Worlds in Ancient Egypt: Material Biographies Past and Present.* Oxford: Berg.
Miller, D. 1987. *Material Culture and Mass Consumption.* Oxford: Blackwell.
Miller, D. (ed.) 2005. *Materiality.* Durham: Duke University Press.
Mills, B.J. 2004. 'The Establishment and Defeat of Hierarchy: Inalienable Possessions and the History of Collective Prestige Structures in the Pueblo Southwest.' *American Anthropologist,* 106, 238-51.
Misak, C. (ed.) 2004. *The Cambridge Companion to Peirce.* Cambridge: Cambridge University Press.
Morgan, L.H. 1877. *Ancient Society, Or Researches in the Lines of Human Progress from Savagery through Barbarism to Civilization.* London: MacMillan and Co.
Munn, N. 1986. *The Fame of Gawa.* Cambridge: Cambridge University Press.
Myers, F. (ed.) 2001. *The Empire of Things: Regimes of Value and Material Culture.* Santa Fe: School of American Research Press.
Olsen, B. 2003. 'Material Culture after Text.' *Norwegian Archaeological Review,* 36, 87-104.
Ortiz, A. 1969. *The Tewa World.* Chicago: University of Chicago Press.
Ortiz, A. 1994. 'The Dynamics of Pueblo Cultural Survival.' In: R.J. DeMaillie, A. Ortiz (eds.), *North American Indian Anthropology: Essays on Society and Culture.* Norman: University of Oklahoma Press, 296-306.
Parmentier, R.J. 1979. 'The Mythological Triangle: Poseyemu, Montezuma, and Jesus in the Pueblos.' In: A. Ortiz (ed.), *Handbook of North American Indians: Southwest, vol. 9.* Washington D. C.: Smithsonian Institution, 609-22.
Parmentier, R.J. 1985a. 'Signs' Place *in Medias Res*: Peirce's Concept of Semiotic Mediation.' In: E. Mertz, R.J. Parmentier (eds.), *Semiotic Mediation: Sociocultural and Psychological Perspectives.* New York: Academic Press, 23-48.
Parmentier, R.J. 1985b. 'Times of the Signs: Modalities of History and Levels of Social Structure in Belau.' In: E. Mertz, R.J. Parmentier (eds.), *Semiotic Mediation: Sociocultural and Psychological Perspectives.* New York: Academic Press, 132-51.
Parmentier, R.J. 1985c. 'Semiotic Mediation: Ancestral Genealogy and Final Interpretant.' In: E. Mertz, R.J. Parmentier (eds.), *Semiotic Mediation: Sociocultural and Psychological Perspectives.* New York: Academic Press, 359-85.
Parmentier, R.J. 1987. *The Sacred Remains: Myth, History, and Polity in Belau.* Chicago: University of Chicago Press.
Parmentier, R.J. 1994. *Signs in Society: Studies in Semiotic Anthropology.* Bloomington: Indiana University Press.
Preucel, R.W. 2006. *Archaeological Semiotics.* Oxford: Blackwell.
Preucel, R.W. & A.A. Bauer 2001. 'Archaeological Pragmatics.' *Norwegian Archaeological Review,* 34, 85-96.
Radcliffe-Brown, A.R. 1957. *A Natural Science of Society.* Glencoe: The Free Press.
Reff, D.T. 1995. 'The Predicament of Culture and Spanish Missionary Accounts of the Tepehuan and Pueblo Revolts.' *Ethnohistory,* 42, 63-90.

Renfrew, C. 1994. 'Towards a Cognitive Archaeology.' In: C. Renfrew, E.B.W. Zubrow (eds.), *The Ancient Mind: Elements of a Cognitive Archaeology*. Cambridge: Cambridge University Press, 3-12.

Renfrew, C. 2004. 'Towards a Theory of Material Engagement.' In: E. DeMarrais, C. Gosden, C. Renfrew (eds.), *Rethinking Materiality: The Engagement of Mind with the Material World*. Cambridge: The McDonald Institute Monographs, 23-31.

Saussure, F. de 1966. *Course in General Linguistics*. In: C. Bally, A. Sechehaye (in collaboration with A. Riedlinger), trans. by W. Baskin. New York: McGraw-Hill.

Schiffer, M.B. & A. Miller 1999: *The Material Life of Human Beings*. London: Routledge.

Sebeok, T.A. 1976: *Contributions to the Doctrine of Signs*. Lanham: University Press of America.

Silverstein, M. 1976. 'Shifters, Linguistic Categories, and Cultural Descriptions.' In: K.H. Basso, H.A. Selby (eds.), *Meaning in Anthropology*. Albuquerque: University of New Mexico Press, 11-55.

Singer, M. 1984. *Man's Glassy Essence: Explorations in Semiotic Anthropology*. Bloomington: Indiana University Press.

Snead, J. & R.W. Preucel 1999. 'The Ideology of Settlement: Ancestral Keres Landscapes in the Northern Rio Grande.' In: W. Ashmore, A.B. Knapp (eds.), *Archaeologies of Landscape: Contemporary Perspectives*. Oxford: Blackwell, 169-97.

Sorrell, T. 1987. *Descartes*. Oxford: Oxford University Press.

Stevenson, M.C. 1894. *The Sia*. Washington, D.C.: Bureau of American Ethnology, 11th Annual Report.

Tambiah, S.J. 1984. *The Buddhist Saints of the Forest and the Cult of Amulets*. Cambridge: Cambridge University Press.

Thomas, N. 1991. *Entangled Objects*. Cambridge: Cambridge University Press.

Tilley, C. 1991. *Material Culture and Text: The Art of Ambiguity*. London: Routledge.

Tilley, C. 1999. *Metaphor and Material Culture*. Oxford: Blackwell.

Tilley, C. 2006. 'Objectification.' In: C. Tilley, W. Keane, S. Küchler, M. Rowlands, P. Spyer (eds.), *Handbook of Material Culture*. London: Sage Publications, 60-73.

Tyler, S.L. 1952. 'The Myth of the Lake of Copala and the Land of Teguayo.' *Utah Historical Quarterly*, 20, 313-29.

Tylor, E.B. 1871. *Primitive Culture*. London: John Murray.

Watson, P.J., S.A. LeBlanc & C.L. Redman 1971. *Explanation in Archaeology: An Explicitly Scientific Approach*. New York: Columbia University Press.

Weiner, A. 1992. *Inalienable Possessions: The Paradox of Giving-while-Keeping*. Berkeley: University of California Press.

White, L. 1935. *The Pueblo of Santo Domingo*. Menasha: American Anthropological Association Memoir No. 38.

White, L. 1964. 'The World of the Keresan Pueblo Indians.' In: S. Diamond (ed.), *Primitive Views of the World*. New York: Columbia University Press, 83-94.

The Hall and the Church during Christianization: Building ideologies and material concepts

Mads D. Jessen

The current chapter will investigate two of the most pervasive characteristics of human cognitive behaviour; firstly, the human ability to generate cultural concepts through the combination of experiential knowledge from different knowledge domains, and secondly, the ability to make manifest these concepts through material culture. In this chapter I will also argue that the interplay between these two traits is fundamental to the functioning of religious concepts – i.e. that any concrete access to abstract concepts must be anchored in the physical world by the means of extrasomatic materials.

In particular, the article will investigate the material environments which frame the socio-ritual activities taking place in Late Iron Age through Early Medieval Scandinavia (ca. AD 500-1200). This period also covers the process of Christianization in Southern Scandinavia, where the traditional belief system was gradually replaced by a Catholic ideology. The alterations, continuations and hybrid forms of material concepts this ideological change produced will therefore figure prominently in the analysis.

Concepts and materiality

Within standard cognitive science the material side of human behaviour has often been regarded a secondary subject matter of only minor relevance, when compared to the processes taking place inside the human brain (e.g. Tooby & Cosmides 1992; Atran 2002; Boyer 2001, Pyysiäinen 2001). Consequently, the proper locus of cognitive studies is considered to be the intricate system of neurons and synapses inside our skull, and the appropriate way to untangle the mysteries of the human mind is to study the human brain (Pylyshyn 1984). For instance, the highly acclaimed *Companion to Cognitive Studies* edited by Bechtel and Graham (2006) does not include an index entry on the words *tool, thing, object, artefact* or even *environment*. In itself this presents a rather conservative attitude towards the cognitive study of human interactions with the diverse range of materialities that surrounds us; especially when taking into account the steadily growing number of publications underlining the significant position the material environment takes in human cognition (Lave 1988; Tomasello 1999, 2001; Barnier *et al.* 2007; Gabora 2007; a.o.), and the increasing attention within the humanities and archaeology concerning the cross-section between mind and matter (Day 2004; Johannsen 2010; Malafouris 2008; Roepstorff 2008; Renfrew 1994, 2004; Sutton 2008, a.o.).

Even though the brain is the principal component in any cognitive operation, it would nevertheless be a serious omission to disregard the countless daily interactions we undertake with the various types of objects surrounding us. The perceptual understanding of or interaction with, for example, particular types of clothes, tools, vehicles or buildings play a vital role in how we conceptualize the world. I would therefore argue that the material environment is not just a symbolic reflection of some particular cultural setting. More likely, material culture presents a constituting element where the experience of the manipulated milieu forms a platform for certain ideological systems. In other words, it becomes an extrasomatic element to think *through* and not just a symbol to think *of*.

In the current chapter, the conceptual integration between material forms such as buildings, artefacts, words etc., and the non-physical and abstract world will therefore be investigated. Special emphasis will be placed on analysing the means by which a significant ideological change can be recognised in the material, i.e. the archaeological record, and in particular how architectural features may influence abstract concept building and concept transmission.

The hall and its context

Before the introduction of the still standing Romanesque churches, one building in particular, is believed to have functioned as a focal point for the ideological circulation in South Scandinavia, namely the Hall. Generally speaking the halls were the main building of the settlement, affording place for the practices connected with, and administration of, social organisation: e.g. kinship management, feasts, social affiliation, and various types of rituals (Andrén 2002,315f.; Gansum 2008,203f.; Gräslund 1992:133-36; Herschend 1998,16f.; 2001, 59f.; Jessen & Holst 2008; Olsen 1966, 83; 1986; Sanmark 2004, 100ff; Lidén 1969,17-21; Price 2002, 61). It often contained the more valuable and exotic artefacts of the settlement, and had a room reserved for functions that were not related to the ordinary household – at least in the ideal sense of a hall. The halls started to take form in the Early Iron Age as a recognizable structural feature within the main building of the large farms; an extra, non-kitchen room as it were. They began to increase in monumentality and exclusive character after AD 200, into finally becoming separate buildings in the Late Iron Age (Bårdseth 2009; Herschend 2009; Løken 2001). These separate buildings would eventually increase in size, particularly in connection with the great manor-type farms of the Viking Age, and would continue to grow as a material and social marker of the status and excellence of the proprietor. In other words, alongside the development of the hall a continuous hierarchization of society took place, which is reflected in the architecture of the building.

Regarding the functional genesis of the hall, it is considered to be a parallel development to the continental hall, which belonged to the aristocracy or the minor kings and royalty, and functioned as an interface between the public and private sphere for the nobility. More exactly, because the cardinal functions of the hall would be social signalling, banqueting, architectural manifestation, religious or other ritual activities, the exact functions would vary and can be regarded as an ideal situation when they appear simultaneously as a complete suite. However, often only a selection of the functions can be registered at any one location (see Herschend 2009:253 for a similar conclusion), and perhaps these functions were not even contained within a single building (see below).

The structural features of the hall, on the other hand, must in some cases be interpreted as evidential of Scandinavian origin. A feature which becomes particularly evident when the architectural adaptation is taken into consideration is the raised platform (mentioned below) in the east Scandinavian material,

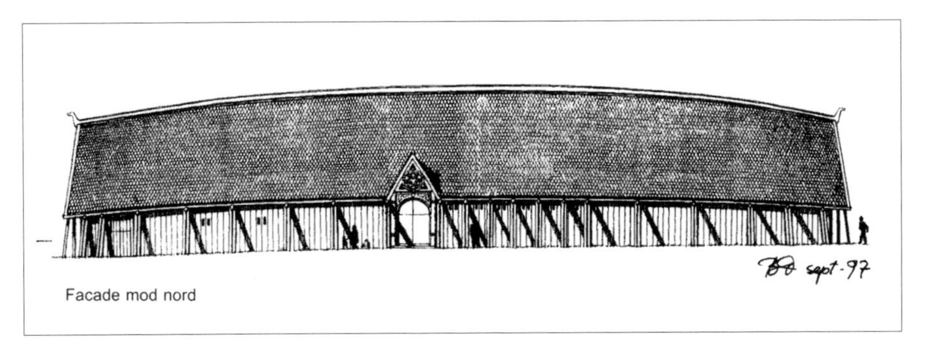

Fig. 1. Reconstruction of the Hall from Lejre. The characteristic curvature of the roof-ridge and the magnitude of the building are clearly presented. To the right of the entrance, the closely placed inclining posts indicate the position of the main room. The particular house behind this drawing was excavated in the early 90s, and has long been considered a unique structure. Renewed excavations at Lejre have, however, revealed a series of at least three additional houses even bigger than this one. (Reprinted by permission of B. Draiby).

and the Jutlandic tradition with hall and stables under the same roof. Such differences portray the Viking Age hall as an inherently composite structure with diverse functions under different contexts. Most likely, the functions of the hall are inspired by the continental situation, while the architectural motivation has a more endemic rooting.

The main architectural feature of the hall is the grandeur of the building itself. In actual physical terms this means a pronounced lengthwise curvature of the walls accompanied by inclining posts on the outside, as well as a house construction with a pronounced arching of the roof ridge. Evidently these architectural features have an instrumental effect on the perception of the buildings. At a distance the arching of the roof would give the building an erect and striving profile, while the curved wall would, on entering and exiting the building, cause a sense of endlessness as the gables cannot be perceived or seen at the doorstep (fig. I). Similarly, when entering the main room of the house, which often occurs from a small anteroom, as this room has no door leading directly outside (Beck 2010,76f.), the curvatures of roof and wall would simulate a somewhat bigger, internal space. In combination, this type of architecture incorporates both concepts of big and high, and even accentuates these elements to the extreme limits of the wooden building material. During the development of the architecture of the hall new solutions were introduced and eventually led to the formation of the timber framed house with trusses as the main roofbearing element. Often these hall buildings span more than 40m in length and 12-14m in breath, which is not at all unusual (Jørgensen 1998). Exactly how the upper parts of the building, the roof for example, are constructed is debated, but a notable height seems to be a generally agreed upon, despite disagreements concerning the construction of the wall (Schmidt 1999, 99ff.; Boëthius 1931,35-47; Larsson & Lenntorp 2004; Jessen & Egeberg, *forthcoming*).

Choosing a strategic place for the hall-building has at several localities been a very important factor. Not just any location in the area would be suitable for the erection of the hall. There clearly was a procedure for selecting a particular site for the building, which often resulted in rather laborious consequences. For example, at the very long hall in Borg (Norway), it is evident that even though the terrain is unsuited for such a large structure the placing of the building overrode more practical parameters (Herschend 2009,396-97). Hence, a levelling of the parcel took place in order to accomodate the large structure (Herschend & Mikkelsen 2003,53). Evidently, the hall-buildings at Uppåkra (Larsson & Lenntorp 2004,3), Uppsala (Nordahl 1993,61-63), Sanda (Åqvist 1996,111) Huseby (Skre 2007,233f.) as well as the main halls at Helgö (Zachrisson 2004,23, see also

Lundström 1970,129ff), Lejre (Christensen 2008) and Tissø (in particular the early Bulbrogård hall-phase) had also been placed in significant environments (Jørgensen *et al.* 2003).[1] At Uppåkra the hall is located at the highest point on a natural ridge, whilst the halls at Tissø and Lejre are built on a plateau and terrace respectively, which would seem to ensure that the buildings fit into – or perhaps even command – the natural landscape around them.

Visually underlining the magnitude of the main hall by placing it atop a terrace or platform seems to be a recurring feature of east Scandinavian hall-buildings in particular. For example, from the latest phase at the Järrestad complex in southwest Scania we find perhaps the most illustrative example of this process. At this locality there a succession of longhouses have been unearthed the youngest of which (around AD 1000) is of an exceptionally large type with no apparent internal roof bearing posts, leaving open an enormous internal space of almost 600m^2 (Söderberg 2003,136ff.+Appendix II). Such a construction is veritably impossible, as a wooden frame will not sustain a roof of such dimensions without some sort of internal support structure. Seemingly, the house was erected on a platform or terrace, now ploughed away, or had the internal posts resting on centrally placed 'sule'-posts, and possibly both.[2]

Similar architectural solutions have been noticed at, for example, Lejre/ Mysselhøjgaard (Christensen 2009), Tissø (Jørgensen 2009), Runegaard (Watt 1983), Toftegaard (Tornbjerg 1998a, 1998b, especially fig. 7), and must have presented several difficulties during the construction phase. Seemingly, this eastern house-type, at this point in time, appears to indicate a formalized structure in which particular purposes and connotations demanded physical presentation. Hence, the considerations put into choosing the right spot or fitting architecture for the building of a hall must have been caused by ideological reasons as the erection of the hall would have been easier elsewhere. However, the raised and/ or prominent position proved to be the main concern, and the principles of construction therefore transgressed mundane functional requirements (contrary to the ideas of Bolvig 1992,10).

In addition, a conspicuous number of the terrace-built halls seem to have another special building attached to the western end of the main building. Two of the locations, namely Tissø and Järrestad, exhibit almost exactly a similar organization of the central building area, i.e., a bigger main building with a smaller annexed building placed within a fenced area (Jørgensen 2002, 2009; Söderberg 2003, 2005). Several of the finds, in particular from the Tissø complex point towards a series of ritual activities taking place here – such as several amulets and pieces of jewellery with mythological motifs – and in general the Tissø residents seem to have been deeply involved in ritual activities (Jørgensen 2009,338-44).

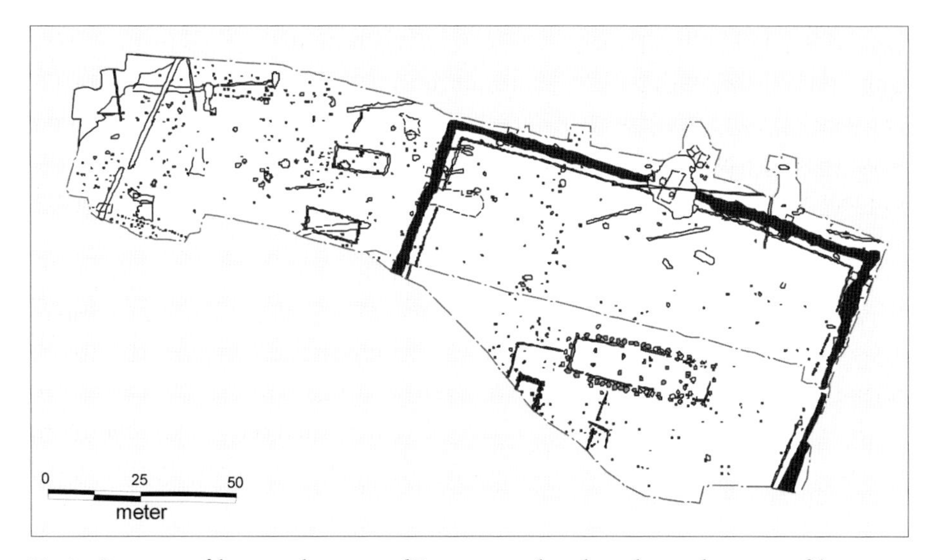

Fig. 2. Overview of the recently excavated Erritsø-complex where the northern part of the rectangular moat and the centrally placed main hall are clearly visible. To the southwest of the hall-building a small fenced enclosure demarcates an area in which the northern half of a smaller building can be recognized. Evidently, the main hall and the small side-house present a coherent structure. (Used by permission from O. Sørensen, Vejle Museum)

In the last couple of decades a whole series of this new building type have been excavated, which all show close connection to the main hall buildings. Presumably the often smaller but solidly built houses must be interpreted as cult houses, and one of the better examples of the kind of 'combined' ritual environment, would be the newly excavated site of Erritsø (Fig. II).

At Erritsø a huge Viking Age hall was excavated and the reminiscent postholes bear witness to a hall-building of considerable proportions, which indicate a visually prominent building. Also the topography follows a similar structure of elevation, as the fortification is placed atop a ridge, one of the highest locations in the Erritsø parish, overlooking the very vital Lyngs promontory from where access across the Little Belt to the island of Funen was possible. Undoubtedly, the topographic considerations figured prominently when the Erritsø complex was established. From the visible spot on the ridge, the residents could easily keep the traffic between the two areas under observation, and passers-by could easily register the fortification and the great hall (Christensen 2009).

As at Järrestad and Tissø, the organization of the Erritsø settlement itself was of a somewhat special character as the central part of the structures were enclosed in a heavy palisade with an additional moat on the outside. Internally the enclosure was dominated by the centrally placed, big hall-building, typical of the Viking age. To the south-west, a small squared fence, attached to the main building, continued around a smaller building. An entrance from the hall-building to the small fenced area guaranteed direct access for the residents, and an opening in the fence towards the east gave access to the main area. It seems that the small house can be regarded as an appendage to the main building, primarily serving as a structural extension of the bigger house. Also with regard to the function of the smaller house this might be the case, due to the fact that the Erritsø complex follows a recurring layout involving a big hall *cum* smaller, fenced-in building, as unearthed at Tissø and Järrestad (*ibid.*).

Besides the three locations mentioned here, which have a conspicuously similar organization, several other sites follow a comparable layout. At Bejdsebakken, in Northern Jutland, for example, the buildings around the main hall (A304) could easily be aligned with the above examples, with offerings in the main postholes of the hall and a secluded and smaller, fenced building to the southwest (Nielsen 2002:fig. 3; Torben Sarauw, pers. comm.). Recent excavations at the well-known sites of Uppåkra and Lejre also appear to suggest an affiliation and combination between bigger and smaller ritual buildings in use at the same time and placed within a limited area (Christensen 2008; Lenntorp & Hårdh 2009). A more uncertain version can be recognized at Vorbasse where the bigger house (house XLI) has a solid enclosure attached to the eastern gable, this way connecting it with a smaller building. Seemingly, this structure is maintained in the repeating phase, where another constellation of an eastern enclosure with a smaller house also appears (Hvass 180,161, 1983,135-36). At Lisbjerg, a possible hall and annexed house might have been positioned under the present Church. The actual layout of the late Viking Age settlement has been severely damaged by the church and churchyard, but at least a hall-building with a small fenced house in the vicinity have been registered (Jeppesen 2005,55). Also the Gudme-site from the late Roman Iron Age exhibits some of the characteristics from the later periods – perhaps in some sort of proto form – with a large main building and an adjacent, smaller, and solidly-built house; again with a significant number of extraordinary objects, which could be of ritual origin (Pentz & Sørensen 2008; Sørensen 1994). The restarted excavations at Uppåkra epitomize in a way the combination of the bigger and the smaller house. However, whilst previously the Uppåkra cultic house (which was the first to be excavated) was interpreted as an exceptional heathen temple, it has lately – *qua* new data from the immediate surroundings of the building – been juxtaposed to the other southeast Scandinavian hall *cum* side-house locations (Larsson 2006b,150; Lenntorp & Hårdh 2009; Herschend 2009,369f.).

What I wish to underline here is that the ritual buildings can, so to speak, 'come in pairs' where the main halls are fitted with a smaller building within an exclusive area – at least in its most formalized version from the 8th to the 10th century, such as at Erritsø[3]. Reasons for placing the smaller building within its own enclosure could be many, but looking at the physical organization of the two buildings in combination, it seems clear that the side-house must have functioned as an extension of the main hall. As mentioned by Jørgensen ... *the prestigious activities such as banquets and ritual meals took place in the eastern part* [of the halls], *while the western part was probably a private area* (Jørgensen 2009,339) ... which suggest that also the small house attached to the western part of the halls could be regarded a semi-private area, perhaps mainly reserved for the residents.

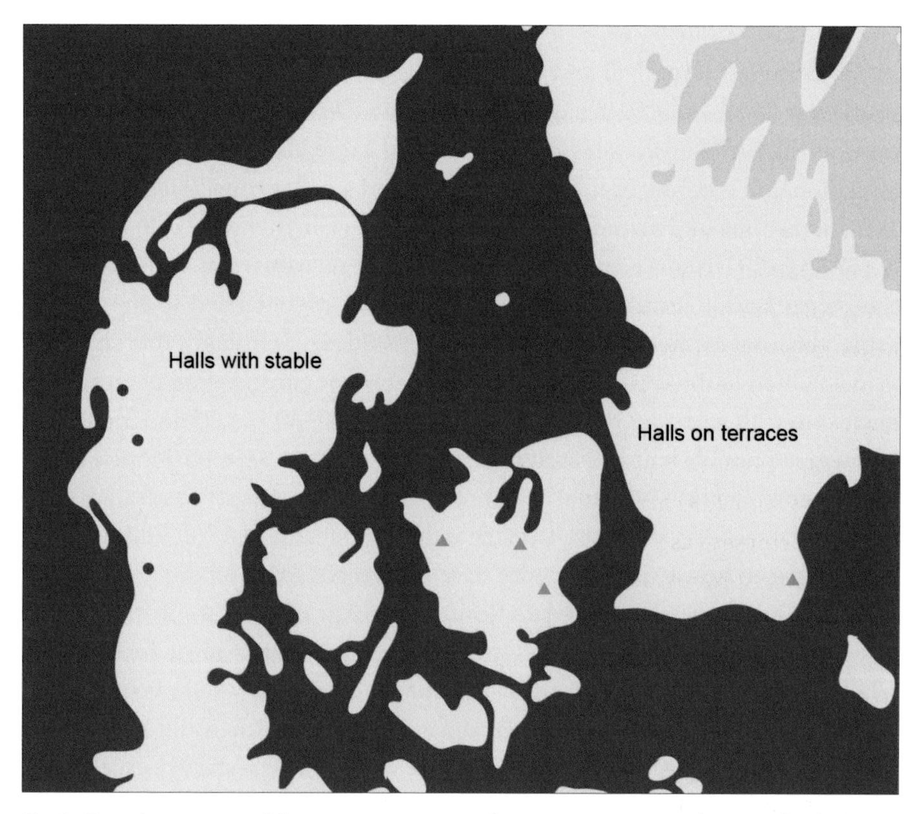

Fig. 3. Distribution map of the two contemporary (approx. AD 850-1000) types of architecture defining the hall buildings. Seemingly, the Great Belt can be regarded as a kind of barrier between the two types of building customs, where the more archaic 'halls with stables' (red dots) are connected to the North Sea areas, while the halls on terraces, exclusively used for human dwelling (green triangles), have an eastern anchor point. The latter group seems to be of a more indigenous Middle Scandinavian type.

Combined, the smaller house and the bigger hall present two aspects of the ritual activities: the monumental hall gives space primarily to the more political sides of ritual life, such as the swearing of alliances or annual feasts, which would be a horizontal negotiation of the ritual relationship centred around the hall-owner, whereas in the cultic side-house, a vertical communication between the divine entities and the believers would take place, such as ritual offerings administered by the hall-owner. To which extent the activities themselves were performed as part of a private or a public event is debatable, but at least the proprietorship is clearly recognized – the resident of the main hall regards the smaller cultic building as part of his domain. In essence, the building organization reverberates the sacral kingship, where the leading character in political affairs figures prominently in cultic affairs as well – a constellation which is reminiscent of the Roman office of the *Pontifex Maximus*[4], but likewise has dominated the Germanic, socio-religious organization (Warmind 1999; Sundquist 2004, 44f.; Dobat 2006).

The western areas

Regarding the Jutlandic areas in the later phase of the Viking Age the architecture of the main buildings also seems to take a different expression than their eastern counterparts. Firstly, the halls follow a more 'archaic', structural tradition where composite functions under the same roof can be expected, and stables, barns or other more pragmatic functions in combination with big open aula-like rooms in another part of the house, is no exception in the main houses in Jutland in the10th century. Such types of architecture (fig. IV) are clearly recognizable at Agerhøj (Jessen & Egeberg, *forthcoming*), Omgaard (Nielsen 1980), Vorbasse (Hvass 1980, 1983) and Gl. Hviding (Jensen 1987). Secondly, a more uniform character emerges as these houses have an almost similar ground plan as well as distribution of rooms – in particular Agerhøj and Gl. Hviding overlap – unlike the more dynamic and diverse house-types found, for example, on Zealand at the same point in time. The general picture of the western hall therefore seems to portray a more normative hall concept, in which an analogous layout becomes dominant in the large rural settlements in the late Viking Age. Thirdly, a more traditional means of displaying wealth and power, such as the use of precious metals and foreign products, are being downplayed in favour of extravagant building strategies, and only few richly-furnished artefacts are found at these locations (see Gl. Hviding (*ibid*) and Østergaard (Sørensen 1998, 2003) for exceptions). The western settlements do not therefore provide evidence of any significant amount of imported goods, votive offerings or production of jewellery, such as often registered on the eastern settlements of comparable size.[5]

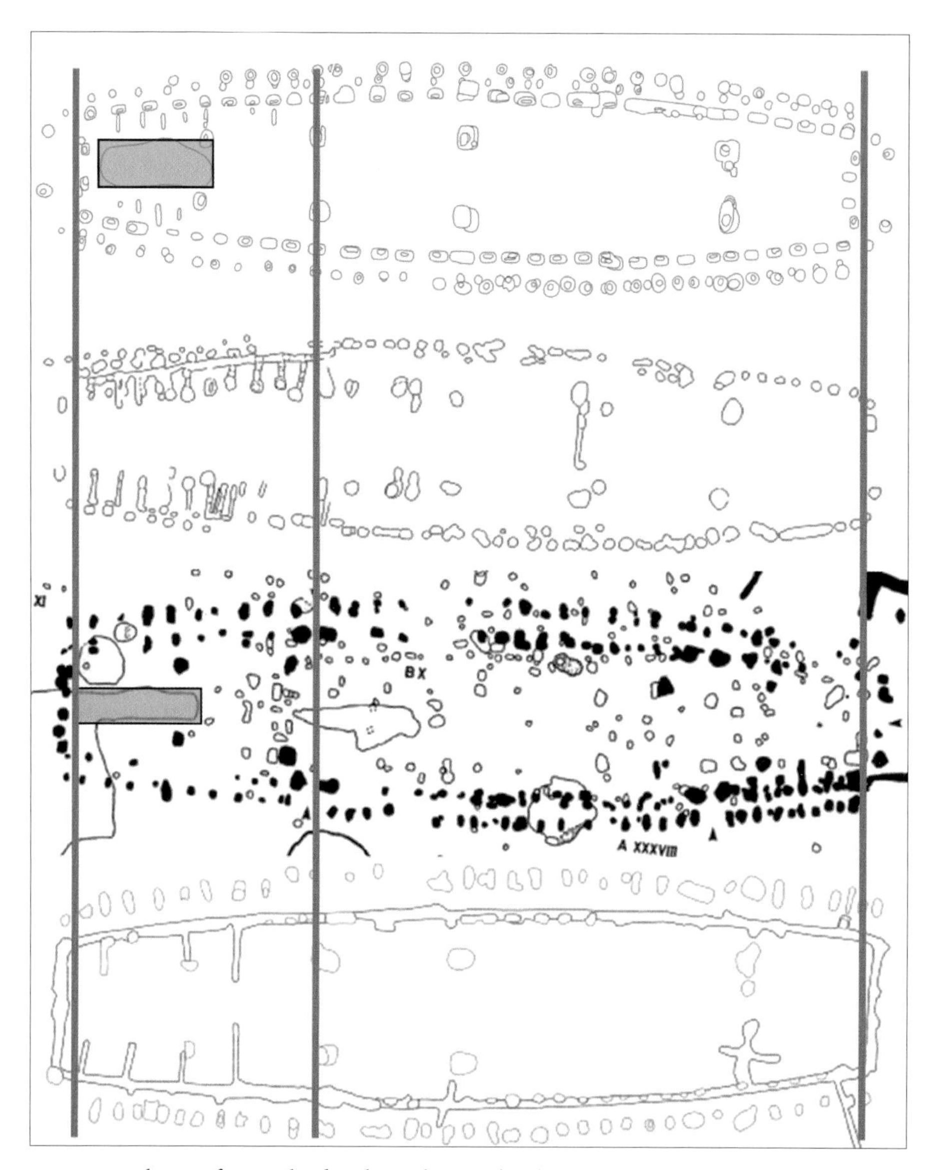

Fig. 4. Four houses from Jutland with nearly complete layouts. The main houses from Agerhøj, Vorbasse, Omgaard and Gl. Hviding (top to bottom) contain a division of the house into a stable end with stalls, and a domestic end with a large, main room. In some cases (Agerhøj and Omgaard) the stable is also recognizable by the shallow ditch (grey marking) generated by removing manure in order to distribute it in the fields (the illustration does not provide accurate dimensions, as the houses are between 34 and 40 meters). (After Hvass 1980, Nielsen 1980 & Jensen 1987).

Nevertheless, these locations found on the Jutlandic peninsula, and regularly accompanied by larger fenced-in private parcels, also demonstrate a clear tendency to 'exaggerate' the dimensions of the main building, often accompanied by a prominent placing in the landscape. Framing influence or authority by large buildings could in a way be said to be more pronounced in these West Scandinavian areas because it seemingly is the principle factor in expressing social power.

Evidentially, the concept of a hall-building could take many hybrid forms, and even if regional groupings can be registered, each settlement had their own particular interpretation, which emphasized different elements taken from an idealized theme. Nonetheless, between east and west a commonality of material expression can be found in the recurring use of big buildings as a means to establish exclusive roofed environments through which the proprietors could position themselves as significant persons. For these reasons, I will focus on the hall building itself, and only to a lesser extent the cultic side-houses, because the hall epitomized the functioning of the sacral kingship, and the cultic annexes, I believe, must be regarded as an integrated part of the main hall, and not necessarily as a functionally independent entity, but an expansion of the ritual activities pertaining to the main hall.

The divine and the earthly hall

In the written, mythological sources there are also several passages describing the magnitude of the buildings that housed the Norse pantheon, and the elevated position as well as spaciousness is a recurring theme. For example in Skirnismál (strophe 3) where Skirnir asks:

> *Tell me now, Frey,*
> *prince of gods!*
> *for I desire to know,*
> *why alone thou sittest*
> *in the spacious hall*
> *the livelong day?*

Odin's grand hall, Valaskjálf, frames the opening scene which is cited here, and a direct relation between the prominent owner and the grandeur of the building is made clear. In several other instances halls belonging to leading persons are characterised as high, magnificent, large, lofty, towering, and other adjectives denominating the significance of the building (see also Beowulf:69+116+713+1016+1926, Grimnismál 4-26; Gylfaginning:2+21+34; Fafnismál/42; Guðrúnarkviða II/13+III/7; Oddrúnar-grátr/3 and many others (Gummere 1909; Thorpe & Blackwell 1907)). There does not seem to be any difference between the words chosen for describing worldly and divine halls, which indicates that the understanding of either sphere is framed by analogous concepts. Indeed, the conceptualization of the physical hall and its celestial counterpart must be understood as mutual reverberations of each other, but presumably grounded in the corporeal experiences that the material building facilitates in real space (see below).

Also, the archeologically known hall-buildings often exhibit a clear tendency to be either very robustly built, or, more likely, to have been unusually high in comparison with contemporary standards for the more mundane buildings. In several of the classical hall-buildings this characteristic architectural feature can be found. Gudme (Jørgensen 2001,76-78; Sørensen 1994:29-31), Helgö (Herschend 1998), Järrestad (Søderberg 2003), Tissø (Jørgensen 1998), Lejre (Christensen 1991), Slöinge (Lundqvist 2000) Uppåkra (Larsson 2006a, 2006b, 2007,) all show excessively large and deeply anchored roof-bearing posts. Posts which would have been suitable for a very high house, perhaps even with a second storey topping the building, as has been suggested in the case of Uppåkra (*ibid.*:21-22).

Over time, the constructional outcome of this building ideology is a diminishing number of roof-bearing posts. Apparently, the architecture of the principal late Iron Age houses was changed by the desire to promote a certain ideological cause, which is grounded in the mentioned aristocratic ideology, where the power affiliation of the main resident in the hall – the sacral king – is administered and arranged in the large central room. Therefore, unconsciously, there existed a pressure upon the hall building itself towards containing at least one big room under the roof of the hall – a room which gradually got bigger, hence pushing out the internal posts in the building, which left behind a large, cohesive room. This pressure eventually broke the very rigid, millennia long tradition of building three-ailed houses and the introduction of the frame-built house took place (Schmidt 1992, 128ff.).

Evidently, the notion of elevation, height and impressiveness figures prominently in the conceptual grounding of the halls. The higher the actual construction and the more elevated a position possible, would only be beneficial to the building *per se*. Visual dominance and grandeur became trademarks of how the hall ought to be experienced. Obviously, assigning such demanding labour investments into underlining the notable position of the hall was directed at signifying the importance of the family residing in the building. Therefore the high position of the hall echoes the high position of the owners. A symbiotic constellation between the position of the building and the hall-owner seem evident. The hall functioned as a physical notion of the qualities of the owner, and an environmental cue for everybody in its presence to experience. Halls are therefore conceptualized as very prominent constructions and most certainly provided a physical presence which was very hard to overlook.

The logic of social physics

> A proud man exhibits his sense of superiority over others by holding his head and body erect.
>
> He is haughty (haut), or high, and makes himself appear as large as possible (*Darwin 1872,262-63*).

What is particularly interesting with this analogous constellation of materiality and authority, described in the previous section, is that it conflates two normally separate social divisions, namely social value and social power and furthermore anchors the constellation in the socio-physical world. A method for investigating this topic more specifically is the relational models theory developed by Alan P. Fiske (1991; 2004, see also Haslam 1994). In his academic production, Fiske has devoted a great deal of attention to the description of the psychology behind social relationships, and he has formulated four divisions of social interaction centred on the different ways social power can be formulated and organized. A four-partite division which he claims to be a universal trait of human interaction, based on numerous anthropological studies around the globe.

Communal Sharing (CS) describes a relationship where people focus on what they have in common and the social interaction is defined by solidarity, equality and sharing of the resources available. Typically this bond exists between the closest of kin or between cohesive groups such as clans or orders. Authority ranking (AR) describes relationships which are hierarchically grounded and organized according to status and/or power differences. Such relationships are normally found in workspaces, the army or other institutionalized settings which adhere to a concise power structure, but can also be found in several other more dynamically defined social settings such as kinship structures. Two additional types of relationships, which are argued to be more recent historical developments, will not be scrutinized further here. They are Equality matching (EM) describing a stringently equal system of rule-based ordering, such as in sports, and Market pricing (MP) which involves a commercially based exchange of commodities or services with assigned values (Fiske 1991,3-12; 2004,3-13; see also Smith 2008).

These four types of interaction should not be viewed as mutually exclusive, but rather be regarded as context defined 'rules of engagement' which define the cognitive models of the social relationship dominating under certain circumstances, and not necessarily comprehensive or stable properties of sets of people. Fiske himself uses a Royal banquet as an example of the intermingled nature and multiple types of relationships in function during one single event.

> At formal functions where rank is marked, guests should arrive in reverse order of rank (subordinates arriving earlier and awaiting superiors) and leave in order of rank (no one leaving before anyone superior to them). Seating at the table also marks rank [AR]. However, the food was purchased and the staff paid in an MP framework. But guests share what they eat and drink – the food and drink is theirs collectively to freely consume. Indeed, eating and drinking together marks and constitute a bond of solidarity among those who partake [CS]. At the same time, participants exchange toasts with each other, matching one-to-one, and may feel obliged to reciprocate the hospitality by later inviting their host to a corresponding dinner [EM]. (Fiske 2004,8).

In the banquet situation all of the four types of relationship orderings are present, but each organize distinct if related situations, thus exemplifying the versatility of both human interactions as well as Fiske's principles of structured interaction. Worth noticing in the Banquet scenario is the apparent use of spatial orderings of authority – the AR relationship – and social power through the seating of the guests.[6] This type of social ordering of space is clearly parallel to the use of spatial configurations underlining status and power in late Iron Age Scandinavia, where the Authority Ranking is often defined by elevation. Apparently, such *social physics* as Fiske denotes these spatial arrangements, can also be found in several other interpersonal settings as the ethnographic record shows, and has been registered both chronologically as well as chorologically, hinting towards a cross-cultural principle of visualizing power.

One of the earliest investigations, but still among the more thorough, concerning posture and spatial ordering was made by Hewes in the 50s. Covering 480 culture groups, of which 34 were registered archaeologically through figurines, carvings, paintings etc., his analysis clearly shows a tendency to have elevated seating on stools or daises as demarcations of authority, and particularly so among masculine groups (1955:237-238). This is supported by several recent investigations which show that the physical organization of buildings (their size and position or the use of platforms and costly materials) also underline the superiority of their owners. Intricate systems of elevation and magnitude operate in Fiji, and elsewhere in Oceania, where people build their houses on raised platforms, whose relative heights correspond to the rank of the owners (Toren 1990:29-39, Firth 1970:194-198). Similarly, in Pre-Hispanic Mesoamerica a common feature in elite architecture was to use terraces or platforms to build houses on in order to accentuate the status of the residents (Hirth 1992:123-4+note 5). Also contemporary use of social physics is a recurring theme, as has been shown Schwartz (1981:62ff) in his investigations of height, furnishing and size of office spaces, just as the use of relative elevation in advertisements to indicate high social positioning follow the same vertical trajectory (Goffman 1976,43-5).

Also more metaphorical or derived instances of physical dominance have been registered. For example, the Moose of Burkina Faso when striving to gain a more privileged social status often turn to witchcraft, such as the intake of potions. Interestingly, these potions are supposed to contain the essence of highness, as they are compounds made of 'high' materials such as rocks collected from the peaks of the highest mountains, or epiphytes growing atop the highest trees (Fiske 2004, 95). Thus, the material qualities of the compounds, or point of collection more correctly, can be used as a physical primer for the social goals of the ascending Moose when becoming part of the persons own body through consummation (see Jessen *in press* for an elaborate account on the use of extrasomatic entities, such as foodstuff, in the transference of magical essence).

Analytically, both the Moose's use of potions as well as the numerous postural and architectural initiatives to attain a particular high or elevated position must be viewed as a metaphorical transference of a particular physical configuration onto a social configuration. It is an underlining of physical highness used to simulate a social status, thus creating an analogy between two normally separate knowledge domains – those of physics and psychology. The outcome is an emergent structure which perhaps can best be defined as a 'social physics' due to the blended character of extrasomatic entities and social knowledge, eventually forming a spatial organization where authority *is* being above or being greater. Importantly, the understanding of the vertical hierarchy, as well as notion of the 'greater' being the more significant, operate at a pre-linguistic level, grounded in perceptual and physical qualities and not on the verbalization of social relations and structures. For example, in the famous *The Great Dictator* by Charlie Chaplin a very vivid caricature of the wish to be seated highest, thus demonstrating superiority, can be found in the scene where 'Hynke/Hitler' and 'Napaloni/Mussolini' visit the barbershop. Both strive to be world leaders and therefore successively raise their chairs to be above the other. Hynke eventually knocks himself out as he reaches the ceiling! No explanation nor conversation accompanies the scene because it is not needed; the logic of the social physics suffices – an elevated position is a superior position.

The concept of the building

> By embodying intelligibility in spatial forms, the individuals in a society create an experiential reality through which they can retrieve a description of certain dimensions of their society and the ways in which they are members of it (*Hillier & Hanson 1984, 198*).

So far, we have established that there presumably exists a panhuman, psychological tendency to demarcate social hierarchies through spatial qualities. From a cognitive point of view this might follow very basic developmental processes, and can therefore be grounded in mundane perceptual features which humans are exposed to during childhood (Barsalou 2008).

When encountering the logic of social physics the experiential input respects two simple formulations; "Control Is Up" and "Important Is Big". Such simple spatial definitions are comparable to some of the ideas promoted in cognitive anthropology and cognitive linguistics. As described by Lakoff and Johnson (1980; 1999), the types of experiential patterning, for example as those recognised in the spatial organisation of the halls, fits the idea of 'primary metaphors'. Primary metaphors are explained as having... "a minimal structure and arises naturally, automatically, and unconsciously through everyday experience by means of conflation, during which cross-domain associations are formed" (Lakoff & Johnson 1999:46), i.e. primary metaphors can be conceived of as very basic conceptual understandings of how we experience the relations things have with each other and with us (Gibbs 2006,120-121). In the case of "Control Is Up" the subjective judgement of course relates to being in control, while the sensorimotor experience is defined by verticality. In everyday life these two types of experiences in combination make you realize that it is by far much easier to control or exert force to something that is beneath you than if it is placed above your head (Lakoff & Johnson 1999,53). Importantly, this realisation is a conflation of two knowledge domains; the one being defined by spatial positioning and the other defined by the subjective understanding of control or authority.

Regarding the "Important Is Big" primary metaphor, the same structure can be identified; a particular sensorimotor understanding pertaining to size is mapped onto the subjective understanding of importance, and again a notion of powerfulness is defined by reference to spatial knowledge (*ibid.* 50). In early development, for instance, children quickly learn that the biggest individuals, often their parents or relatives, are the ones that make the most decisions. Hence, the bigger person is the more important one.

Normally, as Lakoff & Johnson claim, such metaphorical extensions are presented mainly through linguistic behaviour, even though they derive from prelinguistic knowledge about the world. However, the cultural concepts, which are extensions of the different types of metaphors mentioned above, are in the late Iron Age tightly bound to the physical environment and architecture. In fact, there seems to be no way of separating the material crystallisation of "Control Is Up" and "Important Is Big" from the narratives that address the buildings. Both types of cultural media – language and architecture – are responsible for distributing the model through society, and either of them would be more difficult to comprehend if not mirrored in each other. So, even though the possible range of 'culturalizing' the primary metaphors is virtually infinite, the specific expression they have in the present context is rather restricted to the physical environment, and here specifically the hall building. The manifestation of the cultural concept can therefore be aligned with building big and placing high – a physico-spatial definition that transgresses linguistic formulation and relates in actual fact to the physically experienced world.

Many abstract (cultural) concepts are often partly or wholly dependent on knowledge imported from domains which are mainly concerned with spatial or bodily understanding. Simulating basic perceptual/embodied experiences in more elaborate cultural concepts is perhaps even a fundamental aspect in conceptual processing (Gibbs 2006,121-122). As Lawrence Barsalou has argued "...when people form novel concepts productively, perceptual simulation plays a central role" thus pointing to the central position the perceptual modalities take when humans need to confer knowledge about abstract concepts (Barsalou 1999,594). This happens, for example, when taking the perceptual category of elevation and using it to conceptualize hierarchical structure by simulating an actual 'aboveness'. Simulation of the elevated position will often, as has been demonstrated above in the ethnographic and archaeological examples, be enhanced by the use of architectural features ranging from small stools to topographic features, thereby enhancing the perceptual experience and underline the conceptual content of the desired message (i.e. authority ranking). In either case, the conceptual grounding rests on a combination of metaphorical and material qualities which produces an architectural adaptation to the ideological content and *vice versa*.

Through rather straightforward manipulation of the environment an ideological concept has been created, and the cognitive processes behind this creation has combined (or simulated) knowledge about social and spatial qualities, as well as reached beyond the human skull into the cultural, material environment such as architecture.

The question is whether embodied simulation plays any role with regards to more abstract concepts such as social cognition and ideologically related architecture. Gallese and Lakoff (2005) have made a convincing argument for the indispensable structuration provided by the cross-modal mechanisms inherent to embodied simulation in more abstract concepts. The reason for this is the capacity for *abstract conceptual reasoning*, which is basically what happens when an animal simulates, for examples, grasping a cup, when it sees another being grasping a cup (*ibid.* 469). So, when a spatial arrangement, such as vertical positioning according to social position, is played out, the spatial reasoning itself inevitably rests on the cognitive capacity to simulate (i.e. conceptualize) the bodily understanding of an up/down-scale. Without this capacity to make an embodied simulation of the spatial configuration the abstract version of verticality, which in this case refers to an interpersonal convention of authority, would not be possible in the first place. Mapping between two diverse conceptual domains (social rank and 3D space) would require the right understanding of space to combine with the right conceptual inferences, and those inferences could rely on an embodied simulation, because… "the concepts characterised in the sensory-motor system are of the right form to characterise the source domains of conceptual metaphors" (ibid. 470), due to the fact that… "the same circuitry that can move the body and structure perceptions, also structures abstract thought" (ibid. 471). What the right inference would be is of course contextually defined, but the generous examples of 'Control Is Up' and 'Important Is Big', seem to indicate that the conceptual mapping between rank and verticality vouch for a strong inference, which apparently can be applied to a great variety of cultural settings.

The Church and the pre-Christian social physics

Regarding changes of the religious environment taking place in connection with the introduction of a Christian ideology, there presumably existed a period of more or less syncretistic mixing, where both traditional Norse ideals and novel Catholic values were in use at the same time, or at least the former being tolerated and transformed into a Christian ideological understanding. Presumably, the ideological platform which the Church sought to introduce, did not effectuate a general collapse of the well-established conventions, but brought with it a period of hybridisation between the different ideological systems. The most important and weighty pre-Christian traditions did not just vanish due to the gradual incorporation of a Catholic logic. Several aspects of the 'old practices' found new ways of presence in the changing religious environment of the Early Medieval setting (Hultgaard 1992, 68f.; Andrén 2007; Tesch 2007). One such example of a hybrid concept would be the actual building in which the different ritual activities took place. Perhaps even the architectural structuration of the church building itself presents a continuation of pre-Christian traditions.

As pointed out recently by a number of scholars (Anglert 2006a; Nilsson 2003; Sundqvist 2006; Olsen 1967), there are certain architectural features recognizable in the early Romanesque churches which are not strictly related to the divine worship or to the Catholic liturgy either. In particular, the western towers of the early Romanesque churches take such a position, as the different uses of this part of the church often can be related to more profane activities. Storage of seeds collected through taxation, place of refuge in times of conflict, or even as a private area for the patron family has been suggested: for example in connection with private sanctuary or perhaps even more elaborate banquets (Anglert 2006a,171ff., Sundqvist 2006,20-21). For those reasons, it seems clear that the western tower indeed did leave open the possibility for non-Christian activities, and that these activities might be associated with older traditions which used to take place in the Iron Age halls.

But not just the activities in the western towers might present a continuation of the former pagan traditions. Also the physical organisation of the Church can be viewed as an echo of the spatial constellation dominating the hall society. Mats Anglert (2006a) has put forth a very interesting interpretation of the spatial organisation of the early Christian cult in the Scandinavian areas. He explains the structure of the Christian locations at, for example, Simris (Scania) and Rone (Gotland) as a compilation of earlier ideas about how to organize and equip a proper ritual environment. In the earlier pre-Christian milieu a more dispersed structure is dominant, where different social or ritual practices are positioned at different localities in the surrounding area. Importantly, these localities are not placed very far from each other, often within a few hundred meters or less, but seem to be relegated to different, if related, routines within the conglomerate of a pre-Christian cult. Anglert regards the sectioning of 'rooms' in the early churches to correspond to the pagan spatial organisation of different cultic functions, where the western towers in particular correspond to the hall building, due to this rooms' affiliation with the aristocracy. A similar interpretation has been advocated by Olof Sundquist (2006) who considers the western towers to be in almost direct correspondence to the late Iron Age hall. He specifically mentions the elevated position of the first floor in the towers – the so-called *empor* – as an important indicator of the exceptional social and ritual position that the aristocratic sphere held in society and in the church. This floor was often furnished rather lavishly and often had a portal or even a balcony attached, where the persons worthy or powerful enough would be seated. From here the patron ... *sat during the ritual in his promoted position and looked towards the altar, separated from the congregation* (Sundqvist 2006,27).[7]

Ing-Marie Nilsson (2003) has also brought attention to the elevated platforms and benches in the western part of the Romanesque churches, which she believes to be a reference to the high-seat of the Iron Age. In the church this has been transferred to a kinship relation in that a baptism, being supervised by a patron on in the western platform, established a spiritual connection between patron and commoner.

The positioning of the patron personel in the western part of the Church should generate a rather prominent cognitive response in the persons being watched, and the person watching. Importantly, the congregation in the church would of course be people living in the parish and for that same reason presumably also under the influence of the higher – vertical and hierarchical – person in the western tower. This way the patron could express a social position by a rather simple and subtle means – i.e. Control Is Up. Being situated as the higher person as well as being provided with the possibility of overlooking the assembled public evidently provided a distance between the watcher and the people being watched. Likewise the elevated position guaranteed the visibility of the person(s) sitting there. Presumably, being seen by, as well as watching, the people assembled would have been of importance to the persons administering the western part of the early churches (*ibid.*:39-41). In combination with the elevated position it seems very likely that a member of the public in the church would, unknowingly, be convinced or confirmed in believing that the physically higher position of the persons in the western part of the room also warranted him a higher position in the social structure. The cognitive strategy seems evident: correspondence between spatial design and the various levels of social grouping will inevitably relate to the persons using the space (Hillier, Hanson & Graham 1987, 251-53), and the different social segments will be reflected in different spatial segments. In effect, tangible physical zones or structures could potentially belong to particular (and bounded) social groups.

Undoubtedly, the establishment of a church on one's own property, and perhaps even contemporary with a large hall, could be regarded as a conscious act, aimed at changing or consolidating the social order (Anglert 2006a, 168-169, 2006b, 96-98). Structures of strong ideological significance, be they west towers or halls, would be especially valuable to have within ones range of authority, and organizing one's private architecture according to the social physics of elevation and grandeur would in effect sustain and legitimize a traditional hierarchical system *albeit* with a different architectural expression. The western towers take precisely such a position and even exhibit a clear resonance of the traditional sacral kingship (Doig 2008, 130-33).

One therefore clearly recognises the aristocracy manifesting itself in the new Christian environment (McGuire 2008; Wienberg 1993,101ff.), as the special position they held in the late Iron Age was being challenged by the new ritual institution – the Catholic clergy. The relatively numerous western towers that are attached to the earliest churches, evidently became important vehicles of ideological continuity. Apparently the spatial configuration of the towers follows the same metaphorical concepts which dominated the earlier period, but the actualisation of the social physics is slightly changed as the tangible crystallisation of the model no longer is presented through the hall, but through the west towers. It is therefore possible to talk about a sort of conceptual continuity which manifests itself through the physical, sacred environment.

The transference is also partly based on the functions that took place in these buildings, but more pronounced is the social positions that were sought to be maintained. Through the incorporation of the different elements constituting the ideal hall into the composition of the west towers, a more or less unproblematic transference of the social structure dominant in the pre-Christian society could be carried out. Preservation, with modest alterations, of the aristocratic fingerprint on the ritual environment, from traditional to Catholic, became the overall outcome.

Concluding comments

The sort of embodied notion of conceptual understanding that I have been trying to illustrate paints a new picture of how concepts can be conceived; one which is contrary to the classical view advocating disembodied, purely abstract, decontextualised and ontologically separate mental representations. I promote a view which highlights, rather, an adaptable, multimodal and context dependent formulation of basic pre-linguistic and embodied experiences. Such experiences, as the above mentioned primary metaphors, are applicable to a wider range of circumstances, and, as exemplified, can be combined into more complex cultural concepts depending on the context. For example, because space has its own autonomous reality – a reality pertaining to our understanding of our own physical body – incorporation of the environment into the construction of social reality can generate the concept of hierarchy as a vertical dimension. In effect, by being grounded in the mental recollections of an individual's physical experiences the spatial categorization of 'social physics' becomes subjectively meaningful.

Importantly, the archaeological and proto-historical period under scrutiny has also revealed that the cultural concepts at play at a given time are not restricted to mental and/or linguistic formulations, but can equally be recognized and transmitted through material culture. Distribution of the cultural concepts over a broad range of media has several advantages. Firstly, more perceptual modalities will be active in the understanding and uptake of the governing principles of conceptualization. Both visual, auditory, and tactile inputs are affecting the overall internalization of the concepts. Secondly, not only the individual but also the collective platform for conceptual understanding is strengthened; increasing the number of different experiences conforming to the overall model should provide a commonality of conceptual understanding within society. Thirdly, presenting the cultural concepts through materiality creates an enduring experiential unit.

Concepts become stable over longer periods of time – perhaps spanning several generations – which maintain the understanding of the concept in question. Fourthly, physical crystallisation of the concepts also generates an arena for social negotiation; particularly so in the case of the power structural content on display, as mentioned above, where the very spatial grounding of the concepts can become a position for which people contest. Generally speaking, there seems to exist an underlying system of spatial generators in which the simulation of mundane experiences can create the social distribution of a common concept, such as authority ranking. This way, space and – more specifically – architecture functions as a topographic means of ideological communication.

Taken together these points imply that the halls and west towers should not just be viewed as 'derived representations' of the power structure between the late Iron Age and Early Middle Ages. Rather, the significant status of these buildings suggests that they form a fundamental and constituent part of the social transmission and consolidation of the ideological structure prevailing at this point in time. In terms of material means to underline conceptual content, the spatial relational terms generated by architecture function very well as markers of social position, and the buildings were therefore not just a backdrop of social activity, but an intrinsic aspect of it. The cultural concept highlighting importance and control through certain types of physical presence would not function the same way without the tight connection to the spatial organisation of the buildings. Also the dialectic relation between the buildings themselves and the persons administering them underline the necessity of displaying social standing as material capability – these buildings were the true measure of authority.

Notes

1 For a culturally related example, but not geographically Scandinavian, the hall-building at Yeavering shows clear topographical parallels with the mentioned halls. It was purposefully erected on a small hilltop near the river Glen overlooking the Tweed valley and must therefore have been visible from afar (Hope-Taylor 1977, 14-15).

2 A contemporary construction of a platform seems to have taken place at Sanda (Åquist 1996), where the last renovation of the very stable hall-building results in the introduction of a stone-lined terrace at the beginning of the 11th century.

3 The particular configuration of the cultic side-houses in the eastern part of southern Scandinavia might be related to a regional practice, as open air ritual locations from the same period have been found in Jutland as well as in the middle of Sweden (Vædebro (unpubl.) or Götavi (Svensson 2008) for example). At least the small side-houses seem to dominate the cultic arena in Southeast Scandinavia.

4 Literally meaning 'the Greatest Bridge builder', and refers to the major bridges over the sacred river, Tiber, which was also a deity (Encyclopedia Britannica).
5 Due to the different references in the saga literature, Stefan Brink (1996:243) has pointed to the possible difference between hall (*hǫll*) and sal (*salr*). Halls must be the peasant banqueting hall within the house and sal the noble version characterized by a separate building. If so, the western houses could be interpreted as belonging to the peasant's group.
6 Even though it is not explicitly mentioned in the citation, most readers – myself included – will intuitively imagine the more important persons being seated in close proximity to the hosts (which most likely is the case). Perhaps this proclivity should be taken as a sign of the naturalness (or innate expectation) with which humans understand socially ordered space, not to mention the importance of embodied sentiments such as physical closeness or elevation.
7 Authors translation.

References

Andrén, A. 2002. 'Platsernas betydelse. Norrön ritual och kultplatskontinuitet.' In: K. Jennbert, A. Andrén & C. Raudevere (ed.): *Plats och praxis – studier av nordiske förkristen ritual*, 299-342.

Andrén, A. 2007. 'Behind Heathendom: Archaeological Studies of Old Norse Religion.' *Scottish Archaeological Journal, vol. 27(2)*, 105-38.

Anglert, M. 2006a. 'De tidigaste kristna kulthusen.' In M. Anglert, M. Artursson & F. Svanberg (eds.): *Kulthus & dödshus. Det ritualiserade rummets teori och praktik*. Stockholm: Riksantikvarämbetets Förlag, 167-80.

Anglert, M. 2006b. 'Vindinge, torpnam och kristen gårdskult.' In: S. Larsson (ed.): *Centraliteter. Människor, strategier och landskap*. Stockholm: Riksantikvarämbedets Förlag, 77-100.

Atran, S. 2002. *In Gods we Trust. The evolutionary landscape of religion*. Oxford: Oxford University Press.

Barnier A.J., J. Sutton, C.B. Harris & R.J. Wilson 2007. 'A conceptual and empirical framework for the social distribution of cognition: The case of memory.' *Cognitive Systems Research, vol. 9*, 33-51.

Barsalou, L. 1999. 'Perceptual symbol systems.' *Behavioral and Brain Sciences, vol. 22*, 577-609.

Barsalou, L. 2008. 'Grounded Cognition.' *Annual Review of Psychology, vol. 59*, 617-45.

Bechtel, W. & G. Graham (ed.). *A Companion to Cognitive Science*. Oxford: Blackwell Publishers Inc.

Beck, A.S. 2010. *Døre i vikingetidens langhuse. Et forsøg på at indtænke mennesket i bebyggelsesarkæologien*. Master Thesis in Prehistoric Archaeology, University of Copenhagen. http://www.bricksite.dk/User_files/4b696c1219856d63daf77b9ebb68baa1.pdf

Boëthius, G. 1932. Hallar, Tempel och Stavkyrkor. Studier till kännedomen om äldre nordisk monumentalarkitektur. *Studier från Zornska Instituttet fïr Nordisk och Jämförande Konsthistoria vid Stockholms Högskola VII*. Stockholm: C.E. Fritzes Förlag.

Bolvig, A. 1992. *Kirkekunstens storhedstid, om kirker og kunst i Danmark i romansk tid*. København: Gyldendal.

Boyer, P. 2001. *Religion Explained: The human instincts that fashion gods, spirits and ancestors*, London: William Heinnemann.

Bårdseth, G.A. 2009. 'The Roman Age Hall and the Warrior-Aristocracy: Reflections upon the Hall at Missingen, South-East Norway.' *Norwegian Archaeology Review, vol.42(2)*, 146-58.

Christensen, T. 1991. *Lejre – Syn og Sagn*, Roskilde: Roskilde Museum.

Christensen, T. 2008. 'Ældste Lejre?' *SKALK 2008(6)*, 18-24.

Christensen, P. M. 2009. 'Erritsø.' *SKALK 2009(4)*, 9-15.

Darwin, C. 1872. *The expression of the emotions in man and animals*. London: John Murray.

Day, M. 2004. 'Religion, Off-Line Cognition and the Extended Mind.' *Journal of Cognition and Culture. vol. 4(1)*, 101-21.

Dobat, A. S. 2006. 'The king and his cult.' *Antiquity, vol. 80(310)*, 880-93.

Doig, A. 2005. *Liturgy and architecture. From the Early Church to the Middle Ages*. Ashgate: Aldershot.

Firth, R. 1970. 'Postures and Gestures of Respect.' In: J.Pouillon, P. Maranda (eds.): *Échanges et Communications. Mélanges offerts à Claude Levi-Strauss à l'occasion de son 60ème Annivesaire*. Paris: Mouton, 188-209.

Fiske, A.P. 1991. *Structures of social life. The four elementary forms of human relations, communal sharing, authority ranking, equality matching, market pricing*. New York: Free Press.

Fiske, A.P. 2004. 'Four Modes of Constituting Relationships: Consubstantial Assimilation; Space, Magnitude, Time, and Force; Concrete Procedures; Abstract Symbolism.' In: Nick Haslam (ed.): *Relational Modes Theory. A contemporary overview*. London: Lawrence Erlbaum, 61-146.

Gabora, L. 2007. 'The cultural evolution of socially situated cognition.' *Cognitive Systems Research, vol. 9*, 104-114.

Gallese, V., & Lakoff, G. 2005. 'The brain's concepts: The role of the sensory-motor system in reason and language.' *Cognitive Neuropsychology, vol. 22*, 455-79.

Gansum, T. 2008. 'Hallene og stavkirkene – kultbygninger i en overgangstid.' In: K. Chilidis, J. Lund, C. Prescott (eds.): *Facets of archeology: essays in honour of Lotte Hedeager on her 60th birthday*. Oslo: Oslo University Press, 199-213.

Gibbs, R. 2006. *Embodiment and Cognitive Science*. Cambridge: Cambridge University Press.

Goffman, E. 1976. *Gender Advertisements*. New York: Harper Colophon.

Gummere. F.B. 1909. *The oldest English epic, Beowulf, Finnsburg, Waldere, Deor, Widsith, and the German Hildebrand*. New York: Macmillan.

Haslam, N. 1994. 'Categories of Social Relationship.' *Cognition, vol. 53*, 59-90.

Herschend, F. 1998. The Idea of the Good in Late Iron Age Society. (Occasional Papers in Archaeology 15). Uppsala: Uppsala University Press.

Herschend, F. 2001. *Journey of Civilisation. The Late Iron Age view of the human world*. (Occasional Papers in Archaeology, vol. 24). Uppsala: Uppsala University Press.

Herschend, F. 2009. *The Early Iron Age in South Scandinavia. Social Order in Settlement and Landscape*. (Occasional Papers in Archaeology 46). Uppsala: Uppsala University Press.

Herschend, F. & D.K. Mikkelsen 2003. 'The main building at Borg.' In: Munch, Gerd S., Olav S, Johansen & Else Roesdahl (ed.): *Borg in Lofoten. A chieftain's farm in North Norway*. Trondheim: Tapir Academic Press, 41-76.

Hewes, G.W. 1955. 'World Distribution of Certain Postural Habits.' *American Anthropology, vol. 57(2)*, 231-44.

Hillier, B. & J. Hanson 1984. *The social logic of space*. Cambridge: Cambridge University Press.

Hillier, B. J. Hanson & H. Graham 1987. 'Ideas are in things: an application of the space syntax method to discover house genotypes.' *Environment and Planning B: Planning and Design, vol. 14*, 363-85.

Hirth, K.G. 1992. 'Identifying Rank and Socioeconomic Status in Domestic Contexts: An example from Central Mexico.' In: R.S. Santley, K.G. Hirth (eds.): *Prehispanic Domestic Units in Western Mesoamerica. Studies of the Household, Compound, and Residence*. London: CRC Press. Pp. 121-46.

Hope-Taylor, B. 1977. *Yeavering. An Anglo-British centre of early Northumbria*. London: Butler & Tanner Ltd.

Hultgaard, A. 1992. 'Religiøs forandring. Kontinuitet och acculturation/syncretism i vikingetidens och medeltidens skandinaviske religion.' In: B. Nilson& S.Brink (eds.): *Kontinuitet i kult och tro från vikingetid til medeltid*. (Sveriges Kristnande 1). Uppsala; Lunne Böcker. pp. 49-103.

Hvass, S. 1980. Vorbasse. 'The Viking-age Settlement at Vorbasse, Central Jutland.' *Acta Archaeologica, vol. 50*, 137-72.

Hvass, S. 1983. 'Vorbasse – The Development of a Settlement through the First Millennium A.D.' *Journal of Danish Archaeology, vol. 2*, 127-36.

Jensen, S. 1987. 'Gårde fra vikingetiden ved Gl. Hviding og Vilslev.' *Mark og Montre 1986-87*, 5-26.

Jeppesen, J. 2005. 'Lisbjerg; Haldum; Egå.' In: A. Damm (ed.): *Vikingernes Aros. Historie, Kultur, Mytologi*. Jysk arkæologisk Selskab.

Jessen, M.D. *in press*: Material culture, embodiment and the construction of religious knowledge. In L.B. Jørgensen, J. Hughes, M.L.S. Sørensen & K. Salisbury-Rebay (eds.): *Embodied knowledge: technology and beliefs*. Oxford: Oxbow Books.

Jessen, M.D. & M.K. Holst 2008. Om Huse og Slægtskab i Skandinaviens Yngre Jernalder. *Jordens Folk – Etnografisk Tidsskrift, vol. 43(3)*, 44-51.

Jessen, M.D. & T. Egeberg, *forthcoming*: Agerhøj – om bebyggelse og vikingetid i Vestjylland.

Johannsen, N. 2010. 'Technological conceptualizations: Cognition on the Shoulders of History.' In: Malafouris, L., Renfrew, C. (eds.): *The Cognitive Life of Things. Recasting the boundaries of the mind*. Oxford: Oxbow Books, 59-69.

Jørgensen, L. 1998. 'En storgård fra vikingetid ved Tissø, Sjælland – en foreløbig præsentation.' In: Lars Larsson & Birgitta Hårdh (ed.): *Centrala platser, centrala frågor: samhällsstrukturen under järnåldern: en vänbok till Berta Stjernquist*. Stockholm: Almqvist & Wiksell International, 233-48.

Jørgensen, L. 2001. 'From tribute to the estate system, 3rd-12th century: a proposal for the economic development of the magnates' residences in Scandinavia based on settlement structure from Gudme, Tissø and Lejre.' In: B. Arrhenius (ed.): *Kingdoms and regionality: transactions from the 49th Sachsensymposium, 1998 in Uppsala*. Stockholm: Archaeological Research Laboratory. pp. 73-82.

Jørgensen, L. 2002. 'Kongsgård – kultsted – marked. Overvejelser omkring Tissøkomplekstets struktur og funktion.' In: K. Jennbert, A. Andrén & C. Raudevere (ed.): *Plats och praxis – studier av nordiske förkristen ritual*. Lund: Nordic Academic Press, 215-47.

Jørgensen, L. 2009. 'Pre-Christian cult at aristocratic residences and settlement complexes in southern Scandinavia in the 3rd -10th centuries AD.' In: U. von Freeden, H. Friesinger, E. Wamers (eds.) *Glaube, Kult und Herrschaft. Phänomene des Religiösen im 1. Jahrtausend n. Chr. in Mittel und Nordeuropa*. (Frankfurt, Kolloquien zur Vor- und Frühgeschichte Band 12). Bonn: Dr. Habelt Verlag, 329-54.

Jørgensen, L., J.F. Bican, L.G. Thomsen & X.P. Jensen 2003. 'Stormænd, Købmand og håndværkere ved Tissø I det 6-11. århundrede.' *Historisk Samfund for Holbæk Amt 2003*, 50-65.

Lakoff, G. & M. Johnson 1999. *Philosophy in the flesh. The embodied mind and its challenge to Western thought*. New York: Basic Books.

Larsson, L. 2006a: 'Ritual building and ritual space: aspects of investigations at the Iron Age central site Uppåkra, Scania, Sweden.' In: A. Andrén, K. Jennbert & C. Raudvere (eds): *Old Norse religion in long-term perspectives: origins, changes, and interactions: an international conference in Lund, Sweden, June 3-7, 2004*. Lund: Nordic Academic Press, 248-53.

Larsson, L. 2006b: 'Hall, harg eller hof. Ett kulthus i Uppåkra.' *Kulthus & dödshus. Det ritualiserade rummets teori och praktik*. Stockholm: Riksantikvarämbetets Förlag. pp. 143-52.

Larsson, L. 2007. 'The Iron Age ritual building at Uppåkra, southern Sweden.' *Antiquity, vol. 81(311)*, 11-25.

Larsson, L. & K.-M. Lenntorp 2004. 'The Enigmatic House.' In: L. Larsson (ed.): *Continuity for Centuries. A Ceremonial Building and its Context at Uppåkra, Southern Sweden*. (Acta Archaeologica Lundensia, Series in 8°, vol. 48/Uppåkrastudier vol. 10). Stockholm: Almqvist & Wiksell International, 3-48.

Lave, J. 1988. *Cognition in practice: Mind, mathematics, and culture in everyday life*. New York: Cambridge University Press.

Lenntorp, K.-M. & B. Hårdh 2009. 'Uppåkra, investigations in 2005-2008.' In: U. von Freeden, H. Friesinger, E. Wamers (eds.) *Glaube, Kult und Herrschaft. Phänomene des Religiösen im 1. Jahrtausend n. Chr. in Mittel und Nordeuropa*. (Frankfurt, Kolloquien zur Vor- und Frühgeschichte Band 12). Bonn: Dr. Habelt Verlag, 355-58.

Lidén, H.-E. 1969. 'From Pagan Sanctuary to Christian Church. The Excavation of Mære Church in Trøndelag.' *Norwegian Archaeological Review, vol. 2*, 2-32.

Lundqvist, L. 2000. *Slöinge 1992-1996. undersökningar av en boplats från yngre järnålder*. (GOTARC, Serie C, Arkeologiska skrifter, 42). Göteborg: Institutionen för arkeologi.

Lundström, A.1970. 'Find frequency.' In: W. Holmqvist (ed.): *Excavations at Helgö III. Report fir 1960-1964*. Stockholm: Kungl. Vitterhets, Historie och Antikvitets Akademien, 129-46.

Løken, T. 2001. 'Oppkomsten av den germanske hallen – Hall of sal i elder jernalder i Rogaland.' *Viking, vol. 64*. pp. 49-86.

Malafouris, L. 2008. 'Between brains, bodies and things: *tectonoetic* awareness and the extended self.' *Royal Society of London. Philosophical Transactions. Biological Sciences, vol. 363*, 1993-2002.

McGuire, B.P. 2008. *Da Himmelen kom nærmere: fortællinger om Danmarks kristning 700-1300*. Frederiksberg: Forlaget Alfa.

Nielsen, L.C. 1980. 'Omgård. A Settlement from the Late Iron Age and the Viking Period in West Jutland', *Acta Archaeologica, vol. 50*. pp. 173-208.

Nielsen, J.N. 2002. 'Bejdsebakken, a central place near Aalborg in Northern Jutland.' In: B. Hårdh & L. Larsson (eds.): *Central Places in the Migration and Merovingian Periods. Papers from the 52nd Sachsensymposium*, 197-213.

Nilsson, I.-M. 2003. 'Härskarsymbol och högsäte – om betydelsen av västmarkeringar i romanska kyrkor', META 2003(1), 31-49.

Nordahl, E. 1993. 'Södra Kungsgårdsplatån. Utgrävningarna 1988-1991.' In: Wladyslaw Duczko (ed.): Arkeologi och miljögeologi i Gamla Uppsala. Studier och rapporter. Occasional Papers in Archaeology 7. Societas Archaeologica Upsaliensis, Uppsala, 59-63.

Olsen, O. 1966. *Hørg, Hov og Kirke. Historiske og arkæologiske vikingetidsundersøgelser*. København: G.E.C. Gad.

Olsen, O. 1967. 'Rumindretningen i romanske landsbykirker.' *Kirkehistoriske Samlinger 1967*, 235-57.

Pentz, P. & P.Ø.Sørensen 2008. 'Ødelagt kultbæger?' *SKALK 2008(5)*, 24-26.

Price, N. 2002. *The Viking Way. Religion and war in late iron Age Scandinavia*. Uppsala: Uppsala University Press.

Pylyshyn, Z. 1984. *Computation and Cognition: Towards a Foundation for Cognitive Science*. Cambridge: MIT Press.

Pyysiäinen, I. 2001. *How religion works. Towards a new cognitive science of religion*. Leiden: Brill.

Renfrew, C. 1994. 'Towards a Cognitive Archaeology.' In: C. Renferw and E. Zubrow (eds): *The Ancient Mind: Elements of Cognitive Archaeology*. Cambridge: Cambridge University Press, 3-12.

Renfrew, C. 2004. 'Towards a theory of material engagement.' In: E. DeMarrais, C. Gosden & C. Renfrew (eds.) *Rethinking Materiality: the Engagement of Mind with the Material World*. Cambridge: McDonald Institute for Archaeological Research, 23-32.

Roepstorff, A. 2008. 'Things to think with: words and objects as material symbols.' *Royal Society of London. Philosophical Transactions. Biological Sciences, vol. 363*, 2049-54.

Sanmark, A. 2004. *Power and Conversion – a comparative study of Christianization in Scandinavia*. (Occasional Papers in Archaeology 43). Uppsala: Uppsala University Press.

Schmidt, H. 1992. 'Vikingetides huse.' *Nationalmuseets Arbejdsmark 1992*, 122-32.

Schmidt, H. 1999. *Vikingetidens byggeskik I Danmark*. Højbjerg: Jysk Arkæologisk Selskab.

Schwartz, B. 1980. *Vertical Classification. A Study in Structuralism and the Sociology of Knowledge*. Chicago: The University of Chicago Press.

Skre, D. 2007. 'Excavations of the hall at Huseby.' In: D. Skre (ed.): *Kaupang in Skiringssal*. (Norske Oldfunn 22). Aarhus: Aarhus University Press, 233-47.

Smith, E.R. 2008. 'Social relationships and groups: New insights on embodied and distributed cognition.' *Cognitive Systems Research, vol. 9*, 24-32.

Sundqvist, O. 2004. *Kultledera i fornskandinavisk religion*. (Occasional Papaer in Archeaology 41). Uppsala: Uppsala Universitet Press.

Sundqvist, O. 2006. 'Från vikingatida aristokratiska hallar till medeltida stormannakyrkor.' *Bebyggelseshistorisk Tidsskrift, vol. 52*, 20-32.

Sutton, J. 2008. 'Material Agency, Skills and History: Distributed Cognition and the Archaeology of Memory.' In: K. Knappett & L. Malafouris (eds.): *Material Agency: Towards a non-anthropocentric approach*. New York: Springer, 37-55.

Svensson, K. 2008. 'Götavi – en vikingatida kultplats.' In: A. Lagerstedt (ed.): *På väg genom Närke, ett landskap genom historien*. (Rapporter från Arkeologikonsult 2008). pp. 197-210.

Söderberg, B. 2003. 'Järnålderns Järrestad. Bebyggelse, kronologi, tolkningsperspektiv.' In: Bengt Søderberg (ed.): *Järrestad. Huvudgård i centralbygd*. Stockholm: Riksantikvarämbetet Förlag. pp. 109-74.

Söderberg, B. 2005. *Aristokratisk rum och gränsöverskridande. Järrestad och sydöatra Skåne mellan region och rike 600-1100*. Stockholm: Riksantikvarämbetet Förlag.

Sørensen, A.B. 1998. 'Sønderjyllands første Trelleborghus.' *Archaölogie im Schleswig, vol. 6*, 36-41.

Sørensen, A. B. 2003. 'Middelalderens fødsel – tiden 1000-1340 – huse, gårde og bebyggelser.' In: P. Ethelberg, N. Hardt, B. Poulsen & A.B. Sørensen (eds.): *Det Sønderjyske Landbrugs Historie – Jernalder, Vikingetid og Middelalder*. Haderslev: Haderslev Museum/Historisk Samfund for Sønderjylland. pp. 434-57.

Sørensen, P.Ø. 1994. 'Gudmehallerne. Kongeligt byggeri i jernalderen.' *Nationalmuseets Arbejdsmark 1999*, 25-39.

Tesch, S. 2007. 'Tidigmedaltida sepulkralstenar i Sigtuna.' *Sigtuna Dei 2007*, 45-68.

Thorpe, B. & I.A. Blackwell: *The Elder Edda of Saemund Sigfusson and the Younger Edda of Snorre Sturleson*. London: Norræna Society.

Tomasello, M. 1999. 'The Cultural Ecology of Young Children's Interactions with Objects and Artifacts.' In: E. Winograd, R. Fivush, W. Hirst (ed.): *Ecological Approaches to Cognition. Essays in Honour of Ulric Neisser*. London: Lawrence Erlbaum, 153-170.

Tomasello, M 2001. *The Cultural Origins of Human Cognition*. Cambridge, MA: Harvard University Press.

Tooby, J. & L. Cosmides 1992. 'The Psychological Foundations of Culture.' In: J. Barkow, L. Cosmides, J. Tooby (ed.): *The Adapted Mind: Evolutionary Psychology and the Generation of Culture*. New York: Oxford University Press, 19-136.

Toren, C. 1990. *Making sense of hierarchy. Cognition as social process in Fiji*. London: Athlone Press.

Tornbjerg, S. Å. 1998a. 'Toftegård ved Strøby: Arkæologiske udgravninger 1995-98 af en Stormandsbebyggelse.' *Køge Museum 1997*, 5-19.

Tornbjerg, S.Å. 1998b. 'Toftegård – en fundrig gård fra sen jernalder og vikingetid.' In: L.Larsson, B.Hårdh (eds.): *Centrala platser. Centrala frågor. Samhällsstrukturen under järnåldern*. Almqvist & Wiksell International, 217-32.

Warmind, M. 1999. 'Wyryld cyning – veraldargod. Magtens religiøse basis hos germanerne.' In: U. Drobin (ed.): *Religion och samhälle i det förkristna Norden. Ett symposium*. Odense: Odense Universitetsforlag, 229-43.

Watt, M. 1983. 'A Viking Age Settlement at Runegård (Grødby), Bornholm', *Journal of Danish Archaeology, vol. 2*, 137-48.

Wienberg, J. 1993. *Den gotiske labyrint. Middelalderen og kirkerne i Danmark*. (Lund Studies in Medieval Archaeology 11). Stockholm: Almqvist & Wiksell International.

Zachrisson, T. 2004. 'Det heliga på Helgö och dess kosmiska referenser.' In: Anders Andren, Kristina Jennbert & Catherine Raudvere (ed.): *Ordning mot kaos. Studier av nordisk förkristen kosmologi*. Lund: Nordic Academic Press, 243-87.

Åquist, C. 1996. 'Hall och harg. Det rituelle rummet.' In: K. Engdahl & A. Kaliff (eds.): *Religion från stenålder till medeltid*. (Riksantikvarämbetets Arkeologiske Undersökningar. Skrifter nr. 19). Linköping: Riksantikvarämbetet, 105-120.

In Small Things Remembered: Pottery decoration in Neolithic Southern Italy

John Robb & Kostalena Michelaki

Introduction

In 1977 James Deetz, one of the most creative pioneers of processual social archaeology, published a deceptively compact popular book on archaeology entitled *In Small Things Forgotten* (Deetz 1977).[1] Deetz argued that through looking attentively at the minutiae of daily life we can understand the cultural world of ancient people. Unfortunately, archaeologists have done poorly at understanding the small things of daily life. Our traditional rhetorical strategy has been to subordinate material to theory ruthlessly, culling the world of the past for vignettes illustrating currently popular themes. This, of course, relies upon a prior intuition as to which elements of the archaeological record are relevant to our chosen themes. Sadly, this strategy has the collateral effect of squeezing out of one's view things which do not conform to theoretical interests. For example, in the mainstream North American tradition (Hegmon 2003), the cultural world is partitioned between intentional actions by active individuals and the passive reproduction of cultural traditions, and it is the former which get harnessed to the grand themes of politics and change. British post-processualists have generally done better at critiquing these dualisms and at seeing material practices as meaningful. Agency here has generally been understood in terms of social reproduction. However, rather ironically considering the critique of grand narratives, the attention has focused on grand meanings: megaliths, human origins, cosmologies of life and death. In neither tradition has there been theoretical space for understanding agency in things which are habitual rather than intentional, meaningful but not salient, trivial rather than cosmological.

The goal of this paper is to tackle these small things, forgotten by archaeologists. To some extent this means opening oneself to the directions indicated by the archaeological record, much as Evans-Pritchard (1940) went to the Nuer to study social structure and found himself obliged to become an expert on cattle because that is what the Nuer themselves were interested in. To put the problem in concrete terms, our excavations of Neolithic sites in Calabria have yielded an abundance of decorated pottery. We cannot claim, *a priori*, that the way this pottery is decorated, through a happy coincidence, must tell us about the particular Important Anthropological Themes we wish to know about. But neither does this mean it is devoid of meaning and should be ignored, as archaeologists have in fact generally done. Hence the goal of this paper is to try to understand how Neolithic Southern Italians understood the process of decorating their pottery. While this is a vast topic, by a close reading of some pertinent examples, our goal is to explore not the meaning of pottery so much as the meaning of the process of creating pottery, particularly in focusing on the relation between tradition and creativity.

The context: Neolithic Southern Italy and its pottery decoration

The archaeological context of this study is the site of Penitenzeria, located at the southernmost tip of the Italian peninsula. The Neolithic began in Southern Italy around 6000 BC and lasted until about 3500 BC[2], and is well-known archaeologically. People grew and ate domesticated plants and animals, and made the basic repertory of Neolithic material things familiar throughout Europe: pottery, polished stone axes, wattle and daub houses, grinding stones, and a typologically

Fig. 1. Decorated Stentinello wares from Penitenzeria (Bova Marina, Calabria), ca. 5500-5000 BC (BMAP excavations).

simple blade-based lithic industry. Settlement varied; people lived in large ditched villages in some areas, in unditched villages in others and in small, dispersed settlements in others (Cazzella & Moscoloni 1992; Genick 1993; Cremonesi 1992; Malone 2003; Robb 2007)[3].

Our focus here in particular is the Stentinello pottery of Southern Calabria and Sicily, a regional derivative of Impressed Ware which remained in use from the early 6th millennium BC for at least a millennium until the mid-5th millennium. As investigated by the Bova Marina Archaeological Project from 1997 through the present, Southern Calabria was a mountainous and apparently sparsely populated region where people seem to have lived in very small, dispersed villages or even isolated houses. People inhabited a strip of land about 10 km wide between the sea and the apparently uninhabited high mountains of Aspromonte. However, social life was not entirely isolated. People living here could see other areas, such as Sicily across the Straits of Messina to the west, and they participated in a flourishing trade in obsidian, by which obsidian from nearby Lipari passed through their territory to move throughout Southern Italy, the Adriatic, and even Croatia 1000 km away.

Penitenzeria is a site barely 50 meters square where people lived for a few hundred years between circa 5500 and 5000 BC. Excavation has located a thick midden deposit but no structures. However, the site is delimited by cliffs and rock outcrops on all sites, and given the use of space on other Neolithic sites, it cannot have been inhabited by more than a few families at the most. Some daub with stick and reed impressions was found, confirming the presence of houses at the site. Pending further research, the best interpretation of the site is a small cluster of a house or houses; such structures tend to be relatively ephemeral archaeologically unless conditions are favorable for the preservation of house daub, but a spatially concentrated occupation left a dense midden which seems to have been deposited relatively rapidly – up to a meter in the space of less than four centuries. Palaeobotanical and faunal remains reveal a typical Neolithic economy based upon domesticated crops and animals. Over 90 % of the lithics were made of obsidian almost certainly from Lipari, showing an active participation in a regional trade network.

By and large, Neolithic Italian pottery has not fared well at the hands of archaeologists. Italian prehistorians have normally made pottery a focus of intensive and detailed study. However, they have traditionally regarded pottery as a culture-historical indicator of a shared "culture" and used it to trace migrations and less concrete cultural "influences" exerted by one region upon another. More recently, it has been used principally as a chronological indicator for constructing cultural sequences and dating sites. While both approaches are useful, both incur theoretical liabilities in the way of questionable assumptions and neither sheds much light upon the social reasons of why people made pottery in the ways they did. Using pottery as an indication of cultural affiliation, for instance, disregards variation and social choice within an assemblage; using pottery for dating leaves most of any assemblage except for the type fossils uninterpreted. Most Anglo-American archaeologists over the last several decades have failed to engage with pottery as a theoretical topic. Malone (1985) has argued that some pottery styles were prestige wares used for long-distance trade and ritual practices. Although thin-section analyses have uniformly shown that pottery was locally made (Muntoni 2003; Spataro 2002), this usefully opened up the question of contextual usage, particularly of elaborately ornate finewares such as Serra d'Alto wares. Skeates (1998) and Pluciennik (1997) have similarly argued that Neolithic pottery must be analyzed as meaningful material culture. Both present arguments quite compatible with our focus here, particularly with Skeates' contextualised biography of red-painted pottery in the Abruzzo and with Pluciennik's view that pottery constituted a sphere of meaningful social action for particular groups of social actors. However, these stimulating beginnings have not really been followed through with systematic and detailed interpretation.

Pottery, of course, can be analysed from many different angles. Here we want to choose just one focus, that of surface decoration. Pottery decoration has been the archaeologists' *bête noire*. For many of us, pottery makes up the vast majority of our finds. Its decoration is highly variable. It is a completely plastic medium and the decoration cannot be ascribed to any simple practical necessity. Hence pottery decoration demands interpretation. But in spite of a vast range of stylistic, symbolic and ethnoarchaeological analyses (Hegmon 1992; Hegmon 1998; Rice 1987), it is difficult to think of an archaeological phenomenon which is more obviously socially variable and less frequently interpreted to our satisfaction. We would argue that this partly results from a flawed idea of symbols and agency. Archaeologists have tended to assume that when we investigate symbols, their meanings should be large meanings, socially salient, central to social reproduction, cosmologically central, part of a master discourse of some sort: prestige, hierarchy, cosmological order, ancestry. Given this, one has either to tie pottery decoration to such grand themes explicitly (for example Hodder 1982) in a way which unconvincingly magnifies its salience in daily life, or succumb to the lurking suspicion that pottery decoration was, basically, unimportant wallpaper. Neither does justice to the phenomenon. Our goal in this paper is to force open a theoretical space somewhere between intention and structure, between strategy and tradition, where we can understand the material agency of things like pottery.

Pottery as creative action

In a broad sense, our approach to pottery here is to regard it as a social technology, an act of doing in which people exercise agency (Dobres 2001; Michelaki 2006). In pursuing this, one must shift the focus from the final product (the fired pot, used, broken, deposited, recovered and analysed archaeologically) to the process of potting. Over several generations, a handful of potters at the tiny village at Penitenzeria made a series of small bowls. In doing so, they exercised skill, manual and aesthetic reflexes, and critical judgment. It is by probing these qualities of action that we can begin to understand why and how they decorated their vessels as they did.

Skill

To begin with an obvious fact somewhat obscured by the very abundance of pottery in archaeological contexts: Italian Neolithic potting was a seriously regarded craft. The scale of production was probably small; a few potters producing just enough for the village's needs would probably have made at most 10-20 vessels each per year (following Perlés's & Vitelli's (1995) arguments for the Greek Early Neolithic). Though potters would have been recognized for their skills, we cannot imagine potters to have been true economic specialists. Nevertheless, making pots represented a substantial commitment of activity. As a task, potting was embedded in time, space, and material projects. Making a pot committed the potter to a program of several weeks of seasonal activity (it was probably a dry-season task, carried out between spring and autumn), and to composing a range of places, materials, and social relationships. The extended *chaîne operatoire* (Cassano, Muntoni & Barbaro 1995) began with a careful selection of clays from the dozen or so identifiable clay sources available around Penitenzeria. All of these look superficially identical, but only some work well for making impasto pottery; producing *figulina* finewares required knowledge of a specific kind of clay probably found at a single outcrop in the vicinity. Clay was probably ground to powder on grinding stones and mixed with water hauled from nearby springs. Temper (typically crushed metamorphic rock) had to be gathered from several kilometers away and prepared. The paste had to be prepared appropriately for the vessel's use. Potters made at least half a dozen different fabrics. While there was a broad central ground of impasto fabrics with variations of temper, some of which were probably interchangeable, some wares were used for different styles of vessel (e.g. *figulina* wares), and others seem to have been adapted to specific tasks such as cooking wares. The whole process was a series of knowledgeable involvements.

Fig. 2. A "learning sherd"; decoration is slightly less regular than on most sherds and pattern is unusual; inside surface of bowl (not shown) is highly irregular and lumpy (BMAP excavations, Penitenzeria).

Potters took care to create smooth, symmetrically formed, well-finished, thin-walled vessels. In hand-built ceramics, as potters learn their craft, their wares typically become marked by a number of recognizable traits, including the ability to construct larger and more complex vessels, a greater control of symmetry, an even and thin wall thickness, an even rim thickness, and a consistent and attractive surface polish (Kamp 2001). The high level of skill attained by the Penitenzeria potters is marked clearly by the presence of all of these attributes in their works (and underscored by their absence in our own attempts to replicate Stentinello pottery). Not only skill was required but commitment of time; smoothing and scraping the walls to a uniform thinness can take much more time than actually forming the bowl in the first place. A carefully prepared vessel of regular thickness has a greater chance of firing successfully, and the results of this application of skill are immediately visible in the finished product.

Manual craft skills such as how to form a ceramic paste, mold it, decorate it and fire it are taught and conserved in highly local "communities of practice" (Sassaman & Rudolphi 2001). People learn and maintain traditions by working together. That the process was taught to learners (whether children or adult) at Penitenzeria is suggested by one example of a learner's vessel (Figure 2). Here the different stages of the pottery-making process are carried out with different levels of skill. The fabric is fine and identical to that of many other vessels, and may well have been mixed up as part of a large batch by a fully skilled potter. But the vessel is formed poorly; the interior remains lumpy and irregular; uneven wall thickness is often a mark of unskilled but learning potters (Crown 2001). Motor habits such as forming vessels are more difficult to acquire than decorative schemas (Gosselain 1998). Here, while the surface is well-smoothed, the design follows a rudimentary and non-standard layout, although its execution is credible and only slightly more irregular than that of most bowls. Finally, the pot has been successfully fired. Firing pots successfully in an open fire requires skill and experience, and it seems likely that this pot was fired by a more skilled potter as part of a batch. Given the general high quality of fine bowls here, the decision to fire it at all is somewhat surprising, and perhaps an additional indication that a learning potter made it; a more accomplished potter might instead have either remodeled it or consigned it to the scrapheap unfired.

As an anthropological topic, skill is often overlooked; perhaps because we live in a world of specialized labor and standardized material products, we take for granted that ancient people bothered to do things to a stringent and often functionally superfluous standard. This is all the more so when it involves a form of labor we may not perceive as valuable due to gender or other biases (contrast the literature on food preparation with that on hunting, for example). However, technological action is an important exercise of agency; it involves the ongoing engagement of the worker's body, mind, and reflexes with the constantly changing material world (Dobres 2001). In this case, the experience of our Neolithic potters is evident in a highly patterned archaeological assemblage; they were able to match the paste of the fabric with the vessel form, firing procedure, and intended function. Here, we note two pertinent examples of skill, motor actions and timing. Skill is a matter of forming bodily reflexes in conformity with the material world (Ingold 2000). Through training, motor skills become internalized and automatic; the hand knows how to act (Minar & Crown 2001). As noted above, in learning to be a Neolithic potter, one had to acquire the motor reflexes to create thin-walled vessels with walls and rims of even thickness; as the surviving fragments show correction of errors only rarely, these tasks were regularly performed with high accuracy. Secondly, timing is a key element of strategic practice (Bourdieu 1977). Here, as the process of making a specific pot unfolded, potters exercised the keen sense of timing needed to form, decorate and fire clay. Each operation had to be carried out when the paste was at a specific level of moistness, in effect within windows of sometimes less than an hour in a process that extended over several days; as the nascent vessel was continually drying, the potter had to monitor it and act promptly when the moment was right. For example, a pot larger than a medium-sized bowl or a pot of a complex, composite form would have to be made in stops and starts; the lower section would have to dry before it could support the weight of a heavy upper section, and pieces such as necks and bodies would have to dry slightly before being fitted together. Similarly, impressing decoration had to be done after an interval of drying but before the clay hardened too much. The same was true of burnishing, which had to be done when the body was leather-hard, with the additional proviso that the drier the surface, the glossier the resulting shine would be but the less forgiving of mis-strokes the burnished surface would be.

Knowledge and ability can serve as social capital and components of identity. As Sinclair (1995) points out, the ability to execute tasks involving intricate senses of timing, manual control, or planning can be considered iconic of valued personality characteristics such as patience, decisiveness or strength. In Italian Neolithic pottery, some of the more technically ambitious vessels, particularly among the painted buff figulina wares which required a very careful selection and control of clays, coloring agents, and firing, may have been attempted not in spite of but because of their ostentatious difficulty. To the larger community one's identity may have been enhanced by the ability to provide the pottery vessels needed for daily life and social interaction. To the "community of practice" of potters, mastery of these motor and aesthetic skills through long experience would have marked one as an important member of a closely-knit group. All of this suggests the potter as agent: working the material world as creation of the self.

How to create a design: tradition and creativity

So what did our skillful agents actually do? In our assemblage of about 450 rims, there is clearly a modal bowl, a standard formal pattern (Figure 3a). The great majority of the decorated bowls at Penitenzeria whose fragments are large enough to make out the decoration scheme can be seen as a variation upon this basic pattern. Around the rim is a band of interrupted decoration in which small blocks of one stamped motif, usually parallel zig-zag lines or grids, alternate with blocks of other motifs. Below this is an empty space. Below this is an uninterrupted band whose middle is made of zig-zags, fringed upon the top and bottom with a line of stamped motifs, usually triangles. Each pot in a living assemblage necessarily references all other pots in the assemblage; it is clear that designs at Penitenzeria, a site occupied for a discrete span of a few generations, vary much less than they do at Umbro, a nearby site occupied for over a millennium.

Paradoxically, however, at the same time as it is evident that the bowls share a common design, no bowl conforms to it exactly (Figure 3b). It is probably more accurate to see these vessels not as reproducing a single design, a sort of Neolithic blue willow plate, so much as sharing generative rules for how to go about putting together a design. In this sense the potter's reflexes were a kind of habitus (Dietler & Herbich 1998). These generative rules included both prescriptions – "decoration is denser closer to the rim"; "decoration is arranged in horizontal bands which can be broken into segments", and so on – and norms for how much one could –

Fig. 3. (a) the "modal" bowl at Penitenzeria (freehand sketch by J. Robb). (b) range of design variation in actual bowl rims from Penitenzeria (BMAP excavations)

indeed, should – vary the design. While precise quantification is impossible due to the highly fragmented nature of the pottery assemblage, we have the visual impression that almost no small-medium decorated bowl reproduces our hypothetical template exactly, but nor do many vary from this template by more than about three alterations of pattern or substitutions of motif. Thus, the potter's reflex was to improvise creatively within well-defined boundaries, to recombine techniques, motifs, and grammars to create novel designs. No two vessels are ever alike – but creativity and innovation took place within narrow and well-defined limits.

Archaeologically, one important effect of this process is that "potting communities" (*Ibid.*) tended to form distinctive local micro-styles. This is a feature of Stentinello wares often noted (Ammerman 1985; Leighton 1999; Maniscalco & Iovino 2002; Morter 1992); for a parallel example from the Tyrrhenian coast, see Cuda & Murgano (2002). For example, on vessels made in other areas where Stentinello style pottery was used, bands of decoration around the rim were almost always continuous and unbroken. At Penitenzeria, the motifs used in rim bands could be changed, but they conformed to a common local norm that such bands should be discontinuous.

This prolific habit of recombining elements and techniques to create difference is also visible on larger scales too. Between 5500 and 5000 BC, Neolithic Southern Italians decorated their pots in a remarkably florid and varied range of styles; recognized styles in use during this period include several distinct kinds of Impressed Wares, Passo di Corvo bichrome painted wares, Catignano trichrome wares, Matera Scratched Wares, Monte Venere wares, and Stentinello wares, and there may have been early examples of trichromes such as Scaloria, Capri, Ripoli or Serra d'Alto wares too. But while most styles can be associated with a general region, the boundaries between them are normally hazy and potters clearly worked across archaeological "styles". While potters can and do learn new styles, possibly the most important vector of exchanging knowledge about techniques and styles was the movement of potters themselves, generally over short distances but sometimes into surprisingly distant communities (Dietler & Herbich 1998, Gosselain 1998, MacEachern 1998). In Italian Neolithic assemblages, this is likely to be one reason why quite distinctive wares are found on most sites – for example the buff finewares found in combination with Stentinello wares on many sites. Beyond this, we can sometimes spot "mutant sherds" which represent actual acts of recombination. In one example from Matera, someone working within the Matera tradition of scratched decoration, normally used to execute rigidly geometrical designs, tried out a bold non-geometrical design borrowed from trichrome painted pots. In another example from Ariano Irpino, a common Impressed Ware scheme of decorating a vessel with rim bands of "c" shaped impressions was painstakingly reproduced by scratching each motif. Occasionally these recombinations resulted in evanescent local micro-styles. Painted and impressed wares were used together throughout Southern Italy in the 6th millennium, but they seem to have been recognized as distinct kinds of pots and painting and impressing were never combined on vessels. However, for a brief period around the time when painting was introduced, before this rule became standard, one finds potters in central and northern Puglia and the Materano experimenting with using the two techniques together. Similarly, rocker stamping was used all over Italy, but virtually exclusively for large, heavy vessels with decoration randomly spread over their surface. In a small area of Southern Puglia, a miniature version of rocker stamping was substituted as a motif into geometric fineware patterns carried out elsewhere with other impressions.

To summarise, thus, for much of the Early and Middle Neolithic in Italy, the potter's reflex was the regulated, rule-bound creation of difference. That this is not a universal aspect of pottery-making but something culturally specific will be discussed below. The archaeological result of this creative process is nested micro-local, local and regional styles – or fractal styles, if you will. From the archaeologists' point of view, this creates a nightmare. There is an incredible diversity of recognizable but fuzzily bounded styles. But this diversity is cross-cut by shared grammars, common motifs, and family resemblances. Styles such as Ripoli wares (Cremonesi & Tozzi 1985) and Stentinello wares persist for millennia but they constantly evolve. There are distinct and robust patterns visible in the material ("painting is never combined with impressing on a single vessel"; "designs are always denser near the rim"), but it is impossible to define unbreakable rules; somebody was always willing to make an exception. Such inconsiderate habits have caused much wasted ink among pottery typologists. Or, to put it another way, we have yet to tailor our methodologies to fit the specific material these humans generate through their creative tendencies to generate difference. Theoretically, the kind of variation observed, both within a single assemblage such as at Pen-

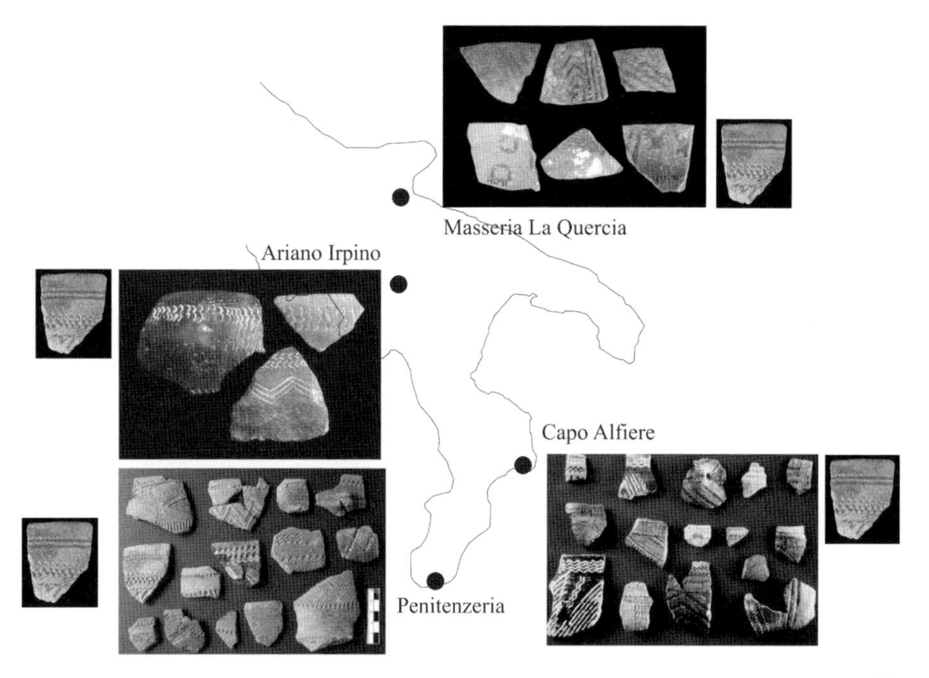

Fig. 4. Same vessel seen in different contexts, all 6th millennium BC. From south to north: (a) decorated bowl from Penitenzeria in its native assemblage, see also Figure 1 (BMAP excavations); (b) Northern Calabrian variety of Stentinello wares, Capo Alfiere (photo Jon Morter); (c) contemporary Incised and Impressed wares, La Starza di Ariano Irpino, Campania (Cambridge University Museum of Archaeology and Anthropology); (d) contemporary painted buff *figulina* wares, Masseria La Quercia, Puglia (Ashmolean Museum, Oxford).

itenzeria and regionally, can be understood only by seeing the potters as creative agents working within, but sometimes against, ongoing traditions.

The phenomenology of potting: Local knowledge

How would pottery decoration have been perceived and understood by Neolithic people? Here we are not focusing upon any potential quasi-iconographic meaning of particular motifs, which we regard both as probably unrecoverable archaeologically and as not necessarily the most salient aspect of decoration in any case. Rather, in keeping with our focus upon the ordinariness of small things, we are interested in considering Neolithic people's general ability to recognize a design as familiar and make sense of it, as part of their fleeting and everyday acts of perception.

To make a pot, potters played with distinctions within the most local frame of reference. We have the constant multiplication of small differences, which creates nested traditions, styles, and micro-styles, a sort of fractal style. However, one's ability to "read" these differences would depend on sharing the frame of reference, the context, of the potter and his or her community. For example, Figure 4 shows a sherd from Penitenzeria, placed in a series of contrasts representing different potential frames of reference at increasing distance northwards from the site (for site descriptions for collections used, see Jones 1987; Morter 1992; Trump 1963). To someone who lived at the site – at least, someone concerned with pottery decoration enough to examine it carefully – the minute distinctions between pots made by different potters would probably have been as individual as the style of someone's writing is to us. Judging by the differences between the neighboring sites of Penitenzeria and Umbro, there seem to have been minute but consistent differences even between very close communities. Someone whose frame of reference was another Stentinello community – perhaps someone from another micro-style area such as the Catania, Siracusa or Crotone areas – would probably have perceived many familiar techniques and motives but a distinctly Calabrian grammar. For example, Stentinello pottery from Sicily tends to have more densely covered surfaces and continuous decorative bands formed from one or two elements rather than broken bands in which motifs alternate. Going further afield, to someone whose frame of reference was the Matera Scratched Ware zone or the refined geometrical Impressed Ware found in Puglia, Stentinello pots would have included generically comprehensible geometric arrays etched into dark surfaces, with a salient difference being the principal technique used to carry out these. Yet further afield, a traveler from the Adriatic coast where most finewares were then being made of buff painted wares may well not have picked up on any of these distinctions within the vast western world of dark impressed bowls.

The point is that every pot incorporated layers of distinction whose penetration depended on local knowledge. One parallel here is with landscapes; it is the locals who know the hidden histories and unseen burials of each piece of land which a stranger sees as generic landscape. Socially, this is not a trivial point. What is central is the link between knowledge, agency, and identity. If academics understand any theme about agency from our own experience, it is that knowledge is a negotiable field of discourse which people mobilize in action and which validates their identity claims. Part of any social interaction – often unconscious but always fundamental to communication and social positioning – is evaluating what our interlocutors know and think about something and how it compares to our own understanding. Shared knowledge is co-identity, gaps in knowledge mark social difference.

If this is so, then Neolithic pottery could not be understood in absolute terms; its meaning was context-dependent, and its context, in turn, was relational, e.g. it was an element of the relationship between the person viewing it and the person making it. Hence, making, and interpreting, a complexly decorated pot was situated agency, agency qualified by identity, history and circumstance. Unlike social information models of style (Wobst 1977), our potters are not signaling pre-constituted identities to people who do not know them. For one thing, much of the fine distinctions are visible only when a pot is not being used, and from close up. This implies that if they are intentionally aimed at anyone, it would be in a context of close inspection and discussion rather than the casual user. Rather, our potters here are colluding with others who understand their pottery to continually reconstitute a field of knowledgeable discourse within which they can think of themselves and be acknowledged as efficacious agents. And it was a local and situated field of discourse.

Some concluding thoughts: Agency, aesthetics, and long term change

To sum up this discussion, let's return to the dreaded question, "What did Neolithic pottery decoration mean?" If we follow the classic Saussurean definition of a symbol, it is doubtful that these patterns "meant" anything in particular. Even if they did carry some explicit iconography now lost to us, this may not have been the real point of the decoration. Instead, we have focused upon two particular aspects of Neolithic potting: the exercise of skill, and the manipulation of difference in creating decoration. In both of these, potters both worked within a community of practice and negotiated their relationship to that community and the ceramic tradition it reproduced. Agency worked in the space between individual and collective, between strategic and traditional. Moreover, pottery decoration constituted a very local form of discourse, and, as with any stock of local cultural capital, the ability to understand it was a measure of the relationship between people. The fact that this form of cultural capital was not harnessed to an exchanged product, political hierarchy, or ritual status does not mean it was not important to people's sense of local identity. In some ways, it is precisely because pottery decoration was a basic background element of ordinary social life – a small thing forgotten – that it formed a persuasive part of the construction of social reality.

We thus have a paradoxical, but, we believe, quite common situation where the principal purpose of exercising that agency was to maintain a field of discourse within which such agency could be exercised. The agency of Neolithic potters throws into relief several important characteristics of agency (see Robb 2007 for more extensive discussion). First, it is culturally defined within specific fields of meaningful action and kinds of persons. We cannot talk about social agency in the abstract as a pure substance or force, like gravity or electricity; we have to understand the agency of being a potter, or a politician, or a parent: each on their own terms and without automatically prioritizing one over another. Secondly, agency is material. Acting materially is not a transparent process of shaping inert matter to a higher will. Rather, material media and their rules enable people to engage in creative activity, and to act creatively we need to embrace the nature of the medium as we construct it. Carrying out a material activity requires belief, commitment, social relations, long-term projects. And our action shapes us in return, by requiring us to acquire knowledge or skill, or by creating long-term social commitments. Hence, pursuing a field of material action becomes at the same time a project of the self: being a potter, as opposed to making a pot. Thirdly, agency is always situated. In strategic models of agency we sometimes are presented with actors who propose to act universally, without constraint or local frame of reference. But this is wrong. People are situated in specific histories and circumstances; action is planned and judged relative to who you are, what situations you are in and what choices you are presented with. Finally, if agency is always relative to a specific field of action; it follows that there must be multiple kinds of agency in any society. If agency relates to different modes of cultural action, it makes perfect sense to suppose that individuals can alternate between multiple forms of agency. Consider ritual; many rituals create spaces to act as different kinds of being temporarily. The same is true for political authority.

This leads to a final ramification of our argument – the question of how different elements of social life relate to each other. As noted above, one traditional approach to the archaeological record is to assume that one or another theme – typically ecology, political process or cultural structure – provides the real bottom

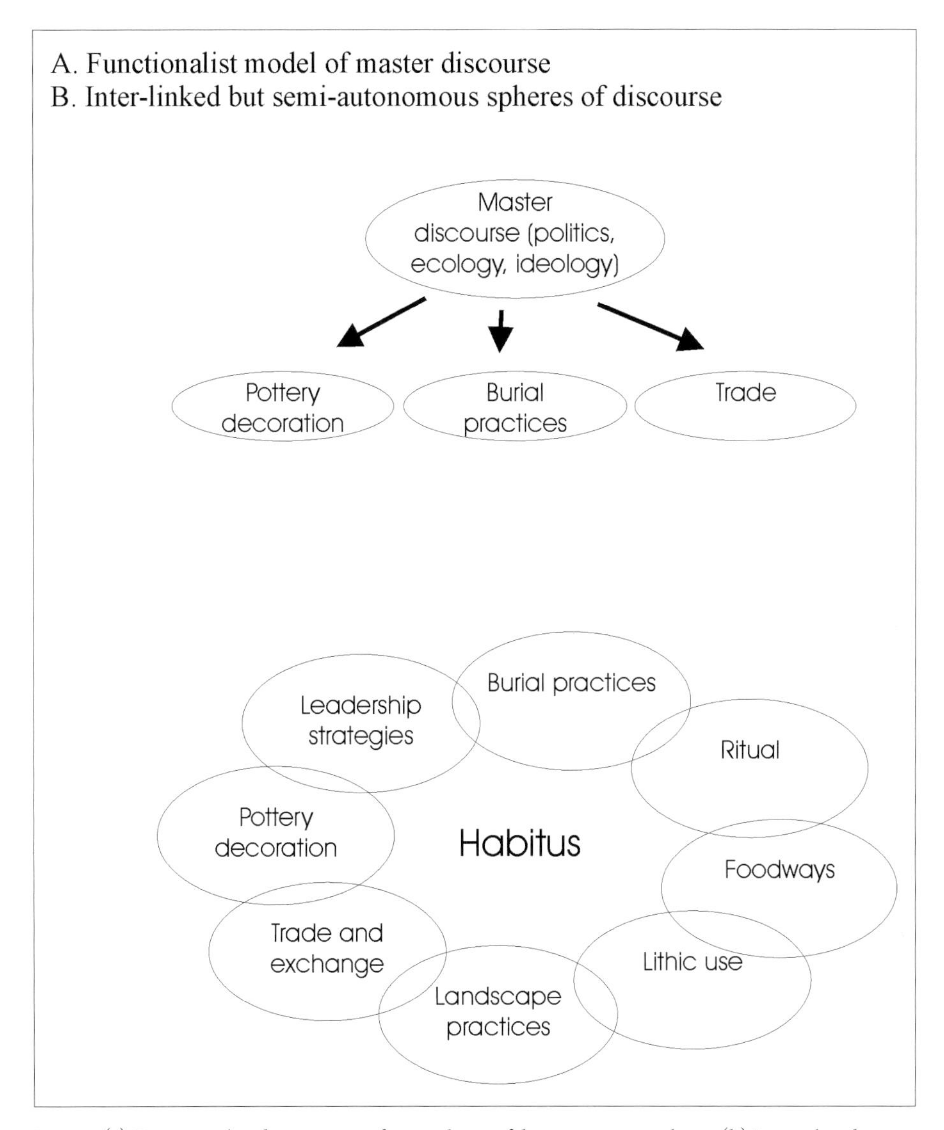

Fig. 5. (a) Functionalist dominance of one sphere of discourse over others; (b) Interrelated, semi-autonomous spheres of discourse.

line for interpretation and to reduce other elements of social life to manifestations or props for it. At the very least, methodologically, we need to understand how pottery worked semantically in human terms before using it for chronology or political analysis. However, unless we are specifically and narrowly interested in pottery decoration *per se*, it is useful to get beyond the phenomenology of pottery to social analysis. The question here is how different areas of agency relate to each other (Figure 5).

Early-Middle Neolithic	Late-Final Neolithic
creation of difference	creation of ceramic similarity
spatially distinct gender symbolism	spatially merged gender symbolism
no common axis of prestige symbolism	common axis of prestige symbolism
trade little and not central to politics	trade increased and integrated into politics

Fig. 6. General contrast of Early-Middle and Late-Final Neolithic in Southern Italy.

Here we will just sketch out a very rapid capsule example, the parallel changes in pottery style and in social organization which mark the end of the Neolithic. This transition in Italy is broadly similar to elsewhere in the Mediterranean, both in terms of pottery decoration styles with the replacement of ornate finewares with plain, often glossy black and red surfaces, and in social organization with a shift to more extended social networks, elaborated burial and trade (Sherratt 1984; 1994).

The kind of pottery we have been discussing, with the proliferation of small-scale differences to create layers of local knowledge, is stylistically heterarchical (Ehrenreich, Crumley & Levy 1995). Because the designs are polythetic and complex, there is no clear single axis of evaluation possible. In comparing any two vessels, there are always common elements to serve as the basis for some relationship and differences to mark social distinction. If we, somewhat artificially, identify a cultural reflex it embodies, it is this heterarchical proliferation of difference. There are other elements which suggest a generally heterarchical organization of agencies in Neolithic Italy (Robb 2007). One is spatially distinct gender symbolizations, with male and female referencing in distinct zones. Another is the lack of anything which looks like a simple, stereotyped axis of prestige, for instance in grave goods. A third is the evidence for heterogeneity in other forms of material culture, notably figurines. Finally, there is the lack of integration of trade into anything which looks like political authority (Morter & Robb 1998; Robb 1994a; 1994b; 2007). In effect, we may have had ritual, trade, material production, and so on, as quite distinct contexts of meaning, identity and power, possibly existing in tension (Figure 6).

Now consider late Neolithic pots in the so-called Diana style (approximately 4400-3600 BC), named after the type site on Lipari (Brea & Cavalier 1960) (Figure 7). Pots like this are basically identical and immediately recognizable over a huge area of Southern Italy and Sicily. Their hallmark is a plain, undecorated, surface, the only adornment is a stereotypical tubular spool-shaped handle (*ansa a rocchetta*) which would have been as immediately recognizable to Neolithic people as it is even to beginning archaeologists; the fineware bowls with red surfaces are particularly distinctive.

Fig. 7. Diana style Late Neolithic wares from Umbro (Bova Marina, Calabria), later 5th millennium BC (BMAP excavations).

What changed? Potters still worked in small local communities of practice, but micro-styles vanished, and this suggests that the link between the potter's production and the tradition it referenced changed. Diana vessels are as carefully and skillfully made as earlier pots – indeed, though they are less ornate, they may have taken more labor to make, as burnishing is a highly time-consuming part of the *chaîne opératoire* – but the goal is different. All surface decoration has been abolished. Instead of an aesthetic of finely tuned difference and layers of local knowledge, the new aesthetic is one of unlayered identification and superficial interchangeability. Effectively, the intention is an immediate recognizability and transactability liberated from the involutions of local knowledge. What pottery surface decoration was intended to accomplish was ready conformity with an inter-regional shared "look".

Again, the social context suggests that this change in aesthetic reflex was mirrored in other spheres of agency (Robb 2007). Most obviously, the obsidian exchange system expanded greatly, with more obsidian moving further. Spatially, people occupied new areas of highlands and offshore islands, probably through pastoral use. The reorganization of burial suggests an increasing emphasis upon genealogy as a form of relating people, and there is the beginning of recognizable axes of prestige distinction in burials which emerge fully in the Copper Age. These have been interpreted as the reorganization of social networks from a heterarchical Great Man-like situation of multiple, narrowly-defined competences to one of fewer, more generalized bases of prominence. The glossy, uniform, reflective look of highly burnished surfaces may itself embody a new synaesthetic association between social value and brightness or gleam.

We are thus not talking about social organization in a structural-functionalist sense so much as cultural styles or reflexes for dealing with multiple agencies. Effectively, the Late Neolithic was the great simplification around fewer, more generalized dimensions of social comparison and evaluation (Robb 1999; 2007). Heterarchy was not replaced by hierarchy; there is little evidence for hierarchy in the Late Neolithic, and heterarchy is common in all societies. But it is simply a different kind of heterarchy, one marked less by the creation of difference and more by isomorphic elements competing for parity. And this change in social reproduction had long-term consequences. Intensification of the Early-Middle Neolithic world ideologically results in something like Malta in the temple period (Robb 2007). Intensification of the Late-Final Neolithic system of social reproduction yields something like the early stratified societies of the Bronze Age. Hence cultural style – a set of reflexes reproduced through pottery decoration among other forms of social action – was an integral element of long-term trajectories of change.

Acknowledgments

We are grateful to our colleagues in the Bova Marina Archaeological Project and to Ruth Whitehouse, Robin Skeates and Mark Pluciennik for discussion of these topics. We thank the *Soprintendenza Archeologica della Calabria*, the Cambridge University Museum of Archaeology and Anthropology, the Ashmolean Museum, and the various funding bodies who have funded our excavations at Penitenzeria and Umbro. John Robb gratefully acknowledges the Leverhulme Trust for a Research Fellowship (2001-2002) which enabled travel and study of Neolithic pottery in museums throughout Southern Italy, and thanks the organizers and fellow participants in the Aarhus conference for a stimulating occasion to discuss these ideas.

Notes

1 We use this title in homage, as for one of us (JR) Deetz's book was a wonderful first introduction to archaeology, and with two decades' retrospect on the development of North American archaeological theory we see it as an important road not taken.
2 All dates discussed in this article are based upon calibrated radiocarbon dates.
3 Robb (2007) provides a broad introduction to the archaeology of the Italian Neolithic.

References

Ammerman, A. J. 1985. *The Acconia Survey: neolithic settlement and the obsidian trade*. London: Institute of Archaeology.

Brea, L.B. & M. Cavalier 1960. *Meligunís Lipàra. Volume I: La stazione preistorica della contrada Diana e la necropoli preistorica di Lipari*. Palermo: S. F. Flaccovio.

Bourdieu, P. 1977. *Outline of a Theory of Practice*. Cambridge: Cambridge University Press.

Cassano, S.M., I. Muntoni & C.C. Barbaro 1995. *Dall'argilla al vaso: fabbricazione della ceramica in una comunità neolitica di settemila anni fa*. Rome: EAN.

Cazzella, A. & M. Moscoloni 1992. *Neolitico ed eneolitico*. Rome: Biblioteca di Storia Patria.

Cremonesi, R.G. 1992. 'Il Neolitico nell'Italia Centrale e in Sardegna', In: A. Guidi, M. Piperno (eds.), *Italia Preistorica*. Roma: Laterza, 306-33.

Cremonesi, G. & C. Tozzi 1985. 'Il Neolitico dell'Abruzzo.' *Atti, Riunione Scientifica dell'I.I.P.P.* 26, 229-38.

Crown, P.L. 2001. 'Learning to make pottery in the prehispanic American Southwest.' *Journal of Anthropological Research*, 57, 451-70.

Cuda, M.T. & R. Murgano 2002. 'Il sito neolitico di Sovereto di Nicotera (RC).' *Atti, Riunione Scientifica dell'I.I.P.P.* 37, 163-74.

Deetz, J. 1977. *In Small Things Forgotten: The Archaeology of Early North American Life*. New York: Doubleday.

Dietler, M. & I. Herbich 1998. 'Habitus, techniques, style: an integrated approach to the social understanding of material culture and boundaries,' In: M. Stark (ed.), *The Archaeology of Social Boundaries*. Washington: Smithsonian, 232-63.

Dobres, M.-A. 2001. *Technology and social agency: outlining a practice framework for archaeology*. Oxford: Blackwell.

Ehrenreich, R.M., C.L. Crumley & J. Levy 1995. *Heterarchy and the analysis of complex societies*. Washington: American Anthropological Association.

Evans-Pritchard, E. 1940. *The Nuer*. Oxford: Clarendon.

Genick, D.C. 1993. *Manuale di Preistoria, Volume II: Neolitico*. Viareggio: Museo Preistorico e Archeologico 'Alberto Carlo Blanc.'

Gosselain, O.P. 1998. 'Social and technical identity in a clay crystal ball', In: M. Stark (ed.), *The Archaeology of Social Boundaries*. Washington: Smithsonian, 78-106.

Hegmon, M. 1992. 'Archaeological research on style.' *Annual Review of Anthropology*, 21, 517-36.

Hegmon, M. 1998. 'Technology, style and social practices: archaeological approaches', In: M. Stark (ed.), *The Archaeology of Social Boundaries*. Washington: Smithsonian, 264-79.

Hegmon, M. 2003. 'Setting theoretical egos aside: issues and theory in North American Archaeology.' *American Antiquity*, 68, 213-44.

Hodder, I. 1982. 'Sequences of structural change in the Dutch Neolithic', In: I. Hodder (ed.), *Symbolic and structural archaeology*. Cambridge: Cambridge University Press, 162-77.

Ingold, T. 2000. *The perception of the environment: essays on livelihood, dwelling, and skill.* London: Routledge.

Jones, G.B.D. 1987. *Apulia*. London: Society of Antiquaries.

Kamp, K.A. 2001. 'Prehistoric children working and playing: a case study in learning ceramics.' *Journal of Anthropological Research*, 57, 427-50.

Leighton, R. 1999. *Sicily Before History*. London: Duckworth.

MacEachern, S. 1998. 'Scale, style, and cultural variation: technological traditions in the Northern Mandara Mountains', In: M. Stark (ed.), *The Archaeology of Social Boundaries*. Washington: Smithsonian, 107-31.

Malone, C. 1985. 'Pots, prestige and ritual in Neolithic southern Italy', In: C. Malone, S. Stoddart (eds.), *Papers in Italian archaeology IV: the Cambridge conference, Cambridge, 1985*. (British Archaeological Reports International Series 244). Oxford: Archaeopress, 118-51.

Malone, C. 2003. 'The Italian Neolithic: a synthesis of research.' *Journal of World Prehistory*, 17, 235-312.

Maniscalco, L. & M. R. Iovino 2002. 'La Sicilia Orientale e la Calabria Centro-Meridionale nel Neolitico.' *Atti, Riunione Scientifica dell'I.I.P.P.* 37, 189-201.

Michelaki, K. 2006. *Household Ceramic Economies: Production and Consumption of Household Ceramics among the Maros Villagers of Bronze Age Hungary*. British Archaeological Reports International Series 1503. Oxford: Archaeopress.

Minar, C.J. & P.L. Crown. 2001. 'Learning and craft production: an introduction.' *Journal of Anthropological Research*, 57, 369-80.

Morter, J. 1992. Capo Alfiere and the Middle Neolithic period in eastern Calabria, Southern Italy. Ph.D. thesis, Department of Anthropology, University of Texas, Austin.

Morter, J. & J. Robb 1998. 'Space, gender and architecture in the Southern Italian Neolithic.' In: R. Whitehouse (ed.), *Gender and Italian Archaeology: Challenging the Stereotypes*. London: Accordia, 83-94.

Muntoni, I.M. 2003. *Modellare l'Argilla: Vasai del Neolitico antico e medio nelle Murge pugliesi*. Firenze: Istituto Italiano di Preistoria e Protostoria.

Perlès, C. 2001. *The Early Neolithic in Greece. Cambridge World Archaeology*. Cambridge: Cambridge University Press.

Pluciennik, M. 1997. 'Historical, geographical, and anthropological imaginations: early ceramics in Southern Italy', In: C. Cumberpatch, P. Blinkhorn (eds.), *Not so much a pot, more a way of life*. Oxford: Oxbow, 37-56.

Rice, P. 1987. *Pottery analysis: a sourcebook*. Chicago: University of Chicago Press.

Robb, J.E. 1994a. 'Burial and social reproduction in the Peninsular Italian Neolithic.' *Journal of Mediterranean Archaeology*, 7, 29-75.

Robb, J.E. 1994b. 'Gender contradictions: moral coalitions and inequality in prehistoric Italy.' *Journal of European Archaeology*, 2, 20-49.

Robb, J.E. 1999. 'Great persons and big men in the Italian Neolithic', In: R. H. Tykot, J. Morter, J. E. Robb (eds.), *Social Dynamics of the Prehistoric Central Mediterranean*. London: Accordia Research Center, 111-22.

Robb, J.E. 2007. *The Early Mediterranean Village: Agency, Material Culture and Social Change in Neolithic Southern Italy*. Cambridge: Cambridge University Press.

Sassaman, K.E. & W. Rudolphi 2001. 'Communities of practice in the early pottery traditions of the American Southeast', *Journal of Anthropological Research*, 57, 407-26.

Sherratt, A. 1984. 'Social evolution: Europe in the Later Neolithic and Copper Ages', In: J. Bintliff (ed.), *European social evolution: archaeological perspectives*. Bradford: Bradford University Press, 123-34.

Sherratt, A. 1994. 'The transformation of early agrarian Europe: the Later Neolithic and Copper Ages, 4500-2500 BC', In: B. Cunliffe (ed.), *The Oxford Illustrated Prehistory of Europe*. Oxford: Oxford University Press, 167-201.

Sinclair, A. 1995. 'The technique as symbol in Late Glacial Europe.' *World Archaeology*, 27, 50-62.

Skeates, R. 1998. 'The social life of Italian Neolithic painted pottery', In: D. W. Bailey (ed.), *The Archaeology of Value*. Oxford: British Archaeological Reports, 131-41.

Spataro, M. 2002. *The First Farming Communities of the Adriatic: Pottery Production and Circulation in the Early and Middle Neolithic*. Trieste: Società per la Preistoria e Protostoria della Regione Friuli – Venezia Giulia.

Trump, D.H. 1963. 'Excavations at La Starza, Ariano Irpino.' *Papers of the British School at Rome*, 31, 1-32.

Vitelli, K.D. 1995. 'Pots, potters, and the shaping of Greek Neolithic society', In: W. K.Barnett, J. W.Hoopes (eds.), *The Emergence of Pottery: Technology and Innovation in Ancient Societies*. Washington: Smithsonian Institution Press, 55-64.

Wobst, H. 1977. 'Stylistic behavior and information exchange', In: C. Cleland (ed.), *For the Director: Research Essays in Honor of James B. Griffin*. Ann Arbor: Museum of Anthropology, University of Michigan, 317-42.

Colourful Meaning: Terminology, abstraction and the Near Eastern Bronze Age

David A. Warburton

Introduction

The late Neolithic and the Bronze Age were the eras in which humans first began to play with yellow gold, white silver, red carnelian, the greens of jade, jasper and malachite, and the blues of lapis lazuli, turquoise and amethyst. Obviously, red and yellow ochre were known long before these semi-precious stones and precious metals came into circulation. However, this paper argues that the precious materials were decisive for the development of the expression of colour in language and that this throws light on the development of cognitive capacities.

The jade axes of Neolithic Europe are as familiar as those of Shang China, where gold and turquoise were also appreciated. The gold, lapis lazuli, turquoise and carnelian in the celebrated treasures of Tutankhamun and the royal cemetery of Ur are likewise well-known. Less familiar perhaps is the fact that today the abstract colour words for *blue* in Greek (*kyaneos* from Akkadian *uqnu*) and Italian (*azzurro* from Persian *lâzuward*) are derived from Near Eastern words for lapis lazuli, the semi-precious stone which lay at the centre of one of the oldest exchange networks known to mankind. For the current writer, this suggests that in the domain of colours, archaeological and philological sources offer a unique insight into cognitive development.

The domain of colours is chosen because one can actually follow – using strict definitions and methodology – the development of an abstract terminology. The terminology can be followed from modern languages back to the earliest written languages, and thus the appearance of abstraction in linguistic terms. Furthermore, the terminology is linked to the archaeological record in a fashion which allows us to proceed from textual sources into prehistory. It thus provides an ideal case study for the emergence of abstraction, which can be related to social science and linguistic definitions and methodology.

The principal challenge here is recognizing both (a) the significance of the archaeological material and (b) the content and application of Berlin & Kay's (1999) *Basic Color Terms*, the dominant paradigm. Although it could be speculated that an oral tradition of abstract colour terms existed before the invention of writing, the Berlin & Kay scheme does not discuss such a possibility. We contend that the nature and origins of abstract colour terminology are at the heart of human cognitive evolution, and that archaeological material offers a window into the cognitive past. This not only allows us to grasp certain essentials in the development of human thought, but also allows archaeological material to contribute to cognitive model building, specifically proposing that the origins of what later became abstract colour terminology lay in precious materials. Furthermore, this particular case also illustrates the problems in drawing on existing social science theories to interpret archaeological evidence, as the ancient evidence actually throws doubt on the dominant paradigm. The author stresses developments in the Bronze Age (rather than farther back in Prehistory) and argues that developments during this period should be taken into account when considering the capacity for abstraction in Prehistory.

Colour theory and colour terminology

In their fundamental volume on colour terminology, *Basic Color Terms*, Berlin & Kay (1999, first published 1969) proposed that human languages divided the spectrum of colours into a range of 11 or fewer colour terms which were more or less the same. They insisted that all terms recognized as BCTs ('basic color terms') be abstract and not related to materials, nor restricted to specific uses. They expected that the words would cover the 'focus' of the colours as represented by the meanings known from English (which correspond for most of the European languages, with the exceptions of Russian and Hungarian – where there are two *blues* and two *reds*, respectively, in contrast to the other European languages). Their basic contention was that there was to be one, and only one, term for each colour in each language, and the spectrum was to be divided identically in all of the advanced languages with a full spectrum of colour terms. Thus *red* was a BCT, *scarlet* was not; Russian *goluboj, light blue,* was excluded assuming that *sinij, dark blue,* covered *blue.*

At the time, the approach was overwhelmingly convincing. For the anthropological, linguistic and philosophical communities – which had assumed that different languages divided the colour spectrum arbitrarily – this was a well documented shock, and transformed the world of colour studies.

They complemented this system of classification with an evolutionary perspective by which the colour terms were acquired in the various languages over seven stages. *White* meant *light* and *black* meant *dark* at the earliest level (Stage I), *red* covered *red-with-yellow* and *green* covered *green-with-blue* (*grue*) before the introduction of separate terms for *yellow* and *blue*, represented by Stage V. The final stages complete the scheme with the remaining colours acquired in no specified order.

I	II	III	IV	V	VI	VII
white black	+ red	+ green (or yellow)	+ yellow (or green)	+ blue	+brown	+pink, purple, orange, grey

Fig. 1. Simplified version of the original Berlin & Kay evolutionary scheme (Berlin & Kay 1999).

Thus, the Dani people of Papua New Guinea use a colour terminology lacking any terms for colours beyond *dark* and *light*, and no words identifiable as BCTs: Stage I. The final stage, VII, is that of languages such as German and English (where the terminology and the division of the spectrum are more or less identical). Languages such as ancient Egyptian and Akkadian were located near Stage III (without *blue*), Greek and Latin (with *blue*) a bit higher, at Stage V.

As applied, Berlin & Kay contend that the evolution of each language heads toward the spectrum of modern English, and that this has happened in the last couple of millennia. The approach has gained the status of a paradigm; the debate is primarily about whether Berlin & Kay are correct or not. The adherents of the original approach are modifying it to accommodate new data and approaches, e.g., 'prototypes', 'saturation', 'intensity', and 'luminosity' which go far beyond the original 'hue-based' approach.[1]

The opponents can be divided into two groups: (a) those philologists, linguists and anthropologists who simply confirm that their interpretations of their material are not compatible with the Berlin & Kay scheme and (b) those studying colour using philosophical, cultural or psychological approaches, viewing colour as a phenomenon without necessarily offering a theoretical construction. Pursuing a cultural and psychological approach, Jameson and Davidoff are among those closest to developing alternative theoretical schools.[2] However, aside from the current author, none of the theoretical approaches to colour as such (as opposed to philologists and linguists working from language and archaeologists working from material) exploits the ancient sources, which should be fundamental to any evolutionary scheme.

The Bronze Age

Although the sun and the sky were visible to the first hominids, Egyptian hymns of the second millennium BC describe the sun as 'rising golden' (*m nbw*) in a 'field of turquoise' (*sḫ.t mfk3t*) (Assmann 1983, 117, 127). Although humans spilled blood and crossed the seas long before they drank wine, Babylonian blood was the colour of carnelian, and Homer's sea was 'wine-dark'. Such expressions could be viewed as poetic – but these languages did not possess other means of making the statement.

These colour terms belong to the urban world of the Bronze Age. The use of a term like 'sky-blue' was unknown. The author argues that this was because it was impossible to develop such forms of expression until after the abstract terms had begun to crystallize – and these forms were dependent upon the beginnings of a colour terminology. In any case there is no evidence of such expressions until much later. Thus, sky and water did not serve as the origin for the expression of the colour blue. Instead of using the surrounding cosmos as the point of departure, the ancients described the sun as being 'gold' or the sky as being 'lapis lazuli' or 'turquoise'.

We argue that the origins of the abstract terms can be found in the precious materials known from the late Neolithic and the Bronze Age onwards. Furthermore, the fundamental importance of abstraction in colour terminology suggests to us that we are also talking about the emergence of abstraction as such.

Exchange

Precious materials (jade, lapis lazuli, carnelian, turquoise, silver, gold) are unknown before the Neolithic, gradually appearing in the archaeological record from the seventh millennium BC onwards – in contrast to ochre, known long before.[3]

Lapis lazuli itself lay at the centre of one of the oldest long distance exchange networks. In the second millennium BC the distribution of lapis lazuli extended from the sources in Central Asia through the Indus, Iran, the Gulf and Mesopotamia to Egypt, Anatolia and the eastern Mediterranean. As Casanova (2002) has shown, this was the end of a long and clearly identifiable development. No lapis appears in the Near East (or anywhere else) during the early Neolithic. Less than 2000 pieces are documented in Egypt, northern Iraq, Iran, Central and South Asia from the period of some 3000 years from its first appearance in an archaeological context (in the late seventh or early sixth millennium in Pakistan) to the beginning of the Bronze Age; a further 2000 pieces appear in the first 500 years of the Bronze Age, and the finds extend into the Gulf, southern Iraq and Syria. The

Fig. 2. Typical fine polished jade axe of alpine jade found in England; Neolithic or Early Bronze Age. Published with permission of the British Museum (ME 121481).

second half of the third millennium experienced an explosion-like development during which tens of thousands of pieces of lapis lazuli appear in archaeological contexts in this same region – virtually all of which was found in a handful of elite tombs. And it was at this time that the use of lapis lazuli, carnelian and other materials as colour terms in poetic texts began (André-Salvini 1995; cf. also the index in Pritchard 1969).

Lapis lazuli and carnelian thus enjoyed a wide distribution (Barthélémy de Saizieu & Casanova 1993; Inizan 1995; Roux 1995), and archaeological evidence confirms the use of white, black, red, green, yellow, blue and brown materials in the millennium immediately prior to the invention of writing, with some of the most striking colours indicated by precious materials. However, in contrast to yellow and red ochre, these precious materials were basically restricted to the households of the elite and remained extremely rare.

However, it is not just our own understanding that designates these materials as precious: lapis lazuli was one of the very few commodities – aside from gold – which had a price superior to that of silver (cf. Michel 1999; 2001b). Thus, these were precious stones for which prices (Michel 2001a; Powell et al. 2003-2005) were negotiated in markets (cf., e.g., Wilcke 2007; Warburton 2003a; 2003b) – markets that were exploited by princes.

A letter written to the king of Mari (a second millennium Syrian city-state) states:

> ... I am seeking precious stones. There is one weighing 25 grams that I can get, but in fact they are only showing me beads of 15 grams, or even less! If my lord decides, I will purchase them. That my lord can have them, please have them bring me the silver which is the price for the beads of lapis lazuli as soon as possible (Durand 2000, 17-18).

The same archives also mention Cretan merchants, thus confirming that commerce was the means by which these words arrived in other languages. In Classical Greek, the adjective *kyaneos* was primarily 'dark blue', and the link to lapis lazuli thereby largely severed. However, the Akkadian word *uqnu* could not be severed from 'lapis lazuli', and it did not mean simply 'blue'. Thus, the Greek is abstract whereas the Akkadian is not – being the precious material itself. Yet the Akkadian is the origin of the Greek, and exchange is fundamental to the system.

Obviously, when palaces made purchases on the market (such as that described to the king of Mari above), the state could not dictate value. From the end of the fourth millennium onwards, states had created systems of measurement (for time, space, weight, etc.), and these incorporated equivalencies whereby a weight of silver could be linked to a quantity of grain and a specific surface area of land, etc. When exposed to the market, these equivalencies could not be dictated, and changed accordingly, and more so from the second millennium onwards.

The origins of prices denominated in silver lie in the fourth millennium when silver appears for the first time both as an artefact and as a word appearing in texts (Reiter 1997, 76, 83-84; Warburton 2003a). The commercial exchange in goods did not take off with the Neolithic, nor with the era of incipient primary state formation, but in the wake of wide-spread urbanization and military conflict from the end of the third millennium BC. Although silver (Prag 1978; Reiter 1997, 75-76) and even credits in silver (Wilcke 2007) are known from before the end of the third millennium, they remained quite rare until then; even as late as the end of the third millennium, neither barley nor silver served as 'money' (Veldhuis 2001, 100). It is only from early in the second millennium that the various systems were linked together in a network of market prices – and from this era onwards, the quantities of silver and lapis lazuli increased by leaps and bounds.

Concrete materials and abstraction

The argument is thus that materials from the Ancient Near East throw light on the development of human cognitive capacities, and in particular on the generation of abstract thought and meaning. Colour and colour terminology will serve as our vehicle in approaching the problem, with the claim that the colour terminology of antiquity can be used to illuminate both subsequent developments (in the last few thousand years) and the capacity for abstract thought in prehistory.

Thus the primary contention concerns (1) the physical materials which led to the preliminary steps permitting the emergence of abstraction. This is linked to the secondary issue (2) of archaeological methodology. Here, the author assumes (2a) that archaeologists frequently rely on the evidence of biological capacity to project active execution into the past, and to assume that signs of this can be found in the archaeological record. This assumes that the biological theory of evolution becomes the explanation of human culture, rendering it impossible to isolate historical developments in cognitive capacities – and above all impossible to understand the processes whereby cultural development leads to the production of meaning. More specifically, the author also notes (2b) that, in the case of colour, archaeologists have applied a theory (that of Berlin & Kay), based on language, to the interpretation of materials as such without recognizing that the theoretical study of abstract terms in language and the actual use of concrete materials are two different matters. Any cognitive approach to the origins and evolution of expression must view archaeological material as providing an essential source of information, and that material should inform theory. Using aspects of ancient colour use and colour theory, the author concludes (3) that the archaeological sources offer a view into the development of the mind as a cultural phenomenon.

From the purely theoretical standpoint, the fundamental question is thus whether our capacity for abstract thought can be projected back to some genetic change rendering us inherently 'cognitive' (as argued by, e.g., Mithen 1999; Klein & Edger 2002), or whether cultural developments have enhanced our cognitive capacity. The author recognizes that the active capacity of the human brain to process information is a biological reality of great antiquity, like the optical capacities of the human eye (and the acoustical capacities of the human ear, and the linguistic capacities of the tongue and vocal chords, cf. Deacon 1997). However, we argue that language and image-based processing dependent upon abstract concepts rely upon a cultural context which facilitates or permits a different type of processing. Without these cognitive processes transforming perceptual input into expression, the acoustical and linguistic capacities will not have been exploited to the maximum. Here, the author argues that, significantly, the evidence suggests that the development of expression had an impact on the classification of colour.

Language, writing and archaeological materials

This becomes extremely important when appreciating that the length of time between the appearance of anatomically modern humans (at least 200,000 years ago) and the invention of writing (ca. 5200 years ago) bears no comparison with the time span between the invention of writing and the discovery of relativity in physics. The contrast becomes even greater when it is appreciated that the earliest written documents indicate the beginnings of a system of measuring time (cf. Englund 1998), and that the beginnings of a mathematically based planetary theory had already been developed in the middle of the first millennium BC (Swerdlow 1998), less than 2000 years after the invention of writing.

That such astronomical observations could have been inherited from Prehistory is rendered improbable by the facts that: (a) many of the observations depend upon understanding of cycles lasting a decade or so (thus requiring external memory storage), and (b) the fact that the mastery is only evident from the second half of the third millennium BC (Krauss 1997). Nothing indicates that such knowledge had existed earlier, and certainly even something as elementary as the length of a year was not resolved until much later. In fact, developments reveal that the ancient scientists were struggling with these and other issues from the third millennium onwards: precise astronomical observations and recording depend upon a relatively accurate understanding of the solar year, as the lunar calendar is wholly inadequate for such purposes. Thus, the invention of writing can be directly related to scientific methodology.

While the diffusion of ideas is potentially debatable in principle, lapis lazuli itself appears in fourth millennium prehistoric cemeteries in Egypt (Hartung 2001, Abb. 54) and Mesopotamia (Casanova 2002), thousands of kilometres from the mines in Afghanistan whence it was extracted. The presence of the Akkadian word for lapis lazuli (*uqnu*) in Greek *blue* (*kyaneos*) demonstrates that the diffusion of objects and ideas clearly applies to colour terminology.

However, there is no reason to believe that all diffusion took place in one direction only, and we will discuss evidence of two other colour words (for *red* and *green*) which points in a different direction. Again, the exchanges are central – and evidently, exchange is incompatible with the evolutionary system proposed by Berlin & Kay.

It follows that the Near Eastern material is not 'illustrative' in the sense of simply providing documentation for an evolutionary phenomenon which is universal and took place everywhere, but rather that the written sources of the ancient Near East are themselves the witnesses testifying to the system leading to the emergence of abstract colour terminology – and evidence that this was radically different than the evolution proposed by Berlin & Kay. In this sense, the Near Eastern material can be viewed as a source contributing to our understanding of cognitive developments.

The invention of writing is widely viewed as a mere detail in linguistic history, but in fact the only language families which can be traced back in any form to a period before the invention of writing are Semitic and Indo-European. The highly limited value of the glotto-chronological methodology of linguistics cannot project any language back to much more than 10,000 years ago at a maximum, but the methodological drawbacks mean that this necessarily opens the door to speculation that languages are tens or hundreds of thousands of years older (cf., e.g., Hombert 2005 for discussions and literature).

However, such speculation lacks support since what evidence there is can be interpreted in very different ways. In principle, the invention of writing reveals that language already existed at this time. However, the earliest texts do not testify to any form of linguistic expression: they are generally economic texts dealing with information in mathematical terms (Englund 1998). Linguistically encoded information only appears several centuries later.

Our source material for the discussion of colour terminology will rely on the earliest known information encoded in those earliest texts, dating from the third and second millennia BC, linking this to archaeological material. And this material seems to suggest that colour terminology is very recent.

Debate

Significantly, the colour terminology of the world's oldest written languages (which are thus by definition the oldest accessible languages) had been studied before the appearance of Berlin & Kay: studies by Schenkel (1963) and Landsberger (1967) had independently concluded that the Egyptian and Mesopotamian languages had only four colour terms: *white, black, red* and *green.*

This convergence was remarkable, and after the publication of Berlin & Kay, the Oxford Egyptologist Baines (1985) observed that the linguistic evidence for the period through the end of the third millennium BC could be matched to the Berlin & Kay sequence as representing Stage III, where the Egyptian and Akkadian words for *green* should be understood as *green-with-blue* (*grue*). This has been accepted among students of colour and ancient languages, and treated as a proof of the validity of the Berlin & Kay theory.

However, Schenkel and Baines both noted that the implications of a colour terminology restricted to four words in ancient Egypt were grave: the Egyptians clearly used a greater variety of colours in their painting (more hues than are included in the 11 BCTs) than in the language (four terms).[4]

Berlin & Kay's approach eliminated words linked to materials or narrow meanings. In searching modern 'primitive' languages, they discovered many different shades of different colours identified by speakers of the 'primitive' languages, but the use was not exclusively a colour use, and when the colour meaning was used, the term appeared in a phrase such as 'like the colour of *x*'. Egyptian, Akkadian and Greek all reveal the same phenomenon (aside from English).

Significant is, therefore, that societies used materials with colours before using BCTs, and where they employed recognized BCTs, they used more colours than BCTs. There is thus a serious cognitive dissonance since colours and terminology do not reflect the same systems of categorization. Apparently, the earliest system of categorization was not based on language. And yet one can follow nuances indicating a gradual increase in colour terminology with an impact on the use of colours. At this point, the importance of blue and green become clear, as blue and green are lacking in Palaeolithic art and artefact assemblages. Thus one can follow a cognitive change whereby increases in vocabulary lagged behind the use of colour in material culture – but the latter likewise broadened the spectrum – yet was entwined in another system of values, beyond mere decoration.

Of great interest to us in this particular context is thus the origin of those words which eventually became the advanced BCTs. In principle, the Berlin & Kay scheme rejects colour terms based on materials. We argue that in terms of the evolution of the terminology, this is not a detail, but rather the fundamental flaw in the BCT system which obscures the understanding of the emergence and evolution of the use of colour and of colour terminology, because prehistoric materials and ancient languages can be drawn together rendering archaeological materials highly relevant to understanding the development of human cognition.

The Achilles heel of the Berlin & Kay scheme is the colour *orange* which they admit as the pinnacle of the scheme, placing it as the 11th BCT in the evolution of the English language. However, they concede that it is related to a material object (an orange). Furthermore, the name of this same fruit is also the name of the relevant colour in both Persian and Arabic, and yet here the word is *burtuqal*. Strangely, the word *burtuqal* refers to the Portuguese sailors who arrived in the Indian Ocean at the end of the 15th century – and yet oranges had arrived in the Indian Ocean from China many centuries before the Portuguese (Warburton 1999). Thus the reason for this term must remain obscure.

However, its obscurity can only be paralleled by the fact that our word 'orange' (both the colour and the fruit, as preserved in Spanish) is borrowed from a word which is preserved in the Sanskrit *naranj*. Obviously it arrived in Europe when the Portuguese sailors returned, and must have been a term they had encountered in the Indian Ocean, and this word spread throughout the Indo-European languages of Western Europe from which Sanskrit had been cut off for millennia. And at the same time, this ancient word was apparently discarded in the Indian Ocean – in favour of a word which had no bearing on either the colour or the fruit.

Whatever the reasons behind this peculiar development, one must note that the most recent addition to the colour terminology of the world is not merely characterized by being a material object, but it is also a loanword of extremely recent origin in two of the linguistically most important and most ancient language families (Indo-European and Semitic).

After the most recent addition to the colour vocabulary of Indo-European, we continue with an ancient word which is probably a recent addition to the vocabulary of our readers, some of whom may have purchased an ink-cartridge with the exotic name of *cyan*. This hitherto obscure word was an alternative word for *dark blue*. The *Petit Robert 2007* identifies its first use in French in 1950; described as 'English', it is explained as being derived from the Greek *kyanos*, 'blue'. This source does not add that it must have reached Greek from Hittite (*khuwannash*) or Ugaritic (*iqnu*), and that it originally came from *uqnu*, which was already a loanword in Akkadian some 4000 years ago. But, at that time, it did not mean *blue*; it was the name of that exotic blue stone called 'lapis lazuli' today.

By contrast, for *azur*, the *Petit Robert 2007* does give the etymology back through Spanish and Arabic to Persian, where *lâzuward* means 'lapis lazuli'. In French, *azur* is only *light blue*, but in Italian *azzurro* is the BCT for *blue*. The stone comes from Afghanistan (where a variety of Persian is spoken), and thus the use of a Persian word is hardly surprising. However, as the stone had to cross Iran and Mesopotamia to reach the Mediterranean, it is hardly surprising that it has left its traces in a number of languages. What is striking is that two different words for the same stone survived in English and French, providing words for *light* and *dark blue*.

Thus, the word for this dark blue stone has quite a history as a wanderer, crossing the boundaries of language families – but above all mixing the categories of 'abstract colour word' (where Berlin & Kay accept it for Greek, Italian and Spanish) and material object (which is the only use Berlin & Kay would allow it in Akkadian and Egyptian), quite aside from different hues.

For Egyptian, Schenkel had excluded the word *ḫsbḏ*/lapis lazuli from his abstract colour words, reasoning that the word was not used as an abstract term in verbal form. In 1963, Schenkel argued that the word *wadj*/green actually covered the *green-blue* part of the spectrum, but Schenkel (2007) has since abandoned this position, accepting that *wadj*/green means *green*. However, Schenkel still maintains that *ḫsbḏ*/lapis lazuli is not *blue*, and that the word referred to the material and not the colour, and where the adjectival form is used, it means *lapis-lazuli-like*, not *blue*.

By contrast, Quirke (2001) accepted *ḫsbḏ*/lapis lazuli as a colour word. Although Baines (1985) accepted that *ḫsbḏ*/lapis lazuli could occasionally mean *blue*, he rejected the use of the Egyptian word *ḫsbḏ*/lapis lazuli as an abstract colour word for *blue* in Egyptian. Obviously, this was partially because Baines accepted the then-current argument that *w3ḏ*/green covered *blue-green*, but significantly, Baines (1985, 283) merely excluded the use of *ḫsbḏ*/lapis lazuli as a colour word by noting that the absence of a word for *yellow* in ancient Egyptian excluded that there could be a separate word for *blue*, specifically because of the acquisition sequence postulated by Berlin & Kay. Baines conceded that some Egyptian colour terms were not merely abstract: his reason for excluding *blue* was the Berlin & Kay theory, whereas Quirke based his conclusion on usage.

Thus, according to Baines, ancient Egyptian was at Stage III of the Berlin & Kay scheme because Egyptian did not have a word for *yellow*, and thus *ḫsbḏ*/lapis lazuli could not mean *blue*. In contrast Schenkel had argued that lapis lazuli was a material and not a colour. Baines had allowed, however, that the universally accepted ancient Egyptian word for *ḥḏ*/white actually was the material silver and was thus not a pure colour word – and both Schenkel and Baines had also allowed as much for *w3ḏ*/green as well. Thus certain words related to materials were accepted as colour terms while others were not, allowing Egyptian to be placed at Stage III.

There has been no theoretically comprehensive attempt to integrate the Mesopotamian evidence into a single coherent scheme; Landsberger identified four terms, of which *black*, *white* and *red* were indisputable. The fourth *warqu*, *green-yellow* was indisputable but did not fit into the *green-blue* which Berlin & Kay demanded. Hitherto, discussion has concentrated on this word, to which we will return.

However, there is a far greater difficulty. The recognized BCT for *red* in Akkadian is *sāmu*, from *sāmtu*, 'the red stone par excellence, carnelian' (*CAD* 15: 127), and thus an adjective derived from a noun, violating the principles of the Berlin & Kay scheme. However, eliminating red from Akkadian would reduce it from Stage III (white + black + red + green) to Stage I (black + white).

Thus, we note that rejecting the adjective *ḫsbḏ*/lapis lazuli allowed Egyptian to be at Stage III, while accepting the adjective *sāmu*/carnelian allowed Akkadian to be likewise set at State III. However, maintaining Akkadian at Stage III depends not only on *sāmu*, but also on *warqu*/green. As noted, Baines had accepted that the Egyptian *w3ḏ* /green actually covered the *green-blue* spectrum, advocating that it was a word for *grue*. And as noted, Baines suggested that it was equivalent to the *warqu*/green of Akkadian. However, Landsberger had argued that *warqu* was *green-yellow*, and had not proposed that it was *green-blue*. According to the evolutionary aspect of the Berlin & Kay scheme, at Stage II the term *red* could cover *red-yellow*, but not a *green-yellow* at Stage III.

Obviously, there are some difficulties with a word meaning *green-yellow*, but Landsberger's documentation reveals that *warqu* does actually mean *green-yellow*. One argument linking the two colours could be the cycle of vegetation which changes seasonally from green to yellow. While reasonable, this would imply that as used in Akkadian it did not have any exclusive 'colour meaning' as required by Berlin & Kay. Thus *warqu* cannot be recognized as a colour term in the sense of the word specified by Berlin & Kay, and Akkadian could not be placed beyond Stage II (black + white + red). And, as noted, even this depends upon recognizing Akkadian *sāmu*/carnelian as *red*, which violates the Berlin & Kay abstraction principle. Yet this latter remains uncontested, for otherwise Akkadian would end up among the most primitive Stage I languages.

Significantly, Schenkel (2007) has since recognized that Egyptian *w3ḏ*/green has a focus in green, and this opens up the possibility that lapis lazuli may have played a role in the blue range at this time. This is fundamental since the entire Berlin & Kay evolutionary scheme is based upon the assumption that the earliest colour terminologies in languages evolved from the three term black+white+red to a four term system by adding *green*-with-*blue*, and not a *green* without *blue*.

The theoretical importance of the colours and the materials

Conceptually, Berlin & Kay's evolutionary scheme is fundamental for archaeologists; of equal importance is that the Berlin & Kay scheme does not discuss the use of colour in society: Berlin & Kay deal only with language. Excluding terms like *blonde* and *scarlet* from the scheme for classifying colour terminology – arguing that these are not abstract BCTs with an exclusive colour range not covered by another word – should be of no significance for the understanding of the use of colours in a society. In this sense the Berlin & Kay scheme cannot be applied by prehistoric archaeologists; in any case they assume that any hypothetical prehistoric languages did not have any BCTs.[5]

However, we stress here that, using the archaeological data, one can reverse the approach. The application of the methodology and principles of the Berlin

& Kay scheme to the linguistic evidence from the earliest accessible languages alone should suffice to eliminate the Berlin & Kay theory as applied to the origin and evolution of BCTs in language. Not only (a) is the basic sequence of hues distorted (by, e.g., misreading *green* and *green-yellow* as *green-blue*), but (b) the application of the system depends upon the arbitrary inclusion (silver in Egyptian, carnelian in Akkadian) and exclusion (lapis lazuli in both) of materials in order to create the illusion of an evolutionary sequence of acquisition of BCTs, and this is compounded by (c) the presence of words related to materials as recognized BCTs (e.g., *kyaneos* and *burtuqal*), when appearing as loanwords. And the fundamental importance of loanwords in basic colour terminology (d) stands in contradiction to an evolutionary scheme inherent to each language.

In the ancient Egyptian language, the current writer recognizes that silver frequently means *white* and that lapis lazuli frequently means *blue* – as is accepted by a number of scholars. Moving beyond this, however, he argues that on occasion (as with silver, but not invariably) gold means *yellow*. In principle, since Baines accepted that silver was *white*, there is no obstacle to gold being *yellow*. Gold is etymologically related to the relevant words for *yellow* in English, Danish and German as well (Shields 1979) and thus it is hardly surprising to find it in Egyptian.

There is, however, a further difficulty, as the author argues that in Egyptian *mfk3t*/turquoise is used for *light blue*. Furthermore, he not only recognizes the term for *green* mentioned above, *w3ḏ*, but also the term generally translated as *red*, dSr.t, as well as a second word for *red*, *rwḏ*.

With *glaukos*, Greek likewise divided the lighter part of blue from the darker *kyaneos*. For the reds, Greek likewise had *rhodos* and *erythros* (as Akkadian has a vast range of reds). With *khashmanum*, Akkadian likewise distinguished a lighter blue (Durand 1983, 222-23), a word derived from the Egyptian word for amethyst (*ḥsmn*) which was never used as a colour term in Egyptian (Warburton 2007a; 2007b; 2008; 2012). Thus, there is another loanword related to a precious material and the colour blue, and indications of a tendency for the ancient languages to divide blues and reds – quite the opposite of combining blue and green, as Berlin & Kay assume for the earliest languages.

Thus the earlier languages divided portions of the spectrum which Berlin & Kay assign to a single term: the modern divisions established by Berlin & Kay were not present in the earliest languages. By imposing their BCTs, variety is eliminated, a difficulty which becomes more serious when recognizing that the application of the scheme to the earliest languages rests on the contradictions in the treatment of materials discussed above.

Materials, exchange and the emergence of abstract colour terms

Thus according to the current author, like other ancient languages, Egyptian (a) had a number of colour terms, few (if any) were purely abstract colour terms; (b) some of which were words for precious materials; and (c) some of which divided colours represented by single BCTs in the Berlin & Kay scheme. Thus interpreted, the Egyptian spectrum reveals a wide range of colours, some possibly abstract and some bound to materials, and other languages reveal exchange.

Although the colours of precious stones served a role in the earliest known written languages, they did not serve as abstract colour terms. Paradoxically, however, at least one of these terms (*uqnu, kyaneos*) survived into the modern world as a colour term. Most significantly, none of these materials (silver, gold, jade, lapis lazuli, carnelian, turquoise, amethyst) was known before the late Neolithic. Thus, one can argue a direct link between the late Neolithic and the Bronze Age, and one can also recognize that the terminology took a leap into the historic period, and that this leap was grounded in precious materials.

We will now return to the Egyptian word *wꜣḏ*, with its focus on green. There is a consensus (Schenkel 2007, 226) that this Egyptian word *wꜣḏ*/green is related to Akkadian *warqu*/green-yellow. The original term is probably Neolithic in origin, with the earlier word entering both Akkadian and Egyptian from elsewhere. The decisive radicals of *wꜣḏ* are *w, aleph* and *č*; those of *warqu, w, r* and *q*; it may be assumed that *aleph* < *r* and that *č* ~ *g*/*q*/*k*. The *w* can easily be eliminated (as it was in Akkadian). The Akkadian radicals *r* and *q* are the same as the consonants *g* and *r* in *green* (in English, German and Danish, for example), being merely metathesized in northern Indo-European (in contrast to Greek, where **orgaō* may preserve the same consonants in the same order as Akkadian and Egyptian, cf. Hannig 2006, 190).

Above, we noted that the jade axes of Europe date to the Neolithic and the very beginnings of the Bronze Age (Klassen 2004). There is one polished basalt axe with a distinctly greenish hue, dating to ca. 7000 BC, from Neolithic Buqras in Syria (Fortin 1999, 188), which would antedate the European jadeite versions by at least one, and perhaps almost two, millennia (Pétrequin 2002), and the Chinese jade versions by more (Liu 2003). As Pétrequin stresses, the European jadeite versions were but the most prominent of the greenstone axes familiar in the Near East and Europe. Hence, there is – at least – a possibility that the word for *green* is in fact related to these axes made of jadeite or greenstone – and also to the words for *green* in the earliest known written languages. Given the demonstrated importance of lapis lazuli and carnelian, this need not be dismissed out of

Fig. 3. Example of use of gold, lapis lazuli and carnelian from the royal tombs at Ur, mid to late third millennium BC. Published with permission of the British Museum (ME 122351).

hand. Thus, we have one more potential candidate for a colour word which was linked to a material at the end of the Neolithic.

A loanword for red

However, there is another word with an even more remarkable distribution. The Egyptian word conventionally translated as *red* (*dšr.t*) was not applied to ordinary Egyptian men, who are, nevertheless, frequently described in art books as being painted dark red. The consistency with which men are painted dark red (or brown) since the third millennium BC cannot be disputed; men are also described as being 'strong' (*rwḏ*).

In the first millennium BC, it is undisputed that a word read as *rwḏ* or *rwt* appears as a colour word in Egyptian, meaning *red* or *rose* or *pink*. It is assumed that this first millennium Egyptian word is a loanword, either from Persian (*ward*) or Sanscrit (*vrdhi*). This word likewise appears in Arabic (*ward*) and Greek (*erythros* and *rhodos*), as well as in German, English and Danish (*rot, red, rød*). Accidentally, the Italian *rosso* is virtually identical to the Akkadian *ruššu,* as is the French *rouge* to the Egyptian *rwḏ* (pronounced *ruwedj*).

The Akkadian and Mycenean (Linear B) sources demonstrate that the word can be traced back at least as far as the second millennium. It is a matter of contention whether or not it appears in second or third millennium Egyptian (Warburton

2007a; 2008; 2012), but the antiquity and distribution of the word cannot be denied. There may therefore have been a near universal term for *red* in Eurasia, and this word probably dated back to the Neolithic.[6]

Red ochre linked to Anatomically Modern humans has been prominently discussed recently by Bouzouggar *et al.* (2007) and Hovers *et al.* (2003), demonstrating the use of colour, exchange networks and communications in the Middle Palaeolithic. The use of a widely distributed word for *red* should thus be of interest. The author does not (yet) propose that ochre lay behind this word for red, but stresses that the distribution of the word implies potentially great antiquity. This word became a BCT in some Indo-European languages, but not in Semitic, yet obviously red had a tremendous impact on human thought, and consequently the importance of the colour rather than the BCT must be recognized.

The use of colour and the evolution of colour terms

Red, therefore, appear to be simultaneously the oldest recognized colour, and also possibly the oldest BCT (for those languages where *red* appears as a BCT). Under these circumstances, it is highly significant that there is no agreement on the words for *black* and *white* in any language family, as these words are rarely shared by many languages and never across language families (as in the case of *red* and *green*). It would thus appear that linguistically and conceptually *red* was of greater antiquity than *black* and *white*, and its widespread use – crossing language families – may mean that it was actually the first colour to have been distinguished in the human mind. For the author, this implies that the definition of *red* may actually have crystallized the colour concept which was then applied retroactively to black and white. Thus, those languages which do not have a word for *red* usually use words for *light* and *dark* (which Berlin & Kay inconsistently then construed as *black* and *white*).

Arguing that the categorization of *red* was the essential step for distinguishing *black* and *white* would mean that the basic or primitive *dark/light* distinction does not warrant treatment in terms of colour terminology, which is the premise of Berlin & Kay. This is methodologically a contradiction, since a word for *dark* cannot substitute for a term for *black* when the fundamental criterion for the evolutionary sequence is the appearance of a 'BCT'. This throws doubt on the acquisition sequence and on the principle of abstraction. Also, it should be evident that the two-fold divisions of *blue* and *red* before reaching stage VII cannot be reconciled with the theory.

Furthermore, the evidence concerning a Neolithic word *green* which would link the Eurasian greenstone axes with *warqu* and *w3ḏ* might even suggest that *green* preceded *black* and *white* as well. Although the use of red is of far greater antiquity than green, it could be argued that the appreciation of green may have had an impact on consolidating the understanding of red, as well as the understanding of black and white – and that these developments can be situated in time. In this sense, the archaeological and philological evidence discussed here for the evolution of the terms would suggest a very different trajectory than that proposed by Berlin & Kay, whereby the appearance of words that later became BCTs for *green* and *red* in some languages may both have preceded the appearance of BCTs for *black* and *white*. In this fashion, the materials and the terms become highly important evidence for the earliest stages of the development. It is in this sense that the application of the Berlin & Kay methodology to the earliest known languages suffers from considerable weaknesses.

Obviously, if dealing with an historical time scale beginning with Ancient Greece or the Hebrew Bible, the development of colour vocabulary in the last thousand years is a long term phenomenon. The same is hardly true if one compares the period from the end of the Neolithic to the time when Anatomically Modern Humans first appeared in the Near East, probably more than 100,000 years ago. However, the antiquity and evolution of colour terminology should not be confused with the use of colour. While recognizing the antiquity of the use of colour, the author agrees that the concept of abstract colours is a recent invention, but argues that it has a cultural origin, based upon the exchange of prestige materials and their names.

However, where Berlin & Kay assume that the languages gradually added colour terms beginning from a poor basic vocabulary, the author assumes that once BCTs emerged, lapis lazuli, turquoise and amethyst were combined into *blue*, and in various forms this word was exported to numerous languages, as *azzurro*, *kyaneos*, etc. Crucial is that *blue* did not exist until after the emergence of the abstract terms, millennia later, and therefore that the materials were intimately linked to the understanding of colour.

Red further undermines the Berlin & Kay theory due to the facts that: (a) a word which did not become a BCT had substantial impact on the understanding of the fundamental colour *red* in various societies, and thus the formation of colour terminology and the use of colour were not solely influenced by the gradual acquisition of the standard BCTs; and (b), the importance of a loanword appearing as a colour term undermines the concept of isolated gradual linear evolution. Thus there are some 20 words for *red* in Akkadian (von Soden 1965-81), and 7 each in Egyptian (Brunner-Traut 1977) and Mycenaen Greek (Blakolmer 2000). This means that a wide variety of colour terms were narrowed down, and that the convergence on 11 terms is the result of interaction as terms were selected and translated (as can be seen in the historically verifiable case of the emergence of the word for *orange* in the Semitic and Indo-European families, and has been demonstrated to be neurologically feasible by Komarova *et al.* 2007).

However, at the same time, one cannot disregard the scientific value of the strict application of the methodology of Berlin & Kay to the earliest languages – regardless of our doubts about their interpretation of the evolution of the terms. The strict application of the abstraction principle in the Berlin & Kay theory means that the most ancient languages really do have a highly limited spectrum of abstract colour terms (if any), and that abstract colour terms as we know them are probably hardly more than a thousand years old. If one recognizes the methodological constraints of the Berlin & Kay theory, then abstract colour terminology has a brief history indeed.

The conceptual import of materials

Thus in the paradigmatic case of ancient Egyptian where silver was *white*, gold was *yellow*, lapis lazuli was *dark blue* and turquoise was *light blue*, the terms were not abstract colour terms, but rather materials which were linked to colours and eventually became colour words, but only when separated from their materials (as, e.g., *azzurro* or *cyan*). The modern loanwords reflect linguistic exchange.

Lapis lazuli also had a commercial value higher than that of silver, but most importantly, it was precious: linked to divinity and royalty, tombs and temples. Prices based on values and equivalencies defined in recognizably economic terms are a recent development. Although Bronze Age market prices followed the earliest Neolithic prestige use of these materials, they preceded the consolidation of colour terminology.

High status and high price jade axes and beads of lapis lazuli are associated with colour, and yet the colour was never separated from the material in the Bronze Age, and likewise, the prestige and price were never separate from the object. The meaning of such an object cannot be interpreted by separating it from the concepts of prestige, price and colour. Abstract prices and abstract colours, if indeed linked to such materials could not exist before the appearance of these artefacts, and all of these articles appear from the end of the seventh millennium onwards.

Accordingly, the ancient colour terminology and materials reveal a great deal about the process whereby modern thought processes appeared, but applying modern theoretical approaches cannot aid us determining how these processes develop. The relevance of the Berlin & Kay paradigm – and the cultural importance of their findings – cannot be denied. However, it can be argued that the stress on abstract terms has limited its pertinence for the understanding of the role of materials and exchange in the creation of terminology.

Far more than mere linguistic evolution, the acquisition sequence is the historical result of interaction and exchange, and this convergence has been strongly influenced by exchanges since the invention of writing. The fact that those using the Berlin & Kay scheme accept English *orange*, Italian *azzurro*, Greek *kyaneos*, Egyptian *ḥḏ*, and Akkadian *sāmu* but deny the importance of the materials and exchange, stressing evolution, indicates the weakness in the system. Obviously the study of colour terminology would benefit from the ancient evidence, as the archaeological and philological evidence suggests that the development of colour terminology lay in the incorporation of *red* and *green* as well as lapis lazuli and gold – and that evolution was not the key.

These points can be added to the difficulties discussed above regarding the sequence of acquisition itself (recognized by the adherents and dealt with in countless variations), and the reality of dual terms for green (Chinese), blue (Russian) or red (Hungarian) already recognized by other scholars (and denied by the Berlin & Kay adherents). As argued here, the ancient evidence implies that the wider range of terms is significant. In effect, therefore, the evolutionary aspect of the Berlin & Kay theory suffers not only from being irrelevant to colour terminology, but also from obscuring the details of the origins of BCTs. This does not deny the existence of the modern division of 11 BCTs and the principle of abstraction: it merely throws doubt on the means by which this abstract system was established.

Conclusions

Silver, gold, turquoise, lapis lazuli, amethyst, jade, carnelian and other materials of colour appear in the archaeological record from the sixth or seventh millennia onwards. We have argued that these play highly significant roles in colour terminology, and stress that they are excluded from the Berlin & Kay scheme of abstract colour terminology. Our contention is not that they were abstract terms, nor do we dispute that Berlin & Kay have provided an excellent methodological tool for the analysis of abstract colour terms. We merely argue that these materials provide a crucial key to the analysis of the emergence of abstract colour terminology, which is the subject of their work. A decisive transformation in the understanding of colours can be observed and traced in the archaeological evidence, revealing origins of abstract values and abstract colours. The archaeological evidence indicates that changes were taking place in a vast arena where ideas and objects were being exchanged and traded.

The biological capacity for the expression of abstraction which made this development possible is as old as anatomically modern humans. We have tried to discuss some of the evidence of how the essential steps taken in the Neolithic and the Bronze Age created the platform for the abstraction which was only achieved quite recently. The archaeological and historical evidence implies that the social interaction and the invention of writing allowed the brain to approach its potential.

Above, we noted that colour words involving lapis lazuli, amethyst and oranges have crossed boundaries, and that this aspect was not incorporated into the Berlin & Kay scheme except where they integrated the loanwords as BCTs into specific languages. The Berlin & Kay scheme was a product of the 1960s as the acquisition sequence was supposed to happen independently in each language. Thus, the addition of *azzurro* in Italian and *blue* in English was viewed and analyzed as an independent evolutionary phenomenon. In fact, almost half of the BCTs recognized by Berlin & Kay for English are loanwords (*blue, brown, orange, purple* and *pink*). These are not the product of independent evolution, and the rest are not colour terms, but allegedly etymologically related to 'grow' or 'shine' (Shields 1979).

Like most, Shields assumed that *green* was etymologically derived from 'grow'. The current author would argue that the jadeite axes gave rise to the concept of the colour green, and that this was then transferred to vegetation – but this will doubtless remain a matter of contention. However, this takes us into one of the fundamental issues in modern colour studies, namely the question of distinguishing whether the primary meaning of a 'colour' word in ancient or 'primitive' languages refers to 'hue' or to 'brightness'. It is frequently proposed that the latter is more common in earlier languages (e.g. Bulakh 2007), and that this is the origin of 'hues'. Since the etymologies of the Indo-European words as understood today do in fact suggest origins in 'brightness', this appears to be a reasonable approach.

However, the undisputed importance of the materials silver, carnelian, amethyst and lapis lazuli in the ancient languages discussed here (to which the author merely adds gold, jadeite and turquoise) would suggest that at least one step is missing in an approach based on origins in 'brightness': where documented, these origins are clearly material and not abstract. The fact that the terms eventually became abstract is a matter of consensus: the issue is the origin and early development, and the degree to which the materials contributed to the development of abstraction, and thus both hues and brightness. An approach which dismisses the importance of materials opens the door to speculation about the origins of colour terminology, and thus to stressing conceptual 'brightness'. However, the lexical evidence in the earliest Near Eastern languages clearly points in the direction of material culture. In Egyptian and Akkadian, certain valuable materials (silver, gold, carnelian, amethyst, turquoise, lapis lazuli) played a role in colour terminology, but these only became BCTs when divorced from their materials and integrated as loanwords in other languages: the final leap – into abstraction – was not accomplished in the Near Eastern languages of the Bronze Age.

Abstraction was based on three aspects of exchange: (1) words, (2) materials, and (3) value. Significantly, if the Berlin & Kay scheme is an accurate representation of modern thought processes, complex abstract colour terminology is not only highly dependent upon language, but also historically contingent. The Berlin & Kay scheme demands that the appearance of the full colour terminology only appeared in the last 500 years, and its application means that the earliest stages lie less than 5000 years ago. These conclusions can be viewed as confirmed by archaeological evidence, rendering it highly probable that abstract terms probably did not exist more than 4000 years ago. Blue and green are virtually missing in Palaeolithic art, but appear as conspicuously employed materials in the Neolithic, and widely employed colours in the Bronze Age, and abstract colour words in the last couple of millennia. In this sense, one can note that the materials, the use of the colours in art, and the development of abstract words had an impact on the classification of colour.

As Jameson and her colleagues (Komarova *et al.* 2007) have shown, the selection of colour terms can be studied and the distribution discovered by Berlin & Kay explained in neurological terms. However, the words and the colours must enter into society before the cultural choices can be made. Archaeological materials, ancient texts and anthropological research indicate the constraints whereby an abstract terminology was gradually created. By contrast, the suggestion that language is inherently human, and that abstract colours are hard-wired in the brain, but only accidentally appeared in language in the last couple of thousand years, does not seem to be a compelling explanation. Yet this is the meaning of the application of the evolutionary aspect of the Berlin & Kay scheme as applied today. Thus drawing on archaeological material when discussing the history of abstraction and human thought, one must reconsider both the antiquity of human language and the fundamental assumptions of Chomskyan linguistics.

Notes

1 The original study was based on interviews with bilingual university students at Berkeley, and thus cannot be viewed as 'random sampling' with 'native speakers.' However, this methodological flaw need not mean that the theory itself is flawed.

2 Cf., e.g., Jameson (in Komarova *et al.* 2007), and Davidoff (2006). For important articles (with references to earlier literature) illustrating the various viewpoints, see Biggam *et al.* (2006), Borg (2008), Hardin & Maffi (1997) and MacLaury *et al.* (2007), as well as the articles edited by Jameson in the *Journal of Cognition and Culture* 5/3-4 (2005).

3 For literature, cf., e.g., Aston *et al.* 2000; Aufrère 1991; Guilaine 2002; Harris 1961; Klassen 2004; Moorey 1999; Nicholson & Shaw 2000.

4 We use the Egyptian evidence here because there are not as many paintings preserved from Mesopotamia and thus it would be difficult to estimate the number of colours they used. In jewellery, both the Egyptians and the Mesopotamians used a wide variety of stones with different colours.

5 This issue is extremely important because archaeologists studying colour refer to the Berlin & Kay scheme when discussing colour in prehistory (e.g. Hovers *et al.* 2003; Jones & Bradley 1999).

6 The '*ras*' in Russian *krasnaya* ('red') is derived from the same root; the *k* is a prefix. Whether a similar linguistic phenomenon (e.g. rarity of the *r*) is likewise the explanation for Chinese *cei* (an alternative word, differing from the standard word, *hong*, for 'red') is more difficult.

N. B. We have no means of knowing where *warqu* and *rwḏ* originally came from. Merely because they first appeared in Egyptian and Akkadian does not mean that they originally came from these languages. Certainly both the Egyptian and Akkadian words for lapis lazuli were loanwords when they first appeared in these languages. However, as neither jadeite axes nor lapis lazuli beads were known before the sixth and seventh millennia BC, the words with these meanings cannot be older.

References

André-Salvini, B. 1995. 'Les pierres précieuses dans la littérature cunéiforme.' In: F. Tallon (ed.), *Les pierres précieuses de l'Orient ancien.* Paris: RMN, 76-87.

Assmann, J.A. 1983. *Sonnenhymnen in Thebanischen Gräber.* Mainz: von Zabern.

Aston, B., J.A. Harrell, I. Shaw 2000. 'Stone.' In P.T. Nicholson & I. Shaw (eds.), *Ancient Egyptian Materials and Technology.* Cambridge: Cambridge University Press, 5-77.

Aufrère, S. 1991. *L'Univers minéral dans la pensée égyptienne.* (2 vols.) Cairo: Institut français d'archéologie du Caire.

Baines, J. 1985. 'Color terminology and color classification: ancient Egyptian color terminology and polychromy.' *American Anthropologist,* 87, 282-97.

Barthélémy de Saizieu, B. & M. Casanova 1993. 'Semi-precious stones working at Mundigak: Carnelian and Lapis Lazuli.' In: A.J. Gail & G.R.S. Mevissen (eds.), *South Asian Archaeology* 1991. Berlin: F. Steiner Verlag, 17-30.

Berlin, B. & P. Kay 1999(1969). *Basic Color Terms: Their Universality and Evolution.* (2nd edn.) Stanford: CSLI Publications.

Biggam, C.P., N. Pitchford, C.J. Kay (eds.) 2006. *Progress in Colour Studies.* (2 vols.) Amsterdam: Benjamins.

Blakolmer, F. 2000. 'Zum Charakter der frühägaischen Farben: Linear B und Homer.' In: F. Blakolmer (ed.), *Österreichische Forschungen zur Ägäischen Bronzezeit 1998: Akten der Tagung am Institut für Klassisiche Archäologie der Universität Wien 2.–3. Mai 1998.* Vienna: Wiener Forschungen zur Archäologie, 225-39.

Borg, A. (ed.) 2012(1999). *The Language of Colour in the Mediterranean.* (2nd edn.) Wiesbaden: Harrassowitz.

Bouzouggar, A., N. Barton, M. Vanhaeren, F. d'Errico, S. Collcutt, T. Higham, E. Hodge, S. Parfitt, E. Rhodes, J.-L. Schwenninger, C. Stringer, E. Turner, S. Ward, A. Moutmir, A. Stambouli 2007. '82,000-year-old shell beads from North Africa and implications for the origins of modern human behavior.' *Proceedings of the National Academy of Sciences* 104, 9964-69.

Brunner-Traut, E. 1977. 'Farben.' *Lexikon der Ägyptologie*, II, 117-28.

Bulakh, M. 2007. 'Basic color terms from Proto-Semitic to Old Ethiopic.' In: R.E. MacLaury, G.V. Paramei, D. Dedrick (eds.), *Anthropology of Color: Interdisciplinary Multilevel Modelling.* Amsterdam: Benjamins, 247-61.

CAD 15 = Chicago Assyrian Dictionary 15 = J.A. Brinkman, M. Civil, I.J. Gelb, A.L. Oppenheim, E. Reiner (eds.) 1984. *The Assyrian Dictionary of the Oriental Institute of the University of Chicago* 15. Chicago: Oriental Institute.

Casanova, M. 2002. 'Le Lapis-lazuli, joyau de l'Orient ancien.' In: J. Guilaine (ed.), *Matériaux, productions, circulations du Néolithique à l'Age du Bronze.* Paris: Errance, 169-90.

Davidoff, J. 2006. 'Color terms and color concepts.' *Journal of Experimental Child Psychology* 94, 334-38.

Deacon, T. 1997. *The Symbolic Species.* New York: Norton.

Durand, J.-M. 1983. *Textes administratifs des salles 134 et 160 du Palais de Mari.* (Archives Royales de Mari XXI). Paris: ERC.

Durand, J.-M. 2000. *Les Documents épistolaires du palais de Mari.* Vol. III. Paris: Cerf.

Englund, R.K. 1998. 'Texts from the Late Uruk Period.' In: P. Attinger & M. Wäfler (eds.), *Mesopotamien: Späturuk-Zeit und frühdynastische Zeit.* (Orbis Biblicus et Orientalis, 160/1 = Annäherungen 1). Freiburg: Freiburg University Press, 15-233.

Fortin, M. (ed.) 1999. *Syrie: Terre de Civilisations.* Quebec: Musée de la Civilisation.

Gage, J. 1999. 'Did Colours Signify? Symbolism in the Red.' *Cambridge Archaeological Journal*, 9, 110-12.

Guilaine, J. (ed.) 2002. *Matériaux, productions, circulations du Néolithique à l'Age du Bronze.* Paris: Errance.

Hannig, R. 2006. *Großes Handwörterbuch Ägyptisch – Deutsch. Marburger Edition.* (Kulturgeschichte der Antiken Welt, 64). Mainz: Von Zabern.

Hardin, C.L. & L. Maffi (eds.) 1997. *Color categories in thought and language.* Cambridge: Cambridge University Press.

Hartung, U. 2001. *Umm el-Qaab II. Importkeramik aus dem Friedhof U in Abydos (Umm el-Qaab) und die Beziehungen Ägyptens zu Vorderasien im 4. Jahrtausend v. Chr.* (Archäologische Veröffentlichungen des Deutschen Archäologischen Instituts Kairo, 92). Mainz: von Zabern.

Harris, J.R. 1961. *Lexicographical Studies in Ancient Egyptian Minerals.* (Institut für Orientforschung, Veröffentlichung 54). Berlin: Deutsche Akademie der Wissenschaften zu Berlin.

Hombert, J.-M. (ed.) 2005. *Aux Origines des langues et du langage.* Paris: Fayard.

Hovers, E., Sh. Ilani, O. Bar-Yosef, B. Vandermeersch 2003. 'An Early Case of Color Symbolism.' *Current Anthropology*, 44, 491-522.

Inizan M.-L. 1995. 'Cornaline et agates: production et circulation de la préhistoire à nos jours.' In: F. Tallon (ed.), *Les pierres précieuses de l'Orient ancien.* Paris: RMN, 21-24.

Jones, A. & R. Bradley 1999. 'The Significance of Colour in European Archaeology.' *Cambridge Archaeological Journal*, 9, 112-14.

Klassen, L. 2004. *Jade und Kupfer*. Aarhus: Aarhus University Press.

Klein, R.G. & B. Edgar 2002. *The Dawn of Human Culture*. New York: John Wiley & Sons.

Komarova, N.L., K.A. Jameson, L. Narens 2007. 'Evolutionary models of color categorization based on discrimination.' *Journal of Mathematical Psychology*, 51, 359-82.

Krauss, R. 1997. *Astronomische Konzepte und Jenseitsvorstellungen in den Pyramidentexten*. (Ägyptologische Abhandlungen, 59). Wiesbaden: Harrassowitz.

Landsberger, B. 1967. 'Über Farben im Sumerisch-Akkadischen.' *Journal of Cuneiform Studies*, 21, 139-73.

Liu, L. 2003. 'The products of minds as well as hands.' *Asian Perspectives*, 42, 1-39.

MacLaury, R.E., G.V. Paramei, D. Dedrick (eds.) 2007. *Anthropology of Color: Interdisciplinary Multilevel Modeling*. Amsterdam: Benjamins.

Michel, C. 1999. 'Les joyaux des rois de Mari.' In: A. Caubet (ed.), *Cornaline et Pierres précieuses. La Méditerranée, de l'Antiquité à l'Islam*. Paris: La documentation française, Musée du Louvre, 401-32.

Michel, C. 2001a. 'Prix.' In: F. Joannès (ed.), *Dictionnaire de la Civilisation Mésopotamienne*. Paris: Robert Lafont, 689-91.

Michel, C. 2001b. 'Le Lapis-Lazuli des Assyriens au début du IIe millénaire av. J.-C..' In: W. H. van Soldt (ed.), *Veenhof Anniversary Volume*. (Publications de l'Institut historique-archeologique neerlandais de Stamboul, 89). Leiden: Netherlands Institute for the Near East, 341-59.

Mithen, S. 1996. *The Prehistory of the Mind: The Cognitive Origins of Art, Religion and Science*. London: Thames & Hudson.

Moorey, P.R.S. 1999. *Ancient Mesopotamian Materials and Industries*. (2nd edn.)Winona Lake: Eisenbrauns.

Nicholson, P. T. & I. Shaw (eds.) 2000. *Ancient Egyptian Materials and Technology*. Cambridge: Cambridge University Press.

Pétrequin, P., S. Cassen, Ch. Croutsch, M. Errera 2002. 'La Valorisation sociales des longues haches dans l'Europe Néolithique.' In: J. Guilaine (ed.), *Matériaux, productions, circulations du Néolithique à l'Age du Bronze*. Paris: Errance, 67-98.

Powell, M.A., P. Vargyas, Th. van den Hout 2003-5. 'Preise.' *Reallexikon der Assyriologie* 10, 609-16.

Prag, K. 1978. 'Silver in the Levant in the Fourth Millennium B.C..' In: R. Moorey & P. Parr (eds.), *Archaeology in the Levant*. Warminster: Aris & Phillips, 36-45.

Pritchard, J. (ed.) 1969. *Ancient Near Eastern Texts Relating to the Old Testament*. Princeton: Princeton University Press.

Quirke, S. 2001. 'Colour Vocabularies in Ancient Egyptian.' In: W.V. Davies (ed.), *Colour and Painting in Ancient Egypt*. London: British Museum, 186-92.

Roux, V. 1995. 'Le travail des lapidaires, Atelier de Khanibhat (Cambay): passé et présent.' In: F. Tallon (ed.), *Les pierres précieuses de l'Orient ancien*. Paris: RMN, 39-44.

Schenkel, W. 1963. 'Die Farben in ägyptischer Kunst und Sprache.' *Zeitschrift für Ägyptische Sprache*, 88, 131-47.

Schenkel, W. 2007. 'Color Terms in Ancient Egyptian and Coptic.' In: R.E. MacLaury, G.V. Paramei, D. Dedrick (eds.), *Anthropology of Color: Interdisciplinary Multilevel Modelling*. Amsterdam: Benjamins, 211-28.

Soden, W. von 1965-1981. *Akkadisches Handwörterbuch*. Wiesbaden: Harrassowitz.

Shields, K. 1979. 'Indo-European Basic Colour Terms.' *Canadian Journal of Linguistics*, 24, 142-46.

Swerdlow, N.M. 1998. *The Babylonian Theory of the Planets*. Princeton: Princeton University Press.

Veldhuis, N. 2001. 'A Multiple Month Account from the Gu'abba Rest House.' *Zeitschrift für Assyriologie*, 91, 85-109.

Warburton, D.A. 1999. '*Sini* "blue" and *burtuqali* "orange".' In: A. Borg (ed.), *The Language of Color in the Mediterranean*. (Stockholm Oriental Studies, 16). Stockholm: Almqvist & Wiksell, 148-51.

Warburton, D.A. 2003a. *Macroeconomics from the Beginning*. Neuchatel: Recherches et Publications.

Warburton, D.A. 2003b. 'Les Valeurs commerciales et idéologiques au Proche-Orient Ancien.' *La Pensée*, 336, 101-12.

Warburton, D.A. 2004a. 'The Terminology of Ancient Egyptian Colours in Context.' In: L. Cleland, K. Stears, G. Davies (eds.), *Colour in the Ancient Mediterranean World*. (BAR International Series, 1267). Oxford: Hodges, 126-30.

Warburton, D.A. 2004b. 'L'impact des échanges en Méditerranée dans le domaine de la terminologie des couleurs.' *Etudes Corses* 59, 145-68.

Warburton, D.A. 2007a. 'La Terminologie des couleurs.' In: J.-C. Goyon & Ch. Cardin (eds.), *Proceedings of the Ninth International Congress of Egyptologists*. (Orientalia Louvaniensia Analecta,150). Louvain: Peeters, 1919-26.

Warburton, D.A. 2007b. 'Basic Color Term Evolution in Light of Ancient Evidence from the Near East.' In: R.E. MacLaury, G.V. Paramei, D. Dedrick (eds.), *Anthropology of Color: Interdisciplinary Multilevel Modelling*. Amsterdam: Benjamins, 229-46.

Warburton, D.A. 2008. 'The Theoretical Implications of Ancient Egyptian Colour Vocabulary for Anthropological and Cognitive Theory.' *Lingua Aegyptia* 16, 213-259.

Warburton, D.A. 2010. 'Colours in Bronze-Age Egyptian Art and Language.' In: V. Brinkmann, O. Primavesi, M. Hollein (eds.), *Circumlithio: The Polychronomy of Antique and Mediaeval Sculpture*. Frankfurt am Main: Schriftenreihe der Liebighaus Skulpturensammlung, 171-187.

Warburton, D.A. 2012. 'Colors in Ancient Egypt.' In: A. Borg (ed.), *The Language of Color in the Mediterranean* (2nd edn.). Wiesbaden: Harrassowitz.

Wilcke, C. 2007. 'Markt und Arbeit im Alten Orient am Ende des 3. Jahrtausends v. Chr.' In: W. Reinhard & J. Stagl (eds.), *Menschen und Märkte*. Vienna: Böhlau Verlag, 71-132.

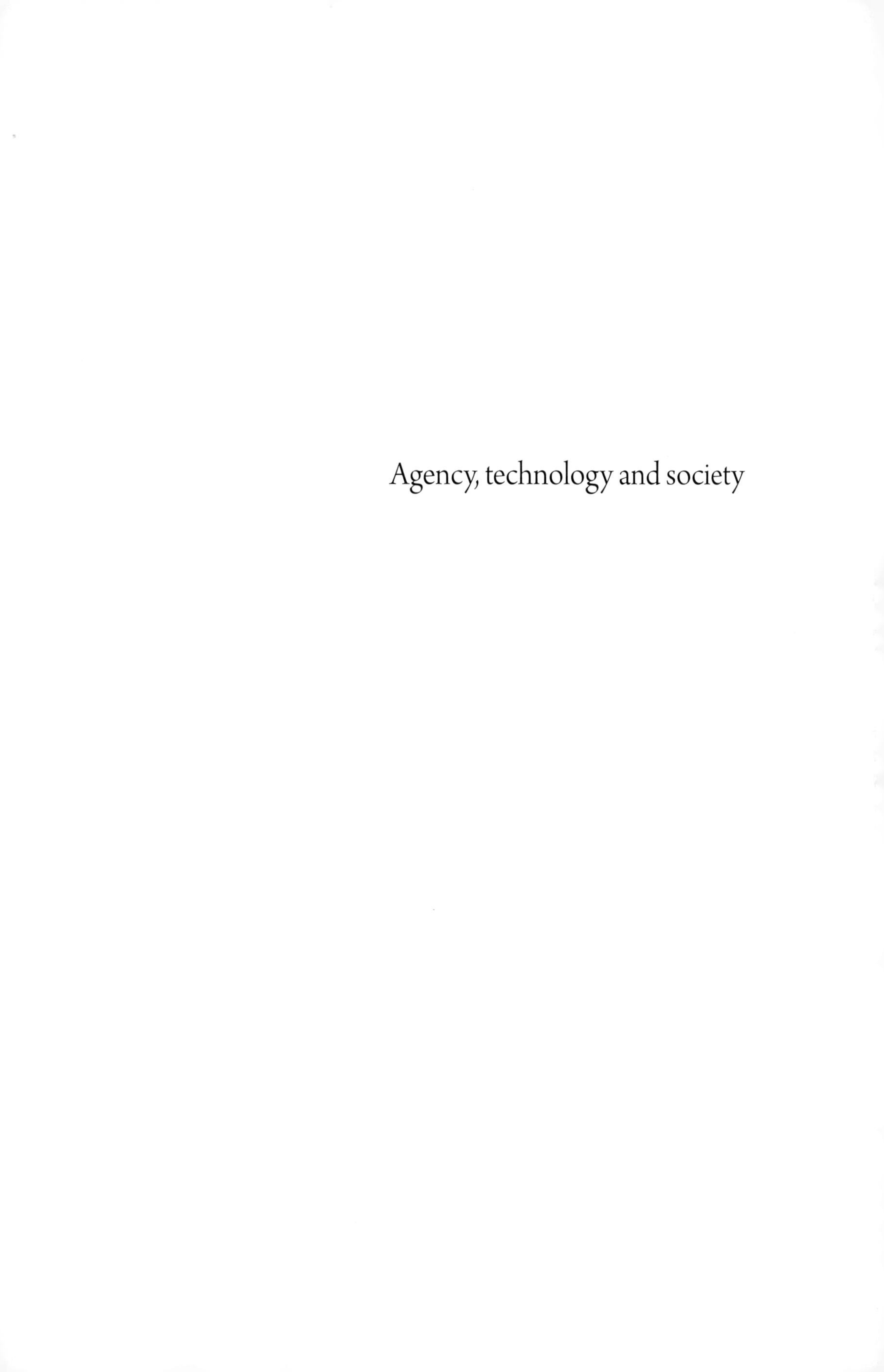

Agency, technology and society

Making Daggers and Scouting for Talents: Situated learning in Late Neolithic Scandinavia

Deborah Olausson

Introduction

Even cursory examination of a collection of Neolithic lithic artifacts will lead to an observation which requires an explanation: for some classes of objects, there are likely to be those which attract our attention and admiration because they are special in some way (Fig. 1). Pelegrin (1990) speaks of elaborate technology when referring to such objects. Had they been unique examples, we would probably explain them as the result of a craftsperson's exuberance or bravado. However, the objects under scrutiny here are not unique – there are sufficient numbers of them to attract our interest and awaken a need to explain why they exist and why we recognize them as special.

Fig. 1. Two thin-butted Neolithic flint axes. Photograph by Bengt Almgren, The Lund Historical Museum.

Fig. 2. An amateur knapper holding an overdimensioned axe he claims to have made. Photograph by the author.

It is conceivable that these extraordinary objects were individual possessions in which their owner for personal reasons invested extra time and care (Fig. 2). A young woman embroidering linens for her dowry might be seen as a nearly contemporary example of such a phenomenon. However, the fact that extraordinary objects occur in some numbers suggests that they might have played a more public role in their contemporary social context. Indeed this is the sort of reasoning archaeologists are fond of using when they identify some artifacts as prestige objects.

We make things for a variety of reasons, most of which involve fulfilling needs. At one end of a hypothetical scale we find needs which are primarily economic; at the other, those which are primarily social. In the first instance objects are involved in economic transactions. A more elaborate item fetches a higher price, while a more common item is cheaper. This model requires demand outside of the family and a scale of production which supersedes family needs. A craftsperson who produces for a market will try to minimize manufacturing time while maximizing prices.

The second kind of demand has primarily social motives. A common explanation for the existence of extraordinary objects, at least in pre-market economies, is that they are prestige objects which served primarily social rather than primarily practical purposes. Enterprising members of transegalitarian societies may use prestige technology in order to transform food surpluses into nonperishable objects that can be used in social transactions. Such objects retain their value as long as they are rare. Aspiring elites are therefore engaged in an ongoing struggle to ensure rarity, thus maintaining control of the prestige objects (Hayden 1995, 18).

Prestige goods are a means by which elites can transform economic surpluses into ways of gaining or maintaining power. The simplest definition of a prestige good is that it is something that everybody wants but not everybody can get. The key attributes, then, are universal desirability combined with limited accessibility. These bear an inverse relationship to each other: desirability *decreases* in direct proportion to an *increase* in accessibility. This is why it is in the best interests of individuals wishing to seize or consolidate power to limit (or at least be seen to limit) accessibility, while at the same time maintaining desirability. Some of the means of limiting the accessibility of crafted objects might be by gaining control over

- sources of raw material
- knowledge
- know-how
- a gifted or talented individual.

In the following, I intend to scrutinize the parameters of know-how and talent in relation to apprentice systems and situated learning. I will explore how know-how is acquired by the individual, and describe two examples of apprentice systems as social structures set up for acquiring know-how. Finally, I will briefly analyze the crafting of Late Neolithic flint daggers in light of the parameters of control mentioned above, in order to evaluate flint daggers as a possible basis for a prestige goods system.

Situated cognition and the many facets of knowing

Jacques Pelegrin (1990) is credited with introducing the concepts of 'knowledge' and 'know-how' into the archaeological discourse (Fig. 3). According to this paradigm, knowledge is situated in the mind and is explicit and declarative, while know-how is experiential and learned by doing (Apel 2001, 27-28). Knowledge can exist independently of individuals, while know-how is inseparable from the practitioner. However, theories of situated cognition, or situativity theory, question this dichotomy. Situativity theory struggles against a functionalist belief in a mind-body dualism. It holds that perception and cognition are not properties or

Knowledge	Know-how
Recipe for action	Embodied practice
Theoretical knowing	Practical knowing
Described by words	Demonstrated by actions
Can be forgotten	Forever part of the body
Can be grasped in seconds	May require years to master
Exists independently from individuals	Inseparable from the practitioner

Fig. 3. The distinction between knowledge and know-how. Based on Pelegrin (1990) and Apel (2001).

possessions of individual minds. Rather they are acts or relations which cannot be disconnected from individual experience within a social context (Kirshner and Whitson 1997; Barab & Plucker 2002). Accordingly, competent action is generated in the contexts of actions, not based on the accumulation of knowledge in individual minds (St. Julien 1997, 261). Thus, it would appear that situativity theory eschews the idea of knowledge as Pelegrin uses it. Theories of situated cognition hold that competence or expertise can only be measured according to the standards set by the context of practice (Barab & Plucker 2002, 169). As the individual develops his/her expertise in a specific domain, he or she gains a more central position in the community (Barab & Plucker 2002, 173). Or as Bereiter (1997) states, 'the course of situated learning typically has the aspect of a progression from being inept and prone to stupid mistakes to being competent and smart' (p. 287). However, expertise in one domain cannot necessarily be transferred to another; expertise is contextually learned and it is also contextually practiced. Although important aspects of what is learned in one situation may transfer to a new situation, the aspects that generally do *not* transfer are those which are involved in 'being smart' (Bereiter 1997). Does this mean that all knowing is contextually bound? Bereiter says no. He suggests that non-situated knowledge does exist. This is knowledge which has been transformed into objects that can be used in an unlimited variety of situations (Bereiter 1997, 298). Therefore it would appear that we may continue to use the concepts of knowledge (explicit and declarative knowing) and know-how (situated and embodied knowing) as Pelegrin proposed them.

Transferring know-how

Knowing, then, is a complicated concept, and how we view knowing has fundamental ramifications for how we think learning takes place. Learning *how* to do something – in theory – is not the same as learning to *do* something – in practice. Crafting, as embodied practice, must be learned by doing. Learning a craft requires practice and more practice until muscles, arms, fingers and brain internalize the know-how necessary for successful performance. The more know-how involved, the more practice will be necessary. The process of embodying know-how requires repetition so that episodes of motor actions become automatic, allowing for the smooth flow which characterizes the proficient performer. Skill acquisition in sports, or in any performance field, involves three stages:

1. Cognitive stage. Learners develop a declarative encoding of the skill. They are exposed to demonstrations of how a skill is correctly performed and they memorize a set of facts relevant to the skill. Declarative knowledge is paramount.
2. Practice stage. Errors in the initial understanding are gradually detected and eliminated and corrections among the various elements required for successful performance are strengthened. In sports, there is rapid improvement at first, less as bodies reach their limits. Procedural and declarative knowledge occur side by side but procedural knowledge dominates at this stage.
3. Automatic stage. Skills become habits and motor responses are automatically triggered. Performance is relaxed, effective, and largely unconscious (Anderson 1990, 259-60; Logan 1985, 369; Vernacchia *et al.* 1992,106).

Repetition progressively frees the mind from attention to details and reduces the extent to which consciousness must concern itself with the process (Moran, 1996, 59). In other words, the greater one's expertise in a domain, the less one needs to think about what he or she is doing.

Giftedness and talent

I have suggested above that achieving control over a gifted individual could be one means of limiting the accessibility of exceptional crafted items. This statement implies that ability is unevenly distributed among individuals and that differences are in some measure present from birth. Is this a viable concept? First, it is necessary to define the terms we are using. Feldhusen & Jarwan (2000, 273-74) define giftedness as a basically genetic endowment that enables the development of special abilities, aptitudes and talents. Talent is a special ability within a domain of human ability such as mathematics or tennis.

Winner & Martino's (2000) article 'Giftedness in Non-Academic Domains: The Case of the Visual Arts and Music' contains interesting insights which are relevant for individuals requiring flintknapping skills. Winner and Martino claim that children who may be labeled 'gifted' in drawing do not pass drawing milestones earlier than typical children. Rather, these children draw in a qualitatively different way. The authors suggest that these children see the world differently, i.e., in terms of shapes and visual surfaces rather than concepts. In the case of both musically and artistically gifted children the unusual abilities emerge early in the child's life: as early as one to two years of age. Winner and Martino conclude that 'the strikingly early age of the emergence of gifts in art and music, and the fact that high levels of skill make themselves known prior to formal training, are strong pieces of indirect evidence for an innate component' (p. 106).

However, not all gifted children grow up to be experts in their domain. This is because the development of exceptional abilities or talent in a particular domain is the product of a combination of the following factors: individual resources, a supportive environment, hard work, and continuous training or practice (Schoon 2000, 214). 'The personality characteristics associated with success in any field are drive, tenacity, and the willingness to overcome obstacles' (Winner & Martino 2000, 108). Furthermore, as I discussed above, expertise is domain-specific and not a universal property. Therefore it is possible for gifted individuals to possess copious amounts of domain knowledge but be unable to use it effectively if they lack the implicit knowledge of a field (Sternberg 2000, 57).

Does practice make perfect? (cf. Olausson 2008) While deliberate practice can affect differences among individuals, there is no evidence that it can *eliminate* these differences. Sternberg concludes that deliberate practice plays a role in the development of high levels of expertise, but it is a necessary and not a sufficient condition (Sternberg 2000, 59). Schneider adds the factor of motivation to those of individual differences and the amount of deliberate practice as being the three key variables for predicting differences in the level of expertise which can be reached within a given domain (Schneider 2000, 173). A quotation from Sternberg can serve to summarize the present consensus: 'The best evidence is in favor of both genetic and environmental origins of intelligence, interacting in ways that are not, as yet, fully known' (Sternberg 2000, 56).

The community of practice

Because in modern Western thought we tend to view the mind and the body as separate entities, we have placed learning in a separate sphere and called it 'education'. Our education systems tend to favor logico-mathematical and linguistic knowledge over bodily-kinesthetic know-how in their curricula. In Swedish schools there has been a trend toward reducing the time spent on instruction in physical activities such as sports. However, recent studies (Ericsson 2003) have shown that bodily-kinesthetic skills are an important component in promoting *all* learning skills, theoretical as well as practical. Learning is not an isolated aspect of our lives; rather it is a practice in which we – our bodies as well as our minds – are continuously engaged with the world around us. Learning is a social practice and it is an aspect of all human activities (Grimm 2000).

In their book *Situated learning. Legitimate peripheral participation* (1991), Jean Lave and Etienne Wenger focus on learning as social practice. They suggest that the community of practice is an intrinsic condition for the existence of knowledge. Learning involves the whole person and it implies not only a relation to specific activities, but also a relation to social communities. The normal process of learning is by legitimate peripheral participation, in which individuals participate in a community of practitioners. Participation is at first peripheral, but as learning progresses the individual's participation increases in engagement and complexity. Learning occurs through apprentices engaging in the real practices of experts. Through this practice, learners move from being peripheral to becoming fully participating members of a community. Children learning to speak are legitimate peripheral participants in the community of practice defined by all who use the language. Through their active participation in using language, the peripheral participants eventually reach the level of those who have mastered the skill.

Formal and informal communities of practice

In what social context does learning a craft take place? Lave & Wenger define a community of practice as 'a set of relations among persons, activity, and world, over time and in relation with other tangential and overlapping communities of practice' (Lave & Wenger 1991, 98). This is a very broad definition which need not imply conscious control or actions limiting access to a community. I believe it is important to differentiate between formal and informal communities, although Lave and Wenger do not really make this distinction. If we use a broad definition of a community of practice, all or most of the skills necessary will be acquired by all participants. Through legitimate peripheral participation, all children are transformed/transform themselves from watchers to doers. This process occurs in informal learning contexts of the household and daily life and access to the community of practice is not consciously limited. In this sense we can see childhood as an extended period of legitimate peripheral participation during which children are expected to make the culture of practice theirs. The skills which are acquired can be mastered – albeit with varying degrees of competence – by all members of the community.

Lave & Wenger concentrate instead on formal communities of practice in which access is restricted and there are recognized boundaries to membership. Such communities limit legitimate access, either through family membership or by formal apprenticeship. These are formalized learning contexts which develop in response to a need for control or a need for long legitimate peripheral participation because the skills to be taught require long practice (Lave & Wenger 1991). Learning does not take place in the learner's own household, although apprentices may receive their training in the artisan family or household, as in the case of the guilds in Montpellier in 13th century France (Epstein 1991, 106; Reyerson 1992, 7).

Expertise in relation to creativity

Lave and Wenger also address the conflict which is inherent in practice, namely the conflict between tradition and innovation. One model of informal learning emphasizes 'scaffolding', meaning the scaffold built around the learner to keep him or her from falling. The learner is expected to carefully observe and follow examples of practice. In this model, the learner is so carefully monitored that he or she has no room for error and no chance for experimentation or innovation (Greenfield 2000). However, if absolute adherence to a template were required in all practice situations, there would be no contingency for change. Lave and Wenger emphasize that there is a motor for change built into the community of practice because the community is composed of individuals (Lave & Wenger 1991, 117).

Should expertise in a domain or a community of practice be judged on the basis of how well the individual adheres to the template, or rather on how well the individual can manipulate the skills in new and creative ways? The consensus here is that expert performance involves a creative element which surpasses automatic responses. Expertise is often characterized by a creative contribution that goes above and beyond the competencies of those who mentored the expert (Singer & Janelle 1999, 137). Winner & Martino (2000) note that the skill involved in being a child prodigy is not the same as the skill of being a domain-altering creator. A prodigy is someone who can easily and readily master a domain with expertise, while a creator is someone who *changes* a domain. They also note that there is considerable evidence that creators do not make domain-altering changes until they have worked at least ten years in their area.

As the community of practice moves through time, newcomers become old-timers and the conflict between the forces that support processes of learning and those that work against them provide the motor of change. Newcomers are caught in a dilemma. They need to engage in the existing practice, which has developed over time. They need to participate in it and to become full members of the community in which it exists. However, they also have a stake in its development as they begin to establish their own identity in its future (Lave & Wenger 1991). I suggest that in this conflict we also find the leeway for individual differences to be expressed and the possibility for the encouragement of gifted individuals. Those possessing both a high degree of know-how and the ability to manipulate this know-how in novel ways are the most talented individuals.

Barbro Santillo Frizell's description of a fraternity of *trullo*-builders yields valuable details about embodied know-how and its social context. Her study focuses on craftsmen in southern Italy who build the so-called *trullo,* a type of conical roof made of limestone slabs and used on traditional rural houses. Craftsmen emphasized that the erection of the domed roof, the most difficult element, requires full bodily engagement and a large measure of know-how. The process of instilling the know-how must begin early in the individual's life in order to ensure its full development. Trullo-building skills are passed on within the family from generation to generation. However, even given the same training and legitimate peripheral participation, not all children in a family become masters at the craft. The informant Santillo Frizell interviewed emphasized that it was important that children have talent for the work. According to him, it was possible to distinguish promising candidates at an early age, and the master's ability to see this was itself described as a skill which could not easily be put into words (Santillo Frizell 2000).

Two examples of learning which is situated in communities of practice

I propose now to illustrate the differences between situated learning in informal and formal communities of practice, respectively, by looking at descriptions of axe-blade-making[1] communities in the Highlands of New Guinea and Irian Jaya.

Several accounts describe axe-blade-making in the Highlands of Papua New Guinea. Among the Tungei, a tribe of about 800 people, axe-blade-making appears to occur in a nonrestricted, informal community of practice. Quarrying expeditions were carried out about every three to five years. All the men in the quarry-owning clans of the Tungei participated in these expeditions, which meant that about 200 men and adolescent youths took part. Burton writes that all clans had to agree to start an expedition at the same time, which emphasizes the consensus-driven nature of quarrying. For the duration of an expedition, men set aside their personal ambition in order to work cooperatively. Individuals were not empowered to find and hoard good axe stones for themselves. Openness and comradship were placed at a premium during quarry expeditions, and axes were left in the open for others to see freely. Each man would get enough stone to make 10-50 polishable roughouts (Burton 1984). Vial (1940) describes a similar organization for inhabitants of the Jimi Valley, another Highland tribe. Højlund (1979) indicates that the pattern Burton describes characterizes many of the Highland tribes. Every male made his own axes and the first stages were carried out at the quarry, followed by later stages of knapping and grinding at the settlement. These accounts describe a situation in which the community of practice is open and nonrestrictive, at least for male members. Youths learn by their legitimate peripheral participation and access to know-how is available to all male members of the tribes in the area.

Dietrich Stout (2002) has described a more restrictive community of practice among the Langda of Irian Jaya, located west of Papua New Guinea. In 1999 there were only seven men who made adzes. This community of practice was more formalized and restricted and it was run by a head adze-maker. Access to suitable stone from the Ey River was controlled by the villages along the river and the head adze-maker in each village had personal authority over quarrying activities. He regulated access to adze production by collecting and redistributing the roughouts made at the quarry. At the settlement, hammerstones and roughouts were stored at his home. Entry into the community of adze-makers was through a period of apprenticeship of up to five years or more. Access to the community was restricted to the close relatives of the masters, usually 'sons' (Langda terminology does not distinguish between sons and nephews). In traditional Langda society apprenticeship began at 12-13 years of age; today beginning apprentices are usually in their mid-20s. Apprentices are chosen on the basis of two factors. One is the interest shown by the potential apprentice; the other is the master's evaluation of his seriousness and commitment. In some cases the master also evaluates knapping attempts before deciding to accept an apprentice. Although access to the formal apprentice system is restricted, younger 'sons' seem to be able to take part in informal legitimate peripheral participation at an earlier age. Perhaps the most successful/interested of these peripheral participants were those who later were chosen to be apprentices.

In traditional societies, the transmission of knowledge and know-how will occur within the home or close to home. While both open and restricted-access communities of practice provide opportunities for individual differences to be expressed, the opportunity for this to occur should be greater in open communities. However, even in formalized communities where access is restricted and kinship-based, there are often mechanisms in place which encourage individuals perceived as particularly gifted or talented, as well as provisions for bringing in individuals who are not related. Among blacksmiths in Kenya, smithing is a hereditary calling and provisions for admitting apprentices are heavily regulated. In those cases where no apprentice candidates are available within the family, they are taken from outside. However these candidates must always come from a family with smith forbears and it is very rare for an individual without smith ancestry to be apprenticed. Such youths are usually chosen from among the sons of the smith's best friends and age-mates (Brown 1995, 119).

My intention in discussing the theoretical issues here has been to point out that learning is an activity which can only be understood in its social context. In his model for dagger manufacture in Late Neolithic Scandinavia, Jan Apel (2001) envisions a restricted-access community of practice under the control of a production fraternity to which only kin were allowed access. Apel suggests that individual differences in ability would be suppressed in this kind of system. I wish to explore if there are ways in which individual talents or interests may be allowed to be expressed, even in formalized, restricted-access communities of practice. In open, informal communities of practice, to which everybody in the group has access, I would expect greater individual leeway and more rapid change. Because of the conflicts between old-timers and newcomers, no community of practice will ever exactly reproduce practice forever (for example, even the Catholic Mass is no longer said in Latin). It is here that I see an opening for individual talent and innovation being employed in social strategies. In the archaeological case study which follows I evaluate Late Neolithic flint daggers in terms of their suitability as prestige goods. Was it possible for any individual or group to gain control over sources of raw material, knowledge, know-how, or a gifted or talented individual who could make flint daggers?

The Late Neolithic, a time of transition

Scandinavian archaeology does not recognize a chalcolithic period. The period preceding the Bronze Age is known as the Late Neolithic and it is divided into an earlier phase beginning in 2350 BC and a later phase from 1950 to 1700 BC. The Late Neolithic I is contemporary with the middle and late Beaker phases in the British Isles, the Veluwe and Epimaritime Beaker phases in the Rhine delta, and the Early Bronze Age in central Europe, while the later phase is contemporary with the Unetice culture in Central Europe (Apel 2001, 10). Although copper objects appear in the archaeological material in Scandinavia as early as the late Mesolithic period (Klassen 2000), the first evidence for domestic casting occurs in the Late Neolithic (Vandkilde 1996; 2005).

Some consider Late Neolithic society to be undifferentiated, while others suggest that the hierarchy visible in the Bronze Age is already underway at this time (Apel 2001; Lekberg 2002; Vandkilde 1996). The subsistence base was agrarian and families lived in two-aisled long-houses. Some farmsteads were clustered into small hamlets while others were more isolated. Deceased individuals were placed in stone cists, in a pit, or interred as secondary burial in older passage graves (Apel 2001; Lekberg 2002; Vandkilde 2005).

Late Neolithic flint daggers

A major innovation in flintknapping emerged at about 2350 BC in southern Scandinavia; namely, bifacial flaking. Previous to this, only one isolated example of a bifacial tool type is known. This is the so-called *dolkstav* ('dagger staff'), a long pointed tool of unknown use found in the Early Neolithic Funnel-necked Beaker Culture. Aside from this isolated example, flintknapping throughout the Early and Middle Neolithic periods is based on quadrifacial forms and on making blade and flake tools. While quadrifacial flint axes are still being made during the Late Neolithic, we now see an explosion of bifacial forms. These include daggers, spearheads, sickles and projectile points (Vandkilde 2005). Of these, the daggers are the type which evinces the greatest degree of artistry and elaboration. Contemporary knappers who have attempted to replicate flint daggers say that they are the most technologically complex chipped-stone tools found anywhere in the world during prehistory (Stafford 1998, 338).

When classifying flint daggers, archaeologists use Ebbe Lomborg's (1973) system of six main types (Fig. 4). Each type has at least two subtypes. Types I to III belong to the earlier Late Neolithic and types IV to VI to the later (Vandkilde 2005, 6). Types I and IV contain examples of the most elaborate and well-made objects; the longest type I dagger known is 45 cm in length (Glob 1952, 64). However, very few daggers are found in mint condition. Most of them show signs of resharpening and/or reworking (Lomborg 1973, 21).

Daggers are numerous and geographically widespread. The most comprehensive and up-to-date registration of flint daggers can be found in Apel (2001, Table 9:2), who lists a total of 13,168 daggers. The majority of these can be found in

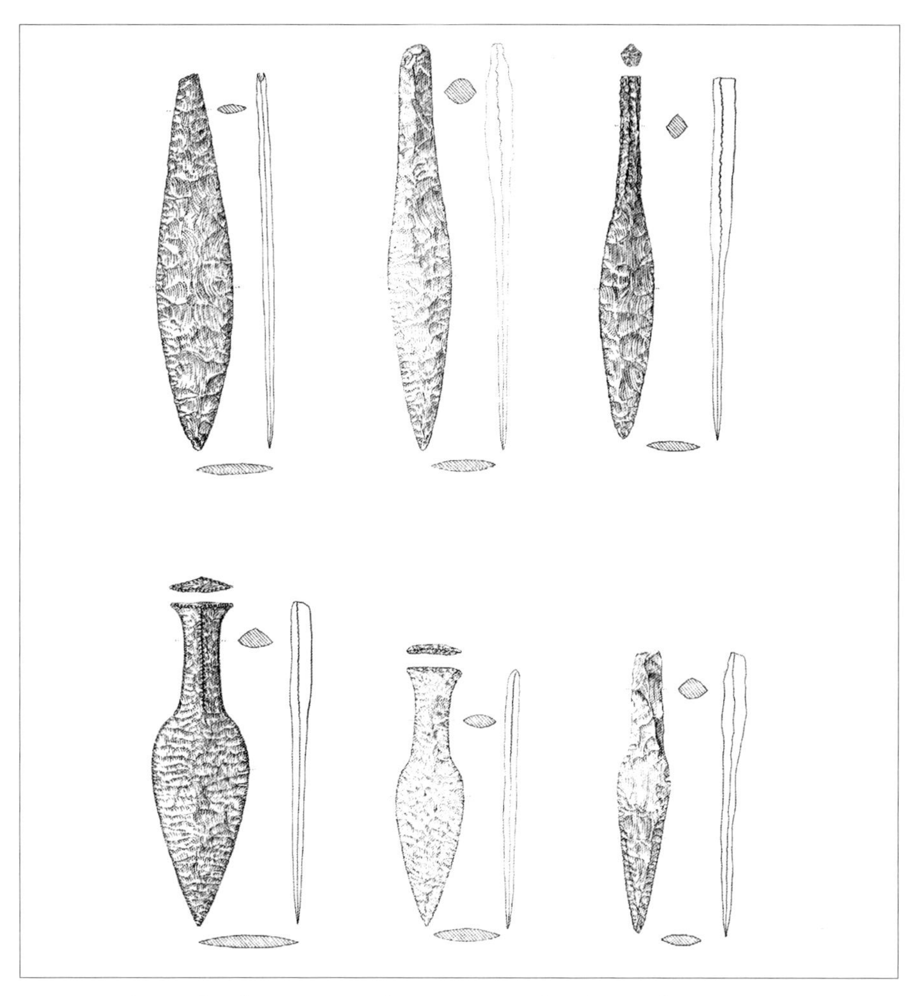

Fig. 4. Lomborg's classification system for Scandinavian flint daggers (reproduced in Apel 2001, Fig. 8:1).

Denmark (*c.* 4200), Sweden (*c.* 4500) and Norway (*c.* 1400), but Scandinavian daggers also occur in Poland, northern Germany, and Finland.

Daggers are more often found in burials and hoards than at settlements (Sarauw 2008). A compilation of the data in Lomborg's catalogue (1973) yields *c.* 430 dagger finds in hoards compared to *c.* 1,360 in burials (no figures for settlement finds are available in this source). Sarauw's investigation of type I daggers showed that most examples in single type hoards are unused or unfinished while most found in burials are resharpened. Daggers found in settlement contexts are usually fragmentary and smaller than those from hoards and burials (Sarauw 2008). Holberg's investigations in Norway confirmed that daggers found on settlements usually show signs of damage and reworking (Holberg 1998, 16). In those instances in which several daggers occur together in burials, it is often possible to distinguish a 'dagger hierarchy'; that is, one or a limited number of large, unused daggers combined with a greater number of daggers showing poor workmanship, reworking, or inferior raw material (Holberg 1998, 13; Sarauw 2008; Weiler 1994, 76).

Those who have studied flint daggers have noted that they show a wide range of knapping quality. I conducted a study of a random selection of *c.* 540 flint daggers of all types from the collections at the Historical Museum in Lund. I recorded knapping quality on a scale from 'poor' to 'excellent'. Some daggers are exceptionally well-made and symmetrical, while others are poorly made and show large numbers of knapping errors (Olausson 2000, fig. 6). Sophus Müller suggested in 1902 that even the finest daggers were intended for use and not made only for the sake of beauty. He pointed to reworked daggers where it was possible to see, from what is left of the original, that they were once first-class objects (Müller 1902, 166).

The majority of the daggers encountered are made from a high quality, glassy flint of Senonian age. Sarauw's investigation of the fragmentary daggers and dagger debitage from the site of Bejsebakken in Jutland showed that most of the daggers were made from a Senonian flint which resembles the kind mined at Skovbakken,

Fig. 5. Senonian flint outcropping at Stevns Klint, Denmark (after Högberg & Olausson 2008).

750 meters from Bejsebakken. However, one broken dagger was made of Danian flint with bryozoans and he states that flintknappers at Bejsebakken were not very demanding in their choice of raw material for making smaller daggers (Sarauw 2008). Similarly, Earle commented that many of the 'household daggers' found during the Thy investigations were made of field flint of low quality (Earle 1997, 165). When he conducted his extensive inventory, Apel discovered rare examples of daggers made of raw materials other than Senonian flint including Danian flint, Kristianstad flint, and even quartzite (Apel 2001, 32).

It seems clear from the appearance of the daggers that they bear some relationship to metal forms. Vandkilde suggests that the type I dagger is modeled on the tanged flat copper daggers of Beaker type (Vandkilde 2005, 15), and many archaeologists have noted the close similarities between the type IVD flint dagger and the triangular bronze dagger from the Unetice Culture (Apel 2001, 251; Callahan personal communication; Stensköld 2004, 66). Most of the flint dagger types are considered imitations rather than copies, however. Daggers were made under the influence of metal forms, but in a distinctly Scandinavian – or should we say 'lithicized' – style (Müller 1902, 132; Stensköld 2004, 92; Vandkilde 2005, 17).

How do daggers measure up as a basis for a prestige goods system?

The manufacture and use of metal increases in scope and complexity during the Late Neolithic, and by the onset of LNII, metallurgy had become an 'integrated part of social life', according to Vandkilde (2005, 11). This must surely have meant a radical shift in the underpinnings of a society which had until that time built its way of life upon objects made of native raw materials such as flint, wood, bone and plant fibers. Unlike these materials, copper and tin could not be obtained locally. Alliances and networks were now open to renegotiation. Networks for obtaining the new raw material, and the know-how for working it, had to be established.

Fig. 6. A replication of a type Ic dagger, made by modern knapper Greg Nunn. The dagger is 32.5 cm long. Photograph courtesy of Greg Nunn.

Flint technology, as epitomized in the daggers, was under threat from this new technology. The ideal prestige good is one where it is easy to restrict access to one or more of the parameters I noted previously. How do daggers measure up?

Control of raw material. As noted above, we know that most of the daggers have been made from Senonian flint, which is glassy and easily worked. This type of flint is readily available on the beaches of Denmark and southern Sweden (Fig. 5; Högberg & Olausson 2008). As discussed previously, daggers made from erratic flints found in surface moraines are also frequent, both at settlements and in burials. Therefore, I suggest that it was not possible for any individual or group to gain control over the raw material for making the majority of daggers (cf. Sarauw 2008). However, localities with nodules of sufficient size and of sufficient quality to serve as raw material for the longest, most elaborate daggers are fewer and these may have been subject to control, as Apel (2001) suggests. The evidence for Late Neolithic flint mines at localities in northern Jutland (e.g. Becker 1959; 1980) may be evidence for this kind of exploitation and control.

Control of knowledge. I maintain that all adult members of Late Neolithic society possessed both the necessary knowledge (recipe for action) and the necessary know-how to make a serviceable flint dagger. My arguments for this position are firstly the large numbers of daggers and secondly that so many of them exhibit poor knapping. I maintain that dagger-making was part of the informal community of Late Neolithic practice. Members of society learned to knap as children (cf. Sarauw 2008), since the ability to do so would have been a necessary survival skill.

The elaboration of certain forms (Fig. 6) indicates that a parallel production system for making extraordinary daggers existed at the same time, however. Joan Gero has noted that social information in things is amplified in the manufacturing sequence by manipulating the number of manufacturing steps that comprise each stage. Incrementing the number of production steps represents inflation in the costs of transmitting social information (Gero 1989, 94). Dagger production technology would seem to be a good example of this process. For instance, several of the subtypes defined by Lomborg (1973) are elaborations on the main typological theme. These subtypes require more production stages and greater knapping finesse (e.g., Type IC; Stafford 2003, 1548). Contemporary knapper Errett Callahan has spent many years trying to replicate flint daggers. He and Jan Apel are attempting, through experimentation and the study of archaeological preforms and finished and unfinished pieces, to rediscover the knowledge necessary for making a type IV flint dagger. They have found, for example, that the so-called stitching on the handles of the best type IV daggers such as those

Fig. 7. Full-sized replica of the Hindsgavl dagger from Denmark, 29.3 cm long. Made by knapper Errett Callahan. Poto-graph courtesy of Errett Callahan.

from Hindsgavl (Fig. 7) or Skatelöv is formed according to specific norms and using specific tools. Stitching on ordinary type IV daggers is done using coarser techniques. In Callahan's descriptions of the type IV system, it is evident that this knowledge is precise, complex and highly standardized (Barrowclough 2004; Callahan personal communication). We can thus envision that the elaborate types were developed in an attempt to restrict access to knowledge or to know-how.

Control of individuals with know-how. Greater morphological complexity re-quires greater know-how, at least where flintknapping is concerned. Size is also an issue here: knappers agree that excessively longer knapped objects are much more difficult to make than shorter ones (Pelegrin 1990; Stout 2002). The aim of Callahan and Apel's work is to make available the knowledge – the recipe for action – necessary for making a type IV dagger. However, those who lack the physical skills to translate this into the appropriate actions will still fail to make anything resembling an elaborate dagger. It seems to me that this is a key ingredient here, since there is no short-cut to accruing know-how; it simply must take time. Callahan has about 50 years of knapping experience and he has been replicating daggers for more than 25 years (Callahan, personal communication).

Granted, as a modern knapper he has not had the advantages of knapping since childhood or hands-on instruction. Nevertheless, achieving the highest levels of proficiency requires time; time which cannot be used in getting food on the table. Stafford, another modern knapper, has suggested that the technical proficiency needed to execute the pressure-flaking stage on a type IC dagger took years to master (Stafford 2003, 1548).

Jan Apel maintains that acquiring the know-how necessary for making the elaborate type IC and type IV daggers requires an apprenticeship system, i.e., a specific type of learning environment. He suggests that certain families set up apprentice systems, thus maintaining control over both the knowledge and the know-how needed for making the elaborate daggers. Perhaps these families were allied with or were themselves members of an enterprising elite who tried to translate these skills, through the medium of elaborate daggers, into symbolic capital (Apel 2001).

Contemporary with the making of elaborate daggers we have the manufacture of ordinary daggers. Here the community of practice was informal and access was open, I believe. Thus, whereas everyone in the society could have had access to the knowledge of how to make a dagger, not everyone could gain the know-how which was necessary to make the most elaborate daggers. In the latter case the community of practice was formal and restricted.

Control of the gifted or talented individual and his or her dagger production. Are full knowledge and long apprenticeship for accruing know-how sufficient to enable any individual to make an elaborate type IV dagger? I do not believe so. The best daggers were only made by the most gifted individuals who also had access to recipes for action (knowledge) and long practice (know-how), as well as motivation and training. The elite who wished to exploit this system would look for a means to ensure that the community of practice for making the elaborate daggers was formal and restricted and attempt to gain control over the community. Furthermore, the elite would wish to find means to ensure that gifted individuals under his/her control were recognized and allowed access to the community. Given the open nature of the community of practice for making most daggers, I think that both of these steps would have been difficult.

Conclusion: endings and beginnings

As a basis for a prestige goods system, daggers were only partially successful. Dagger-making was carried out in two types of communities of practice. Flint-knapping know-how was necessary for survival and the knowledge and the know-

Fig. 8. Stitching on the handle of an experimentally made type IV dagger. Photograph by the author.

how needed for making everyday daggers belonged to an open and informal community of practice. Some of the more elaborate daggers are evidence of attempts to control know-how, perhaps in order to restrict access to a community of practice. We see these sorts of elaborations on daggers of type IC and type IV. Trying to restrict access meant 'upping the ante' on knowledge and/or on know-how by making the dagger more and more elaborate so that the community of practice for making them could be restricted. But there were only limited means of increasing the complexity of making daggers. The only options were to increase the manufacturing stages or to create details on them which only the individuals with the most knowledge, the most know-how, and/or the most expertise could reproduce (Fig. 8). But if elaborate dagger forms became too complicated, for instance if too few knappers were able to make them, then it became impossible to make enough to satisfy social demands.

Copper/bronze technology proved much more suitable as a social medium for prestige goods. In this case it was fairly simple to limit access to the parameters of raw material, knowledge, and know-how, and the community of practice could be easily restricted and brought under the control of an aspiring elite. It is easy to understand why social complexity accelerated once the system got underway.

Acknowledgements

I would like to thank the organizers of Excavating the Mind for a most inspiring conference. Jan Apel read and commented on an earlier draft of this article. The comments of two anonymous reviewers and the editors greatly improved the article. I wish also to thank Jan Apel, Errett Callahan and Greg Nunn for permission to use their illustrations.

Notes

1 Since authors have not made a distinction between axes and adzes in their descriptions, I will follow the terminology used by the author. From a technological point of view and based on the documentation, I judge that axe blades and adze blades are comparable.

References

Anderson, J.R. 1990. *Cognitive Psychology and its Implications.* New York: W.H. Freeman & Co.

Apel, J. 2001. *Daggers Knowledge & Power. The Social Aspects of Flint-Dagger Technology in Scandinavia 2350-1500 BC.* (Coast to Coast Books 3). Uppsala: Uppsala University, Department of Archaeology & Ancient History.

Barab, S.A. & J.A. Plucker 2002. 'Smart People or Smart Contexts? Cognition, Ability, and Talent Development in an Age of Situated Approaches to Knowing and Learning.' *Educational Psychologist,* 37(3), 165-82.

Barrowclough, D.A. 2004. 'The secrets of the craft production of Scandinavian Late Neolithic flint daggers.' *Lithic Technology,* 29(1), 75-86.

Becker, C.J. 1959. 'Flint-mining in Neolithic Denmark.' *Antiquity,* 33, 87-92.

Becker, C.J. 1980. 'Hov, Gem. Sennels, Amt Thisted, Jütland.' In: G. Weisgerber (ed.), *5000 Jahre Feuersteinbergbau.* Bochum: Deutschen Bergbau-Museum, 457-464.

Bereiter, C. 1997. 'Situated Cognition and How to Overcome It.' In: D. Kirshner & J.A. Whitson (eds.), *Situated Cognition. Social, Semiotic, and Psychological Perspectives.* Mahwah, N.J.: Lawrence Erlbaum Associates, 281-309.

Brown, J. 1995. *Traditional Metalworking in Kenya.* (Oxbow Monographs 44). Oxford: Oxbow Books.

Burton, J. 1984. 'Quarrying in a tribal society.' *World Archaeology,* 16(2), 234-47.

Earle, T. 1997. *How Chiefs Come to Power.* Stanford: Stanford University Press.

Epstein, S. 1991. *Wage Labor and Guilds in Medieval Europe.* Chapel Hill, N.C.: University of North Carolina.

Ericsson, I. 2003. *Motorik, koncentrationsförmåga och skolprestationer: en interventionsstudie i skolår 1-3.* (Malmö Studies in Education Sciences 6). Malmö: Malmö Lärarhögskola.

Feldhusen, J.F. & F.A. Jarwan 2000. 'Identification of Gifted and Talented Youth for Educational Programs.' In: K.A. Heller, F.J. Mönks, R.J. Sternberg, R.F. Subotnik (eds.), *International Handbook of Giftedness and Talent.* New York: Elsevier, 271-82.

Gero, J. M. 1989. 'Assessing social information in material objects: how well do lithics measure up?' In: R. Torrence (ed.), *Time, Energy and Stone Tools.* (New Directions in Archaeology). Cambridge: Cambridge University Press, 92-105.

Glob, P.V. 1952. *Danske Oldsager.* Copenhagen: Nordisk forlag.

Greenfield, P. 2000. 'Children, material culture and weaving.' In: J. Sofaer Derevenski (ed.), *Children and Material Culture.* London: Routledge, 72-86.

Grimm, L. 2000. 'Apprentice flintknapping.' In: J. Sofaer Derevenski (ed.), *Children and Material Culture*. London: Routledge, 53-71.

Hayden, B. 1995. 'Pathways to Power. Principles for Creating Socioeconomic Inequalities.' In: T.D. Price, G.M. Feinman (eds.), *Foundations of Social Inequality*. New York: Springer, 15-86.

Holberg, E. 1998. 'Flintdolkene – Symboler i en brytningstid.' *Arkeo*, 2, 10-17.

Högberg, A. & D. Olausson 2008. *Scandinavian Flint. An archaeological perspective*. Aarhus: Aarhus University Press.

Højlund, F. 1979. 'Stenøkser i Ny Guineas Højland.' *Hikuin*, 5, 31-48.

Kirshner, D. & J.A. Whitson 1997. 'Editors' Introduction to *Situated Cognition. Social, Semiotic, and Psychological Perspectives*.' In: D. Kirshner, J.A. Whitson (eds.), *Situated Cognition. Social, Semiotic, and Psychological Perspectives*. Mahwah, N.J.: Lawrence Erlbaum Associates, 1-16.

Klassen, L. 2000 *Frühes Kupfer im Norden. Untersuchungen zu Chronologie, Herkunft und Bedeutung der Kupferfunde der Nordgruppe der Trichterbecherkultur*. Højbjerg: Jutland Archaeological Society.

Lave, J. & E. Wenger 1991. *Situated learning: Legitimate peripheral participation*. Cambridge: Cambridge University Press.

Lekberg, P. 2002. *Yxors liv. Människors landskap*. (Coast to Coast Books 5). Uppsala: Uppsala University, Department of Archaeology & Ancient History.

Logan, G.D. 1985. 'Skill and Automaticity: Relations, Implications, and Future Directions.' *Canadian Journal of Psychology*, 39(2), 367-86.

Lomborg, E. 1973. *Die Flintdolche Dänemarks*. Copenhagen: The Royal Society of Northern Antiquaries.

Moran, A.P. 1996. *The Psychology of Concentration in Sport Performers. A Cognitive Analysis*. Hove: Psychology Press.

Müller, S. 1902. 'Flintdolkene i den Nordiske Stenalder.' *Nordiske Fortidsminder I*. Copenhagen: Gyldendalske Boghandel, 125-80.

Olausson, D. 2000. 'Talking Axes, Social Daggers.' In: D. Olausson, H. Vandkilde (eds.), *Form, Function and Context. Material culture studies in Scandinavian archaeology*. Stockholm: Almkvist & Wiksell International, 121-33.

Olausson, D. 2008. 'Does Practice make Perfect? Exploring the question of craft skill as a factor in aggrandizer strategies.' *Journal of Archeological Method and Theory*, 15(1), 28-50.

Pelegrin, J. 1990. 'Prehistoric Lithic Technology: Some Aspects of Research.' *Archaeological Review from Cambridge*, 9(1), 116-25.

Reyerson, K. 1992. 'The adolescent apprentice/worker in Medieval Montpellier.' *Journal of Family History*, 17(4), 353-71.

Santillo Frizell, B. 2000. 'Händernas tysta vetenskap. Om apuliska kupolbyggares yrkeskunnnde och dess reproduktion.' In: E. Hjärtner-Holdar, C. Risberg (eds.), *Hantverkets roll i samhället--produktion och reproduction*. (Rapport R0004). Uppsala: UV GAL, 69-78.

Sarauw, T. 2008. 'Early Late Neolithic Dagger Production in Northern Jutland: Marginalised production or Source of Wealth?' *Bericht der Römisch-germanischen Kommission*, 87, 252-72.

Schneider, W. 2000. 'Giftedness, Expertise, and (Exceptional) Performance. A Developmental Perspective.' In: K.A. Heller, F.J. Mönks, R.J. Sternberg, R.F. Subotnik (eds.), *International Handbook of Giftedness and Talent*. New York: Elsevier, 165-77.

Schoon, I. 2000. 'A Life Span Approach to Talent Development.' In: K.A. Heller, F.J. Mönks, R.J. Sternberg, R.F. Subotnik (eds.), *International Handbook of Giftedness and Talent.* New York: Elsevier, 213-25.

Singer, R.N. & C.M. Janelle 1999. 'Determining Sport Expertise. From Genes to Supremes.' *International Journal of Sport Psychology,* 30, 117-50.

St. Julien, J. 1997. 'Explaining Learning: The Research Trajectory of Situated Cognition and the Implications of Connectionism.' In: D. Kirshner, J.A. Whitson (eds.), *Situated Cognition. Social, Semiotic, and Psychological Perspectives.* Mahwah, N.J.: Lawrence Erlbaum Associates, 261-79.

Stafford, M. 1998. 'In search of Hindsgavl: experiments in the production of Neolithic Danish flint daggers.' *Antiquity,* 72, 338-49.

Stafford, M. 2003. 'The parallel-flaked flint daggers of late Neolithic Denmark: an experimental perspective.' *Journal of Archaeological Science,* 30, 1537-50.

Stensköld, E. 2004. *Att berätta en senneolitisk historia.* (Stockholm Studies in Archaeology, 34). Stockholm: Stockholm University, Department of Archaeology and Classical Studies.

Sternberg, R.J. 2000. 'Giftedness as Developing Expertise.' In: K.A. Heller, F.J. Mönks, R.J. Sternberg, R.F. Subotnik (eds.), *International Handbook of Giftedness and Talent.* New York: Elsevier, 55-66.

Stout, D. 2002. 'Skill and Cognition in Stone Tool Production. An Ethnographic Case Study from Irian Jaya.' *Current Anthropology,* 43(5), 693-715.

Vandkilde, H. 1996. *From Stone to Bronze. The Metalwork of the Late Neolithic and earliest Bronze Age in Denmark.* Højbjerg: Jutland Archaeological Society.

Vandkilde, H. 2005. 'A Review of the Early Late Neolithic Period in Denmark. Practice, Identity and Connectivity.' www.jungsteinSITE.de

Varberg, J. 2005. 'Flint og metal – mellem stenalder og bronzealder i Sydskandinavien.' In: J. Goldhahn (ed.), *Mellan sten och järn.* (Gotarc Series C, Arkeologiska Skrifter, 59). Gothenburg: Univeristy of Gothenburg, 67-80.

Vernacchia, R.A., R.T. McGuire, D.L. Cook 1992. *Coaching Mental Excellence: "It Does Matter Whether You Win or Lose... ".* Dubuque, Iowa: Brown & Benchmark.

Vial, L.G. 1940. 'Stone axes of Mount Hagen, New Guinea.' *Oceania,* 11(2), 158-63.

Weiler, E. 1994. *Innovationsmiljöer i bronsålderns samhälle och idévärld.* (Studia Archaeologica Universitatis Umensis, 5). Umeå: Umeå University, Department of Archaeology & Sami Studies.

Winner, E. & G. Martino 2000. 'Giftedness in Non-Academic Domains: The Case of the Visual Arts and Music.' In: K.A. Heller, F.J. Mönks, R.J. Sternberg, R.F. Subotnik (eds.), *International Handbook of Giftedness and Talent.* New York: Elsevier, 95-110.

Decision-making and Structuration: A study of the minds behind private statues in New Kingdom Egyptian temples[1]

Annette Kjølby

The creation of an ancient Egyptian statue was not the work of a single artist. The process involved the cooperation of several individuals, including the person commissioning the statue, as well as the leader of the workshop and the producers. These individuals or groups of individuals were all competent agents in their own field, all knowledgeable of the rules and resources they acted upon, but acting with different intentions, motivations and knowledge of the basis for and implications of their actions.

This paper discusses aspects of the decision-making process for the creation of the private statues placed in Egyptian temples during the New Kingdom (1539-1075 BC).[2] It considers the identification and positioning of the agents, the motivations for and intentions with the choices made, including the agents' awareness of the conditions of action, as well as how daily decision-making related to longer-term practices and the structuration of Egyptian Society.

The decision-making process

A decision-making approach to the study of objects is based on the view that all artefacts result from decisions made by human agents situated in a given space and time. The approach consequently focuses on the creation phase of the 'life histories' of the artefacts (e.g. Appadurai 1986). This does not imply that the statues are viewed as passive products of human agency. They were actively used by, as well as influencing, the people who produced and lived with them, and were thus involved in shaping the society of which they were a part.[3]

Decision-making is defined here as the choices or decisions made during the creation of a statue. A choice implies that the agent was faced with more than one possibility (e.g. Lemonnier 1993, 7). A particular motif, material or size was chosen rather than another, the cutting of the statue was made in a specific fashion, and the conventional representation of an elite Egyptian was selected from among other possible ways of materializing a human figure in three dimensions.

As demonstrated by recent discussions of agency in archaeology, there is no agreement about the use of the term 'agency' or how this should be applied in studies of the past (e.g. Gell 1998; Dobres & Robb 2000; Barrett 2001; Dornan 2002; Hodder & Hutson 2003, 99f.; Kjølby 2009). Following the definition offered by Giddens, I use the concept of agency to apply to: 'events of which an individual is the perpetrator', and 'whatever happened would not have happened if that individual had not intervened'. Agency, thus, refers not to 'the intentions people have in doing things but to their capability of doing those things in the first place (which is why agency implies power)' (Giddens 1984, 9ff).

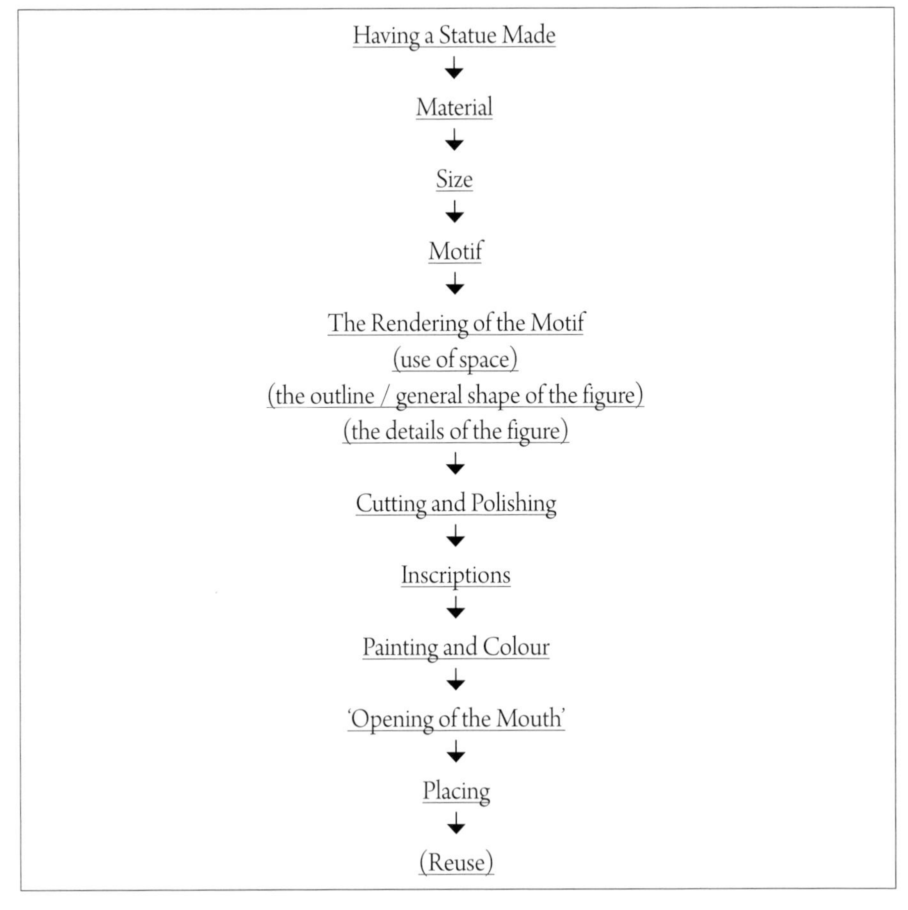

Fig. 1. The Decision-making Process for the creation of Egyptian private statues.

This definition of agency is useful for a study of decision-making as it implies that everybody involved in the decision-making process should be viewed as agents. That is they were empowered to make at least some of the choices that resulted in the statues, and through the implementation of their decisions they were tacitly or strategically engaged in the reproduction of social practices stretching across time and space. The definition thus stresses the analytical difference between the agents' capability to act, the motivations and intentions of the individual agents, and the consequences of their actions. Consequently, it encourages an analysis that identifies the possible agents; studies their knowledge, motivations and intentions, and their involvement in the material and conceptual world; and which, finally, seeks to understand whether the reproduction or change of social practices were intended by the agents or the unintended consequences of the decisions made.

Outlining *a* or *the* decision-making process for a specific type of object must always be an abstraction of the multitude of processes behind the individual objects. The decision-making process established for the creation of Egyptian statues (fig. 1) is based on a *chaîne opératoire* for the construction of stone statues (Kjølby 2001, Table 3; 2007a, 199 (fig. 9.2)),[4] which counts for the majority of the preserved New Kingdom private temple statues.

The sequence of the decisions listed may have varied in each individual case, but these are the overall considerations faced by those involved in the creation of the statues. The detailed operational sequence or *chaîne operatoire* is, of course, more elaborate including, for instance, the many phases of the working process of the sculptors and painters.

Identification and positioning of the people commissioning the statues

One step in dealing with decision-making processes is to consider the identification and positioning of the agents. In most cases it is only possible to identify the agents at a group level, thus discussing the positioning of 'the people commissioning the objects', 'the sculptors', 'the apprentices', etc.

Identification of the people commissioning the objects is largely based on written sources. Dedication texts on statues, the placement of the king's name on the body of statues, as well as a few inscriptions from New Kingdom tomb chapels show that the king occasionally donated statues to his subjects as a 'reward' or 'favour'. This counts for approximately 1/5 of the New Kingdom private statues from the Karnak Temple Complex (Kjølby 2007a, 95ff.; see also Burkhardt *et al.* 1984, 118-19, 323-24). Whether the donation of a statue generally implied that the king was taking part in the other phases of the decision-making process, for instance in deciding the motif, size or material, is, however, uncertain.

Statues could also be commissioned by the statue owner himself or occasionally by one of his relatives, as demonstrated by the dedication texts of private individuals on some statues (e.g. Legrain 1906, nos. 42131 and 42134; 1909, nos. 42162, 42176, 42183, 42187).[5] The inscriptions on the statues usually give the titles of the people represented and, in the cases including a donation, of the donor as well, thus providing a basis for studying which social groups had statues made for themselves or their relatives.

Not surprisingly, a run-through of titles preserved on the statues from the Karnak Temple Complex shows that amongst the owners of private statues we find some of the most prominent individuals of the central and local administration as well as of the administration and priesthood of the Karnak Temple or the House of the god Amun. Thus, we find viziers, mayors, viceroys of Kush, high stewards of the king, his family members, or of Amun, royal tutors, overseers of the treasury, overseers of all work of the king or of Amun, high priests of Amun, as well as other high-ranking priests and members of the administration of the House of Amun. However, other statues were placed there by – or on behalf of – less prominent individuals, such as a servant and steward of the high priest of Amun, royal scribes, a scribe of the treasury of Amun or a sistrum player of the barks of Mut and Min (Kjølby 2007a, 62ff.).

The majority of these statue owners would have had access to statues or skilled labour and materials through their office either as a royal favour or through their authority of office (also Eyre 1987b, 183ff.). Less prominent owners could possibly commission a statue at their own expense or by offering their services to the craftsmen or leaders of the workshops. Written evidence from Deir el-Medina, which housed the workmen constructing the New Kingdom royal tombs, shows that the inhabitants were spending part of their spare time producing and exchanging various artefacts, amongst which were wooden statues (Cooney 2006; Janssen 1975, 246-48; Steinmann 1991, 157, note 54; Wente 1990, 139 (no. 175); Eyre 1987b, 199). This clearly demonstrates that at least some private individuals could commission statues by state-employed craftsmen working 'out-of-office'. Whether this practice also applied to craftsmen working in temple or state workshops is undocumented but surely conceivable.

It is possible that statues were sometimes prefabricated in temple or state workshops without a specific receiver in mind. Prefabrication is known for other objects and even for a few tombs (e.g. Baud 1935, 245ff.; Eyre 1987b, 197ff.)

and may be indicated by a few private temple statues as well (Bernhauer 1999b no.1.5-8; Legrain 1909 no. 42174). The fact that most statues were produced with conventionalised or idealised facial features characteristic of a specific reign makes it conceivable that such prefabrication was common, although not easily documented. If statues were occasionally prefabricated the people deciding on the motif, size or material in these cases would have been the leaders of the temple, quarry or palace workshops,[6] although they may have followed the king's commission of a certain amount of statues with specific motif, size, material and style.

In a few cases it is possible to identify and discuss the role played by a specific individual agent in statue making. This is best illustrated by the case of Senenmut, a high official during the reign of Queen Hatshepsut (1473-1458 BC). At least 25 statues representing Senenmut are known (Bernhauer 1999a-b; Dorman 1988, 188ff.; Meyer 1982, 28ff.). Most of these were placed in temples and introduced new motifs in private sculpture, including ones showing him as a royal tutor, with a measuring cord, with a sistrum, with a naos and with a god or royal emblem, respectively.

In short, it was Senenmut's favourable positioning in place and time that provided him with the opportunity to choose new motifs for his statues. Senenmut's offices included those of steward of the god Amun, royal high steward, high steward and tutor of the princess Nefrure and, at least for a period, leader of all the work of the king and Amun (e.g. Dorman 1988, 203ff.). They would thus have allowed him to have at his disposal a large workforce and valuable materials, as well as direct access to the queen, temples and talented craftsmen. Senenmut was moreover favoured by Hatshepsut, as reflected in the placement of his tomb in relation to her mortuary temple in Deir el-Bahri, as well as by the large amount of discrete inclusions of his portrait on the walls of this temple (Dorman 1988, 66 ff; 1991; Hayes 1957, 80-84). Finally, he lived at a time during which innovation in private monuments seems to have been accepted, and in which officials may have had more influence than in other periods (e.g. Bernhauer 1999a, 117; Dziobek 1998, 144ff.; Hornung 1995).

Positioning in place and time alone does not, however, result in innovation. The innovation in the repertoire of private statues should be conceived as the combination of favourable positioning and a creative mind. The creative agency of Senenmut is indicated by three of his statues on which an inscription announces that he had invented two two-dimensional motifs drawn above the inscriptions and identified as cryptograms showing the names of Hatshepsut (Dorman 1988, 175; Drioton 1938; Meyer 1982, 156-71). Drawing on his knowledge of the world, of which he himself was a part, Senenmut used his creative abilities in transforming already existing concepts into three-dimensional images, thus using these images in the negotiation of his social identity and position in Egyptian society. Presumably this transformation of ideas into images happened in close cooperation with one or more of the master sculptors of his time and had to be authorized by the regent herself.

Identification and positioning of the producers

While the identification of the people commissioning the statues relies largely on written documents, a reconstruction of the working process and the identification and positioning of the craftsmen involved in this process is based on material as well as written sources.

First of all, unfinished statues are useful for an understanding of the working process. A collection of unfinished stone statues from the workshop in the valley temple of king Menkaure at Giza (c. 2500 BC) allows for the construction of a *chaîne opératoire* for the production of stone statues (Kjølby 2001, table 3). This sequence applies to statues produced during the Old Kingdom, but there is no reason to believe that this should have been seriously altered for the New Kingdom, as indicated by unfinished products from workshops at Amarna (examples in Arnold 1996).

In the unfinished statues from the Menkaure workshop the excavator identified eight 'states' or stages in the production of a statue. Based on his description of these 'states' and of the statues (Reisner 1931, 108ff., pl. 62), the stages involved in the production of a statue may be summarised as follows: First, the stone was roughly blocked and subsequently roughly sculpted, this work being guided, at least initially, by lines indicating the shape, displayed by Reisner's states I-IV. The details were then sculpted as displayed by states V-VI. Finally the statue was polished, during which process the final details of the toes and fingers, as well as the sharp lines around the eyes, were defined as displayed by state VII. The shape and details of the statue were now completed and the inscription was cut into the stone (State VIII). As indicated by some finished statues (e.g. O'Neil *et al.* 1999, 269ff.), the statues would usually be painted, and inscriptions could be added before the statue was completely polished.

Reisner believed that the work displayed by states I-IV was carried out by the apprentices, following the guidelines drawn by their master, while the work displayed in states V-VIII was carried out by the master himself, as these latter states are not marked by guidelines (Reisner 1931, 115). On the unfinished statues from the New Kingdom workshops at Amarna (e.g. Arnold 1996), correction lines were, however, also used for the later phases of production, thus guiding

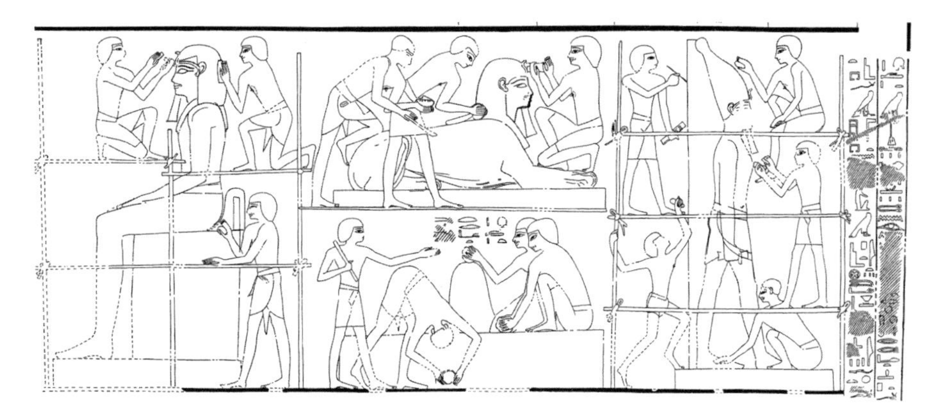

Fig. 2. Workshop scene from the tomb of Rekhmire (Davies 1943, pl. LX)

the sculpting of eyes, facial lines and other details. This practice indicates that either the masters in the Amarna workshops used guiding lines for themselves, or the corrections were to be executed by trained sculptors working under their command. The amount of unfinished statues in workshops seems, however, to be in favour of the latter.

Two-dimensional representations from private tombs depicting statue producers at work support the impression that the production of stone statues was a cooperative process. An illustrative New Kingdom example comes from the tomb of the vizier Rekhmire (fig. 2).

This workshop scene is part of a section depicting Rekhmire inspecting work in the Temple of Amun in Karnak and shows groups of sculptors and painters producing royal colossal statues and an offering table. The accompanying text is not informative as to the actions carried out and does not give the titles of the people involved. Relevant for the present argument is that for each of the objects several people seem to be working together. Although this and other scenes from the New Kingdom showing statue production generally show the production of royal statues, team work is also seen in older workshop scenes depicting the production of private statues (Drenkhahn 1976, 52ff.; Eaton-Krauss 1984; Wild 1966, pl. CLXXIII).

The division of work and cooperation of the workforce indicated by these examples is paralleled by the evidence for the construction of relief decoration in the New Kingdom royal tombs in the Valley of the Kings. A relief, or even a single figure in a relief, was not the product of one 'artist', but the product of several craftsmen, mastering different stages in the production. In the tomb of Horemheb (c. 1319-1292 BC) the uncompleted decoration thus displays several phases of the working process seemingly carried out simultaneously by different craftsmen working side by side in the tomb (Kjølby 2001, table 2; Teichmann 1971, 32-36). The evidence from the tomb walls is supported by written records. Here it is learned that the workforce, literally the gang, involved in the construction of a king's tomb included: 'quarrymen' who cut out the tomb; 'plasterers', who Černý (1973b, 36ff.) argues were making the plaster, not applying it to the walls; 'draughtsmen' or 'painters' and 'chief draughtsmen' or 'chief painters'; as well as 'relief sculptors' and 'chief relief sculptors' (Černý 1973a; also Valbelle 1985, 99ff.).

Combining these data it seems reasonable to conclude that the production of a statue was usually made not by a single 'artist', but by teams of craftsmen or artists working under the supervision of one or more 'masters', who themselves referred to an administrative leader of a temple or state institution (see also Drenkhahn 1976, 52ff.; Steinmann 1980; 1982a, 1984).

It may then be suggested that statue production usually included the following agents: After the statue had been commissioned, a master craftsman or leader of craftwork gave the general outlines for the work, while a draughtsman (possibly the master himself), made the lines to be followed when cutting the statue. The first crude phases were conceivably cut by the new apprentice(s), while the master or a trained supervisor working for the master added red or black marks indicating the corrections to be made. When the rougher stages were finished, the statue awaited completion by the more skilled sculptors and then – perhaps – the master craftsman himself took over the last phases of polishing and finishing the details. A draughtsman-scribe (possibly the master craftsman himself) added the inscriptions to be cut and polished by the sculptors, and finally the statue was painted, thus including a painter and for some materials a plasterer to prepare the surface.

The people involved in this cooperative process of statue creation were evidently not equally positioned with respect to which decisions could be made. While those commissioning the statues decided that the statue should be made and possibly which motif, size, material and inscriptions to use, the master or the experienced draughtsmen and sculptors working on the basis of rules of representation made the day-to-day choices concerning the rendering of the motif and how to cut and polish the statues.

Knowledge, consciousness and decision-making

In the daily decision-making of statue creation the agents were drawing on their experience as competent actors. They knew the rules and resources that formed the basis of their actions, and used this information reflexively when acting in the world (Giddens 1984). The knowledge of the agents involved in the process differed, needless to say, depending on their positioning in time and space. It was shaped by their experience from living and learning in the world and thus reflected the 'constitution of human beings as persons' (Ingold 2000, 3). Often their knowledge would have been used tacitly or habitually, but it could also be used discursively, thus giving the agents the opportunity to act strategically (see below).

As an example of how the knowledge of the agents may be analysed I will briefly consider the choice of motif (for a study of the choice of motif see Kjølby 2007a). A logical first step is to register the motifs available to the decision makers in order to study how existing motifs were interpreted and used by the agents, thus influencing their decision-making. Ideally, this includes a study of the motifs used in the agents' own time as well as in earlier times – including the access to and visibility of older statues and the motifs which were available in other media (e.g. wall decoration, hieroglyphs). Furthermore, an analysis of the relationship between motif and social position of the owner may provide an understanding of the use of different motifs. This may, finally, be combined with a study of the religious, social and ideological aspects known by the agents and thus influencing the choices made.

An examination of these aspects will, however, mainly give an impression of how the positioning in time (i.e. a given time period) would have influenced the knowledge of the agents. In order to understand the decision-making process one must also consider how agents were influenced by their positioning in the narrower time-space contexts of social encounters (Giddens 1984, 70f.). This will be exemplified by a discussion of the artists or craftsmen.

Becoming an artist and the transmission of knowledge

The artists' or craftsmens' knowledge was passed on from one generation to the next by a learning process based on watching and imitation, trial and error. Regarding the sculptors, the wall decoration from the tomb of Huya in Amarna shows a master sculptor instructing or correcting his pupil. Here Iuti, Queen Tiye's overseer of sculptors (c. 1350 BC), is painting or making guiding lines on a statue of a princess, while another sculptor is watching him (fig. 3).

As the cutting of a stone statue is a process of reduction and thus irreversible, it is most unlikely that the new apprentices were allowed to sculpt during the later stages of the working process outlined above. Rather it must be assumed that they obtained their know-how and skills of working the stone by assisting in the initial rough shaping of the stone – using trial pieces for practicing the sculpting and finishing of facial details, fingers, the draping of the cloth, and so forth. Several

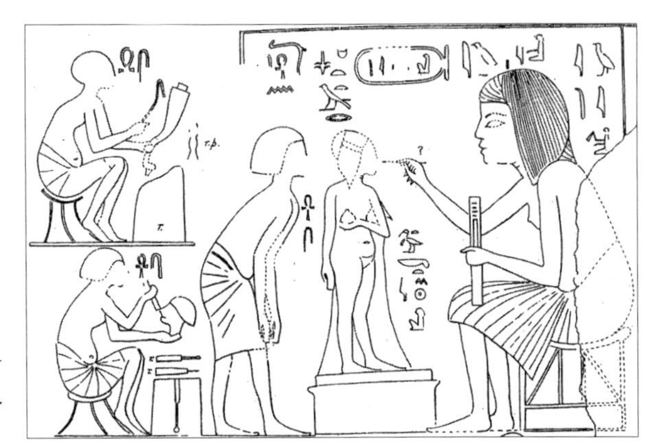

Fig. 3. Iuty instructing or correcting a pupil (Davies 1905, pl. XVIII)

such two-dimensional trial pieces showing the exercises of draughtsmen, painters and relief sculptors have been preserved, particularly from Deir el-Medina and from Amarna (Jørgensen 1998, 156-59; Vandier d'Abbadie 1937-1959). Only after mastering this technique as fully trained sculptors were they allowed to work on the details and finish of the statues.

Through their training the craftsmen acquired the skill of working the stone, the movements being stored in their minds and in their bodies (e.g. Ingold 2000, 349-61). They learned the rules of representation, how to render a motif correctly, when to work strictly by the rules and when to use their creativity. In the end their experience in being a craftsman and getting about in the world placed them in a position whereby the majority of daily choices made by these 'ordinary' sculptors and painters were generally made tacitly and habitually.

Whether a sculptor, draughtsman or painter, a craftsman was thus expected to fulfil certain demands. The few records, in which people involved in the production of relief and statuary give an account of their work, do not focus on the work produced by a person, but on how he had worked to the satisfaction of his lord or patron (Drenkhahn 1995, 338) or on the skills he possessed, as seen in the unique stele of Irtysen (or Iri-irusen), an overseer of craftsmen (or artists), painters (or draughtsmen) and sculptors (Barta 1970). Although made several centuries earlier, the stele provides an insight into the self-awareness of a master craftsman, that is also useful for an understanding of the New Kingdom. Summarised, Irtysen emphasises how he masters certain techniques, such as the preparation of colour and the cutting of a relief, as well as the prescriptions given for the correct rendering of human and animal figures (Barta 1970; Drenkhahn 1995, 339-40). In other words even this master seems to have seen himself not as an 'artist' but as a craftsman, mastering certain techniques and ways of representation.[7]

This does not imply that the qualities of sculptors, and with them painters, went unrecognized. In the world of the Egyptians these qualities were, however, the ability to make an everlasting image of the person represented. One term for sculptor was '*sankh*', that is 'life maker' or 'one who brings to life' (e.g. Steinmann 1980, 152) and the sculptor and painter were participating in the so-called 'opening of the mouth' ritual carried out to make an image effective. This ritual was performed in the workshop when the manufacturing of a statue had been completed (fig. 1) and included a long chain of actions involving, amongst others, the ritual opening of the mouth of the statue (Drenkhahn 1976, 63-64; Otto 1960; Roth 2001; also Gell 1998; Meskell 2004). Irtysens inscription also refers to this particular role of the craftsmen, stating that he knows the secrets of writing (the divine words) and how to conduct ceremonies (Barta 1970, 78ff.). The sculptor's ability to create living and lasting images from non-living materials was, however, founded in his knowledge of the right way to make an image, and the statues were not – at least not in writing – attributed to a specific sculptor.

In order to do their work correctly, the producers of Egyptian images made use of several prescriptions and 'guiding tools'. They followed rules of representation and applied a standardised grid or system of guidelines as an aid in representing the figures according to the correct proportions of a given period (Robins 1994). At least in some workshops the sculptors also used models. Noteworthy in this regard is a famous bust of Queen Nefertiti, the wife of Akhenaten (c.1353-1336 BC). Found in a sculptor's workshop it was most probably used as the 'correct image' of the queen and a guideline for the production of statues (e.g. Arnold 1996).

The transformation of art during the reign of Akhenaten most clearly demonstrates how the producers of relief and statuary were able to change their style on demand. During this reign the conventions for the motifs as well as the proportions of the human figure were radically changed as was the religious system (e.g. Freed *et al.* 1999; Robins 1994, 119ff.). On a rock-cut stele at Aswan it is claimed that one of the sculptors involved in the transformation, the master sculptor Bak, was personally instructed by the king. This statement is, however, quite conventional (Krauss 1986), and does not document that the new style and decorative program was mainly the product of the king himself, although it is highly conceivable that only the king would have been empowered to change the decorative program and style as drastically as was the case during the reign of Akhenaten. In either case the craftsmen of Akhenaten's reign quickly mastered the new rules aided by the changed structure of the grid and probably also by the use of model statues.

The acquired mastering of correct proportions, motifs, poses and way of representation limited the producers' creative influence on the final object, as did the division of work among several people. The producers of private statues were thus not positioned to make choices that deviated from the traditional or conventional aspects of statue production. The personal touch of the experienced and master sculptors was expressed, however, in the final character of the product, in the details and quality of workmanship.

Motivation, intentions and levels of consciousness

From these examples of the position of the agents involved in statue making, it follows that the intentions and motivations of the sculptors or painters were different from those of the people commissioning the statues. An investigation of the motivations for, and intentions behind, the choices made therefore adds to our understanding of the decision-making process and the part played by the statues in Egyptian society. Analytically, motivations can be defined as religious, social, ideological, political, economic, practical, aesthetic and unconscious, some of which will be exemplified below.

As the different agents involved in the decision-making process were not equally aware of the conditions of their actions, I find it useful to include Giddens' treatment of consciousness as an element in the discussion of agency and the agents (Giddens 1984). Giddens divides human consciousness into three "layers": discursive consciousness, practical consciousness and the unconscious. Whereas the unconscious is protected from the other layers by a bar of repression, the border between practical and discursive consciousness is fluctuating and permeable. Much agency is carried out in a routine or habitual manner, that is with a *practical consciousness* of how to get things done and get about in everyday life. If confronted, agents will, however, usually be able to account for their actions, thus having a *discursive consciousness* of the conditions of their actions. Agents with a discursive knowledge of the conditions of their actions may use this knowledge to act strategically with the intention of maintaining or altering social practices and thus the structure of the world they live within.

Based on the discussion of the positioning and constitution of the agents, I suggest that most of the decisions made by the sculptors, painters and other craftsmen were largely motivated by practical, social, and perhaps economic factors. Their main intention would have been to do their job correctly, thus pleasing their patrons, keeping their job, receiving their reward, maintaining their living conditions and social position, or even advancing as a result of their achievements. Included in the motivations of these agents might then have been the discursive recognition of the possibility of negotiating their social position through their work, although many of their decisions were made from a practical consciousness and bodily experience of how to get along as an artist (i.e. how to work the material, how to render the motif correctly, etc.).

The people commissioning the objects were motivated by other factors. Private statues were intended to ensure the immortality of the represented and were thus religiously motivated. The immortality of the person represented was supported by the preservation of a bodily materialization (the statue), the preservation of his identity (ensured by the inscriptions and arguably the statue type and features) and the receiving of offerings (as established by the inscriptions, by the involvement of the statue in cultic activities, and for temple statues also by the location in the temple of a god or king), to mention some crucial religious functions of the images.[8]

Artefacts are, however, also useful in the negotiation of identity (e.g. Wiessner 1988), and the private temple statues provided a good medium for negotiating the social position of the owner or the relation between the donor and the receiver of a statue and could thus also be socio-politically motivated. The person commissioning a statue would have been aware of the signifying value of a specific motif, material, size, or way of representation, and could use this knowledge strategically to communicate the identity of the person represented. Social as well as religious signifiers in the statues could thus be used in the self-thematization of the statue owner,[9] which is seen for instance in the use of scribal statues reserved for elite males, and tutor statues indicating a close relation to the royal family (e.g. Bernhauer 1999; Scott 1989), but also in various other aspects. Furthermore, through the act of donating a statue to another person, the king, son, or other person related to the person represented negotiated his or her relation with the statue owner, and thus his own place in society.

The placement of statues in temples could also involve a practice in which an individual donates property or resources to a royal statue in a temple or to the temple itself. This in turn ensured the redistribution of offerings to the statue or mortuary cult of the donor, and in some cases his relatives, and may also have provided the donor with other economic benefits (e.g. Haring 1997, 142ff.; Kozloff & Bryan 1992, 138-39). In this sense the statues were at least in some cases economically motivated although this partly served the religious end of securing the offering cult of the donor. Economic or practical motivations may also have guided some choices of material and size, with the intention of reducing costs in terms of material or working effort, as may have been the case for statues made from a material found locally in the place of installation (Kjølby 2007a).

While the discussion of the decision-making process is largely concerned with practical and discursive consciousness, it is also important to consider the unconscious motivation and cognition involved in agency as exemplified by the

Egyptian way of rendering a person in three dimensions. Rather than showing things the way they appear to the eye, with oblique views and foreshortening, Egyptian representations depict the mental image of the object in question and may be understood as 'based on frontal images' (in German *Geradvorstellig*) as suggested by Heinrich Schäfer early in the 20th century (Schäfer 1986). This is seen most clearly in two-dimensional images in which the Egyptians combine different views of an object in one drawing. Thus the two-dimensional human figure is usually depicted with a combination of frontal (e.g. eyes, shoulders) and side views (e.g. facial contour, the feet) thereby including the most characteristic aspects or frontal images of the figure elements. Although less apparent, the same principles apply to three-dimensional works, where the different elements would be drawn on the respective surfaces of the stone block as a guideline for the sculptor, who would then approach the statue frontally from the front, back, sides and top. Schäfer suggested that, in three-dimensional images, the representation based on frontal images resulted in *Richtungsgeradheit* (1986, 310ff), meaning that the statues were directionally straight. Arms and legs could be shown in different positions, but were always placed according to a fixed axis without the figure twisting or turning.

Directional straightness and a representation based on frontal images does seem to apply to most Egyptian statuary and, working from an ethnocentric position, Schäfer believed that this was the instinctive way of representation, not only by the Egyptians, but by all cultures and persons not influenced by 5th century BC Greek art. Several observations, however, reveal that the directional straightness in Egyptian three-dimensional images was not made by instinct (i.e. unconsciously), but should be seen as the result of choices made from a practical or discursive knowledge of the correct or accepted way of representation.

This is illustrated by a group of figurines dating to the early New Kingdom (e.g. Aldred 1961, 90, fig. 162-63; Freed *et al.* 1999, 264 (no. 208); Kozloff & Bryan 1992, 361-62, pl. 42).[10] The figurines show servants carrying a jar, which most likely contained unguents, and some of the figures are bending and turning to the side under the weight of the jar. In the collective mind of the Egyptians of this time, three-dimensional images following other representational principles were thus present and provided an alternative to the directionally straight representations used for the statues of primary individuals. However, this does not imply that the people involved in the production of formal statues would have considered this alternative way of representation an option for the images of kings, gods or the elite. The rendering of these followed long established conventions. It would not have been up for debate, but would have been applied tacitly by the draughtsmen and sculptors from a practical knowledge of how to produce a correct formal image.

Paul John Frandsen (1997) has argued that the motif elements included in an Egyptian image were the inalienable properties of the mental image or prototype it was meant to represent. Applying this view to three-dimensional images, I would suggest that by the early New Kingdom the long established directional straightness of formal images had become an inalienable property of the prototype of a *statue of* an elite Egyptian. As the focus of private statues was on their materialization of the *kind of individual* depicted, they had to conform to this conventional way of rendering an elite Egyptian. In contrast, the focus of the above-mentioned servant figurines was not on the person but on *the activity carried out*. Consequently the figurines displayed the inalienable properties of the mental image of 'carrying', 'bringing' or an equivalent activity, and the figures would not have to conform to the rules of frontality and directional straightness but were allowed to bend to the side under the weight of the jar.[11]

Decision-making and structuration

The embodied daily choices and actions of those involved in statue creation resulted in various short-time effects. First of all, the person represented received a statue which served as his materialization in a temple, thus extending his presence in the world of the living through time and space and ensuring him various benefits crucial for his perpetual existence. Furthermore, in the process of statue making the social positions of and relations between the people immediately involved in the process, that is the patrons, statue owners and craftsmen, were reproduced. The people commissioning and receiving the statues used them in the confirmation and negotiation of religious and social identity. Additionally, through the working process and organisation of work the sculptors and painters were tacitly enrolled and maintained in their social role in life. Through their skill and talent, however, they were able to negotiate their position within the group and in society as such.

The agency involved in statue creation also played a part in the reproduction of wider social practices. The repeated negotiation of identity involved in the practice of statue creation had an impact not only on the people involved in the individual cases of statue production but on Egyptian social structures in general. Thus, as long as statues were commissioned and produced the social differentiation and relations between elite and craftsmen were maintained. In addition, the presence of the statues in the lifeworld of the Egyptians contributed to the maintenance of various other aspects. The repeated visual exposure of the Egyptians to conventional representations in statues and on other monuments contributed to the continual reproduction of the mental images of 'an elite

Egyptian' and 'the Egyptian elite', as well as to the conception of the exclusive position, and the religious and social roles of members of the elite. Likewise the conventionalised rendering of men and women contributed to the maintenance of Egyptian concepts of male and female and thus gender roles.

It goes without saying that the day-to-day production of conventional images, using traditional motifs, materials, colours and ways of representation, was also continually involved in the reproduction of Egyptian representational practices. While this may, to some extent, have been intended by the people who laid out the rules for correct representation and accepted motifs, it was largely the unintended result of choices made by the participants of the individual cases of statue creation, who would usually have acted with quite different intentions. Thus the commission of specific motifs or materials and the craftsmen's knowledge of how to produce and work these ensured the continual use of motifs and materials. Likewise the daily practice and passing of knowledge from one generation of craftsmen to the next ensured that the practice was carried on.

However, the training and maintenance of the craftsmen's skills were based at temple and state institutions, and representational practices were maintained only as long as the central powers supported the system, as clearly demonstrated by the decrease in the quality of workmanship and amount of statuary produced during periods of socio-political instability. Likewise, while the reproduction of representational practice was largely the unintended consequence of the everyday activities of the craftsmen, the craftsmen were subordinate to the will of their patrons. Thus, strategically positioned individuals with awareness of the power of images in producing reality could alter representational practices in order to restructure society. This is most notable during the reign of Akhenaten when the repertoire of motifs and the way of representation were changed in order to restructure the socio-political and religious practices and structures of Egyptian society, but also by periods such as the early Middle Kingdom or the 26th Dynasty when inspiration was sought in monuments from the remote past, probably as a means to re-establish the social order of earlier times (e.g. Freed *et al.* 1999; Maneulian 1994; Robins 1997, 90ff.).

Finally, the creation of the statues and their involvement in the life of the Egyptians would have contributed to the reproduction of various religious practices and Egyptian views on the relations between the various beings inhabiting their world. To the Egyptians the world was inhabited not only by the living but also by the deceased and the gods who participated in some situations as real social actors. Private statues as well as other monuments presented focal points for the interaction with the deceased and may in the moment of interaction have been experienced as real embodiments or containers of the individuals represented.[12]

The statues extended the personhood of the depicted beyond the real lifespan of the individual represented and would have ensured his presence in the life of the living, not only as memory traces but materialised in the statue. As a result the statues contributed to the reproduction of various religious practices, including the presenting and redistribution of offerings, the relations between the living and the dead, and would in some cases also have served as intermediaries between men and god, thus serving in the reproduction of these relations.

Conclusion

The creation, use and presence of New Kingdom private temple statues involved several agents acting and thinking together. The embodied agency and cognition involved in statue creation affected not only the individuals directly involved in the process, but influenced the stretching of ideas and practices as well as the recollection and presence of individuals across time and space. The paper thus links the decision-making and day-to-day agency of the people involved in the creation of private statues to the longer term practices and structuration of Egyptian society and to the part the statues played in the life of the Egyptians.

Notes

1 The author wishes to thank Paul John Frandsen, Bo Dahl Hermansen, Ole Herslund, Charlott Hoffmann, Rune Nyord, and the reviewers, as well as my students in the spring 2005 course 'Introduction to Archaeological Theory and Method' for their valuable comments on the paper.
2 Kjølby 2007a, 2007b. Dates according to Baines & Malek 2000.
3 For material agency and agent/patient relationships involving the statues and the raw materials used for the statues, see Kjølby 2007a, 219ff; Kjølby 2009.
4 I use the term *chaîne opératoire* to describe the detailed operational sequence involving the many stages of, for instance, the cutting and polishing of the statue. For a discussion on the use of the term see Dobres 2000, 154ff.
5 'Statue owner' is used here to refer to the person represented.
6 For the location of workshops in the New Kingdom, see conveniently Arnold 1996; Drenkhahn 1995; Eyre1987b; Kozloff & Bryan 1992, 136ff.; Philips 1991; Steinmann 1984.
7 For the position or self-image of the artists or craftsmen in various periods see also Anthes 1941; Baines 1994, 73; Barta 1970; Davis 1989, 94ff.; Drenkhahn 1976, 1995; Eyre 1987a; 1987b; Junker 1959; Müller 2005; Smith 1946, 351ff.; Steinmann 1991; Wilson 1947.
8 For views on the function of the statues, see e.g. Assmann 1991, 93ff.; Bernhauer 1999a; Kayser 1936; Kjølby 2007a; Kozloff & Bryan 1992, 237ff.; Otto 1948; Schulz 1992; Verbovsek 2005.
9 On self-thematisation and self-preservation see Assmann 1996; 1991; for a study of signifiers and material anchors in the statues, see Kjølby 2007a, 136ff.

10 It has been observed that, when carefully examined, several statues are modelled turning very slightly to the left (Wildung 1990). Wildung suggests that this may be an attempt to put life into the otherwise seemingly static images.

11 The inclusion of inalienable properties was, of course, only one of several cognitive factors underlying the choices made in the making of Egyptian images. For instance, on a cognitive level the combination of motifs and choice of design elements may be explained in terms of conceptual blending (Fauconnier and Turner 2002; Kjølby 2007a, 136ff.).

12 This is generally interpreted in terms of the German concept of *'Einwohnung'* (which may be translated "installation" or "indwelling").

References

Aldred, C. 1961. *New Kingdom Art in Ancient Egypt*. London: Alec Tiranti.

Anthes, R. 1941. 'Werkverfahren ägyptischer Bildhauer.' *Mitteilungen des Deutschen Instituts für ägyptische Altertumskunde in Kairo*, 10, 77-121, Taf. 17-20.

Appadurai, A. (ed.) 1986. *The Social Life of Things: Commodities in Cultural Perspective*. Cambridge: Cambridge University Press.

Arnold, D. 1996. 'The Workshop of the Sculptor Thutmose.' In: D. Arnold, L. Green, J. Allen (eds.), *The Royal Women of Amarna*. New York: The Metropolitan Museum of Art, 41-83.

Assmann, J. 1991. *Stein und Zeit. Mensch und Gesellschaft im alten Ägypten*. München: Wilhelm Fink Verlag.

Assmann, J. 1996. 'Preservation and Presentation of Self in Ancient Egyptian Portraiture.' In: P. der Manuelian (ed.), *Studies in Honour of William Kelly Simpson* I. Brooklyn: Museum of Fine Arts, 54-81.

Baines, J. 1986. 'Translator's Introduction.' In: H. Schäfer (ed.), *Principles of Egyptian Art* (transl. and ed. by J. Baines; German 4th ed. 1963 edited by E. Brunner-Traut). Oxford: Griffith Institute, xi-xx.

Baines, J. 1994. 'On the Status and Purposes of Ancient Egyptian Art.' *Cambridge Archaeological Journal* 4/1, 67-94.

Baines, J. & J. Malek 2000. *Cultural Atlas of Ancient Egypt*. Abingdon: Andromeda Oxford Limited.

Barrett, J.C. 2001. 'Agency, the Duality of Structure, and the Problem of the Archaeological Record.' In: I. Hodder (ed.), *Archaeological Theory Today*. Cambridge: Polity Press, 141-64.

Barta, W. 1970. *Das Selbstzeugnis eines altägyptischen Künstlers (Stele Louvre C14)* (Münchner Ägyptologische Studien, 22), Berlin: Verlag Bruno Hessling.

Baud, M. 1935. *Les dessins ébaucheés de la necropole Thebaine (au Temps de Nouvel Empire)*. (Memoires publiés par les membres de l'Institut Francais d'archéologie Orientale du Caire, LXIII). Cairo: Imprimerie de l'Institut Francais d'Achéologie Orientale.

Bernhauer, E. 1999a, b. *Innovationen in der Privatplastik der 18. Dynastie*. (vol. 1-2). Vienna: Doctoral dissertation, University of Vienna.

Borchardt, L. 1912. 'Ausgrabungen in Tell el-Amarna 1911/12. Vorläufiger Bericht.' *Mitteillulngen der Deutschen Orient-Gesellschaft*, 50.

Borchardt, L. 1913. 'Ausgrabungen in Tell el-Amarna 1912/13. Vorläufiger Bericht.' *Mitteillulngen der Deutschen Orient-Gesellschaft*, 52.

Borchardt, L. & H. Ricke 1980. *Die Wohnhäuser in tell el-Amarna*. (Ausgrabungen der Deutschen Orient-Gesellschaft in Tell el-Amarna, 5). Berlin: Gebr. Mann Verlag.

Brunner-Traut, E. 1986. 'Epilogue. Aspective.' In: H. Schäfer (ed.), *Principles of Egyptian Art* (transl. and ed. by J. Baines; German 4th ed. 1963 edited by E. Brunner-Traut). Oxford: Griffith Institute, 421-46.

Burkhardt, A., E. Blumenthal, I. Müller & W.F. Reineke 1984. *Urkunden der 18. Dynastie. Übersetzung zu den Heften 5-16.* Berlin: Akademie-Verlag.

Černý, J. 1973a. *A Community of Workmen at Thebes in the Ramesside Period.* (Bibliothéque détude, vol. L, Institut francais d'archéologie orientale du Caire). Cairo: Institut Francais d'Archéologie Orientale du Caire.

Černý, J. 1973b. *The Valley of the Kings.* (Bibliothéque détude, vol. LXI, Institut francais d'archéologie orientale du Caire). Cairo: Institut Francais d'Archéologie Orientale du Caire.

Černý, J. & A. H. Gardiner 1957. *Hieratic Ostraca.* Oxford: University Press.

Davies, N de G. 1905. *The Rock Tombs of el Amarna. Part III. The Tombs of Huya and Ahmes.* (Archaeological Survey of Egypt, 15). London: Egypt Exploration Society.

Davies, N. de G. 1943. *The tomb of Rekh-mi-Re' at Thebes.* (Publications of the Metropolitan Museum of Art, Egyptian Expedition, 11, I/II). New York: Metropolitan Museum of Art.

Davis, W. 1989. *The Canonical Tradition in Ancient Egyptian Art.* Cambridge: Cambridge University Press.

Dobres, M. 2000. *Technology and Social Agency: Outlining a Practice Framework for Archaeology.* Oxford: Blackwell.

Dobres, M. & J. Robb 2000a (eds.). *Agency in Archaeology*. London: Routledge.

Dobres, M. & J. Robb 2000b. 'Agency in Archaeology: paradigm or platitude?.' In: M. Dobres, J. Robb (eds.), *Agency in Archaeology*. London: Routledge, 3-17.

Dorman, P. 1988. *The Monuments of Senenmut: Problems in Historical Methodology.* London: Kegan Paul International.

Dorman, P. 1991. *The Tombs of Senenmut. The Architecture and Decoration of Tombs 71 and 353.* (Publications of the Metropolitan Museum of Art Egyptian Expedition, XXIV). New York: The Metropolitan Museum of Art.

Dornan, J.L. 2002. 'Agency and Archaeology: Past, Present and Future Directions.' *Journal of Archaeological Method and Theory*, 9/4, 303-29.

Drenkhahn, R. 1976. *Die Handwerker und ihre Tätigkeiten im Alten Ägypten.* (Ägyptologische Abhandlungen, 31). Wiesbaden: Otto Harrasowitz.

Drenkhahn, R. 1995. 'Artisans and Artists in Pharaonic Egypt.' In: J.M. Sasson (ed.), *Civilizations of the Ancient Near East*, I. New York: Charles Scribner's Sons, 331-43.

Drioton, E. 1938. 'Deux cryptogrammes de Senenmout. *Annales des Service des Antiquités de l'Égypte*, 38, 231-46.

Dziobek, E. 1998. *Denkmäler des Vezirs User-Amun.* (Studien zur Archäologie und Geschichte Altägyptens, 18). Heidelberg: Heidelberger Orientverlag.

Eaton-Krauss, M. 1984. *The Representation of Statuary in Private Tombs of the Old Kingdom.* (Ägyptologische Abhandlungen, 39). Wiesbaden: Otto Harrasowitz.

Eaton-Krauss, M. 2001. 'Artists and Artisans.' In: D.B. Redford (ed.), *The Oxford Encyclopedia of Ancient Egypt.* New York: Oxford University Press, 136-40.

Eyre, C.J. 1987a. 'Work and the Organisation of Work in the Old Kingdom.' In: M.A. Powell (ed.), *Labor in the Ancient Near East.* (American Oriental Series, 68). New Haven: American Oriental Society, 5-47.

Eyre, C.J. 1987b. 'Work and the Organisation of Work in the New Kingdom.' In: M.A. Powell (ed.), *Labour in the Ancient Near East.* (American Oriental Series, 68). New Haven: American Oriental Society, 167-221.

Fauconnier, G. & M. Turner 2002. *The way we Think. Conceptual Blending and the Minds Hidden Complexities.* New York: Basic Books.

Frandsen, P.J. 1997. 'On Categorization and Metaphorical Structuring: Some Remarks on Egyptian Art and Language.' *Cambridge Archaeological Journal*, 7/1, 71-104.

Freed, R., Y.J. Markowitz & S.H. D'Auria (eds.) 1999. *Pharaohs of the Sun. Akhenaten, Nefertiti, Tuthankhamen.* London: Thames and Hudson.

Giddens, A. 1984. *The Constitution of Society. Outline of the Theory of Structuration.* Cambridge: Polity Press.

Haring, B.J.J. 1997. *Divine Households. Administrative and Economic Aspects of the New Kingdom Royal Memorial Temples in Western Thebes.* (Egyptologische Uitgaven, XII). Leiden: Nederlands Instituut voor het Nebije Oosten.

Hayes, W.C. 1957. 'Varia from the Time of Hatshepsut.' *Mitteilungen des Deutschen Archäologisches Institut Abteilung Kairo*, 15, 78-90.

Hodder, I. & S. Hutson 2003. *Reading the Past. Current Approaches to Interpretation in Archaeology.* (3rd ed.). New York: Cambridge University Press.

Hornung, E. 1995. 'Die Königliche Dekoration der Sargkammer.' In: E. Dziobek (ed.), *Die Gräber des vesirs User-Amun Theben nr. 61 und 131.* (Archäologische Veröffentlichungen, Deutches Archaeologisches Institut Abteilung Kairo, 84). Mainz: Philipp von Zabern, 42-47.

Ingold, T. 2000. *The Perception of the Environment. Essays in livelihood, dwelling and skill.* London: Routledge.

Junker, H. 1959. *Die Gesellschaftliche Stellung der ägyptischen Künstler im Alten Reich.* (Östereicher Akademie der Wissenschaften. Philosophisch-historische Klasse Sitzungsberichte, 233/1). Wien: Rudolf M. Rohrer.

Jørgensen, M. 1998. *Catalogue. Egypt II (1550-1080 B.C.).* Copenhagen: Ny Carlsberg Glyptotek.

Kayser, H. 1936. *Die Tempelstatuen ägyptischer Privatleute im mittleren un im neuen Reich.* Heidelberg: Druck der Johannes Hörning G.m.b.H.

Kjølby, A. 2001. *Diskursive Afbildninger. Beslutningsprocessen ved fremstillingen af ægyptisk kunst.* University of Copenhagen: unpublished MA-dissertation.

Kjølby, A. 2007a. *New Kingdom Private Temple Statues: A Study of Agency, Decision-making and Materiality.* University of Copenhagen: unpublished PhD-thesis.

Kjølby, A. 2007b. 'Decision Making Processes: A Cognitive Study of Private Statues in New Kingdom Temples.' In: J.-Cl. Goyon & C. Cardin (eds.), *Proceedings of the Ninth International Congress of Egyptologists.* Leuven: Peeters, 991-1000.

Kjølby, A. 2009. 'Material Agency, Attribution and Experience of Agency in Ancient Egypt.' In: Nyord, R. & A. Kjølby (eds.), *'Being in Ancient Egypt' Thoughts on Agency, Materiality and Cognition.* (BAR International Series, 2019). Oxford: Archaeopress, 31-46.

Kozloff, A.P. & B.M. Bryan 1992. *Egypts Dazzling Sun: Amenhotep III and his World.* Cleveland: The Cleveland Museum of Art.

Krauss, R. 1986. 'Der Oberbildhauer Bak und sein Denkstein in Berlin. *Jahrbuch der Berliner Museen* 28, 5-46.

Legrain, G. 1906a. 'Nouveaux Renseignement sur les Dernières Découvertes faites a Karnak.' *Receuil de Traveaux*, XXVIII 3-4, 137-61.

Legrain, G. 1906b. *Statues et statuettes de rois et de particuliers*, I. (Catalogue Général des Antiquités égyptiennes du Musée du Caire Nos 42001-42138). Cairo: Imprimerie de l'Institut Francais d'Archaeologie Orientale.

Legrain, G. 1909. *Statues et statuettes de rois et de particuliers*, II. (Catalogue Général des Antiquités égyptiennes du Musée du Caire Nos 42139-42191). Cairo: Imprimerie de l'Institut Francais d'Archaeologie Orientale.

Lemonnier, P. 1993. 'Introduction.' In: P. Lemonnier (ed.), *Technological Choices. Transformation in Material Cultures since the Neolithic*. London: Routledge, 1-35

Manuelian, P. der 1994. *Living in the past. Studies in Archaism of the Twenty-Sixth Dynasty*. London: Kegan Paul International.

Meskell, L. 2004 'Statue Worlds and Divine Things.' In: L. Meskell (ed.): *Object Worlds in Ancient Egypt. Material Biographies Past and Present*. Oxford: Berg, 87-115.

Meyer, C. 1982. *Senenmut. Eine Prosopographische Untersuchung*. (Hamburger Ägyptologische Studien, 2). Hamburg: Verlag Borg GmbH.

Müller, M. 2005. 'Die Königsplastik des Mittleren Reichs und Ihre Schöpfer: Reden über Statuen – Wenn Statuen Reden.' To appear in *Imago Aegypti*, I (expected release June 2005).

O'Neil, J.P., C. Ziegler & D. Arnold (eds.) 1999. *Egyptian Art in the Age of the Pyramids*. New York: Metropolitan Museum of Art.

Otto, E. 1948. 'Zur Bedeutung der ägyptischen Tempelstatue seit dem Neuen Reich.' *Orientalia*, 17, 448-66.

Otto, E. 1960. *Das Ägyptische Mundöffnungsritual*. II (Ägyptologische Abhandlungen, 3). Wiesbaden: Otto Harrassowitz.

Pendlebury, J.D.S. 1951. *The City of Akhenaten, Part III* (2 vols.). (Egypt Exploration Society, 44). London: Egypt Exploration Society.

Phillips, J. 1991. 'Sculpture Ateliers of Akhenaten.' *Amarna Letters*, I, 31-40.

Reisner, G. 1931. *Mycerinos. The Temples of the third pyramid at Giza*. Cambridge, MA: Harvard University Press.

Ricke, H. 1967 [1932]. *Der Grundriss des Amarna-Wohnhauses*. (Ausgrabungen der Deutschen Orient-Gesellschaft in Tell el-Amarna, 4). Osnabrück: Otto Zeller.

Robins, G. 1994. *Proportions and Style in Ancient Egyptian Art*. London: Thames and Hudson.

Robins, G. 1997. *The Art of Ancient Egypt*. Cambridge, MA: Harvard University Press.

Roth, A.M. 2001. 'Opening of the Mouth' In: D.B. Redford (ed.), *The Oxford Encyclopedia of Ancient Egypt*, vol. 2. London: Oxford University Press, 605-09.

Schäfer, H. 1986. *Principles of Egyptian Art* (transl. and ed. by J. Baines; German 4th ed. 1963 edited by E. Brunner-Traut). Oxford: Griffith Institute.

Schulz, R. 1992. *Die Entwicklung und Bedeutung des kuboiden Statuentypus. Eine Untersuchung zu den sogenannten "Wurfelhockern"*, I-II. (Hildesheimer Ägyptologischer Beiträge, 33-34). Hildesheim: Gerstenberg Verlag.

Smith, W.S. 1946. *A History of Egyptian Sculpture and Painting in the Old Kingdom*. London: Oxford University Press.

Steinmann, F. 1980. 'Untersuchungen zu den in der Handwerklich-künstlerichen Produktion beschäftigten Personen und Berufsgruppen des Neuen Reichs. I. Katalog der Berufsbezeichnungen und Titel.' *Zeitschrift für Ägyptische Sprache*, 107, 137-56.

Steinmann, F. 1982a. 'Untersuchungen zu den in der Handwerklich-künstlerichen Produktion beschäftigten Personen und Berufsgruppen des Neuen Reichs. II. Klassifizierung der Berufsbezeichnungen und Titel.' *Zeitschrift für Ägyptische Sprache*, 109, 66-72.

Steinmann, F. 1982b. 'Untersuchungen zu den in der Handwerklich-künstlerichen Produktion beschäftigten Personen und Berufsgruppen des Neuen Reichs. III. Bemerkungen zu den an Titel und Berufsbezeichnungen angeknüpften Angaben über Dienstverhältnisse etc..' *Zeitschrift für Ägyptische Sprache*, 109, 149-56.

Steinmann, F. 1984. 'Untersuchungen zu den in der Handwerklich-künstlerichen Produktion beschäftigten Personen und Berufsgruppen des Neuen Reichs. IV. Bemerkungen zur Arbeitsorganisation.' *Zeitschrift für Ägyptische Sprache*, 111, 30-40.

Steinmann, F. 1991. 'Untersuchungen zu den in der Handwerklich-künstlerichen Produktion beschäftigten Personen und Berufsgruppen des Neuen Reichs.' *Zeitschrift für Ägyptische Sprache*, 118, 149-61.

Teichmann, F. 1971. 'Das Werkverfahren.' In: E. Hornung (ed.), *Das Grab des Haramheb im Tal der Könige*. Bern: Francke Verlag, 32-37.

Valbelle, D. 1985. *'Les Ouvriers de La Tombe' Deir el-Médineh à l'époque Ramesside*. Cairo: Institut Francais d'archaéologie orientale du Caire.

Vandier d'Abbadie, J. 1937-1959. *Catalogue des ostraca figurés de Deir el Médineh*, 4 vols. (Documents de Fouille de l'Institut Francais d'Archáologie Orientale du Caire, 2). Cairo: Imprimerie de l'Institut Francais d'Achéologie Orientale.

Verbovsek, A. 2005. *"Als Gunsterweis des Königs in den Tempel gegeben… ". Private Tempelstatuen des Alten und Mittleren Reiches*. (Ägypten und Altes Testament 63). Wiesbaden: Harrasowitz Verlag.

Wente, E. 1990. *Letters from Ancient Egypt*. (Society of Biblical Literature Writings from the Ancient World, 1). Atlanta: Scholars Press.

Wiessner, P. 1988. 'Style and Changing Relations between the Individual and Society.' In: I. Hodder (ed.), *The Meaning of Things. Material Culture and Symbolic Expression*. London: Harper Collins, 56-63.

Wild, H. 1966. *Le Tombeau de Ti. Fasc. III. La Chapelle (2. Partie)* (Memoires publiés par les membres de l'Institut Francais d'archéologie orientale du Caire, 65). Cairo: Imprimerie de l'Institut Francais d'Achéologie Orientale.

Wildung, D. 1990. 'Bilanz eines Defizits. Problemstellungen und Methoden in der ägyptologischen Kunstwissenschaft.' In: M. Eaton-Krauss, E. Graefe (eds.) 1990. *Studien zur ägyptischen Kunstgeschichte*. (Hildesheimer Ägyptologischer Beitrage, 29). Hildesheim: Gerstenberg Verlag, 57-80, Taf.7-14.

Wilson, J.A. 1947. 'The Artist of the Egyptian Old Kingdom.' *Journal of Near Eastern Studies*, 6, 231-49.

Combined Efforts: The cooperation and coordination of barrow-building in the Bronze Age

Mads Kähler Holst & Marianne Rasmussen

The challenges of being stronger together than apart

Cooperation is a fundamental constituent of human society. It is a precondition for the execution of large and complex tasks and it develops and maintains social relations and group identities in the effort to obtain higher common objectives. It implies a harmonization or adjustment of the intentions of two or more individuals and, for the individual, cooperation can be considered a strategy of social interaction that is complementary to competition, involves alternative cognitive processes, and advances very different modes of engagement as well as social institutions.

Within any society cooperative and competitive strategies will be employed concurrently in different situations, and in new social encounters there will often be an initial stage of inconclusiveness as to which approach to use. The contrary effects of the two strategies entails, however, that further development of the social relations generally calls for an open adherence to either of the two. The balance between cooperation and competition in the history of individuals and communities is in this way generally assumed to have a decisive influence on the course of conflicts, including the possibilities of resolving them, and here cooperation is generally assumed to promote the more constructive outcome. This makes cooperation a very basic mode of interaction with an evident socially formative role (Axelrod 1984; 1997; Deutsch 1973; Goffman 1963; Hardin 1982; Olson 1965).

Despite the obvious overall advantages it is far from given that attempts to cooperate will succeed. The cooperation implies giving and taking, sometimes to the extent of consigning individual sovereignty, and the long-term benefits of cooperating may appear less evident than the short term benefits of pursuing egoist interests, or the vulnerability entailed in a one-sided initiation of cooperation. Therefore cooperation requires communication to clarify and try the positions and motives of the involved parties and to facilitate an agreement on objectives and a settlement of obligations and rights. The process may involve the construction of new loyalties and identities at odds with existing ones. It presupposes mutual trust, and a basic understanding between the contracting parties as well as the more tangible logistical basis of the cooperation including established principles of coordination. For stability it depends on the development of sanctions against defectors and free-riders, which creates a close link to the establishment of group identities and norms (Bendor & Mookherjee 1990; Bicchieri 1990; Elster 1989, 187ff).

While cooperation is a universal social phenomenon, the specific form of the cooperation will in this way inevitably refer to the present social structures, such as the available norms, ethics, institutions, infrastructure, technology and the existing social networks. Thereby cooperation both forms society and carries in its organization an impression of existing social structure. The disclosure of the various expressions of cooperation occurring in a society would in consequence seem an indispensable part of a characterization of that society and its history.

The recognition of the socially embedded nature of cooperation and its close interplay with institutions and norms with an often very long history draws attention to an apparent bias in the present theoretical debate on cooperation (Henrich 2006). On the one hand, there has been an intense focus on abstract, universal evolutionary aspects of cooperative behaviour closely associated with the development of game theory and agent-based modelling (Axelrod 1984; Richerson *et al.* 2003; Sugden 2001). On the other hand, there is a scarcity of detailed empirical studies of the character and organization of cooperation in specific societies in the past and the concrete long-term historical courses of the development and shaping of collective action. Empirical studies of modern small-scale societies reveal significant cultural variation in choices of interaction strategy, and indicate much more complex courses of development of cooperation and closer relationships between the social context and the character of the cooperative behaviour than assumed in the generalized models (Henrich *et al.* 2005). This discrepancy makes the study of the forms of cooperation and their social conditions and consequences a natural topic for further attention in archaeology.

Part of the explanation for the lack of detailed analyses on cooperation in past societies seems to be of a methodological nature. In archaeology the apparent significance of cooperation often contrasts the restricted possibilities of performing the detailed analyses and controlled experiments employed to characterize cooperation in other disciplines today. These analyses presuppose a high relative-chronological resolution and a complete and coherent representation of actions, which is rarely obtainable archaeologically due to the fragmented and partial character of the available sources. Consequently, the characterization of cooperation in an archaeological, and particularly a prehistoric archaeological context will normally have to rely on different methodological premises and with a focus on the few fortunate instances where a detailed insight into the cooperative efforts can be obtained.

One area where prehistoric cooperation and its organization and social context has been a relatively prominent topic, is in connection with monumental architecture, from pyramids to megalithic monuments (e.g. Černy 1973; David 1996; Whittle 1997, 142ff). Even without the actual cooperation being discernible, the size of the works and the complexity of the constructions here echo a comprehensive number of participants and an elaborate coordination of their efforts. When the construction sequence of the monuments is accessible further details about work processes and activity sequences can be approached and, on rare occasions, even the basic organization of the work with indications of various building teams. This allows basic propositions on the nature of cooperation in a historical perspective.

In South Scandinavia the large Bronze Age barrows constitute an example of these possibilities. The barrows of the period were constructed almost entirely

Fig. 1. A modern attempt to reconstruct small barrow models of grass sods at the Historical-Archaeological Experimental Centre at Lejre on Zealand in 2001. As with the Bronze Age barrows the sods are carefully placed with the vegetation surface downwards and according to rigid principles, which ensures a stable construction (Photo: Ole Malling).

of grass and heather sods taken from the surrounding landscape (Fig. 1). Under fortunate circumstances these sods are still clearly recognizable under excavation, with each new sod slightly overlapping the preceding (Fig. 2). This allows an exceptionally detailed reconstruction of the building sequence, down to the relative-chronological order of the individual sods. Starting with a recent barrow excavation in South-western Jutland,

this article presents examples of the information that through the excavation of this type of monument can be obtained on the historic cooperation. In addition, the social significance of the cooperation, as witnessed in the barrow structures, is discussed. Attention is thus directed at the barrow-building process and the monument builders rather than the normal subjects of analyses in connection with the Bronze Age barrows: the burial and the deceased.

The South Scandinavian Early Bronze Age and its barrows

The Early Bronze Age of South Scandinavia from 1700-1100 BC was apparently characterized by a growing social complexity. There are indications of an increasing interaction between the settlements including the establishment of long dis-

Fig. 2. Part of the excavation of the Bronze Age barrow Skelhøj in southern Jutland. In the sections and plans of the barrow the individual sods are still recognizable as the vegetation surfaces of the sods stand out as thin, dark layers, which allow a delimitation of the individual sods (Photo: Per Poulsen).

tance contacts. Some degree of functional specialization of the settlements can be recognized (Rasmussen 1995, 104f), and a still more varied inventory in the burials is assumed to represent an increasing social differentiation, continuing a tendency already evident in the Late Neolithic (Kristiansen 1987; Randsborg 1974; Vandkilde 1996). And finally, new, more elaborate and architecturally complicated monumental constructions appear in the form of large barrows with composite building sequences.

This development occurs on a setting of dispersed and relatively small settlements, normally consisting of just one or two long houses, and with an assumed duration of only a few decades. There is no evidence of a stable hierarchical settlement structure until the Late Bronze Age, even if the sizes of the long houses vary considerably already in the Early Bronze Age with some houses reaching 500 m^2 in size and 200-250 m^2 constituting the average (Boas 1993; Ethelberg 1993a; 2000; cf. Artursson 2005). Rather than a strategic assertion of power this variation could, however, just as well represent differences in household structures and demographic variation from settlement to settlement, which would seem to be supported by the occurrence of sectioning of the large houses with separate cooking areas in the individual sections indicating multiple social groups within the same building (Rasmussen 1999) (fig. 3). The dispersed settlement pattern may be interpreted as reflecting some form of neolocal residence structure, where new households emanate from one or two existing households, most probably when selected members from the younger generation establish themselves. In this way, there would have been strong links in the form of kinship relations between the settlements, but economically and in everyday practices

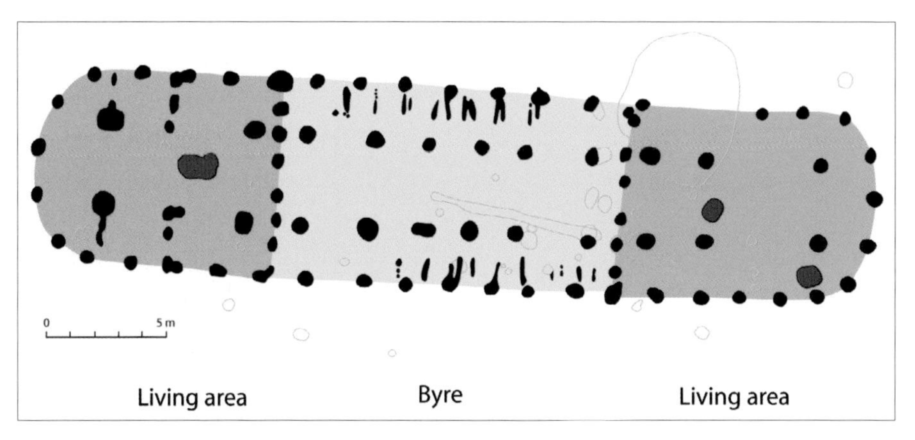

Fig. 3. Late 2nd millennium BC Bronze Age long house from Legård in Northwestern Jutland with a tripartite internal arrangement. Black indicates postholes and stall partitions, while red represents cooking and fire pits. Redrawn by Louise Hilmar after Mikkelsen & Kristiansen (1997).

each settlement appears to have operated relatively autonomously, which seem to be a general pattern in large parts of North-western Europe. This autonomy would have made the household a very basic social unit in the Bronze Age society, an inference also supported by the central role of the household in later periods right into the Middle Ages, even after the appearance of villages (Gerritsen 1999; Holst 2010).

At the beginning of the Early Bronze Age, as in the preceding Late Neolithic, by far the majority of the activities we can identify in the archaeological record appear to have been within the capacity of just one household or to have occurred in the meeting of two. The new large barrows, however, represent something entirely different. With diameters of up to 70 m and heights of more than 10 m, and an apparently short construction period, they must have entailed a comprehensive and evidently successful cooperation of several settlements.

The cooperation implies the formation of new relations or a further development of existing relations between the settlements, thus making the large barrows an important source to understanding the increasing complexity of the Bronze Age. They are, on the one hand, the places where the required inter-group relations become apparent to us. And, on the other hand, the large barrows must in themselves have made an important contribution to the development of these relations, as the monuments constituted one of the most distinct scenes for the performance and negotiation or coercion of the relations.

The characterization of barrow-building cooperation

As mentioned in the introduction there are methodical problems in analysing cooperation archaeologically. An excavation of a barrow does obviously not provide the active dynamic cooperation of the past. Even if the barrows in many ways appear as an evident source to the study of cooperation in the Bronze Age, their testimony is still fragmented and partial, and dependent on our de- or encoding already during excavation. This process relies on an apprehension of what important questions are and how they may be answered. In connection with the characterization of the cooperation in barrow-building, at least three components seem essential: Firstly, an idea of the concrete objectives or intentions of the barrow builders; secondly, an identification of participants or groups of participants; and thirdly their practices. When translated into specific objectives for the excavation based on an assessment of how these components may be recovered, this leads to three themes (Holst *et al.* 2004):

The first theme concerns the overall architecture of the barrow. Here the different indications of control, planning and correction of the shape of the mound are considered in relation to room for variation, gradual adaptation and asymmetry. This may provide the basis for an idea of the significance of the final shape of the mound as opposed to the importance and meaning of the building process itself and its accompanying activities. Of specific interest are the structures in the barrow, which seem to reflect preconceived plans of design. Physically constructed templates, such as the fences of Lusehøj on western Funen, represent an obvious case (Thrane 1984). However, more indirect indications may also be uncovered in the analysis of the construction sequence. For example, evident structures in the composition of the barrows can be the result of several relative-chronologically discontinuous building events which may never have appeared as a recognizable whole during the construction. These structures seem to presuppose some form of external physical model or non-physical template. A simple example could be the alignment of successively added structures reflecting a reference to a main axis in the monument. The widespread occurrence of common elements in the architecture and burial customs of the South Scandinavian Bronze Age barrows represents another indication of the existence of relatively well-established and widespread ideas about the barrows. On the other hand, it must be acknowledged that there is also a considerable variation in the architecture, which clearly indicates that these concepts were not strictly prescriptive.

With regards to the cooperation, this first architectural theme contains the common and presumably explicitly defined objective. However, in the archaeological record it is mixed together with the ability of the builders to achieve this goal, and a separation of these two aspects is often complicated. In practice, the distinction presupposes an attempt to identify the original idea or template of the architecture in contrast to the actual end result. This separation is often problematic, as it entails risks of projecting modern architectural ideals on the monuments of the past. Still, a tentative identification of the template of the building may be achieved in part a) through a comparison of the many excavated barrows, for the purpose of identifying common architectural ideas; and in part by b) a reading of the construction process in an attempt to recognize a meaningful pattern in shape adjustments in relation to an assumed template for the architecture. In this way, we also gain insight into how successful the builders were in achieving their objective.

The second theme concerns the practical organization of the barrow-building and the technical solution of its logistical and constructional challenges. Here the objective is the identification of the different types of tasks involved in the building, as well as the traces of labour division among teams and the structures and means of transport required for the construction process. These aspects may reveal basic social relations between the builders and provide an insight into the technical knowledge and know-how associated with the barrow-building.

In the analyses of the cooperation aspect this second theme concerning the practical organization offers basic information on the structural framework of the cooperation. It defines the cooperating entities and their modes of engagement such as the degree of integration and correlation of their efforts. This includes the discrimination of a particular specialization, where the identifiable participants or groups took care of separate, discrete functions, or if they operated parallel and attended to the same functions – though possibly still with some organizational division and grouping of the participants. The integration may be studied both in the concrete physical meetings of the operations of two or more groups as well as in a comparison of the functionally identical operations of separate groups, i.e. the uniformity or variability in the performance.

The analyses of the practical organization may also provide an idea of the extent to which the general idea of the barrow was recognizable in the various tasks and work groups of the monument construction, and may indirectly reflect important aspects of the cooperation. Clear references, for example, between the overall ideas and the individual tasks may be expected to support a dissemination of a feeling of responsibility for the work. And, particularly in connection with a monument where cosmological references are often a prominent part of the architecture, it may also provide an ethical dimension to the efforts, which as a general principle can be seen as supporting the cooperation (Bendor & Mookherjee 1990).

The third theme is very basic and concerns the building routines and the manual skills which can be defined. They are first and foremost accessible through the stratigraphical analyses of the sequence of sod-laying. This may, under favourable circumstances, provide an insight into the operations of individual builders or groups within the overall barrow-building, and it may also disclose the degree of rigidity and regularity in the practices in comparison to their adaptability and creativity.

For the analyses of the cooperation this theme provides an insight into the flow and regulation of the building process. It gives an impression of the degree to which the individual actions and interactions were routinized or required continuous monitoring and adjustments by the participants. These properties are important for understanding the character of the cooperation and its degree of negotiability (Goffman 1963, 198ff).

Furthermore, the basic building practices may provide an idea of how important the integration of the tasks of individual workers was for the overall objective of the work: i.e. by relating the degree of consistency in the work procedures to the extent the presumed overall architectural objectives were achieved.

The three themes represent an analytical structuring of the various interpretational constructions made during the excavation, for the purpose of capturing three different aspects of the barrow-building, i.e. the concrete architectural objectives, the participants, and their practices. Though all three themes seem accessible, it is important to emphasise that it always will only be a partial representation that can be derived. This it not least problematic in connection with the objectives of the cooperation, where the architectural aspects would most likely have constituted a concrete physical manifestation of more abstract overall intentions associated with the concepts of burial within a Bronze Age cosmology.

Skelhøj

From 2002 to 2004 the well-preserved Early Bronze Age barrow Skelhøj in Southwestern Jutland near Ribe was completely excavated. It is radiocarbon dated to the 15th century BC and is situated in a group of 26 barrows along the northern side of the Kongeå River. Several renowned archaeological Bronze Age finds have been recovered from the group (Boye 1896, 98ff; Kristiansen *et al.* 2003; Thrane 1963). With a diameter of 30 m and an original height of 7 m (at the time of excavation 5 m), Skelhøj belongs to the large barrows, and could be expected to have involved a considerable building team and a well-developed organization and planning.

The mound was investigated by a series of sections and plans through the monument (fig. 4). The excavation revealed a complex building sequence and also allowed the reconstruction of the basic organization of the work (Holst *et al.* 2004). The barrow was constructed in one continuous process, without recognizable intermissions. The exact duration of the work is difficult to estimate, but it probably was no longer than a few months.

The existence of an idea and a plan of the barrow seem to penetrate the monument from the beginning of the construction. Even before the coffin was positioned, a structure was imposed on the construction in the form of a segmentary pie-division of the building site, with a centre in what was to become the central burial (fig. 5). Furthermore, the burial was aligned with the E-W-axis of the pie-division in accordance with a predominant E-W-symbolism evident in a large number of Early Bronze Age barrows. This is generally assumed to reflect a metaphorical link between the burial architecture and a cosmology, in which the journey of the sun occupies a prominent position (e.g. Goldhahn 2004, 45ff; Kaul 1998; Randsborg & Nybo 1986). In Skelhøj the metaphor seems particularly strongly expressed, as the segment division together with the circular form of the barrow establishes a spoked-wheel-template on the building site, and exactly the spoked-wheel is a frequent sign in the iconography of the Bronze Age, generally

Fig. 4. The Skelhøj barrow during excavation in 2002. The shape reflects the extensive use of various types of sections and plans to disclose the construction sequence of the barrow (Photo: Mads Holst).

assumed to represent central aspects of Bronze Age cosmology such as the sun and a prominent repetitive or cyclical concept of the world (Kaul 2004: 250ff; Thrane 1963a, 103; Tilley 1999, 146ff).

This structure, however, had wider implications than just a symbolic reference to a cosmology. Through the remaining construction process it came to govern the building practices of the mound as it acted as a physical division of the building work. All actions in the building process respected this initial segmentation of the building ground. Varying provenance of the sods, separate access pathways, and small variations in the basic building practices from segment to segment, all point towards the segments as representing discrete groups of builders, with each group procuring the sods in a different part of the surrounding landscape; having their own pathways into the mound; and having responsibility for the construction of each their section of the mound. The segmentation would thus serve as a clear separation of different building groups, and there were very few activities which transgressed borders. Stratigraphical observations indicate that there was contemporaneous work underway on the different segments, but that the work was not entirely synchronised. One segment could be ahead of the neighbouring segments.

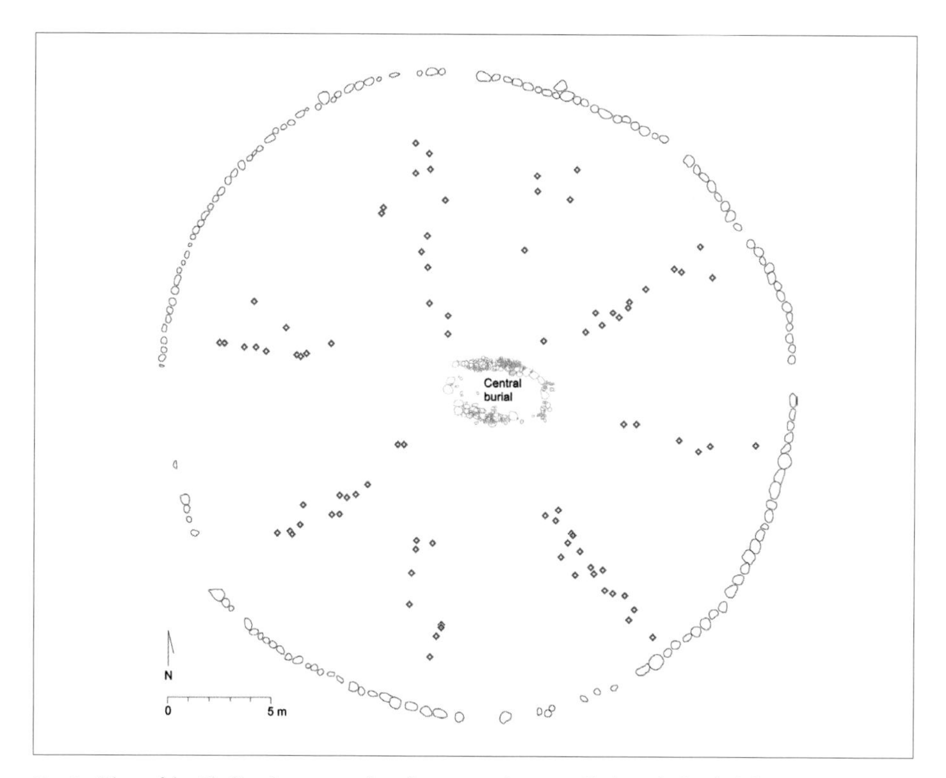

Fig. 5. Plan of the Skelhøj barrow with red points indicating all identified radial divisions observed in the fill of the barrow. Together these observations draw the contours of a maintained segmentation of the barrow from the onset of the construction to its completion (Graphics: Mads Holst).

The building within the different segments, however, followed the same basic course, which is clearly visible in the main sections through the barrow (fig. 6). During the first stage, a primary barrow cover was constructed around the central burial. At the completion of this stage a number of modifications is evident, which were apparently all directed at establishing as perfect a spherical shape as possible. This primary stage was then immediately – or after a very short intermission – covered by a series of four shells gradually increasing the size of the barrow.

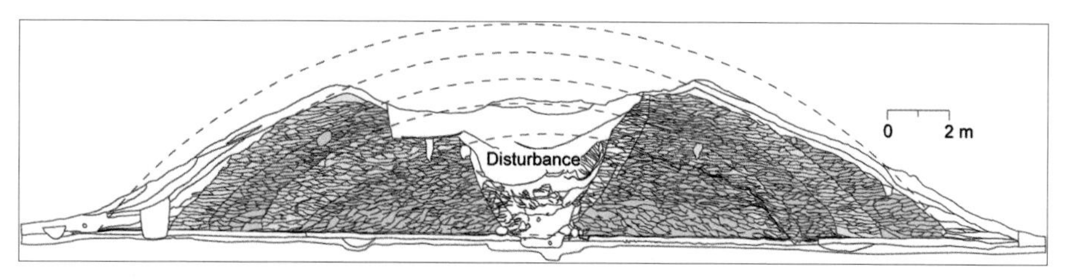

Fig. 6. Drawing of the main section through Skelhøj with outlines of the estimated original extents of the barrow and the shell-extension principle emphasised (Graphics: Peter Jensen & Mads Holst).

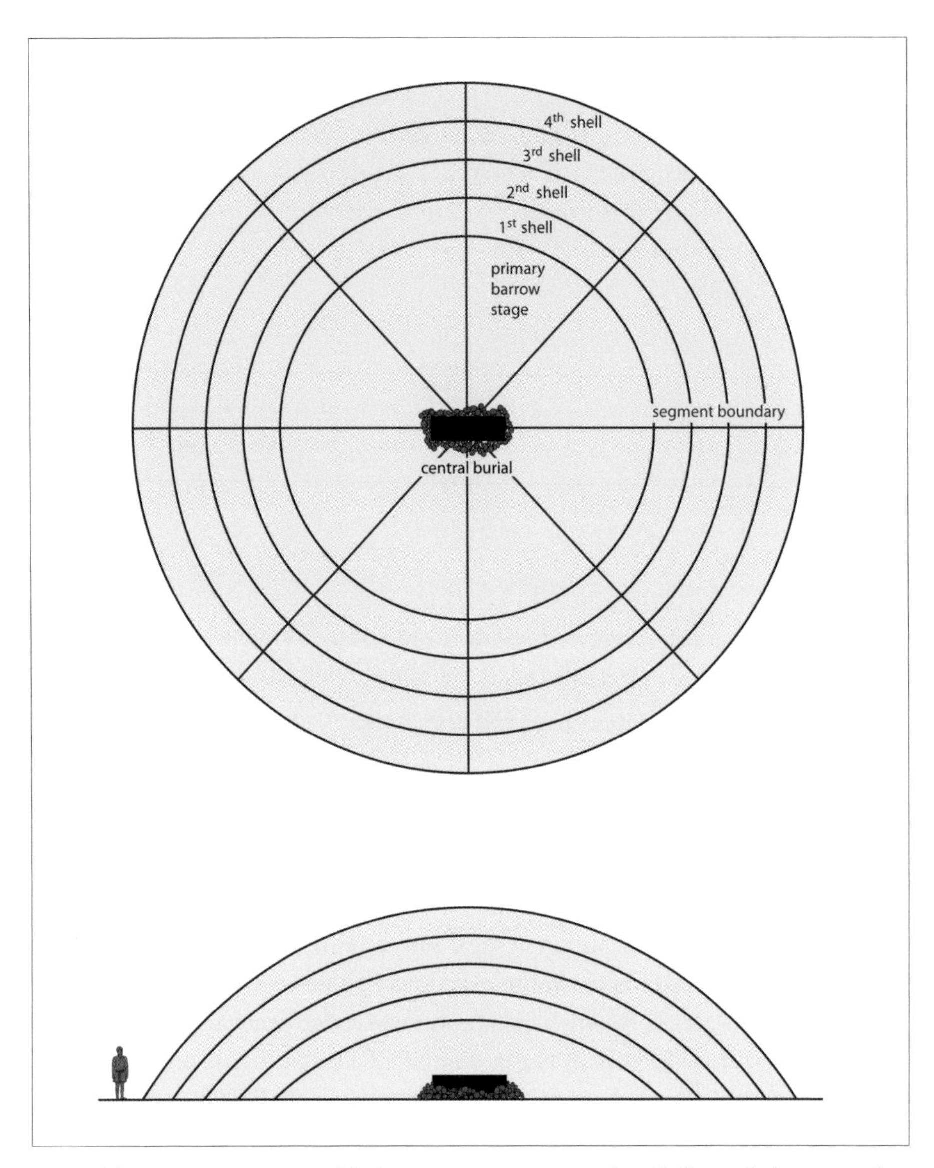

Fig. 7. Schematic representation of the basic construction principle in Skelhøj with the two overlain structuring principles, the concentric shells which steered the gradual extension of the barrow, and the radial segmentation of the building site, which appears to have served as a basis for an organization of the builders into groups (Graphics: Mads Holst).

The architectural plan in this way had two overlain dimensions: a dimension of labour division represented by the radial segment division, and another dimension structuring the progression of the work, and which was manifested in the shells (Fig. 7).

The documentation of the sods also allows the reconstruction of the basic building routines of the workers within each segment. These routines reveal a limited number of quite strictly maintained rules. All sods in the shells were, practically without exception, placed horizontally with the vegetation downwards. The sods were relatively standardized in size approximately 25 x 35 cm and 10-15 cm in thickness, which meant that each sod weighed approximately 15 kg, and it is conceivable that they were carried to the building site by the individual builders one at a time.

The construction of each segment was initiated by a demarcation of the outer boundary with a row a sods. Then the space between the row and the previous shell was filled by carefully constructing further rows on the inside. In the next layer the procedure was repeated, and building directions were maintained. Simply by following these principles, the shape of the mound could be maintained without the need of extended control or coordination of the individual segments. To a large extent, the building teams could in this way operate independently of each other.

The architectonic plans and the practical building principles should in principle have led to the intended form and matter of the monument, provided that problems and irregularities did not arise during the construction. However, naturally enough trouble did arise – also on numerous occasions. The problems were mainly associated with the maintenance of the geometrical order implanted and intended in the barrow. Variation in sod types led to uneven surfaces, whose irregularity propagated out into a growing area as the barrow size increased. There were small slides and erosion in connection with larger rainfalls, and the lacking coordination of the construction in the segments caused asymmetry.

An individual solution for each of these problems can be identified. Even surfaces were re-established by a break in the sod row routines enabling a new level surface to be established. The erosion deposits at the base were smoothed out before new shells were initiated and supports were added to prevent slides. Errors in the meeting of segments were corrected by defining new curvatures at the commencement of a new shell. Generally the repairs take place at specific points in time, that is, between the routines either at the commencement of a new layer or a new shell.

The number of people participating in the event, as well as its duration, is difficult to estimate. Larger rain episodes can be identified as wash layers in the sections of the barrow, and they suggest with some uncertainty a construction within perhaps a few months. The narrow work surfaces of the shells can only have allowed a limited number of people to operate on each segment at a time, which in combination with the supposed duration of the building project may suggest a total number of between 100 and a few hundred participants.

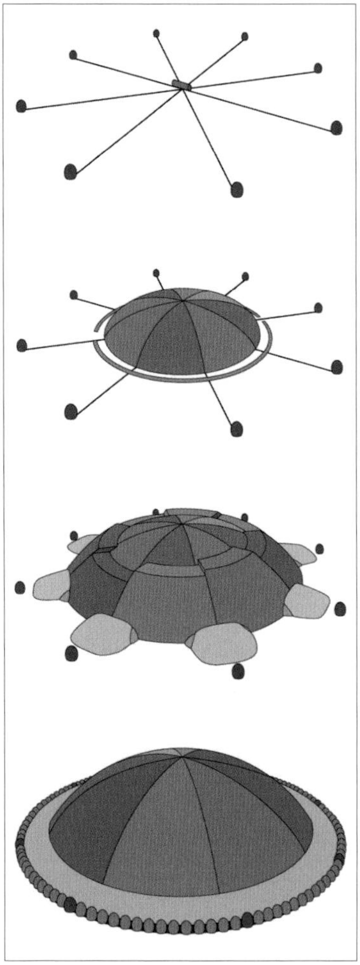

Fig. 8. Reconstruction of the basic construction sequence of Skelhøj with its complex composition of different construction elements (Graphics: Lars Thomsen).

The nature of barrow cooperation

Skelhøj reveals a rigidly structured but also strongly purposeful organization and construction sequence. At first glance, the organization of the barrow construction appears highly complex. A primary barrow stage and four shells with eight segments in each, makes 40 different construction parts (Fig. 8). But from an operational angle, there may be very good reasons for the organization ending up like this. All the various construction principles can be seen to support two major purposes. Firstly, they maintain the geometric symmetry of the barrow. Secondly, they facilitate the logistics and the practical cooperation.

The symmetry is obtained primarily by structuring actions in nested routines: the construction of rows, leading to the construction of layers, leading to the construction of shells. Thereby the perfect shape of the primary barrow stage could gradually be up-scaled by incremental steps, whereby any irregularity could easily be discovered at an early stage and counteracted before it came out of control. At the same time the regularity of the sod-laying ensured a highly stable interlocking construction.

The logistics and practical cooperation are also supported by the routines, but primarily by the segment division. It apparently provides a clear structuring of the participants' tasks in the construction event. If we consider the cooperation *between* the assumed groups, the independence of each group is a prominent feature. They follow the same rules and construction sequence, and as such the independence is not an autonomy, but there is a strong symbolic as well as practical segregation. The overall plan of the monument is realized through the building practices of the individual groups, while adjustments, repairs and coordination between the groups are restricted to a few natural intermissions in the construction process. The work is organized in a way which maximises the independent operation of these groups at the expense of a more centralized coordination of the barrow-building. This does not happen by granting them complete autonomy but, on the contrary, by establishing some very simple routines, which all the teams must follow rigidly. The abstract planning and the extended control are minimized. Operations *within* the groups seem to be characterized by a well-developed and integrated cooperation. Individuals are not evident in the basic building practices, and the regularity of the sod-laying suggests a very fluent procedure, which was with reluctance interrupted when modifications were required.

The cooperation at Skelhøj is, in this way, based upon what may be termed a nested, decentralized division of the builders into groups, with the individual groups largely operating independently. However, still some form of superior body exercised a limited and targeted control, apparently not of the building styles of the individual groups, but of the overall shape and mutual coherence of the result of the individual groups' efforts. It is a type of organization which represents a middle course between a centrally controlled and enforced way of cooperating and an entirely decentralized solution with the individual groups operating autonomously (Simon 1969; Bendor & Mookherjee 1987), and one which seems to have ensured an efficient and stable cooperation for the numerous participants.

The contrast between the integrated cooperation within the groups and the accentuated segregation of the segment groups makes it reasonable to suggest an existence of the groups also beyond the barrow-building event. They must represent entities who were accustomed to cooperating, and within which the basic rules and principles of coordination were already established. The most obvious interpretation would appear to be that there was a link between the segment groups in the barrow and the settlement groups in the society beyond. The prominent introduction of segmentation in the symbolism and practices of the barrow appear as a strong indication of generally recognized importance of groups in Bronze Age society.

The cooperation of the barrow construction may in this way seem to contain a clear reference to the organization of the settlements. This reference could also have been present in basic building practices. Some of the practical operations involved in the barrow construction would have been performed frequently in a settlement context. Cutting and transporting sods may have been a required part of the clearing of new fields for cultivation. Constructions with sod walls have been recorded at a few well-preserved Early Bronze Age settlements, and could have been a much more frequent phenomenon than the often badly preserved sites at first seem to suggest. In practice that would have made the participants in the barrow-building primarily refer to well-known everyday situations and structures. They would first and foremost have operated together with people with whom they normally operated, and they would have engaged in activities, which were well known. This had two major advantages that facilitated the extended form of corporation represented by the large barrows. Firstly, the basic building of the barrow would largely have concurred with well-established schemes; and secondly, it incorporated and reinforced existing social norms.

The general preference of schematically consistent structures over inconsistent or foreign structures may be an important part of the explanation of how the quite complex barrow-building organization emerges. Also the fact that they are more easily communicated and comprehended would have supported these elements in the spread of the building principles from one area to another (Fiske & Taylor 1991; von Hippel *et al.* 1993; Schneider 1991). And exactly this last property, the comprehensibility, also suggests that despite the apparent complexity resulting from their application, they did in fact make the work process much more intelligible to the participants; something which was even further facilitated by the strict rule-like routines (Henrich *et al.* 2005).

Altogether the Skelhøj excavation suggests a form of cooperation, which had strong references to existing social groups and practices within them. In fact to a wide extent it seems like a relatively simple combination of these, while the inter-group cooperation appears comparatively undeveloped and untested. Still the combination had a complex outcome, and the large barrows in many respects constituted a new form of practical cooperation, which may have established a model for other types of interaction in the Bronze Age also, and thereby play a role in the formation of social structures.

Beyond the barrow

The architectural and constructional approach to the barrows puts a strong emphasis on the cooperative elements of the Bronze Age burial practice. This contrasts the otherwise prevalent concept of the monuments and the period. For decades there has been a strong and somewhat one-sided focus upon the competitive aspects of South Scandinavian Late Neolithic and Bronze Age society in general. This appears most explicitly in connection with theories on the establishment of hierarchical structures and the emerging of elites. Even though reciprocal relations are discussed in connection with exchange on an elite level, it is normally presented as part of a competitive struggle for prestige, and in the interpretation of the organization of local communities there has been a clear emphasis on the establishment of dominating relations on a group of "commoners" by members of the elite (Kristiansen 1982; 1984; Larsson 1986; Vandkilde 1996). Also the building of barrows and the barrow itself as a monument have been viewed as expressions of these competitive strategies (Gröhn 2004, 356; Säfvestad 1993).

The analyses of the barrow-building provide an alternative aspect of social interaction with a focus on the cooperative processes occurring during the construction. Some asymmetric relations may clearly be recognized in the building organization. There are certain elements of control of the building process and the plan required a relatively advanced knowledge, which may have served as a basis for emphasising asymmetric relations between the knowledgeable few and the ordinary participants as suggested in other contexts in the South Scandinavian Bronze Age, such as flint working (Apel 2001; Olausson this volume). Also the nested organizational structure would seem to correspond well to some of the ideas contained in the concept of the decentralized chiefdom (Kristiansen 1991). However, there are also a number of elements in the construction that seem to indicate a strong emphasis on more symmetric relations between the participants.

There is the symbolic emphasis on the independence of the supposed work groups and the parallel construction sequences they follow. The fulfilment of the architectural intentions are achieved through the building practices of the individual teams and corrections are restricted to natural intermissions in their building practices and take the form of adaptive corrections of the practices. This suggests that the individual groups or representatives from them participated in the comparison of and adaptation to the architectural plan. The minor variation in the building principles from segment to segment also indicates that each group entered the barrow-building event with an already developed knowledge and experience of their own, which they applied during the construction. And even though part of the plan of the barrow may have been attended to by a particularly knowledgeable minority, the performance of the construction required at least a basic and probably an elaborate understanding of the plan by all the builders. The construction thus contains a strong element of shared knowledge as well as knowledge dispersal.

The building process with its rigid structure of nested routines, the symbolic element of the architecture, and its reference to and thereby implied use of a Bronze Age cosmology fulfils some of the classic traits of ritual in a relatively strict sense of the word (Turner 1969). In this respect, all the builders are participants in the ritual actions – there is not a clear distinction in the construction between performers and spectators. Rather than being a forum for imposing asymmetric control relations, the barrow-building in this way becomes an expression or accentuation of existing symmetric social relations, and it did so on the scene where cosmological understandings were probably most clearly expressed in the South Scandinavian Early Bronze Age: in the assembly of a barrow burial. Thus, it metaphorically linked this understanding of Bronze Age social relations to a wider and shared understanding of everything. That does not mean that the symmetric relations recognized in the barrow-building necessarily had a superior truth-value over asymmetric relations, evident in other contexts in the Bronze Age. Just as the emphasis on asymmetric relations should be considered as strategic assertions, so should the architectural accentuation of the symmetric relations.

It is important to stress, however, that the chosen emphasis on cooperative elements did not just have symbolic implications. It was also a transformation of certain social relations into a building organization, which enabled the construction of the barrow by facilitating cooperation. In this way, the emphasis on either symmetry or asymmetry, cooperation or competition, independence or dependence had considerable and real consequences in the Bronze Age as well as in our interpretations today. The almost ostentatious assertion of the independence of the groups in the construction process could thus very well have been evoked by the coexistence of two well-developed but alternative and partly conflicting strategies of social interaction in the Bronze Age society, a competitive one and a cooperative one, probably associated with different sets of norms. The construction of the barrow clearly relied on the cooperative set of rules, and the architectural prominence of the symmetric relations between the participating groups would have helped to ensure that everyone played by the same rules.

Thus, instead of the outcome of strategies of domination, the barrow-building appears as an integrative process where symmetrical relations between well-defined social groups were emphasised just as much as the asymmetrical – if not even more. Taking into account the intensification in barrow-building and the appearance of the large barrows, this suggest that not only did the Bronze Age see an increase in competitive strategies but also an alternative, parallel strengthening of strategies of cooperation – most likely based on existing social networks – in which it seems natural that kinship relations would have played a prominent role (Johansen *et al.* 2004). Rather than the rigidly ranked and controlled society, which is propagated in most studies of the Scandinavian Bronze Age, the construction sequence at Skelhøj suggests a much more ambiguous and dynamic interplay between the various groups, where their reciprocal roles were not entirely well-defined and universal, but at least to some extent flexible and manipulable, a concept occasionally summarized in the term of heterarchy (Crumley 1987; Levy 1995).

Constructed cooperation

The close link between the form of cooperation and the social organization seen in the structure of the Skelhøj barrow emphasises the need of context-based studies to understand the specific and extremely varied expressions cooperation takes. It may also contribute to the understanding of some remarkable and apparently culturally unrelated similarities in architecture across time. The radial segment division of the barrow, for instance, seems to be a recurring phenomenon over wide distances in time and space. In Denmark it reappears in the Viking Age monumental barrows at the Royal seat of Jelling after an interruption in monumental barrow-building of almost two millennia (Krogh 1993, 176ff). In Ireland a similar situation is found with segment divisions appearing in both the Neolithic monument of Townleyhall and in the Iron Age Navan Fort (Eogan 1963; Waterman 1997). There are no indications of a cultural transmission of the barrow-building principles between these examples, and there are other ways of constructing the barrows in periods and areas between them. The common building principles may instead echo basic similarities in the relation between social structure and the principles of participation in the monument construction. Thus the segmentation may, in accordance with the interpretation of Skelhøj, be seen as the barrow-builders' underlying self-perception of society as based upon relatively small and autonomously operating groups, which may also have coincided with the primary groups of everyday cooperation. In such a situation, the construction of the monuments would clearly have exceeded the capacity of these primary groups. Thereby the monuments came to embody a striking contrast between, on the one hand, tasks requiring a well-integrated, coordinated effort and, on the other hand, a basic understanding of, and perhaps even insistence on, society as compartmentalized. The architectural similarity could thus reflect that the efforts to establish a proficient cooperation beyond and between the normal and well-established social groups of cooperative practice entailed very similar challenges, and perhaps a relatively narrow range of possible and schematically patent organizations, which would ensure a successful outcome. And given the intended basic spherical or truncated conic shape of the monument, there was a similar narrow range of feasible ways of implementing this organization in the building processes, of which one was architecturally manifested in the radial segmentation of the barrow-building.

Monumental architecture is one of the fora where the higher level of social interaction, exceeding the groups of everyday practices, becomes most apparent in the archaeological record. This is partly because of its substantial material component, but by all appearances, also because the monument building was, in fact, one, if not *the*, prime forum of actual cooperative meeting for these groups. Furthermore, monument construction was generally not a singular occurrence but a recurring event, and consequently entailed the possibility of developing institutionalized ways of cooperating. The monument construction thereby obtained a potential formative role in the development of new modes of cooperation. It appears significant in this connection that archaeologically more extensive and complex modes of cooperation often become evident in the construction of monuments with strong and carefully prepared references to a developed cosmology: in the case of Skelhøj indicated by the architectural incorporation and practical use of the spoked-wheel structure.

This combination of cosmology and construction seems to constitute strong support for the development of cooperation in several ways. First, as mentioned above, the architectural references to the cosmologically significant icons assisted a schema-reading of the unusual event, which may have improved the comprehension of the task at hand by metaphorically linking the event to well-known structures. Secondly, the strong ritualization of the event provided a strong operative framework for the participants including their interaction, which lowered the mental resources that had to be allocated to the monitoring of and adaptation to each other, and guided the attention towards the construction (Goffman 1963, 198ff). Finally, the link between the development of the new forms of cooperation and an explicit understanding of order in the world, explicitly or implicitly empowered the construction work with an ethical or normative dimension. Failure to comply with the rules of coordination thus entailed the considerable risk of being conceived as an immoral act.

By implementing and ethical dimension within game-theoretical studies of cooperation there has recently been an increased focus on the role of norms and morals for the choices of individuals, which may restrain competitive behaviour and instead support cooperative practices (Bendor & Mookherjee 1990; Henrich 2006; Pillutla & Chen 1999). The use of various forms of regulated games as basis for the characterization of the cooperation, however, implies that the norms are generally considered as background property of the individuals in the form of a tacit mental template internalized by well-established ways of interacting in everyday activities in the society and largely unconsciously transferred by the individuals to the game (Henrich *et al.* 2004; 2005; Lesorogol 2007).

Elements of this process may arguably be recognized in the construction of Skelhøj with its apparently strong implementation of well-established group operations from everyday life beyond the barrow construction, which seems to have facilitated a fluent and efficient operation of the individual work teams. Still, the monumental construction in itself was not an everyday activity, and particularly the construction of the large monuments must to a wide extent have implied exceptional challenges both organizationally and conceptually for all involved. The new forms of cooperation implied would not have been immediately consistent with existing schemes for cooperation. It seems that in this situation a much more directed and reflected use of norms or ethics to support the cooperation may have been initiated. The strong architectural references to cosmological concepts and the very distinct and unmistakable application of these references in the organization of the labour imposed a prominent ethical dimension to the work, and it inserted the individual activities in a larger explanatory framework. By interlinking the cooperation with cosmology a normative structure was established, which would have directed both the operations of the builders and their perception of the work. In this sense, the cosmological concepts were both the initiating motive and the operative means of the barrow construction.

This interpretation suggests a relatively well-developed sense of the role of the normative schemas in supporting cooperation as well as an ability to utilize this property purposively and efficiently in the development of new modes of cooperation by assisting a definite schema-reading of an unusual – if not exceptional – situation, through strong metaphorical links in the architecture between well-established cosmological schemas and the modes of cooperation. It emphasises an active constructivist element in the role of the norms in the support and development of cooperation in addition to the more passive prescriptive effects of norms often identified in studies of cooperative behaviour.

Through the detailed studies of the monument building it may in this way be possible to go beyond the relatively obvious fact that elaborate cooperation took place, and begin to distinguish the premises for this cooperation and the various tangible as well as abstract elements combined to enable the cooperation. In combination with the role of the monuments as one of the primary forums for the development of the more complex forms of cooperation, this entails that the analyses of the monument building may open for a more general approach to the interpretation of the long-term interplay between forms of cooperation and emerging social complexity in the shape of the development of institutions exceeding the groups of everyday practice.

Acknowledgements

The investigation of Skelhøj is part of an interdisciplinary research project funded by the Danish Research Council for the Humanities. The archaeological part of the project is a collaboration between the Historical-Archaeological Experimental Centre in Lejre, the National Museum in Copenhagen, the Section for Archaeology at Aarhus University, the Institute of Geography at Copenhagen University, the Museum of Sønderskov, and the Danish National Heritage Agency. A further range of institutions participate in the environmental and preservational analyses (http://skelhoej.natmus.dk). We would like to thank sincerely all the many participants in the Skelhøj excavation for both their efforts in uncovering the construction of Skelhøj during excavation and the contributions to the discussions on, among many other things, the interpretation and implications of the barrow-building organization, and not least for contributing to a cooperative endeavour with all its challenges.

References

Apel, J. 2001. *Daggers Knowledge & Power. The Social Aspects of Flint-Dagger Technology in Scandinavia 2350-1500 BC.* (Coast to Coast Books 3). Uppsala: Uppsala University, Department of Archaeology & Ancient History.

Artursson, M. 2005. 'Byggnadstradition.' In: P. Lagerås & B. Strömberg (eds.), *Bronsåldersbygd 2300-500 f. Kr.*. (Skånska spor – arkeologi längs Västkustbanan). Lund: Riksantikvarieämbetet. Lund, 20-83.

Axelrod, R. 1984. *The evolution of cooperation.* New York: Basic Books.

Axelrod, R. 1997. *The Complexity of Cooperation. Agent-based models of competition and collaboration.* Princeton: Princeton University Press.

Bendor, J. & D. Mookherjee 1987. 'Institutional Structure and the Logic of Ongoing Collective Action.' *American Political Science Review*, 81(1), 129-54.

Bendor, J. & D. Mookherjee 1990. 'Norms, Third-Party Sanctions, and Cooperation.' *Journal of Law, Economics, & Organisation*, 6(1), 33-63.

Bicchieri, C. 1990. 'Norms of Cooperation.' *Ethics*, 100(4), 838-61.

Boas, N.A. 1993. 'Late Neolithic and Bronze Age Settlements at Hemmed Church and Hemmed Plantation, East Jutland.' *Journal of Danish Archaeology*, 10, 1991, 119-35.

Boye, V. 1896. *Fund af Egekister fra Bronzealderen i Danmark. Et monografisk Bidrag til Belysning af Bronzealderens Kultur.* Copenhagen: Andr. Fred. Høst & Søns Forlag.

Černy, J. 1973. *A Community of Workmen at Thebes in the Ramesside Period.* Cairo: IFAO.

Crumley, C.L. 1987. 'A Dialectic Critique of Hierarchy.' In: T.C. Patterson & C.W. Gailey (eds.), *Power Relations and State Formation.* Washington DC: American Anthropological Association, 155-69.

David, R. 1996. *The Pyramid Builders of Ancient Egypt – A modern investigation of the Pharaoh's workforce.* London: Routledge & Kegan Paul.

Deutsch, M. 1973. *The resolution of conflict. Constructive and destructive processes.* New Haven: Yale University Press.

Eogan, G. 1963. 'A Neolithic habitation-site and megalithic tomb in Townleyhall townland, County Louth.' *Journal of the Royal Society of Antiquaries of Ireland*, XCIII, 37-81.

Elster, J. 1989. *The Cement of Society. A Study of Social Order.* Cambridge: Cambridge University Press.

Ethelberg, P. 1993. 'Two more House Groups with Three-aisled Long-houses from the Early Bronze Age at Højgård, South Jutland.' *Journal of Danish Archaeology*, 10, 1991, 136-55.

Ethelberg, P. 2000. 'Bronzealderen.' In: P. Ethelberg, E. Jørgensen, D. Meier & D. Robinson, *Det Sønderjyske Landbrugs Historie, Sten- og Bronzealder*. Haderslev: Haderslev Museum & Historisk Samfund for Sønderjylland, 135-280.

Fiske, S.T. & S.E. Taylor 1991. *Social cognition*. New York: McGraw-Hill.

Gerritsen, F. 1999. 'To build and to abandon. The cultural biography of late prehistoric houses and farmsteads in the southern Netherlands.' *Archaeological Dialogues*, 6(2), 78-114.

Goldhahn, J. 2004. *Från Sagaholm till Bredarör – hällbildsstudier 2000-2004*. (Gotarc Series C, Arkeologiske Skrifter, 62). Gothenburg: University of Gothenburg.

Goffman, E. 1963. *Behavior in Public Places. Notes on the Social Organization of Gatherings*. London: The Free Press of Glencoe, Collier-Macmillan Ltd.

Gröhn, A. 2004. *Positioning the Bronze Age. In social theory and research context*. (Acta Archaeologica Lundensia Series in 8°, 47). Lund: Almqvist & Wiksell.

Hardin, R. 1982. *Collective Action*. Baltimore: The John Hopkins University Press.

Henrich, J. 2006: 'Cooperation, Punishment, and the Evolution of Human Institutions.' *Science*, 312, 60-61.

Henrich, J., R. Boyd, S. Bowles, C. Camerer, E. Fehr, H. Gintis (eds.) 2004: *Foundations of human society: Economic experiments and ethnographic evidence from fifteen small-scale societies*. Oxford: Oxford University Press.

Henrich, J., R. Boyd, S. Bowles, C. Camerer, E. Fehr, H. Gintis, R. McElreath, M. Alvard, A. Barr, J. Ensmiger, N.S. Henrich, K. Hill, F. Gil-White, M. Gurven, F.W. Marlowe, J.Q. Patton, D. Tracer 2005: '"Economic man" in cross-cultural perspective: Behavioral experiments in 15 small-scale societies.' *Behavioral and Brain Sciences*, 28, 795-855.

von Hippel, E., J. Jonides, J.L. Hilton, S. Narayan 1993. 'The inhibitory effect of schematic processing on perceptual encoding.' *Journal of Personality and Social Psychology*, 64, 921-35.

Holst, M. K. 2010. "Inconstancy and stability: large and small farmsteads in the Iron Age village of Nørre Snede.' *Siedlungs- und Küstenforschung im Südlichen Nordseegebiet*, 33, 155-179.

Holst, M.K., M. Rasmussen, H. Breuning-Madsen 2004. 'Skelhøj. Et bygningsværk fra den ældre bronzealder.' *Nationalmuseets Arbejdsmark*, 2004, 11-25.

Johansen, K.L., S.T. Laursen & M.K. Holst 2004. 'Spatial patterns of social organization in the Early Bronze Age of South Scandinavia.' *Journal of Anthropological Archaeology*, 23, 33-55.

Kaul, F. 1998. *Ships on Bronzes. A study of Bronze Age religion and iconography*. (Studies in Archaeology and History 3). Copenhagen: Publications from the National Museum.

Kaul, F. 2004. *Bronzealderens religion. Studier af den nordiske bronzealders ikonografi*. Copenhagen: Det Kongelige Nordiske Oldskriftselskab.

Kristiansen, K. 1982. 'The formation of tribal systems in later European prehistory: northern Europe 4000-500 BC.' In: C. Renfrew, M. J. Rowlands & B. A. Segraves (eds.), *Theory and Explanation in Archaeology*. New York: Academic Press, 241-80.

Kristiansen, K. 1984. 'Krieger und Häuptlinge in der Bronzezeit Dänemarks. Ein Beitrag zur Geschichte des bronzezeitlichen Schwertes.' *Jahrbuch des Römisch-Germanisches Zentralmuseums*, 31, 187-206.

Kristiansen, K. 1987. 'From stone to bronze – the evolution of social complexity in Northern Europe 2300-1200 BC.' In: M. Brumfield & T. K. Earle (eds.), *Specialization, Exchange and Complex Societies*. Cambridge: Cambridge University Press, 30-51.

Kristiansen, K. 1991. 'Chiefdoms, states, and systems of social evolution.' In: T. Earle (ed), *Chiefdoms: Power, Economy, and Ideology*. Cambridge: Cambridge University Press, 16-43.

Kristiansen, S.M., K. Dalsgaard, M.K. Holst, B. Aaby & J. Heinemeier 2003. 'Dating of prehistoric burial mounds by ^{14}C analysis of soil organic matter fractions.' *Radiocarbon*, 45(1), 101-12.

Krogh, K. 1993. *Gåden om Kong Gorms Grav. Historien om Nordhøjen i Jelling.* (Vikingekongernes monumenter i Jelling, Bind 1). Herning: Poul Kristensens Forlag.

Larsson, T. 1986. *The Bronze Age Metalwork in Southern Sweden. Aspects of Social and Spatial Organization 1800-500 BC.* (Archaeology and Environment 6). Umeå: Studia Archaeologica Universitatis Umensis.

Lesorogol, C.K. 2007. Bringing Norms In. The Role of Context in Experimental Dictator Games. *Current Anthropology*, 48(6), 920-26.

Levy, J. 1995. 'Heterarchy in Bronze Age Denmark: Settlement Pattern, Gender, and Ritual.' In: R. M. Ehrenreich, C. L. Crumley & J. Levy (eds.), *Heterarchy and the Analysis of Complex Societies.* (Archaeological Papers on the American Anthropological Association, 6). Washington DC: American Anthropological Association, 41-54.

Mikkelsen, M. & K. Kristiansen 1997. 'Legård.' *Arkæologiske Udgravninger i Danmark,* 1996, 168.

Olsson, M. 1965. *The Logic of Collective Action.* Cambridge, MA: Harvard University Press.

Pillutla, M. & X. Chen 1999. 'Social norms and cooperation in social dilemmas: The effects of context and feedback.' *Organizational Behavior and Human Decisions Processes,* 78, 81-103.

Randsborg, K. 1974. 'Social stratification in Early Bronze Age Denmark: a study in the regulation of cultural systems.' *Praehistorische Zeitschrift,* 49, 38-61.

Randsborg, K. & C. Nybo 1986. 'The Coffin and the sun.' *Acta Archaeologica,* 55, 161-84.

Rasmussen, M. 1995. 'Settlement Structure and Economic Variation in the Early Bronze Age.' *Journal of Danish Archaeology,* 11, 1992-93, 87-107.

Rasmussen, M. 1999. 'Livestock without bones. The long-house as contributer to the interpretation of livestock management in the Southern Scandinavian Early Bronze Age.' In: J. Ringtved & C. Fabech (eds.), *Settlement and Landscape. Proceedings of a conference in Århus, Denmark, May 4-7 1998.* Aarhus: Jutland Archaeological Society, 281-90.

Richerson, P.J., R.T. Boyd & J. Henrich 2003. 'Cultural Evolution of Human Cooperation.' In: P. Hammerstein (ed.), *Genetic and Cultural Evolution of Cooperation.* Cambridge, MA: MIT Press, 357-88.

Schneider, D.J. 1991. 'Social cognition.' *Annual Review of Psychology,* 42, 527-61.

Simon, H. 1969. *The Sciences of the Artificial.* Cambridge, MA: MIT Press.

Sugden, R. 2001. 'The evolutionary turn in game theory.' *Journal of Economic Methodology,* 8, 113-30.

Säfvestad, U. 1993. 'Högen och bygden – territoriell organisation i skånsk bronsålder.' In: L. Larsson (ed.), *Bronsålderns Gravhögar.* (University of Lund, Institute of Archaeology Report Series, 48). Lund: University of Lund, 161-69.

Thrane, H. 1963a. 'Hjulgraven fra Storehøj ved Tobøl i Ribe Amt.' *Kuml,* 1962, 80-112.

Thrane, H. 1963b. 'To Egekistegrave fra Tobølegnen.' *Kuml,* 1962, 113-22.

Thrane, H. 1984. *Lusehøj ved Voldtofte – en sydvestfynsk storhøj fra yngre broncealder.* (Fynske Studier XIII). Odense: Odense Bys Museer.

Tilley, C. 1999. *Metaphor and Material Culture.* Oxford: Blackwell Publishing.

Turner, V. 1969: *The Ritual Process. Structure and anti-Structure.* London: Routledge & Kegan Paul.

Vandkilde, H. 1996. *From Stone to Bronze. The Metalwork of the Late Neolithic and Earliest Bronze Age in Denmark.* Aarhus: Jutland Archaeological Society.

Waterman, D. M. 1997. *Excavations at Navan Fort 1961-71.* (Northern Ireland Archaological Monographs, 3. Completed and edited by C. J. Lynn). Belfast: Department of the Environment for Northern Ireland.

Whittle, A. 1997. *Sacred Mound, Holy Rings. Silbury Hill and the West Kennet Palisade Enclosures: A Later Neolithic Complex in North Wiltshire.* (Oxbow Monograph 74). Oxford: Oxbow.

Literacy: A tool of modernity and community in Vanuatu

Janet Dixon Keller

Dedicated to: Takaronga Kuautonga

Where does technology begin and end? How might material, functional, cognitive, intellectual, socio-cultural, political, ideological, historical, and embodied features of productive activity co-contribute to scholarly perspectives? Research on technology has focused variably on material and functional properties (e.g., Skibo & Schiffer 2001), on the relations between society and technological practice (e.g., Goody 2000; Star 1995), on interactional shaping of techniques (e.g., Suchman 2001; Suchman & Trigg 1993; Brown *et al.* 1989), on mind in productive activity (Keller & Keller 1996; Shore 1996), or more holistically on knowledge and instrumental acts within their contextual, social, embodied, and historical milieux (Chaikin & Lave 1993; Engeström 1987; Hutchins 1995; Ingold 2000; Vincenti 1990). The more complexly relational an approach, the more likely the analysis is to capture contingent and emergent properties providing a glimpse of processes that vest technology in persons and their actions. However, the wider the relations considered, the more vulnerable are the results to a critique of 'porridge functionalism' (Goody 2000, 9); everything influences everything else in unspecified ways. Porridge may be a useful dish, however; less a jumble than a product of contingent relations such that ingredients, cooking time and temperature, culinary complements, and participants engaged in cooking and consuming a meal co-contribute in largely specifiable ways to emergent experiences of taste and sociality. The dinner is in the details and the details are in the doing (Sutton 2001).

I will argue here that integrated synthesis combining structural features of practice with contingent details of production can usefully illuminate technology (Wilson 2004). Such an approach can account for situated and emergent variability in form and process, conflicts and tensions embedded in activity, and, at the same time, provide a basis for comparative analysis through attention to defining elements. As developed here, integrated synthesis suits ethnographic research especially well for two reasons: technological practices can be observed in ethnographic settings and participants can comment on their activities. How successfully such relational analyses may generate inferences about past practices is, of course, one of the issues addressed in the present volume.

I will examine technology through literacy practices in Vanuatu, a recently independent republic of the southwest Pacific. For my purposes literacy will be evidenced by the ability to read and write in any mode. More specifically, I will take 'writing' to mean the ability to communicate in graphic form, to set down by one method or another a series of legible symbols intended to represent linguistic elements that can be deciphered or interpreted by others. The processes of deciphering and interpretation constitute 'reading'. So defined, 'writing' and 'reading' can be instantiated variously and investigated with respect to mental, material, socio-cultural, political, practical, embodied, and historical contingencies. Such definitions can be used comparatively to identify instances of literacy without importing assumptions as to the further entailments of the skills. For example, the interdependence of learning and literacy skills, frequently accepted in the mainstream of Western societies, can be and is challenged elsewhere (Stewart 1996; Wogan 2004), including in some arenas in Vanuatu. The present investigation targets interpenetrating social relations and communicative practices that have shaped literate technologies in this archipelago.

The great debate involving literacy in anthropology focuses on an argument for universal intellectual and social entailments of writing (e.g., Goody 2000) as against an argument for the contingent, historical shaping of literate practices within particular socio-cultural milieus (e.g., Heath 1983; Scribner & Cole 1981; Street & Besnier 1994). The former takes literacy to be an independent driver transporting social practices and cognitive skills along predictable routes. The latter argues for relational constructions of literacy where subjective ends and improvisational means take shape within social ecologies. Evidence from Vanuatu suggests the debate actually polarizes what might better be conceived as interconnected realms; the first capturing structural continuities and socio-historical trends while the latter elaborates the grounded, subjective texture of technology in use. Neither realm alone gives a full understanding of the technologies of literacy.

Background

The data for this paper derive from intermittent fieldwork over 30 years in Vanuatu. My research focused primarily on spoken genres of language use, but literate applications frequently came to my attention over the years. Ultimately as I worked with Takaronga Kuautonga in an effort to inscribe oral literatures of Futuna, Vanuatu, issues of literacy became paramount.

The population of the recently independent Republic of Vanuatu constitutes over one hundred ethnically and linguistically distinct communities with a total of just over 200,000 citizens (estimate based on Lal & Fortune 2000). The indigenous Melanesian and Polynesian languages are, for the most part, mutually unintelligible. The colonial languages, English and French, as well as Bislama, a Melanesian Pidgin, serve as lingua francas. English and French are the languages of education, while all three languages have been declared national languages and serve in various capacities for governmental, commercial and journalistic ventures. Everyday discourse may mix vernaculars with lingua francas but the vernaculars predominate in private spheres and rural settings.

Literacy practices, introduced by colonial powers, Britain and France, and Christian missions of the nineteenth and twentieth centuries, offer privileged access to formal Western settings for learning. The business of religious, media, governmental, commercial and educational institutions entails implementation of intellectual technologies facilitated by Western modes of reading and writing. Archival record keeping involving both nominal lists and relational tables, cartography, text based inferencing, and the 'neutral' questioning posture of science are all present in institutional settings (Goody 2000, 145-48). These practices emerged not as products of indigenous literacy, but rather as transfers of knowledge and implementation of practices from the West. These state level applications of reading and writing, whether enacted by hand, by typewriter or by computer, are associated with activities of a learned, cosmopolitan community and illustrate modernizing trends widely associated with literacy.

However, the literacy skills at issue in institutional settings have also been appropriated by citizens of Vanuatu to promote the development of writing and reading in modes that incorporate vernacular language practices. See, for example, Figure 1 where the end of the school year celebration (*Tafakarava school*) is announced in writing on a board. The languages pulled into this public bulletin include English, Bislama and the vernacular of Futuna Island, Vanuatu. The vernacular predominates but is accentuated with borrowings from Bislama (*salem* 'sell') and English. All three languages are used together to convey an open invitation to attend events that reflect the still colonial cultural mixing of the 1970s. The celebration focused on the calendar of the Western school involves feasting, singing and dancing in the tradition of local ritual events, with Western flourishes such as the carol singing, a market, and the written character of the announcement itself.

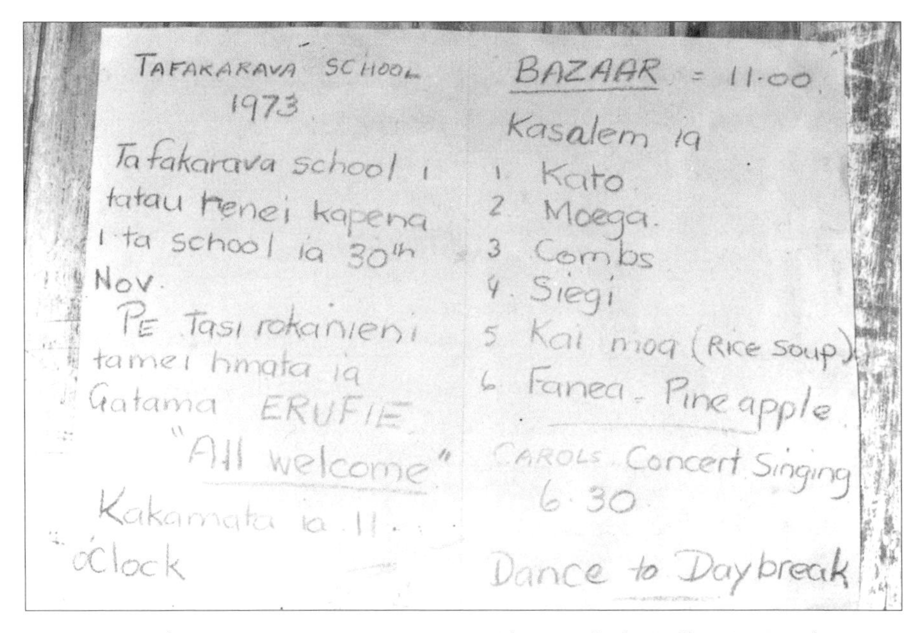

Fig. 1. Vernacular Literacy, Futuna, Vanuatu 1973. Photography by William R. Dougherty. Reprinted with permission.

Other areas where literacy has taken shape include letter and sermon writing or the creation of cultural archives. In each of these arenas new forms of literacy appropriating the tools from school for everyday ends is emerging. As a result of the *ad hoc* processes involved, vernacular literacy is not usually standardized. Religious and secular materials offer different orthographies or stylistic choices for a given language while individuals develop personal preferences as well. Although there have been vernacular literacy initiatives in recent years, few of these have had significant impact. As elsewhere (Scribner & Cole 1981; Heath 1983; Street & Besnier 1994; Besnier 1995; Schieffelin 2000; Kulick 1992), citizens of Vanuatu have taken hold of pen, pencil or keyboard to create their own vernacular, literate practices (Street & Besnier 1994). It is to the details of these processes as exemplified by members of the community of Futuna, Vanuatu that I now turn.

Literacy in practice

Futuna is an island in the southern district of the Vanuatu archipelago. The people of this island and their descendents number between one thousand and fifteen hundred. They speak a Polynesian Outlier language as their native tongue. Many people from the island of Futuna also speak English, French and/or Bislama as a result of schooling, work, and other diasporic experiences. The Futuna community is currently distributed throughout the archipelago wherever people find careers, educational opportunities or create new families through intermarriage. Some even travel further in these pursuits. A recent past Prime Minister is a Fijian educated migrant to Port Vila who hails from Futuna, while members of the capital city Futuna community are otherwise visible in government, business, religious and educational spheres. For many members of the cosmopolitan community of Port Vila, literacy reflects a mastery of Western intellectual technologies, but the consumption of literacy does not stop there. I will focus on four primary arenas in which literacy in the language of Futuna is subject to variations that augment or constrain the Westernizing trajectory. The relevant domains include: inscribing traditional oral narrative, letter writing, electronic communication via e-mail, and cartography.

Transforming oral literature to written form

In Vanuatu literacy is quintessentially a tool of the colonial languages, English and French. Little published literature is available in the vernaculars and early education in these languages has been hobbled by this lack. Still, among those of Futuna descent there are many who have applied the tools of Western literacy to their own vernacular language use. The mix of indigenous and Western values toward language yields potentially novel applications. One practice is the inscribing of ancestral stories and song lyrics as a mnemonic device or to archive exemplars of ancestral wisdom and cultural heritage. This practice of writing down what has been elusive and contextual in performance bridges in novel ways proprietary rights to narrative, spoken or sung, with the desire to make expressions of ancestral wisdom available for posterity.

Oral narratives and musical lyrics are rooted in the local cosmology; each text expressing parts of an intellectual heritage that centers on the island of Futuna. Ancestral realms of the sky and underworld encompass the living as envisioned in Figure 2.

The Futuna community is further encircled by foreign and supernatural others inhabiting islands and mists on the horizon. The supernatural spheres protect traditions of the homeland and shape individual subjects (Keller & Kuautonga 2007) within their community-oriented, reciprocity based way of life. Individuals, families, moieties, and villages are heterogeneous yet united and mutually constituted through reciprocal exchange practices that create and maintain a sustainable mosaic of peoples and places (see Rakau n.d.; Keller & Kuautonga 2007). Linking the island society with spiritual others above and below, and with

Fig. 2. A graphic rendering of the encompassment of the land of Futuna by clouds above and the underworld below. This supernatural sphere forms a protective shield for the land and lifeways Futuna. © 2007 Keller and Kuautonga.

human others on its margins, is risky, for in moving beyond the local order of life the dangers of the supernatural or foreign realm are encountered. Yet this linking offers access to resources. Crossing boundaries is therefore sanctioned and governed by an etiquette designed to enrich local traditions through ideas and artifacts of others while limiting the impacts of external influences by maintaining control over novelty in the hands of the people of Futuna.

This is a community heritage embodied in narrative performances (Keller & Kuautonga 2007), yet the oral narratives have been prized, not only as community property, but also as part of the heritage of particular individuals, families or villages constituting distinctive elements of the mosaic. For performances, members of the Futuna community were once authorized to tell or sing narratives associated with their places, kin and expertise. Today there is tension and ambiguity as people renegotiate their relationships with the verbal arts. Some would like their heritage tales and songs to circulate more widely, yet many, including those who advocate for greater access to the arts, still feel the proprietary rightness of ties between narrative and family that protect access to knowledge. This conflict can be seen as people seek to tell their tales, but hesitate to expound on figurative meanings, as youth groups request permission from elders to perform traditional music publicly without seeking understanding of the hidden meanings of the lyrics to which they give voice, or as novel genres of music and narrative replace traditional genres seen as the provenience of elders.

It is not just in the words but in ties between words and hidden meanings that the power of narrative knowledge lies. The surface of a tale or song should allow its substantive message to remain concealed from outsiders (Feld 1990, 106; Firth 1990; Kaeppler & Love 1998; Luomala 1955; Nero 1992). Individuals hesitate to reveal the unspoken wisdom for fear of revealing knowledge and thus losing power. One defers to others who may defer to still others when questions focus on issues of meaning. This becomes particularly clear in the processes of anthropological inquiry and literate rendering of oral traditions.

My initial recognition of the unstable ambiance associated with literacy and local narrative emerged during a project initially conceived as a documentary effort to preserve and make available a repertoire of traditional oral literatures for islanders' contemporary use. The project was co-designed in collaboration with Takaronga Kuautonga, cultural fieldworker from Futuna for the National Museum and Cultural Center, who is knowledgeable about and interested in customary practices. Responding to the Vanuatu Cultural Center's initiative for research on indigenous languages, we transcribed vernacular texts and translated into English a series of popular local tales and songs. However, because many of the original composers and performers were no longer living, the process of entextualization was more complicated than simply returning to these authorities for assistance. During the active engagement that ensued we found the project transformed from one of documentation to one of co-inscription in the creation of a secular literary genre that developed in ways unanticipated at the outset.

While working together largely in the capital city of Port Vila, we took two opportunities to return to Futuna to interview narrators and elders familiar with the narrative repertoire at issue. In one visit, we called upon an elderly gentleman to request assistance in unraveling figurative lyrics of a song composed during a distant moment of resistance against nineteenth century evangelism. Today performing the song has become primarily a participatory experience. The past is relived by performers and audience through emotional and embodied enactment but without attention to specific meanings or precise historical significance of the lyrics (Thomas 1992).

As we probed for significances hidden within now obscure lyrics, the gentleman we were visiting excused himself to retrieve a notebook seldom shared or considered to be of interest to others. Here he had penciled or penned the lyrics to numerous songs. We turned to the composition we were working on. His orthography differed some from ours, but words and lines matched closely. Gradually, line-by-line, he located ancient named places mentioned in the lyrics for us, situating the text in the land, and he offered clues to the meanings of tropic figures.

As we worked over hours, the notebook never left his hands. Our consultant's eye-sight, dimmed perhaps a bit by age, contributed to his struggle to read his own rendition of the ancestral text, but his reverence for the repository was profound. One might say he had created an archival resource, yet it was secreted away within the walls of his house closed to public access. Far from constituting a common resource available for commentary, critique, even negotiation and revision as a universalizing model of literacy might expect, the notebook was a concealed, personal treasure; an almost diary- like repository of largely unrealized import to the community. Paradoxically the writer felt unable to share his work openly with others. The notebook reflected a felt or embodied conflict (Sullivan & McCarthy 2004) occasioned by literacy with its potential for preservation and circulation of a dynamic past that once written down becomes *unmoored* from the knowledge of narrative ownership and authority of the era of composition.

In continuing to pursue the meaning of this same song, we talked to others and found ourselves respectfully, but firmly, referred to yet others who would know the story better. Finally, sitting down with one member of an original group of performers of a composition from a 1973 recording, we asked about the significance of its central metaphor, lobster trapping. Why is this song about lobster trapping composed in the 1850s so loved and long lived? Is there meaning beyond the literal lyrics? Gradually our consultant realized that though we had written the lyrics on paper and translated them into a second language we were nonetheless ignorant of their deeper meanings. As this consultant unpacked metaphors for us, equating the fear lobsters must have of underwater traps with the fear the people of Futuna felt for evangelical calls to conversion in the nineteenth century, rich layers of significance emerged.

In the somewhat obscure lyrics of the song:

> 'Nigkohlika a-ika i ai, akoe kotagimai
> koafe.
> 'The lobsters (people) fear it (the trap),
> you (evangelists) return discouraged.'

Paraphrasing our consultant's interpretation of the metaphor: people were frightened, startled by ideas that urged heresy from beyond the island against ancestral wisdom (and she flinches, still feeling the tension attributed to this experience as she speaks). The possibility of falling into the trap of foreign ideas represented a total immersion, a loss of that boundary crossing etiquette and control so essential to safe travels between realms. This could only occasion the beginning of the end of Futuna lifeways and early evangelists could only be discouraged at the lack of willingness on the part of the people of Futuna to convert.

This song, composed and performed originally in the 1850s (Keller & Kuautonga 2007), offered an opportunity for critical reflection on then current spiritual and political crises. The trope of "lobster trapping" voiced a community dialogue on evangelism while keeping outsiders, those without knowledge of the language, in the dark. For those who understand the ancient lyrics today, the song still has a gleeful resonance with this subterfuge.

In addition, although one of our consultants mentioned above did not write, she recognized that in this case writing lacked the power of knowing to be gained from life's experience. (For a similar perspective see Scollon 1994, 215 cited in Wogan 2004, 117). Whether written or spoken, the verses themselves served only as a cue for the already knowledgeable, evoking for them alone the context and memories of early resistance to mission efforts. Common sense perhaps, but the implications of this critique of literacy transformed our documentary assumptions for the narrative project. Working with community members, boundaries of written and oral genres began to blur in the construction of what was emerging as a uniquely performable written resource. Our process became one of reaccentuating oral narratives through literacy to create a genre of 'writing-for-reading-out-loud' (Bakhtin 1981; Schieffelin 2000, 297) with the potential to reaccentuate tradition and encourage inference, debate and discussion that would replenish background knowledge once attributed to narrators and audience alike (Bakhtin 1981). In the process Takaronga developed a facility with editing that not only incorporated predicted forms of engagement with written texts (Goody 2000, 149-50), but acquired an emphasis on performance that took shape as 'editing-for-listening'. Figure 3 is an example of an edited page of Takaronga Kuautonga's work. The initial transcript reproduces an oral performance. Takaronga revises with future performances in mind, creating dialogue from third person narrative and adding

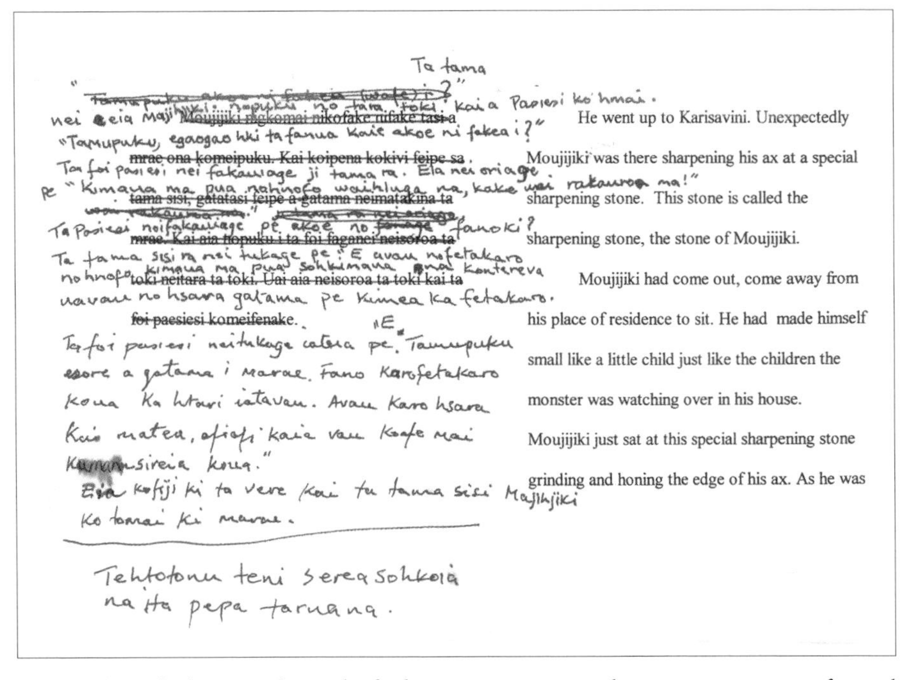

He went up to Karisavini. Unexpectedly Moujijiki was there sharpening his ax at a special sharpening stone. This stone is called the sharpening stone, the stone of Moujijiki.

Moujijiki had come out, come away from his place of residence to sit. He had made himself small like a little child just like the children the monster was watching over in his house. Moujijiki just sat at this special sharpening stone grinding and honing the edge of his ax. As he was

Fig. 3. Editing-for-hearing. The work of Takaronga Kuautonga as he revises a transcript of an oral performance with future audiences in modern settings in mind. The revisions expand the text corresponding to the final paragraph of the translation in the right hand column.

background for imagined new audiences in novel settings. This text then becomes a literate rendering as a basis for retelling.

In one case, Takaronga felt it imperative that he retell a particular tale told again and again to him by a grandfather. He did not discount earlier recordings of other versions, but identified the narrative as one for which he felt a particular kin based affinity that compelled him to recount the story as he remembered it. Motivated by a strong desire to convey the ancient narratives in the vernacular as fully and richly as possible to an audience of young people of Futuna descent now living – many of them having been born – in urban settings outside their home island, Takaronga would perform written utterances for me and at the same time for himself, imagining his audience's reaction while he considered the information and stylistic elements listeners might need to grasp the significance of a passage or catch the humor intended. He used my lack of deep ancestral knowledge to test possibilities for evoking desired insights. As he edited my computer-generated texts, whole pages were rewritten in penned lines time and again.

Each word and literary technique was subject to his scrutiny. Repetition, for example, was preserved and emphasized as an element of engagement. Passages initially in third person narrative were transformed into dramatic dialogue to encourage audience identification with characters and their plights. Implicit inferences were more richly cued in explicit text, a common step everywhere oral literatures are inscribed (Goody 2000, 47-62; Scribner & Cole 1981), and one that might have been achieved in many ways, such as overtly summarizing the 'gist' of a narrative up front (Scribner & Cole 1981). However, the task of making details explicit in the service of engendering proper interpretations takes on a particular character in our work where the power of language resides in its dual potential to reveal and conceal (Ewing 2006; Feld 1990; Firth 1990; Keller & Lehman 1991). In local speech styles a story must be developed in words that indexically cue but do not directly reveal their deepest significance. The art of writing here maintains the value for oral literature on indirection rather than making explicit information required for understanding. The inscriber enriches the clues to meaning in an attempt to maintain the oral practice of saying just enough to cue reflection of deeper significances.

As an example, in telling of a monster who sets out to destroy the island population, Takaronga orally in his telling makes no mention of motivation. Nor is motive ever explicit in other oral versions recorded. The written text as edited by Takaronga, however, mentions the monster's desire to establish himself as *sole occupant* of the land; a key to understanding the character as an inversion of the human desire for community. Without explicit mention of self-interest at the root of the tale's horrors, the story is easily heard as a fantastical portrayal of evil and good of mythical proportions but lacking any connection to reciprocity as the means of maintaining a community mosaic. Once the desire of the monster to reign alone is made explicit, the implications for a mutually supportive life way are accessible by inference.

At another point, it is related that after killing nearly everyone in a village the monster hoards children to fatten and consume. The edited text adds an explicit passage noting the paradoxical love the children acquire for their captor, who feeds and nurtures them. Hearing of this emotional dynamic allows the modern audience to infer a critical and unwritten theme of the tale, the difficulty in freeing oneself from a protected and nurturing environment to accept the risks of maturity and independence. The message is especially pertinent for young people whose dependence on others is extended during years spent acquiring a Western education. The inserted passage gives voice to the temptation to succumb to nurturing overtures of others (including bearers of foreign aid in today's political scenarios as well as over-extended parental nurture). When the story is read-out-loud audiences should reconstruct an essential link between *independence* and *reciprocity* at the moral foundations of the ni-Vanuatu (of Vanuatu) sense of community.

These examples are mustered to illustrate the processes entailed by the employment of 'literacy-for-telling'. Writing here becomes an instrument in an art intended to empower the vernacular language and the indigenous community publicly. Literacy is used to enhance present access to intellectual (oral) resources from the past. Pen and paper become tools not only of effective performance, but of imagined consumption. Unpredicted by those who focus on the historical trends associated with literacy, the setting of the literate document discussed above is still that of face-to-face engagement.

Literacy has been wrested from its exogenous origins, documentary emphasis, didactic potential and presumptions of referential transparency, to accentuate complex relations between surface forms and underlying meanings. Paradoxically, Takaronga intends his writing for an audience who has largely replaced traditional values by modern sensibilities. Yet in an effort to return their heritage to these community descendents, he adapts the modern tool of writing to a local vision of oral engagement. He creates a new genre blurring written and oral practices. His is a written medium for being read-out-loud that anticipates (re-)connecting the generations through narration and dialogue.

The result is a hybrid product that derives from prior oral exchanges to envision future oral dialogues mediated by techniques for writing by hand and computer. The anticipated result is renewed circulation of discourses centered on aesthetic, socio-political and historical wisdom. It is an emergent genre that promotes community and challenges the values of institutionalized literacy perceived in contrast to promote the individualized and autonomous learning associated with Western inspired schools (Rakau n.d.).

Countering a general tendency associated with inscribing oral literatures, the intention in Takaronga's work to initiate a secular literate canon is secondary (see Bauman & Briggs 2003) to the invitation to critical dialogue. The literate product is intended to remind an audience of diverse, nonliterate resources and to encourage individuals to reinvigorate a heteroglossic discursive practice as true to local *kastom,* where each family performs its own tales in its own ways and comments on the compositions performed by others. The written tale is intended as inspiration to continuing tradition while at the same time it expands critical practices commonly associated with formal processes of entextualization (Goody 2000, 131).

In inscribing what he knows, Takaronga indeed creates a product characterized by the typical properties of literate renditions: his tale is told primarily through language, and as a written text it has a particular form that can be returned to repeatedly (Goody 2000, 47-62). But such a structural account is skeletal, falling far short of addressing one consultant's earlier recognition; that a written document does not offer an entrée to ancestral wisdom, but only reinforces the insight of those already knowledgeable. The universalizing account misses the manipulation of technology toward particular ends; in this case, the crafting of surface forms to promote intellectual engagement and learning through 'writing-for-reading-out-loud-and-talking-together', rather than transparent conveyance of information. The blurring of oral and written genres that emerges here anticipates local forms of critical thinking reflecting customary forms of narration and negotiation. This illustrates 'regulated improvisation' to use Bourdieu's terms (1977,11), practices characterized by structural elements that define the technology at issue as literacy, and yet yield an integrated synthesis of structure and contingency with its own historically particular character.

Writing letters, fax, and e-mail

Letter writing and e-mail provide other illustrations of the protean constructive potential for technology in action. Letter writing and e-mail are media adapted to professional and personal communication in Vanuatu as in the West. However, focusing on details illustrates nuances of these technologies in use and suggests a trajectory still in development.

Following a fieldwork stay on Futuna in the early seventies, I began a correspondence with community members that continues to the present. Personal letters arriving from Futuna in the 1970s largely shared a common style; news prefaced by an optional greeting with an optional opening discussion establishing common ground from a previous exchange. There might be a modest disclaimer suggesting that the writer has nothing too important to convey. Almost every letter comments on the well-being of local residents noting those who are ill or have passed away. The author usually begins by inquiring into my health and the well being of my family and moves to a list like mentioning of happenings in the community. If there is a more specific purpose to the letter than maintaining ties by sharing recent tidings, then a request or thank you tends to come toward the end. Requests are modest, expressing interests in items such as fabric yardage or a wristwatch, unlike the more general, abstract expectations of extravagant cargo associated with written *poms* 'forms' in some communities of Papua New Guinea (Kulick 1992, 174). The Futuna letters typically close with a brief valediction and signature although both are occasionally omitted, the author assuming his or her identity is clear.

There are no stories, and few descriptions of nonroutine events. Letters are not a venue for airing serious personal problems or feelings. Affective commentary may be included as embellishment in the opening or closing lines, but only rarely are events given affective force (cf. Besnier 1995). Letters may or may not invoke spiritual references as suits the author. The primary language is Futuna with occasional loan words in English or Bislama. One to two pages of careful penmanship is typical.

Everyone is empowered to write such personal notes; some through younger scribes, others with their own hand or an office typewriter. The letters are diversionary. Their substance is social, including the recipient within a circle of events: marriages, births, accidents, feasts, deaths, subsistence, and responses to the challenges of local weather. As is typical of face-to-face interactions, these communications serve as a way of maintaining ties and resource access. Literacy is a tool of conventional social engagements here. Letters fill in blanks against shared background expectations with separate items introduced successively by the phrase, *Ma te foki*, 'and this too'.

A translation by me of a typical letter follows:

1974

Dear Lifa Janet,
And so this too we two saw the letter that you sent here
for us we both enjoyed it very much We say
Thanks to you And this too we all are well
only some sickness has taken us And this too the young one
Is Very well she's begun to go all about she remembers Lifa
And this too Isu (a pet dog) is well she already gave birth and her puppies
are many and fofotu (a pet cat) is well too now I will tell you
about the fish pulled in by my husband one tuna
two king fish. One nufau (species unknown to me) lots of Little fish and
flying fish he got at night netting by torch light I am stuffed with them all
The tides for the flying fish have started at night and this too
you know the child of your friend
the youngest she died in the month of June
And this also everyone in Ibau is well
And this too that is all of our news

The topics introduced in this note are those that would be the substance of conversational exchanges were writer and reader able to be together. Requests, which might be added to a longer version of such a letter, were a secondary motivation for correspondence.

In the 1980s and 1990s letters are more often typed or even printed from a computer. A few are longer and share a greater variety of news including discussions of the political scene in the country post independence (1980) or mention educational and professional developments for correspondents who had entered urban contexts. The occasion for letter writing continues to be a socially defined endeavor that takes advantage of literate means to extend the community circle and keep everyone informed. As above this is oral practice gone literate.

Yet typical oral or written style is not coercive. One person in particular who corresponded with me modified the usual genre of letter writing at an early age. He wrote in the 1970s when in secondary school in Port Vila. We did not know each other personally but he established his identity via kin relations in opening remarks. His was the only letter I ever received from a member of the Futuna community whom I did not know personally. The letters have elements of the usual style but he takes the occasion to write primarily in English, the language of his education. The primary motive for his letter was a request for a pen pal for himself, and then later, for others.

This letter writing style is unique on several counts. The young author initiates correspondence with someone he only knows indirectly and he uses the opportunity to write in both English and Futuna, displaying and practicing his bilingual skills. His letters, more than those of others writing at the same time, are clearly instrumental. The pen pal requests have a more time sensitive quality to them than was usual: 'anyone who is willing to write to me in the near future (underlining added)'. He also notes that he hopes to hear from me before returning to Futuna for the school holiday period.

Later, at the turn of the millennium this same author wrote several times after we had met. This more recent correspondence is entirely in the language of Futuna reflecting a new-found pride in the vernacular. Again the author writes for a specific purpose. The first of these letters is brief and to the point bracketing a query regarding developing plans for a joint project with polite mention of everyone's well being and asking after my family's health as well at the outset. After only a few business oriented sentences in closing he notes:

> Ejikai foki tasi anea ka tukua kaie ka tukua ana pe ERUFIE ta nopogi iatakoe.
> There is nothing else to say except to say have a GOOD day.

There is no news beyond the direct query that serves as the main purpose of the letter. This example and a few others like it, prioritize the instrumental potential of letter writing, and minimize the social engagement typical of other letters.

By comparing the corpus of letters received over three decades, it becomes clear that the postal system offers an occasion for employing literacy to extend usual social contexts as well as for genre development within professional social milieus. In the former case literacy is applied as a medium for social engagement and community maintenance. The practices associated with this writing style import conversational rules of polite engagement among community members expressed in the vernacular language. Establishing common ties, opening personal discussions and highlighting useful community information all occur in oral exchanges in similar fashion. The list like presentation, with *ma te foki* 'and this too' introducing successive items, presumes the social context that serves as background for successive related events. Entreaties in such contexts tend to be moderate and appropriate to the relationships involved. Unlike narrative writing, there is no critical dialogue or reflection promoted by the correspondence. No hidden meanings beneath the surface.

In professional correspondence business is handled directly and swiftly in a manner reflective of operations in the modern office. It is the context of the business that writer and recipient of the letter have in common that shapes the background. The language of choice depends upon the intended recipient's linguistic competence and the author's language politics. And the text is brief and to the point.

In both cases, the writer takes control of instrumental means for contemporary purposes that stretch over long distances. Rather than a driver of possibilities, writing is clearly a tool to be manipulated in the service of ends defined independently of the technology itself.

FAX and e-mail, by contrast, have not been utilized as extensions of personal or professional conversations or letter writing for most people of Futuna. Both technologies are expensive and difficult for many potential users to access. These modes of communication are reserved for only the briefest and most vital messages perhaps in the way one might traditionally have sent a messenger on foot along difficult trails to announce pressing news. In particular, e-mail has become the medium for long distance communication of deaths or otherwise highly urgent and time sensitive communications.

The social etiquette displayed by typical letters is truncated in e-mail exchanges which tend to be only a few sentences not unlike the professional letter. The content presumes a shared social background; that of commonly known individuals or professional goals. The chosen language for electronic transmissions varies with audience and author competencies and political commitments. The technology and its computerized means of inscription, foreign as these are, do not force an *a priori* assumption about the language to be used.

Although a critical dialogue is not engendered by fax or e-mail correspondences, like the previous discussion of 'writing-for-reading-out-loud', I have witnessed community members from Futuna who, on receiving e-mail, prefer to have them printed out and read aloud by an intermediary rather than deciphering the texts on a computer screen. Even such direct and explicit messages demand a virtual imagining of the context shared by writer and recipient, a task that takes time and mulling over to make a message sensible. An answering note, if elicited at all, will be constructed as a direct response, even mirroring the original style, and is likely to be dictated to someone comfortable with the keyboard and screen only after careful deliberation.

Despite extensive use of many other modes of technology such as: video and aural tape recording, telephone and air travel, there seem to be, at the moment, economic barriers, unease, and some resistance to electronic communication. A fully integrated synthesis and a sense of local ownership (see Meadows 1995; White 2000) has yet to emerge in public arenas in Vanuatu outside specific office contexts where e-mail communications have already been interwoven into professional practice. I suspect the wider usage will come, but true to local tendencies the process will synthesize the defining properties and potentials of the technology with established socio-political priorities and customary etiquette familiar to residents of Vanuatu through a process of 'regulated improvisation' (Bourdieu 1977, 11, 54). I look forward to the genres that emerge in ni-Vanuatu e-mails of the future.

Cartography

Finally, cartography proved, surprisingly at first for me, to be an arena where literacy is not only shaped by local values and practices, but also strongly resisted and, at points, prohibited. Graphic technologies for mapping and inscribing features, analogous to Western plat books indicating personal rights in land, reef or sea, are unquestionably inappropriate in the eyes of many members of the Futuna community.

Discussions of cultural geography and resource management with members of the Futuna community revealed that inscriptions that might connect families and individuals to real resources at any given moment entailed an unqualified, negative consequence. The creation of such a written and graphic record was perceived to jeopardize flexible relations of people to land through negotiation of use rights and longer-term responsibilities for resources. A graphic record, it was argued, would 'fix' rights to resources in perpetuity on the basis of a presumptively authoritative document. The document could enable outside intervention in local management strategies by providing a momentary record taken to reflect a permanent state of affairs. The outcome would be politically divisive rather than supportive of flexible community practices. For the particular purpose of recording personal, family and community interests in real resources, it was widely assumed that writing or graphic representation would result in the imposition of an absolute and unchanging record with the potential to compromise processes of requesting and granting permission for resource use or negotiating relationships to land and sea. Local kinship ties and interpersonal respect employed in negotiating use rights would be undermined. This ideological assumption of permanence (a common Western association with literacy) entails a closing off of interpretive possibilities in the eyes of those from Futuna. The same presumption of fixity is evident for none of the other applications of literacy explored in Vanuatu, nonetheless, it is firmly held in this realm of personal and community interests in resources.

In principle, inscribing ancestral narratives could also lead to the establishment of a canon diminishing the circulation of competing versions of local narrative heritage. Indeed Goody suggests as much is likely (2000, 56) in his general treatment of the consequences of literate technology, and Bauman & Briggs (2003) document the process in their attention to the Grimm brothers. But for the people of Futuna, although tension and ambiguity surround possibilities for inscribing traditional lore, in practice islanders have imagined ways to commit oral literature to paper without cutting off dialogue. The ideology of permanence does not even apply to written Biblical texts in Vanuatu, for Christian lessons are debated vigorously and openly, in vernacular or European languages. This interpretive, dialogic process enables community discussions of spiritual notions and opens possibilities for competition among Christian denominations. Personal choices in Christian religious affiliation may even be based on divergent views that arise in such discussions.

What might be the particular contingent synthesis that results in resistance to cultural and community cartography? There are plenty of maps and photographs of the Futuna landscape, its surrounds, and inhabitants that are not seen to jeopardize the local mosaic. It is, however, in the explicit association of specific sites of land, reef, and sea with individuals or families that danger is paramount. While there exists a general well-known association of families and district resources on the island of Futuna, at any moment rights to specific resources are in dispute, some areas are off limits in observance of mourning, and micro-climatic variations compromise productivity in localized niches. In the context of such variability, individuals are always flexibly employing their kin networks to ensure access to subsistence resources somewhere on the island.

What is at stake in the establishment of a potentially permanent record is the very livelihood of the community itself; the ability of individuals to interact reciprocally and respectfully to access resources through complex kinship networks and to exchange their localized harvests. If the process of resource access were 'fixed' by freezing a momentary configuration on paper, the subtle negotiation and interpersonal etiquette that create and maintain community would be undermined. The mosaic of heterogeneous individuals, families and village groups could be subjected to an 'authoritative' document. Too much is at risk to allow the construction of a product that might or might not be subject to dialogic revision, and that, even if it were open to contestation, might give advantage to some as against others.

This foresight, on the part of community members, to limit, contain, and control the possibilities for literacy is remarkable. We see local ownership of technology here (cf. Meadows 1995) – not by constructive application as in narrative or epistolary genres, but by persistent and well-considered resistance; a resistance based on an historically derived knowledge of the power of outsiders to intervene and usurp local prerogative. Here again the properties of literate technology alone fail to drive social praxis while mutually constitutive and mutable relations among people and places shape possibilities.

Conclusions

In this brief look at uses of literate skills by members of the Futuna community, I have argued that variation in human action even within small communities and subgroups is to be expected (Block 1985; Ingold 2000). In the process of consuming widely distributed tools, agents exercise choice as they create or recreate, innovate or accept practices evident in their larger social milieus to put into the service of immediate and contingent ends (de Certeau 1984; Wertsch 1998; 2000). It is this local ownership that requires a focus on details in scholarly accounts of technology and allows the constants that pinpoint a given technology to be understood as positioned within and subject to networks of social forces, relations of power, and situated and strategic options (Garro 2000, 297).

There is no question but that literacy in Vanuatu has facilitated many of the technologies of the intellect that Goody (e.g., 2000) finds more generally associated with reading and writing: organization of information through literate strategies of naming, listing, archiving, and tabling; mathematical and logical applications; argumentation; the questioning postures of science, critical reflection, editorial revisioning, and rebalancing implicit and explicit information. In the case of Vanuatu, as perhaps everywhere, few of these modes of reasoning are unique to applications of literacy but rather combine customary practices with literate potentials. In the details of use of the skills of literacy we find, further, innovations where issues of identity, power, and purpose shape practices in distinctive ways.

When members of the Futuna community adapt to their vernacular, skills learned in association with Western settings prioritizing English and French, they almost inevitably turn the literate product to customary, community ends. Maintaining social ties, transmitting urgent information, writing for reading-out-loud, and recording heritage narratives for performance, are all motivated by the project of promoting the traditional social mosaic. Resistance to literate applications as well is developed in the service of perpetuating complex patterns of interaction that create community. Each application or its refusal involves wider relations in integrated syntheses, relations that speak to the protean and strategic potential at the very core of technology (Wilson 2004).

The typical (Goody 2000), the unusual (Robbins 2001), and the subversive product all reflect a mix of factors in their productive histories. The puzzle is in discovering the mix. When Goody claims that 'Each society, each group, each individual adapts the bicycle to his own context, *but only within limits*' (Goody 2000, 136, italics added), perhaps the unicycle, immobile exercise bike, lawn ornament, bicycle generator, moral prescriptions against cycling, recycled components, and the disarticulated frame used idiosyncratically are forgotten? The limitations Goody imagines would be better understood in conjunction with the degrees of freedom available to individuals to influence the conditions of their existence. Indeed forces of society, technology, and prior history offer structural moorings, but it is in the day-to-day, contingent practices of individuals that these forces are reproduced or transformed.

It is useful to remember that literate skills always belong to someone; they are not an abstract force but concrete possibilities subject to the goals of those employing them and to the characteristics of the milieus in which they are applied (Sutton 2006; Wertsch 2000). Perhaps this personal ownership of practice is easy to miss in a contemporary world of superficially homogeneous and comparable modernities. If we look closely, however, the concrete and conceptual relations of actual practice not only reveal divergent technical outcomes selectively facilitated by literacy, but also demonstrate the bricolage that results in a pool of applications from which future extensions of literacy will be socially inspired. Literacy (and other technologies) is always 'in the making' (Ingold 2000; White 2000). The inertia of habitus and the potential for 'regulated improvisation' (Bourdieu 1977, 11, 54), authoritative directives, affordances of the material world, cultural filters, social scaffolds, and individual or community initiatives co-create ever developing ecologies for writing and for reading.

A material record reflects only a moment (of greater or lesser duration) in such a process. Whether, and to what degree, an archaeological record may offer clues to productive cognitive and cultural relations such as those identified here will likely vary with the richness of each case, but at the very least ethnographic evidence for versatility and virtuosity in technological practice offers a set of wide questions that need to be asked about the past in order to accentuate the counterpoint to universalizing tendencies found in the contextual experiences of human life.

Acknowledgments

The conference was organized by the Department of Prehistoric Archaeology in cooperation with the Centre for Cultural Research, University of Aarhus. Special thanks to Helle Jensen, Mads Jessen and Niels Johannsen who made the conference possible and to many participants for helpful comments. I appreciate the readings and responses of Rob Moore, Laurel Monnig, David Sutton, Peter Wogan, Elizabeth Spreng, Steve Maas, Tzu-kai Liu and Charlie Keller whose advice has improved my ability to use literate tools for particular ends. I also thank Rolf Kuschel and Torbin and Hanna Monberg who hosted me during a wonderful lay over in Copenhagen that was full of good food and inspiration. The University of Illinois and the William and Mary Hewlett Foundation funded segments of the project. The community of Futuna, Takaronga Kuautonga and Ralph Reganvanu, past Director of the Vanuatu Cultural Center, have supported this work with enthusiasm. I am grateful for opportunities to learn from them all. I have dedicated this work to Takaronga for the vision he has opened to me through our collaborations.

References

Bakhtin, M. 1981. *The Dialogic Imagination*. M. Holquist (ed.). C. Emerson & M. Holquist (translators). Austin: University of Texas Press.

Bauman, R. & C. Briggs 2003. *Voices of Modernity: Language Ideologies and the Politics of Inequality*. Cambridge: Cambridge University Press.

Besnier, N. 1995. *Literacy, Emotion and Authority: Reading and Writing on a Polynesian Atoll*. Cambridge: Cambridge University Press.

Bloch, M. 1985. 'From Cognition to Ideology.' In R. Fardon (Editor) *Power and Knowledge: Anthropological and Social Approaches*. Edinburgh: Scottish Academic Press.

Brown, J.S., A. Collins, P. Duguid 1989. 'Situated Cognition and the Culture of Learning.' *Educational Researcher*, 18(1), 32-41.

Bourdieu, P. 1977. *Outline of a Theory of Practice*. Cambridge: Cambridge University Press.

Chaiklin, S. & J. Lave 1993. *Understanding Practice*. Cambridge: Cambridge University Press.

de Certeau, M. 1984. *The Practice of Everyday Life*. Translated by S. Rendall. Berkeley: University of California Press.

Engström, Y. 1987. *Learning by Expanding: An Activity-Theoretical Approach to Developmental Research.* Helsinki: Orienta-Konsultit Oy.

Ewing, K. 2006. 'Revealing and Concealing: Interpersonal Dynamics and the Negotiation of Identity in the Interview.' *Ethos* 34(1), 89-122.

Feld, S. 1990. *Songs and Sentiment: Birds, Weeping, Poetics and Song in Kaluli Expression.* (2nd ed.) Philadelphia: University of Pennsylvania Press.

Firth, R. 1990. (with Mervyn McLean) *Tikopia Songs: Poetic and Musical Art of a Polynesian people of the Solomon Islands.* Cambridge: Cambridge University Press.

Garro, L.J. 2000. 'Remembering What One Knows and the Construction of the Past: A Comparison of Cultural Consensus Theory and Cultural Schema Theory.' *Ethos*, 28(3), 275-319.

Goody, J. 2000. *The Power of the Written Tradition.* Washington D.C.: Smithsonian Institution Press.

Heath, S.B. 1983. *Ways with Words: Language, Life and Work in Communities and Classrooms.* Cambridge: Cambridge University Press.

Hutchins, E. 1995. *Cognition in the Wild.* Cambridge, MA: MIT Press.

Ingold, T. 2000. *The Perception of the Environment: Essays in Livelihood, Dwelling and Skill.* London: Routledge.

Kaeppler, A. & J.W. Love (eds.) 1998. *Garland Encyclopedia of World Music.* (Vol. 9). New York: Garland Publishing Co.

Keller, C. & J. Keller 1996. *Cognition and Tool Use: The Blacksmith at Work.* Cambridge: Cambridge University Press.

Keller, J. & F.K. Lehman 1991. 'Complex Concepts.' *Cognitive Science*, 15, 271-91.

Keller, J. & T. Kuautonga 2007. *Nokonofo Kitea: We Keep on Living this Way.* Myth & Music of Futuna, Vanuatu. Belair: Crawford House Publishing Australia & Honolulu: University of Hawai'i Press.

Kulick, D. 1992. *Language Shift and Cultural Reproduction: Socialization, Self and Syncretism in a Papua New Guinea Village.* Cambridge: Cambridge University Press.

Lal, B.V. & K. Fortune 2000. *The Pacific Islands: An Encyclopedia.* Honolulu: University of Hawai'i Press.

Luomala, K. 1955. *Voices on the Wind: Polynesian Myths and Chants.* Honolulu: Bishop Museum.

Meadows, M. 1995. 'Ideas from the Bush: Indigenous Television in Australia and Canada.' *Canadian Journal of Communication*, 20(2), 197-212.

Nero, K.L. (ed.) 1992. The Arts and Politics: Special Issue. *Pacific Studies*, 15(4), 1-349.

Rakau, F. n.d. (circa 1997). 'Background Paper IV.' In: *The Cross and the Tanoa: Gospel and Culture in the Pacific.* Suva: South Pacific Association of Theological Schools, 80-98.

Robbins, J. 2001. 'God is Nothing But Talk: Modernity, Language and Prayer in a Papua New Guinea Society.' *American Anthropologist*, 103(4), 901-12.

Schieffelin, B. 2000. 'Introducing Kaluli Literacy: A Chronology of Influences.' In: P. Kroskrity (ed.), *Regimes of Language: Ideologies, Politics and Identities.* Santa Fe, NM: School of American Research, 293-327.

Scribner, S. & M. Cole 1981. *The Psychology of Literacy.* Cambridge, MA: Harvard University Press.

Scollon, R. 1994. 'Cultural Aspects in Constructing the Author.' In: D. Keller-Cohen, (ed.), *Literacy: Interdisciplinary Conversations.* Creskill, NJ: Hampton Press.

Shore, B. 1996. *Culture in Mind.* New York: Oxford University Press.

Skibo, J. & M.B. Schiffer 2001. 'Understanding Artifact Variability and Change: A Behavioral Framework.' In: M.B. Schiffer (ed.), *Anthropological Perspectives on Technology.* (Amerind

Foundation New World Studies Series, 5). Albuquerque: University of New Mexico Press, 139-50.

Star, S.L. 1995. 'The Politics of Formal Representation: Wizards, Gurus and Organizational Complexity.' In: S.L. Star (ed.), *Ecologies of Knowledge: Work and Politics in Science and Technology*. Albany, NY: SUNY Press, 88-118.

Stewart, K. 1996. *A Space by the Side of the Road: Cultural Poetics in an "other" America*. Princeton: Princeton University Press.

Street, B. & N. Besnier 1994. 'Aspects of Literacy.' In: T. Ingold (ed.), *Companion Encyclopaedia of Anthropology: Humanity, Culture and Social Life*. London: Routledge, 527-62.

Suchman, L. 2001. 'Building Bridges: Practice Based Ethnographies of Contemporary Technology.' In: M.B. Schiffer (ed.), *Anthropological Perspectives on Technology*. (Amerind Foundation New World Studies Series, 5). Albuquerque: University of New Mexico Press, 163-78.

Suchman, L. & R. Trigg 1993. 'Artificial Intelligence as Craft Work.' In: S. Chaiklin & J. Lave (eds.), *Understanding Practice*. New York: Cambridge University Press, 144-78.

Sullivan, P. & J. McCarthy 2004. 'Toward a Dialogical Perspective on Agency.' *Journal for the Theory of Social Behavior*, 34(3), 291-309.

Sutton, D. 2006. 'Cooking Skill, the Senses and Memory: The Fate of Practical Knowledge.' In: C. Gosden, E. Edwards, R. Phillips (eds.), *Sensible Objects: Colonialism, Museums and Material Culture*. (Wenner-Gren International Symposium Series). Oxford: Berg, 87-118.

Sutton, D. 2001. *Remembrance of Repasts: An Anthropology of Food and Memory*. Oxford: Berg.

Thomas, A. 1992. 'Songs as History.' *Journal of Pacific History*, 27(2), 29-36.

Vincenti, W.G. 1990. *What Engineers Know and How They Know It: Analytical Studies from Aeronautical History*. Baltimore: Johns Hopkins University Press.

Wertsch, J. 1998. The Russian Revolution: Official and Unofficial Accounts. In: J.F. Voss & M. Carretero (eds.), *International Review of History Education, Vol. 2: Learning and Reasoning in History*. London: Woburn Press, 39-60.

Wertsch, J. 2000. 'Narratives as Cultural Tools in Sociocultural Analysis: Official History in Soviet and Post-Soviet Russia.' In: T.J. Csordas & J.H. Jenkins (eds.), Theme Issue: History and Subjectivity. *Ethos*, 28(4), 511-33.

White, G.M. 2000. 'Histories and Subjectivities.' In: T.J. Csordas & J.H. Jenkins (eds.), Theme Issue: History and Subjectivity. *Ethos*, 28(4), 493-510.

Wilson, R.A. 2004. *Boundaries of the Mind: The Individual in the Fragile Sciences*. Cambridge: Cambridge University Press.

Wogan, P. 2004. *Magical Writing in Salasaca: Literacy ad Power in Highland Ecuador*. Boulder, CO: Westview Press.

Archaeology and the Inanimate Agency Proposition: a critique and a suggestion

Niels Johannsen

For a long time in archaeology, *agency* has been synonymous with *human action*. While it might well be argued that most archaeologists still tend to understand agency that way, a fundamental dissatisfaction with this notion of agency has been growing on the theoretical scene of the discipline during the last ten years or so. Some archaeologists have begun to worry that the equation of agency with human action stands or falls with an untenable anthropocentric premise that blocks the way for any full acknowledgement of non-human materiality as a causal constituent in the cultural lives of human beings. For all the attention given to the social, ideological and communicative importance of human 'material culture', it is argued, non-human materiality has remained causally deprived and stigmatized within the dominant analytical frameworks centred on *the human agent* (e.g. Boast 1997; Boivin 2004; Jones 2002; Knappett 2002; Olsen 2003; Robb 2004). Robin Boast, one of the pioneers of this reaction in archaeology, noted that 'If we insist that the objects become a static representation of our consciousness, then we deny the possibilities of examining them as partners in the social conversation of being – we deny things the agency that is their due' (Boast 1997, 190). A few years later, Carl Knappett sensed the particular difficulty of distinguishing agents from objects in the age of biotechnological implants and virtual reality and suggested that 'Agency clearly needs rethinking, if no useful distinction can be made between a "pure" human mind and body (subject) within which agency resides, and an external world of objects onto which agency is projected' (Knappett 2002, 98). Similarly, Bjørnar Olsen proposed that 'To understand how collectives – societies – work, we have to relearn to ascribe action, goals and power – or to use that old mantra, *agency* – to many more agents than the subject, as well as to ballast epistemology – and ontology – with a new and unknown actor; the silent thing' (Olsen 2003, 88-89). For these authors, among others, the obvious way to fully acknowledge the causal significance of non-human materiality for humans is to admit that inanimate objects and structures are active agents in their own right – that they have *agency*. In other words, we should broaden our concept of agency to include what is perhaps most cogently termed *inanimate agency*. For simplicity's sake, this proposition may be referred to as the 'Inanimate Agency Proposition' (IAP).

At surface level the idea of inanimate agency seems quite clear. However, much of the recent literature promoting this revision of *agency* in archaeology has remained relatively vague on its more specific ontological commitments. It has often been difficult to identify what exactly revisionist proposals are meant to imply in terms of the practical operation of causal factors (e.g. Martin 2005, 283-84). Perhaps this lack of clarity or explicitness is what has led some commentators to suspect that propositions on the agency of inanimate things have been adopted primarily because of their suitability as rhetorical levers in the academic game of persuasion and self-promotion (Johnson 2006, 125). But, as we shall see below and as stressed by Olsen (2006a, 147-48) in reply to Johnson, closer examination reveals that the commitments of the IAP, in archaeology and elsewhere, go far beyond the rhetorical. The issue at stake – our 'problem of agency' – is not a simple matter of 'terminology'. *Agency* has been, and remains, one of the strongest structuring elements of ontological thought in archaeology as more widely in the study of human life and culture, and exactly for that reason it is worthwhile, even necessary, to devote energy to discussing the semantics and employment of this particular concept. Whatever we choose to do with it, the repercussions on archaeological ontologies will be significant. Given this condition, the interesting question is not whether we can put many different meanings into the concept of agency – clearly, we can – but whether the semantic content that we do choose to include provides us with a concept that is *useful* for archaeological analysis and reflection. Archaeologists, then, need to ask themselves whether the Inanimate Agency Proposition provides a useful way forward in their ontological thought?

This paper attempts to provide an answer to that question by reviewing the content and implications of the IAP in archaeology and its foundations outside the discipline. After a brief sketch of the concept's pre-history in archaeology, I examine concrete statements on *agency* published by proponents of the IAP in archaeology. Subsequently, in order to clarify the commitments entailed by these statements, I review the theoretical developments in anthropology and the sociology of science and technology that these archaeological contributions were inspired by, and explicitly refer to. I identify and discuss a number of problems with these developments which result partly from their ontological commitments and their temporal scales of analysis, and the theoretical link between them. This review leads me to question the viability of the IAP as a strategy for achieving the stated aim of introducing proper causal credit to the inanimate world into archaeological (and other) analyses of human life and culture. Boast, Knappett, Olsen and other proponents of the IAP seem right in suggesting that the concept of agency needs to be revised, and most archaeologists share their ambition of improving our understanding of the human entanglement in material practices and environments. But the specific revision suggested by these authors represents one particular strategy among many potential strategies towards this aim – one which, I contend, turns out to be fundamentally counterproductive on closer analysis.

As discussed further below, archaeological variants of the IAP inherit a number of serious analytical limitations from their main sources of inspiration, Gell's anthropology of art and agency and the socio-philosophical actor-network theory of Callon, Latour, Law and others. Briefly put, Gell's analysis is torn internally by an unresolved struggle between two theoretical attractors: its ideological foundations in the study of human agency, on the one hand, and, on the other, a temptation to dissolve the boundary between human and inanimate forms of causation and thus wield the full conceptual power that this gave in a given intellectual environment. Actor-network theory's perspective on agency is more settled, but its theoretical starting point in the study of human linguistic communication leads to a one-sided and synchronistic emphasis on *relations* that fosters a materially styled but fundamentally *immaterial* conception of causal power. Paradoxically, in two rather different ways, both frameworks end up as elaborate promotions of the implicit, anthropocentric assumption that *real causal significance is human-style significance*, or at least significance that does not depart fundamentally from our own. Thus, while the idea of 'inanimate agency' is sometimes staged as the ultimate way of doing justice to non-human materiality, I argue that it comes closer to doing the opposite, i.e. that it does causal justice neither to humans as animate organisms, nor to the very material 'otherness' of inanimate entities, which gives them much of their power in human lives and relations. Further, I argue that it is perhaps not so much *matter*, as it is *time*, specifically several levels of 'history', which is being marginalized in present thought on agency. In the concluding part of the paper, I explore the possibility of an alternative revision of the concept of agency. The trend of recent years, including the IAP, has been towards a gradual broadening of this concept (cf. Dobres & Robb 2005) or, perhaps rather, an increasing *packing* of the concept – 'concentrating things difficult to think in a small conceptual space' (Robb 2004, 131) – but I will propose a more delimited, less ambitious notion of *agency* that is more attuned to the historicity and implications of both organic life and inanimate matter, and which thus takes qualitative, *a priori* differences (not only relations) between things to matter in the situatedness of human being and activity.

Revising agency in archaeology

Questions concerning the nature of and conditions for human agency have long been a main hub for epic narrative, zealous deconstruction and general controversy in the study of human life and culture. Linked to the broader and fundamental problem of stability and change in human societies, the debate on agency has focused not least on the capacity of human individuals and groups to take (or deliberately not take) their lives in different directions than people around them and before them – what we may call the 'freedom/constraint problem'. A motivating issue for such founding figures as Karl Marx, Émile Durkheim and Max Weber, this has remained a core problem of social theory in recent decades, whether framed under the auspices of practice theory, structuration theory, actor-network theory or some other, more or less prominent paradigm. Archaeologists, like all other scholars of human life and culture, have made implicit or explicit theories and assumptions about human agency since the birth of their discipline. The explicit concept and discussion of 'agency', though, only found its way into the central discourse of archaeological theory during the 1980s, when the freedom/constraint problem became one of the most significant concerns of a disciplinary rebellion against eco-functionalism and systems theory.

It is beyond dispute that the concept of *agency*, in archaeology as in the wider human sciences, has served as one of the most effective conceptual remedies to prior academic hegemonies of structures and systems. When the concept started to become popular in archaeology, it was unambiguously synonymous with *human action* (e.g. Hodder 1982; 1986; Johnson 1989; Shanks & Tilley 1987a; 1987b), and human action was, in turn, perceived in relation to social and ideological 'structures' corresponding to (mental) culture. This rendering and employment of *agency* as an explicit concept was inspired primarily by the rejuvenation of practice perspectives that took place in sociology and neighbouring disciplines during the 1970s and 80s, not least in the works of Pierre Bourdieu and Anthony Giddens, whose writings became widely influential among archaeologists during the latter decade and onwards (Dobres & Robb 2000b). For Bourdieu as well as Giddens, agents were humans and agency thus synonymous with human action (Bourdieu 1977; 1990; Giddens 1979; 1984). As already noted, the concept, particularly and most explicitly in Giddens' work, was introduced as a decisive supplement and corrective to the omnipotence of 'structures' which had characterized the dominant causal accounts of human social life during much of the 20th century (Giddens 1979, 2).

But agency was never meant by these authors to replace the notion of structure; rather, despite significant differences between the emphases of their approaches, Bourdieu and Giddens shared a fundamental interest in the complex, never-ending *dialectic* between human action and the (social) structures that they saw as both enabling, constraining and being produced and challenged by agency. As pointed out in one of the first archaeological articles dedicated by its title to the topic, '...a study of *agency* cannot be separated from a study of *structure*... agency is a manipulation of an existing structure, a structure that is external to the individual in the Durkheimian sense and appears to that agent as a synchronic construct, as something to be drawn upon' (Johnson 1989, 206, emphases added). Many contributors to the archaeological debate have continued to discuss agency with variants of this premise as a starting point and have thus treated the concept as fruitful when applied and discussed *as part of* the more or less coherent theories developed in practice sociology (e.g. Barrett 2000; Barrett & Fewster 2000; Dobres 2000; Dobres & Hoffman 1994; Dornan 2002; Glørstad 2008; Hegmon & Kulow 2005; Joyce & Lopiparo 2005; Kristiansen 2004; Silliman 2001; Smith 2001). However, in archaeology – as perhaps more widely – the idea of *agency* turned out to be powerful enough to gradually smother the conceptual twin that it was brought up with. A decade after the statement quoted above, Johnson (2000, 213) noted how the structure side of the dialectic was already being neglected (also Olsen 2006a, 148), and it was no coincidence that it was agency, and not agency *and* structure, which defined the title of an influential edited volume at the turn of the millennium (Dobres & Robb 2000a). Agency had become 'the buzzword of contemporary archaeological theory' (Dobres & Robb 2000b, 3) and was increasingly treated as a concept that could stand on its own, something that could be picked up and taken in all sorts of directions whilst not necessarily being restricted by the theoretical context of its initial growth (cf. Dobres & Robb 2005, 162). For the understanding of causal relations in human life and culture, *agency* had become the name of the game. As we shall see below, recent steps towards revision of this concept in archaeology continue this movement away from the dialectical models of ontological reality with which it was tightly integrated when it gained currency in the discipline.

The gradual development in the theoretical status of agency outlined above interacted with another theoretical trend in setting the stage for the Inanimate Agency Proposition, to which we shall return shortly. In parallel with the focus on agency from the early 1980s onwards, archaeologists were (and are) struggling to find theoretical tools for fully bringing out the many ways in which things, structures and materials are significant to human beings far beyond their utility in satisfying the most basic of Maslowian needs. The big attempt of the 1980s and 90s was to see 'material culture' as a powerful means of communication working very much like language or, more specifically, text. The avant-garde of archaeological theory turned to theoretical work in structuralist linguistics and, subsequently, poststructuralist semiotics and textual analysis for models that could help clarify how the communication of ideological and social agendas and identities took place in the past. In addition to delivering communicative ontologies for past societies, this perspective also suggested that archaeologists were in practice *reading material culture* in order to be *reading the past* (Hodder 1986; Tilley 1990; also Tilley 1991). As the poststructuralist critique gained momentum in the discipline, such *reading* – in past as well as present – was increasingly perceived as practices of *construction* rather than *decoding*.

There can be no doubt that the textual-semantic perspective of this theoretical conjuncture – which we might call archaeology's First Semiotization of ontology – was stimulating and productive for the discipline as a whole (cf. Olsen 2006b). Indeed, had it not been for this development, it is difficult to imagine that equally competent archaeological interpretations of the communicative roles of material things and practices could be produced today. But limitations of the textual analogy were being discussed from the very beginning and throughout the 1980s and 90s (e.g. Buchli 1995; Conkey 1990, 10-11; Hodder 1986, 123; Miller 1982, 19-23; Olsen 1997, 181, 217; Shanks and Tilley 1982, 134), and gradually these considerations turned into frustration. In many ways 'material culture' is not really like text, and there seemed to be little actual room for the particular *material* qualities of things, structures and practices when viewed through the lens of textually styled, infinitely malleable communication of (predefined) mental culture. The knowledge archaeologists gained from the sophisticated textual models of communication came at a price. As part of an incisive diagnosis of the problem, Olsen noted that:

> 'Unfortunately, this knowledge did little to help us understand what material culture is, the 'nature' of it so to speak, or to understand the role it plays in human existence on a more fundamental ontological level ... Things do far more than just speak and express meanings [cf. Joerges 1988:224]; and at some point it just stopped being fun conceiving everything as a text that writes itself, the past as a never-ending narrative, an endless play of signifiers without signifiedes [e.g. Olsen 1987, 1990]' (Olsen 2003, 90).

For archaeology, which for good reasons never perceived quite the same theoretical freedom to liberate itself completely from the things and materials of culture as some of its disciplinary neighbours, the textualized pseudo-materiality that accompanied the strong interest in cultural meaning became a distinct feature of the discipline's encounter with the linguistic turn. More broadly in the study of human culture, this theoretical turn formed the (preliminary) highpoint of a much longer-standing tradition for treating the actual physical things, structures and substances of non-human materiality as secondary to ethereally flexible mental culture – 'immaterial culture' – and for depriving them, in this way, of causal significance in the cultural lives that archaeologists among others wanted to understand (cf. Boivin 2004; Olsen 2003; Schiffer 1999). The Inanimate Agency Proposition constitutes an attempt to instantiate a clear break with this problematic tradition, i.e. a theoretical effort to give back causal significance to the non-human material world in the study of human life and culture. Given that the problem of 'immaterial culture' culminated within the same theoretical climate where *agency* had become a shorthand for causation (or at least for causation worth studying), it is perhaps not entirely surprising that archaeologists and others should turn to this concept for a cure. However, if we are to take the IAP seriously and evaluate its viability beyond its immediate appeal as a solution in the context outlined above – and this seems necessary – closer examination of its character is required.

The Inanimate Agency Proposition

The proposition that we should broaden the concept of agency to include the causal influence of inanimate things, structures and substances has taken various forms in archaeology. As already mentioned, most proponents in the discipline have drawn on one or both of two main sources of inspiration for this development, viz. the anthropological work on art and agency by Alfred Gell and the sociological and philosophical 'actor-network' perspectives developed by scholars like Michel Callon, John Law and, not least, Bruno Latour. Like Gell's grappling with the concept of agency, some archaeological discussions have taken non-Western, indigenous notions of materiality and causation as an important starting point. The introduction to a recent journal special issue notes that 'Animate objects and non-human beings are active members of many societies today, and presumably were so in the past' (Brown & Walker 2008, 297) and proceeds to suggest that:

> 'Object agency is defined as the causal consequences objects (artifacts, architecture, and landscape features) have on the course of human activity, and includes animate objects as well as the performance characteristics of material things (e.g., the thermal shock resistance of heavily tempered cooking pots). This broad definition allows room for culturally distinct understandings of who and what can act, while acknowledging the agency inherent in the physicality of objects ...' (Brown & Walker 2008, 298).

Further, if the object in question is perceived as animate, its agency is 'autonomous, purposeful, and deliberate, and arises from sentient qualities possessed by the object, such as consciousness or a life-force' (Brown & Walker 2008, 298). In other words, all things have causal consequences and thus *agency*, but things/beings perceived by someone as animate have particular forms of agency. While Linda Brown and William Walker are thus suggesting that we somehow operate analytically with (at least) two forms of agency, no *a priori* assumptions can be made about the application of these respective forms because, as their starting point implies, it is up to people in the cultural context studied (or in prehistoric situations, presumably, the archaeologist?) to define which applies in particular cases, i.e. to define what is perceived as animate vis-à-vis inanimate in that context.

Like Brown & Walker, John Robb (2004) has advocated operating with more than one form of agency – but Robb takes a slightly different position, arguing that archaeologists need to distinguish clearly between two different criteria of *agency*, since 'analytically, confounding them creates a tangle of complexities' (Robb 2004, 132). By the first criterion identified by Robb, exerting agency implies 'having some effect on the course of human events' while by the second, agency is understood as 'a quality of actions governed in some sense by intention, volition, or consciousness.' Further, he notes that:

> 'By the first criterion almost anything that affects human life has "agency" – people, dogs, rocks, Alfred Gell's car, the moon's gravitational field. By the second criterion, essentially by definition, only humans have agency, which becomes an aspect of experience rather than causation' (Robb 2004, 131-32).

Instead of Gell's (1998) notions of 'primary agency' (exerted by humans or sometimes other intentional beings like deities) and 'secondary agency' (also exerted by inanimate things), Robb suggests that we '... call the intentional and conscious aspects of action "conscious agency", and the ability to shape future events "effective agency"' (2004, 132). Though Robb (2004, 131) wants to show how material things structure human life 'in concrete ways which cross the traditional conceptual boundaries of subject-object, active-passive, and agent-environment', he thus maintains a clear distinction between the kind of agency that all things (including humans) can exert, and the kind of agency that only humans, by virtue of their *consciousness*, can exert.

Another contribution that has placed human thought centrally in the debate is Lambros Malafouris' elaborate argument for 'material agency' (2008). In contrast to Robb, however, Malafouris identifies the assumption of internal conscious will or, more specifically, prior *intentionality* as an element of and precondition for human agency as a main source of confusion in the debate. Taking an 'extended mind' perspective on human thought, Malafouris argues that the intentionality involved in most human activities is not the kind of conscious deliberation that is posited by traditional, internalist analyses, i.e. involving explicit, declarative cognitive content, firmly situated in the human brain and preceding subsequent action in clearly identifiable order. Rather, most intentionality involved in human activities is constituted by 'intentions in action' which do not precede action but unfold *with* the action. Malafouris suggests that such intentions in action are not in general situated internally in the human agent but in the 'extended' human mind, i.e. in a mind that cross-cuts the bodily and external components involved in activity (2008, 31). On this premise, the project of identifying one or more distinctly human form(s) of *agency* associated with intentionality crumbles: '... if intentionality is not an internal property, it cannot be used as the criterion for the attribution of agency to humans' (Malafouris 2008, 33). For Malafouris, the failure of 'intentionality' in providing a litmus test facilitating distinction between the causal contributions of humans and those of inanimate things exposes the futility of such distinctions:

> 'With respect to agency there is nothing to be found outside the tension of mediated activity and this is precisely the area to which we should look for its manifestations – human or material. Agency is a property or possession neither of humans nor of nonhumans. Agency is the relational and emergent product of material engagement. It is not something given but something to become realised. In short, as far as the attribution of agency is concerned, what an entity (wheel, sheep or tree ...) *is* in itself does not really matter; what does matter is what it becomes and where it stands in the network of material engagement' (Malafouris 2008, 34).

And further:

> 'Agency is a temporal and interactively emergent property of activity not an innate and fixed attribute of the human condition. *The ultimate cause of action* in this chain of micro and macro events is none of the supposed agents, humans or non-humans; it *is the flow of activity itself* (Malafouris 2008, 35, emphases added).

For Malafouris, then, agency is not a force, capacity or property driving activity but a product *of* activity; and the cause of the action that feeds into activity is (sic) activity itself.

Malafouris' views on 'the problem of agency' are in many respects closely related to those expressed in a number of contributions from authors inspired more explicitly by actor-network theory (ANT) and its fallout. In one such contribution, Knappett (2002, 115) has suggested that 'Agency, far from being the preserve of the individual mind and body, is distributed across networks, networks that invariably include both humans and non-humans'. Similarly, building on criticism of prevailing human-centred ontologies, Olsen has proposed that we adopt:

> '... a more egalitarian regime, a symmetrical archaeology, founded on the premise that things, all those physical entities we refer to as material culture, are beings in the world alongside other beings, such as humans, plants and animals. All these beings are kindred, sharing substance ("flesh") and membership in a dwelt-in world. They are, of course, different, but this is a difference that should not be conceptualized according to the ruling ontological regime of dualities and negativities; it is a non-oppositional or relative difference facilitating collaboration, delegation and exchange' (Olsen 2003, 88).

This is, Olsen (2003, 98) suggests, in the distinct vocabulary of ANT, 'a democratic and inclusive regime, everything can become actors (or actants) by being included into a network and assigned properties to act'.

Other, very clear examples of such inspiration from ANT have emerged with a recent series of papers by Timothy Webmoor and Christopher Witmore (e.g. Webmoor 2007; Webmoor & Witmore 2008; Witmore 2007). Aligning themselves tightly with this school of thought, not least the work of Latour, these authors argue that the problems with traditional, human-centred notions of agency originate in one of our most deeply entrenched assumptions, i.e. in distinctions between the (active) subject and the (passive) object, not least that between humans and 'nonhumans'. Such distinctions are, they argue, products of a modernist 'purification project' with the agenda of (artificially) parsing the world into discrete and controllable entities (Webmoor & Witmore 2008, 56-57, 60). Like Olsen, they find solution in ANT's 'principle of symmetry', the principle by which 'humans and non-humans should not be regarded as ontologically distinct, as detached and separated entities, *a priori*' (Witmore 2007, 546; also Webmoor 2007, 564; Webmoor & Witmore 2008, 57). Anticipating the scepticism that this levelling may provoke in some readers, Webmoor asks:

> 'What is the root justification for treating humans-things, or "naturescultures", as entangled? With modernist thought, such categories were viewed as separate because of differences due to inherent qualities or essences. The inferred possession of these qualities placed an entity into one category or the other. First and

> foremost among such qualities was "intentionality" or "consciousness"... So, if humans possess intentionality, nature, as substratum, does not. Discussions of agency and meaning are slotted, in this either/or ticking of attributes, under human or society; while time, environment and objects, lacking intentionality, are slotted into nature and things. The problem, as brought most illustratively to light in the "trenches" of actually studying how such divisions are (or are not) utilized in scientific practice, is that such "essences" prove un-demonstrable and are furthermore often "mixed" in actual research. The best examples come from technoscience where human research goals and models and the capacities of instruments create grey areas where *both* are responsible in an indissoluble manner for research outcomes [e.g. Haraway 1997; Latour 1999: 145-73; Pickering 1995]' (Webmoor 2007, 570).

Pressing the issue of responsibility for practical outcomes further, Webmoor takes up Latour's gun-man example, asking:

> '... is it the gun in the hands of an individual which kills people? Or the individual with a gun in the hand? Neither, symmetrically speaking, is quite right: it is the special assemblage, or "cyborg", of gun + individual which is uniquely responsible for killing, and which is *sui generis* reducible neither to human intention nor to mechanical function' (Webmoor 2007, 571).

For Webmoor and Witmore, then, *agency* (or its ANT sibling 'actantiality') is not something associated either with (animate) subjects or (inanimate) objects (as *a priori* distinctions, those very categories are rejected) but the causation that emerges from the combinations, or 'mixtures', of humans and non-humans, who are thus equally and 'indissolubly' responsible for the particular courses of events. Since this perspective dissolves the 'units' employed in dialectical models of ontological reality, they argue, it illustrates the fundamental flaws of perceiving the unfolding of human/non-human life across time as such a dynamic (Webmoor & Witmore 2008).

Various forms of the Inanimate Agency Proposition have been exemplified above. While these examples do not provide an exhaustive picture of all the forms this proposition has taken in archaeology, they do suffice to illustrate the main variants and to show the substantial breadth of variation among propositions here subsumed under this heading. Perhaps the most obvious conclusion to draw is that the IAP is not one, but several, to some extent disparate propositions integrated in several different approaches to ontology. Some of these points of variation are not mere nuances but make major theoretical differences. Consider, for instance, the contrast between the closing remarks of two contributions, both of which are suggesting that we broaden our notions of *agency* to include the influence of inanimate things – Robb (2004, 138) concluding with a twist on a Marxian theorem, 'humans make our own history, in conditions not of our own choosing but certainly of our own making' and Olsen (2007, 586) concluding with the opposite statement that '...the claim of a symmetrical archaeology becomes very different from that of Marx (and Childe): man did not make himself.' As I shall set out in more detail below, these differences among archaeological IAPs to a large extent reflect differences between their main sources of inspiration drawn from anthropology and sociology. In fact, critical discussion of the value and implications of IAPs in archaeology must start with the realization that their central solutions and problems are ones that its proponents have adopted from these sources.

But, first, we should note that though the contributions in this small sample are very far from representing any unanimous view on or application of the concept of agency, the contributions do share the basic IAP, i.e. the proposition that *agency* is not simply a property of humans but equally, or instead, something distributed across humans (and other animate beings[1]) and, crucially, inanimate objects, structures, substances etc. In each their way, these contributions thus champion a radical change in the ontological connotations of the concept of agency. A concept that was for many synonymous with human (capacity for) action is for many now simply synonymous with *causation*. As evident from the discussion and quotations above, this semantic shift is meant to further proper acknowledgement and better understanding of the overwhelming significance that all the non-human, material entities and configurations of the world have in the cultural lives of human beings. However, as also noted already, the Inanimate Agency Proposition is one among many potential paths towards such an objective, and it is an open question whether it is a productive one. Below, I shall attempt to evaluate more closely whether it is likely to be so. This entails considering the foundations and arguments of the IAP carefully in order to clarify its ontological commitments and consequences. The foundations, arguments and commitments, as to some extent the consequences relevant for archaeological ontology, are best exposed by looking beyond the disciplinary boundaries of archaeology to those intellectual contexts where the ontological programmes underlying this proposition were conceived and have been laid out in much greater substance and detail.

Foundations, arguments and commitments of the IAP

As already noted, the Inanimate Agency Proposition in archaeology has drawn on two main sources of inspiration: Gell's anthropology of art and agency and the socio-philosophical actor-network theory developed by Callon, Latour, Law and others. Needless to say, all contributors to the debate in archaeology have relied on a wider range of work when making this proposition (e.g. Haraway 1997; Pickering 1995), but these two bodies are, by far, the most influential sources of the IAP in archaeology. Below, I review and critique these two lines of thought on agency, and subsequently discuss the challenges and problems that they may bring with them into archaeological ontology.

Gell's Art and Agency

Alfred Gell's thought on agency has had significant impact in archaeology (a random sample of different contexts might include: Bille & Sørensen 2007; Brown & Walker 2008; Gamble 2007; Jones 2002; Knappett 2002; Robb 2004). Gell's work with this concept was part of his wider project of reorienting anthropological analysis and understanding of the role of *art* in human societies away from the traditional, semantic and aesthetic focus of Western art studies and towards a focus on *the efficacy of art*, something that Gell saw as driven more often by the ability of an art object's 'formal', material qualities to instil a sense of astonishment and awe in those confronted with it and thus beguile them. Examining such cases as the impact of the spectacular prow-boards of Trobriand canoes in *kula* exchange situations, and the virtuosity of the wood carving underlying these objects, Gell came to the important realization that the creation and display of art, like other forms of purposive practice, could most usefully be thought of as a form of *technology*. Arguably, the most incisive and convincing presentation of this argument – and of Gell's overall project – was given in his 1992 paper on *The technology of enchantment and the enchantment of technology*. But later, as signalled by the title of his most elaborate and influential statement on the topic, *Art and Agency*, published in 1998, Gell's conceptual strategy for dealing with the efficacy of art changed, when the concept of *agency* acquired a central role in the theoretical framework he was developing.[2]

As laid out in the opening pages of his book, Gell wanted to create a more comprehensive theory of (visual) art that was distinctly *anthropological*, which for him implied a theory fundamentally about *social relationships*. For Gell, 'The simplest way to imagine this [was] to suppose that there could be a species of anthropological theory in which *persons* or "social agents" are, in certain contexts, substituted for by *art objects*' (Gell 1998, 5). 'Simplest' here refers probably not just to Gell's own imaginative context but also to that of his colleagues. Needless to say, Gell's ambition was to produce a way of thinking about art *in* human social relations that would work not only for himself but equally for (many of) his anthropologist colleagues. As he acknowledged explicitly, his suggestion that art objects could be considered in this context as 'persons' represented no substantial departure from 'the entire historical tendency of anthropology', since Tylor, Frazer and Mauss, 'towards a radical defamiliarization and relativization of the notion of "persons"' (Gell 1998, 9). But Gell still needed a conceptual tool that could make anthropological minds fully realize how grounded the efficacy of art objects in social interaction is in (the specific materialities of) the objects themselves. What could really make anthropologists take the causation of art objects *themselves* – and not just the human agents manipulating them – seriously? In the context of mid-1990s (British) anthropology, it is perhaps not entirely surprising that Gell chose the concept of *agency* to do this work for him. Art objects, Gell suggested, should be regarded as entities with agency in their own right – as agents.

Measured by the impact of Gell's work, it is beyond dispute that he chose wisely. The success lay in Gell's application of a contagious magic of his own: by bringing the abstraction that anthropologists and others were already using to acknowledge the causal powers of humans – without which they would have nothing to study – into conceptual contact with their evaluation of the causal powers of (inanimate) objects, the latter were admitted to a well-established field of analytical significance. But as admirable as this theoretical manoeuvre is, it created significant problems for Gell. In the second chapter of *Art and Agency*, where Gell devotes considerable focus to the latter concept of this title, he seems fundamentally torn between two agendas. On the one hand, Gell (1998, 16-17) makes clear that his notion of *agency* does not need to satisfy the analytical demands of philosophers (most of whom Gell appears to take as rather secluded champions of scientific reasoning), i.e. that he is not concerned to meet standards of logic and analytical coherence by which the academic community might hold him responsible had he wanted his concept of agency to make a claim for 'general validity'. As he puts it, 'For the anthropologist, the problem of "agency" is not a matter of prescribing the most rational or defensible notion of agency, in that the anthropologist's task is to describe forms of thought which could not stand up to much philosophical scrutiny but which are none the less, socially and cognitively practicable' (Gell 1998, 17). On the other hand, realization of Gell's project of formulating 'an anthropological theory of art' is difficult to imagine without at least some recourse to claims of proposed general validity. And, indeed, Gell's argument soon exposes this ambition of his overall project as fully intact when, further down the same page (p. 17), he claims that 'Art objects are not "self-sufficient" agents, but only 'secondary' agents in conjunction with certain specific (human) associates ....' Here Gell takes precisely the kind of analytical stance that he has just deemed irrelevant for his purposes a few lines above. But then, on the next page, 'Not only is the car a locus of the owner's agency, and a conduit through which the agency of others (bad drivers, vandals) may affect him – it is also the locus of an "autonomous" agency of its own' (Gell 1998, 18). What exactly Gell intends to imply with the inverted commas framing the *autonomy* of the car in this context remains opaque.

This exchange between Gell's two epistemological faces unfolds over several pages and makes up a substantial part of his core discussion of the concept of *agency*. The argument sways back and forth between granting authority to various 'folk' notions of agency and granting authority to Gell's own attempts to make professional judgements about general ontological states and conditions, instantiated as claims with apparent, proposed general (anthropological) validity. But Gell clearly senses the internal division of his perspective and, in the end, feels compelled to settle things with an argument that he thinks could satisfy his analytically minded colleague (if not the philosopher). In a section devoted to 'paradox elimination', Gell confronts what he expects to be the main criticism levelled against his proposition that art objects should be considered agents, i.e. the objection that to treat *art objects as agents* is to ignore that these objects clearly do not possess the *intentionality* that humans do (1998, 19). Gell responds by emphasizing that humans as intentional beings always act in and with material environments, wherefore '..."things" with their thing-ly causal properties are as essential to the exercise of agency as states of mind' (Gell 1998, 20). He goes on to suggest that because ascriptions of *agency* are experientially based (i.e. retrospective), it makes little sense to ascribe agency categorically to particular types of entities:

> 'We recognize agency, *ex post facto,* in the anomalous configuration of the causal milieu – but we cannot detect it in advance, that is, we cannot tell that someone is an agent before they *act as an agent,* before they disturb the causal milieu in such a way as can only be attributed to their agency. Because the attribution of agency rests on the detection of the effects of agency in the causal milieu, rather than an unmediated intuition, it is not paradoxical to understand agency as a factor of the ambience as a whole, a global characteristic of the world of people and things in which we live, rather than as an attribute of the human psyche, exclusively' (Gell 1998, 20).

Arguably, there are several alternatives to the two understandings of agency which Gell here posits as those available. More to the point, however, the logic of his argument seems difficult to follow in a world where (all) people (always) bring experientially based categorical prejudices to any given situation: in practice people *do* attribute agency to some entities *a priori* because past experience has told them that entities of this kind/category have the capacity to do so and so. The kind of scenario for agency ascription that Gell envisages is an artificial, virginal situation in which the individual (human) agent making such judgment confronts the world in isolation from her own life history, from the life histories of contemporary individuals with whom she is socially embedded and from the whole corpus of accumulated experience passed from previous generations through historical time. Considering Gell's overall project, it is paradoxical that he comes to base part of his argument on the premise of a solitary mind deprived of any personally and culturally established system of classification and thus confined to the permanent naiveté of a synchronic empiricism.

Irrespective of the objection I have just raised, it is clear that Gell's initial response to his prospective critics is one that seriously questions the relevance of employing 'intentionality' and other cognitive capacities as distinguishing criteria in defining *agency*. In this light, Gell's next move is surprising:

> 'I am prepared to make a distinction between "primary" agents, that is, *intentional beings* who are categorically distinguished from "mere" things or artefacts, and "secondary" agents, which are artefacts, dolls, cars, works of art, etc. through which primary agents distribute their agency in the causal milieu, and thus render their agency effective' (Gell 1998, 20, emphasis added).

Here Gell takes a significant step back towards the kind of theory 'premised on the intentional nature of agency' (1998, 19) that his discussion has just taken issue with. With his dual concept of agency, Gell's well-known response to the challenge posed by intentionality to 'the agency of art objects', Gell to a large extent accepts an 'intentionality-based' definition of *agency* but supplements it with a different, 'secondary' kind of agency. However, he is quick to retort: 'But to call artefactual agents "secondary" is not to concede that they are not agents at all, or agents only "in a manner of speaking"' (1998, 20). To explain this further, Gell turns to discuss the agency associated with the thousands of anti-personnel mines planted in the fields of Cambodia by the Khmer Rouge, emphasizing that 'The soldier's weapons are *parts* of him which make him what he is' (1998, 20-21) and that, without the landmine, '...this agent (the soldier + mine) could not exist' (1998, 21). With this example, Gell takes us back, once again, towards the relational or distributed notion of agency as 'a global characteristic of the world of people and things' (1998, 20), concluding that 'Anti-personnel mines are not (primary) agents who initiate happenings through acts of will for which they are morally responsible, granted, but they are objective embodiments of the power or capacity to will their use, and hence moral entities in themselves' (Gell 1998, 21).

There are obvious questions to ask to the specific way that Gell chooses to give prominence to artefacts here. How can artefacts be *moral entities in themselves* but not morally responsible? What does it take for an artefact to qualify as a moral entity? Were the machetes used in the Rwanda genocide moral entities too? Is the blind man's stick a moral entity, and does it change its moral character if raised with the intention of violence? Are all artefacts moral entities? What about non-artefactual objects like rocks? But Gell immediately evades these thorny issues by reverting to his assurance that he is not trying to satisfy 'philosophers' (once again cast as isolated, somewhat obdurate guardians of logic and analytical coherence):

> '"Agency" is usually discussed in relation to the permanent dispositional characteristics of particular entities: "here is X, is it an agent or not?" And the answer is – "that depends on whether X has intentions, a mind, awareness, consciousness, etc." The issue of "agency" is thus raised in a classificatory context, classifying all the entities in the world into those that "count" as agents, and those that do not. Most philosophers believe that only human beings are *pukka* agents, while a few more would add some of the mammals, such as chimpanzees, and some would also include computers with appropriately "intelligent" software. It is important to emphasize that I am not raising the question of "agency" in anything like this "classificatory" sense. The concept of agency I employ is relational and context-dependent, not classificatory and context-free' (Gell 1998, 21-22).

Gell, apparently relieved by this assurance from dealing with the sort of questions just raised above, proceeds to explain how the 'exclusively relational' character of his notion of agency is predicated on the idea that *agency* always implies a corresponding 'patiency':

> 'To be an "agent" one must act with respect to the "patient"; the patient is the object which is causally affected by the agent's action. For the purposes of the theory being developed here, it will be assumed that in any given transaction in which agency is manifested, there is a "patient" who or which is *another "potential" agent,* capable of acting as an agent or being a locus of agency' (Gell 1998, 22).[3]

The relationality at play in Gell's framework is clear enough in the conditioning mutual implication of that which causes and that which is affected, and in the interchangeability of these roles. But his claim that this relationality renders his treatment of the concept of agency 'non-classificatory' is puzzling. Gell's overall 'classes' of *agency* and *agent* are very inclusive indeed, but they are not empty. To Gell, potential agents are all entities which can affect something else causally (i.e. all entities, full stop), and the concept of agency thus, in all essence, a synonym of *causation*. Further, his specification of these concepts into 'primary' and 'secondary' species of agents/agency alludes to exactly the kind of permanent, entity-based characteristics that he claims to avoid and thus represents a more static employment of classes than the one explicated in his principled argument on classification. In short, Gell here confuses his desire for a very broad conceptual employment of *agency*, one that lies indistinguishably close to *causation*, with convenient liberation from the problems of classification that any ontological (or other) theory faces. But then, a few pages further into the book, he affirms that 'A theory of the kind being developed here consists primarily of a device for ordering and classifying the empirical material with which it deals, rather than offering law-like generalizations or predictions therefrom' (Gell 1998, 28).

As illustrated above, Gell's central theoretical encounter with the concept of agency in the first chapters of *Art and Agency* was charged with internal conflicts. And the uneasy relationship with this concept which Gell passes to his readers in the opening chapters continues to mark the remaining parts of his book (though the frequency of the oscillations decreases somewhat). Following his main discussion of agency, Gell presents an elaborate discussion of 'indexes', which he defines as 'material entities which motivate abductive inferences, cognitive interpretations etc.' (1998, 27) and as 'objectifications of agency distributed in the causal milieu' (1998, 38) – i.e. entities which affect human (or sometimes spiritual) agents by virtue of *reflecting* or *implying* the agency of other human (or spiritual) agents in their social environment. This notion of 'the index', which Gell adopts from Pierce but develops and extends over several chapters, competes with that of 'the secondary agent' over very similar conceptual space, but the causal relationships posited by Gell's 'indexicality' are considerably less fuzzy than those connoted by the 'secondary' part of his 'agency'. It is hard to avoid the impression that the former, though not entirely consistent, fares considerably better than the latter. Nonetheless, despite the perspective made available by the concept of indexicality, much of the discussion in Gell's subsequent chapters, where he is more extensively immersed in case studies, gives causal prominence to artefacts and decorations in social transactions in a decidedly more 'agentive' manner. As noted previously by Robb (2004, 138), 'the further into Gell's book one reads, the more autonomous things become'. But then, in the concluding pages of the book, where Gell adopts a more diachronic perspective on works of art and starts to develop temporally sensitive notions of mind and agency, he seems to drift somewhat back towards a stronger causal emphasis on human beings, where (art) objects and structures are thought of as tools and indexes of the initiatives and traditions of human individuals and collectives.[4] In fact, Gell's closing argument (along with his whole notion of indexicality) in many ways seems more compatible with his previous perspective of 'art as technology' (1992) than it does with large parts of the book that it rounds off.[5] Note that I am pointing here to a certain element of covariation through the second, more empirically involved part of Gell's book – that of his analytical emphasis concerning *agency* with the temporal scope of his empirical focus, i.e. the scale(s) of analysis employed. As illustrated further by the discussion of actor-network theory below, this correspondence is not likely to be coincidental.

Gell's work on *agency* simultaneously reveals the brilliance of its author and the theoretical perplexity of a deeply anthropocentric tradition trying to come to terms with the immense causal significance of distinctly non-human entities. Conceptually, the solution of parsing the concept of agency into two subspecies, a 'primary' and a 'secondary' agency, was less a cure than a palliative. As noted early on by Gosden (2001, 164-65):

> 'Objects can be seen as active, but they are active in the manner of objects not in the manner of people. To call objects secondary agents is make them look like people, but with certain deficiencies of intention ... Calling objects secondary agents detracts attention from Gell's main point, which is that we should concentrate on the effects of objects and the formal qualities of objects which were aimed at creating effects'.

Gell seems to have been caught in a dilemma. In some parts of *Art and Agency* he goes very far in dissolving the boundary between the causal contributions of human and inanimate entities. Yet, something keeps Gell from taking the conceptual step fully and eschewing categorical distinction between the two from his analytical framework. As exemplified above, his most explicit motivation for retaining any such relates to 'intentionality' as something that sets human agents apart, but he also refers sporadically to their 'autonomy' and 'self-sufficiency'. However, apart from his relatively straightforward acceptance of the standard assumption of 'intentionality' as an obvious hallmark of human agency, Gell says surprisingly little about *why* he feels the need to distinguish human and inanimate causation categorically. Perhaps the clearest answer to this question emerges as part of his discussion of indexes, where his explanation of this distinction is elaborated:

> 'It will be apparent that "indexes" are, normally, "secondary agents" in this scene; they borrow their agency from some external source, which they mediate and transfer to the patient. It will be equally apparent that "artists" are normally "primary" agents. *They initiate actions on their own behalf.* This is true even if, as is often the case, they act under the direction of patrons. The artist may be a socially subordinate agent, a hired hand, but unless the artist wills it, the index he has been hired to make will never come into existence (Gell 1998, 36, emphasis added).

For Gell, it seems here, the central thing that sets 'the primary agent' apart from the art object with which it shares its causal milieu is not a feature of its context but, rather, *a capacity specific to the entity itself*, i.e. to the artist, a human organism: the capacity to initiate and execute (or refrain from) action 'on its own behalf'.[6] What Gell does not seem to consider is that it is perhaps not so much 'intentionality', 'free will' or some other, highly complex cognitive subset of (human) motivation that gives human beings this capacity as it is something much more basic about *organic life*. As we shall see below, this theme concerning the capacities of 'entities' is one that plays an equally central, if rather different and more explicit role in the arguments on agency provided by the other main source of inspiration for the Inanimate Agency Proposition in archaeology.

ANT: actor-network theory

As has been the case with Gell's anthropology of art and agency, recent contributions advocating revisions of the concept of *agency* in archaeology have drawn substantially on perspectives developed in 'actor-network theory', or ANT (e.g. Boast 1997; Jones 2002; Knappett 2002; 2005; 2008; Martin 2005; Olsen 2003; 2007; Watts 2007; 2008; Webmoor 2007; Webmoor & Witmore 2008; Witmore 2007). As indicated by the references here, the impact of ANT in archaeology is a very recent phenomenon – for the most part one coterminous with that of Gell's work, with which it has shared much of its momentum – but ANT itself has a significantly longer history. 'Actor-network' perspectives started to develop as a distinct branch of the sociology of science and technology during the early 1980s, when its key proponents began an effort to reform sociological inquiry in what we might broadly call a *pragmatic* direction, one intended to shift focus from analytical high-level distinctions (like 'agency vs. structure') towards localized, 'bottom-up' analyses of processes of social interaction and negotiation involving configurations of humans *and* all the other material parts making societal practice possible (Callon 1986a; Callon & Latour 1981; Callon & Law 1982; Latour 1983; 1987; Law 1986). Since then, ANT has grown into a multifaceted and extremely ambitious critique that questions many of the foundational conventions and structuring principles of Western social theory and epistemology. One of the main thrusts of ANT has been to problematize esoteric, immaterial notions of 'the social' and of 'culture' and replace them with a thoroughgoing recognition of the constitutive part that technologies play in holding human societies together. On that account, few would contest that this 'sociology of associations' has succeeded where many have failed in setting *things on the agenda*. Among ANT's most productive contributions we might count its demonstrations of the role of technology in distinctly human, 'remote' or indirect forms of social positioning, persuasion and power exertion – significant in all societies but increasingly with larger scales of organization – (e.g. Callon & Latour 1981; Latour 2000; Strum & Latour 1987),[7] its studies of how constellations of technology, power and exchange are (re)negotiated, and how they reach (once again) some form of 'closure' (e.g. Latour 1987; Law & Callon 1992) and its consideration of how sociotechnical networks can come to exhibit degrees of irreversibility (Callon 1991). The scope of ANT, however, is very wide and there are many more facets to this field than those touched upon here. Nonetheless, as the discussion below will focus specifically on ANT's conception of *agency*, it will bring us into contact with some of the most fundamental aspects and problems of its ontological project.

Contrary to Gell's work on agency, which was largely presented in one book and published posthumously (and thus not subject to revision by its author), the ideas on agency developed in ANT's studies of science and technology are distributed across a large number of articles and books. Accordingly, any attempt to discuss the character of *agency* in ANT (as the collective product of a school of thought) will, necessarily, have to be pieced together from a sample of writings published by some of the field's central figures. Even so, ANT's views on agency are in many ways more settled and, partly for that reason, significantly less complex than Gell's writings on the matter. One central thing that we may note initially is that ANT's take on causal relationships has a starting point which differs fundamentally from most of its alternatives in the social sciences. In the words of John Law (1999, 4), '... actor-network theory may be understood as a *semiotics of materiality*. It takes the semiotic insight, that of the relationality of entities, the notion that they are produced in relations, and applies this ruthlessly to all materials – not simply to those that are linguistic'. As stressed by Law, the implications of this starting point are far-reaching:

> 'In this scheme of things entities have no inherent qualities: essentialist divisions are thrown on the bonfire of the dualisms. Truth and falsehood. Large and small. Agency and structure. Human and non-human. Before and after. Knowledge and

power. Context and content. Materiality and sociality. Activity and passivity. In one way or another all of these divides have been rubbished in work undertaken in the name of actor-network theory' (Law 1999, 3).

The qualities of entities, in other words, are constituted in their relations with other entities. Of course, what Law suggests is not that entities have no *a priori* qualities *at all* – that would deny any form of stability of different ontological kinds (such as humans and non-humans) across different scenarios and would thus preclude, or at least invalidate, the structuration of the world through classification which is a precondition for any (conceptual) thought and talk about *anything* (such as humans and non-humans) to begin with – an overtly absurd scenario of cognitive paralysis. Rather, what seems to be suggested is that, *a priori* – i.e. prior to its involvement and shaping or 'transformation' in the relations of a given network configuration with other entities – an entity has no (significant) *causal qualities*; the character of its causal role and impact in a certain context of relations is not to any considerable degree determined by an inherent character (or 'essence', in the vocabulary chosen by Law) as 'human', 'pillow' or 'giraffe'.

Agency, in the view just expressed, is something that an entity can acquire, not something it simply possesses in its unitary self. As such, there are no distinctly human forms of agency or, for that matter, any distinctly non-human forms of agency. Indeed, in order to avoid the entrenched connotations of the concepts *agent* and *agency* to alternative, dialectical perspectives (which posit *a priori* causal qualities of entities), ANT has proposed that the entities or 'operating parts' of ontology be conceptualized as 'actants' and 'actors'.[8] An *actant* is 'whatever acts or shifts actions' (Akrich & Latour 1992, 259), i.e. potentially any entity. *Actors*, like actants, are 'entities that *do* things' (Latour 1992, 241) but, crucially, the actor is an 'actant endowed with a character' (Akrich & Latour 1992, 259), which may be non-human or human. This endowment with character or 'competences', or what we might call the 'definition' of the actor (which is never definitive), occurs through its 'performances' in one or many 'trials' (e.g. Callon 1986b, 30-33; Latour 1999b, 17-19). Actors, then, are not so much the 'input' of a given configuration of relations as the 'output' produced by the 'summing up' of those relations. Again, it is important to stress that no *inherent* difference between entities performing as actants and those performing as actors is posited – the relevant difference is one between two levels in a pragmatic hierarchy of specification with regard to acquired, performative roles. In the words of Latour, '... actantiality is not what an actor does ... but what *provides* actants with their actions, with their subjectivity, with their intentionality, with their morality' (Latour 1999b, 18). Any given entity can be specified from actant to actor, and unspecified back.

The view of agency sketched above grounds ANT's causal principle of ('generalized') *a priori* 'symmetry', which has already been mentioned. Since agency is emergent, and there is nothing prior to the interactions through which it is created, ANT is committed to treating human and non-human causal contributions to any given ontological scenario 'symmetrically' (Callon 1986a; Latour 1993, 95-96). Of course, as acknowledged recently by Latour (2005, 76), talking about 'symmetry' between humans and non-humans is somewhat awkward in a framework where the ontological status of an entity is argued to be flexible according to its position in practice, since such *symmetry* would seem to presuppose – even emphasize – something like (dual) 'stably different entities' for it to exist between. Nonetheless, this concept has been important in ANT's effort to shift humans from the privileged causal position they hold in traditional social theory. This may be useful point at which to revisit Latour's famous 'gun-man' case (Latour 1999, 176-93), which is probably the most well-circulated argument for *causal symmetry* provided by ANT.[9] Latour contrasts two positions in the US debate on fire arms in civil society: 'Guns kill people' is the parole of those who want to restrict their distribution, and 'Guns don't kill people: *people* kill people' is the reply of the National Rifle Association, which promotes the possession of guns (for self-defence) as a constitutional right. The anti-gun segment emphasizes the risk of accidents and the fact that the possession of guns makes it easier for people to turn their aggressions (most of which would also be there in the absence of guns) into extreme violence but downplays the fact that guns do nothing that they are not made to do by the particular humans handling them. The NRA performs the opposite manoeuvre; it emphasizes the fact that humans have a choice (that they decide whether to hold the gun and pull the trigger) but ignores the practical difference that guns make given the prevalence of aggressions – and unsuspecting children – amongst humans (that killing is physically much easier and perhaps socially more convenient with a gun than is barehanded strangling).

Latour intervenes:

> 'Which of them, then, the gun or the citizen, is the *actor* in this situation? *Someone else* (a citizen-gun, a gun-citizen)'... This translation is wholly symmetrical. You are different with a gun in your hand; the gun is different with you holding it. You are another subject because you hold the gun; the gun is another object because it has entered into a relationship with you. The gun is no longer the gun-in-the-armory or the gun-in-the-drawer or the gun-in-the-pocket, but the gun-in-your-hand, aimed at someone who is screaming. What is true of the subject, of the gunman, is as true of the object, of the gun that is held. A good citizen becomes a criminal, a bad guy becomes a worse guy; a silent gun becomes a fired gun, a

> new gun becomes a used gun, a sporting gun becomes a weapon … If we study the gun and the citizen as propositions, [however,] we realize that neither subject nor object (nor their goals) is fixed. When the propositions are articulated, they join into a new proposition. They become "someone, something" else … It is neither people nor guns that kill. Responsibility for action must be shared among the various actants' (Latour 1999, 179-80).

Latour's alternative to the anti- and pro-gun diagnoses is to see agency as *distributed* between citizen and gun, and, for Latour, such distribution is constitutive of human agency:

> 'There is no sense in which humans may be said to exist as humans without entering into commerce with what authorizes and enables them to exist (that is, to act). A forsaken gun is a mere piece of matter, but what would an abandoned gunner be? A human, yes (a gun is only one artifact among many), but not a soldier – and certainly not one of the NRA's law-abiding Americans. Purposeful action and intentionality may not be properties of objects, but they are not properties of humans either. They are the properties of institutions, of apparatuses, of what Foucault called *dispositifs*. Only corporate bodies are able to absorb the proliferation of mediators, to regulate their expression, to redistribute skills, to force boxes to blacken and close' (Latour 1999, 192).

There can be no doubt that Latour's gun-man case – like Gell's landmine case – was carefully picked, since scenarios involving technologies of molestation and murder activate some of our strongest feelings and verdicts about causation. But Latour's reference to the historically oriented work of Foucault is paradoxical and draws attention to a central weakness in his argument: Latour's *agency* is distributed in *space* only, not in *time*. Though Latour writes at length about the contingency of the societal constellations that put a given human being into the position of being able to fire a gun, he settles the *causal* account of the gun-man case in the neatly sealed moment of the shooting incident, where (not when) the 'hybrid actor' (gun+human) releases the bullet. The *provenance* of the gun is conspicuously absent in Latour's causal zoom-in on the virtually synchronic point of 'material semiosis' when the killing is done.[10] But if we relax our temporal zoom – even just a little by archaeological standards – this causal setting is invaded by a host of human agents without whom Latour's hypothetical but depressingly topical man would never have had a gun in his hands. Humans *acquire* guns, guns which have been developed, refined, produced and distributed *by humans* through a long historical process. Before anyone comes into possession of a gun, a long chain of people gained a profit from manufacturing that lethal implement and making it available, legally or illegally. Before anyone is endowed with the destructive potency of this mechanism, a whole series of populations and politicians – humans by the millions – decided to sanction the extensive circulation of these tools in their societies. Latour presents us with the apparent choice between ascribing causal responsibility to the citizen *or* the gun. But this is a highly selective framing of the problem, which serves to prepare the stage for the solution already given by the principle of symmetry (distributing responsibility symmetrically between the two). Both framing and solution, unfortunately, draw attention away from the causal and ethical responsibilities of the long chain of human actors whose agency made firing a gun an option in Latour's scenario. The gun being fired could have done nothing differently – the North American collective of humans could.[11]

On the surface, Latour's gun-man setting fits ANT's causal principles well with its relatively simple, local and temporally well-controlled (almost laboratory-like) observation of operating parts 'inter-acting'. However, the conclusion of *causal symmetry* between humans and non-humans, which is arguable by this more or less synchronic reckoning, seems very difficult to sustain as soon as we allow *history* into the equation. What Latour's carefully selected case provides is most of all a powerful illustration of this analytical limitation to ANT. Here it is important to note that, somewhat paradoxically, the more elaborate case studies of ANT have in general *not* been particularly synchronic in their foci – in fact, most would qualify as diachronic or 'longitudinal' in many disciplines (e.g. Callon 1986a; Latour 1988; 1996a; Law & Callon 1992) and a few are decidedly historical in scope (e.g. Law 1986). As it happens, many of the empirical expositions of these studies have a distinctly *dialectical* ring to them. But, as we have seen above, when it comes to principled statements on causality, the same authors are not informed by their engagement with diachronic evidence; on the contrary, they remain unshakably devoted to the principle of symmetry, *a priori* and, in practice, far beyond.

This is not entirely surprising, for the diachronic evidence is squeezed by synchronicity at two levels in ANT: not only does the synchronic settling of causal accounts tend to confirm symmetry, as we have just seen – the principle of symmetry is itself already an artefact of a synchronic emphasis, namely that which sustains the very extensive, relational malleability of entities and their agency in ANT's scheme. Consider Callon & Latour's (1992, 356) adage 'One is not born a scallop, one becomes one' (see Callon 1986a for the full argument), which might as well have read 'one is not born a human, one becomes one'. As should be clear from the discussion above, this statement is not meant simply to point to ontogenetic development as a basic condition of organic existence but to question *the significance of* (differences in) starting points or, rather, *inheritance* for such developments. However, it seems difficult to deny that this bold challenge excises a central part of scallop and human life alike from our conceptual framework. If, for a moment, we turn the counterfactual method – a favoured form of reasoning in ANT (e.g. Callon & Law 1995, 484; Latour 1992, 228) – on this proposition, one wonders whether the mother expecting a human child – but then giving birth to a scallop child, would be much consoled by our assurances that 'she may turn out human enough in due course'? Much like the counterfactual tales of ANT, the absurdity of this scenario brings out how something (in this case the physiological qualities passed from parents to offspring), which makes a *significant* difference for particular possibilities and outcomes, may be ignored or trivialized in the interest of promoting other analytical agendas (in this case those of ANT itself) with maximal force.[12]

The problems in accommodating historical grounding that we have just encountered begin to indicate that the 'metaphysical freedom of the semiotician' sought by ANT (cf. Latour 2005, 55) comes at a price. The entities of ANT's causal accounts (as opposed to those of its empirical scenarios) have no history. Or, to be more precise, the only history deemed significant for ANT's causal entities is that which unfolds under, and *begins with*, the temporally well-constrained analytical glance of the actor-network analyst (e.g. Latour 1999a, 182).[13] These entities bring nothing with them from the past preceding the analysis which enables or constrains their particular roles in practice, which defines their *causal qualities* to any notable degree – for if they did, the doctrine of *a priori* symmetry would shatter. 'Human entities' would come to the analytical situation as material products of human procreation and subsequent ontogeneses possible from that starting point, and would bring particular material qualities – and thus, it would seem, a finite spectrum of causal qualities – that these specific processes had granted. 'Gun entities' would come to the analytical situation as material products of *human* activities of innovation, manufacture, use, maintenance and repair (utilizing geologically, synthetically and, sometimes still, biologically formed raw materials), and would, likewise, bring particular material qualities that these specific processes had granted, resulting in a *different* but equally finite spectrum of causal qualities. Both humans and guns would be causally important, but *agency* would be distributed in a diachronic and asymmetrical manner, and the overall account would have to be very different. Histories of how entities came into being, of their geneses, it seems, are not only causally irrelevant for ANT, but theoretically compromising.

ANT's disregard for the material histories of entities captures the main paradox of its ontological programme. On the one hand, ANT wants to break away from the long humanistic tradition of treating non-human material parts of society as epiphenomenal to the 'true' substance of sociality and culture allegedly existing somehow locked away in the mental worlds of individuals but nonetheless shared and negotiated in strangely esoteric realms of intersubjectivity. That is, ANT wants to re-materialize the ontology of human *being* – and this, needless to say, entails lots of empirical confrontation with material entities and their histories. On the other hand, ANT also wants to eradicate assumptions about *a priori* differences between entities as causal contributors; it wants to *start* its analyses in a world of causal symmetry or, less dualistically, causal isomorphism. This somewhat peculiar marriage of theoretical agendas depends crucially on a particular philosophical manoeuvre: the *causal qualities* of entities must be severed from their *material qualities*, i.e. from the ties of their material histories. Once this liberatory action has been executed, ANT's causal entities are free to behave remarkably similar to those of abstract systems of communicative symbolization, which really do seem to 'take their form and acquire their attributes as a result of their relations with other entities' (Law 1999, 3-4; also Latour 1991). And, equipped with causal entities behaving according to such principles, the actor-network theoretician has achieved the 'freedom of the semiotician' necessary to exercise his 'semiotics of materiality' without being constrained in causal attribution by the material pre-givens of the entities involved. In short, ANT wants materiality but not the constraints of material history.

Whatever one thinks of the metaphysics involved in this theoretical arrangement, it is hard to see that there is anything particularly *re-materialized* about the chastely relational ontology that results from this projection of linguistic dynamics to extra-linguistic substance. At the very least, this is materiality of a very specific kind. Entities of abstract systems of communicative symbolization are characterized by their material *compatibility* and *flexibility*. Shifting such entities around, breaking them up and mixing them has all sorts of semiotic consequences but is in general *materially easy* (this is a main source of the system's power). While this may also be the case with non-linguistic entities, it seems that, by comparison, elements of *incompatibility* and *inflexibility* are remarkably pervasive among material entities of the extra-linguistic world. Of course, ultimately, all material entities are composed of different elements or 'entities' (we could pass the buck till the smallest units known by physics), and many biotic processes operate with recursive combinatorial complexity that matches or surpasses that of human language. But at the analytical scales relevant to studying the cultural lives of humans (e.g. those employed by ANT) very few domains of ontology share *the ease of re-configuration* found in abstract systems of communicative symbolization. Most entities of the extra-linguistic world, like guns and humans, were not made to travel effortlessly in a system (or network) of continuous recombination utilizing a globally shared format and flexibility of configuration. In general, the material qualities of entities do have significant implications for their causal qualities, *a priori*. No matter what the relations, a speed bump would never work as a blind man's stick, and, unlike the blind man or the driver, neither bump nor stick could ever sense a need to find its way or slow down. ANT's purist insistence on relational flexibility, unfortunately, leaves little room for such diversity among the material entities of our world.

As should be evident above, ANT's perspectives on *agency* are shaped by the agendas of a much larger project – one whose ambitions are hard to overestimate. In some respects, the ontological relationism offered by ANT constitutes a much further-reaching kind of constructivism than those forms of epistemological relationism which most scholars of human life and culture have come to accept in some variant or to some extent (cf. Latour 1991, 129). As noted by Pickering, '...worrying about the dualisms of subject and object, nature and society goes pretty deep. The foundations of modern thought are at stake here; this is precisely the point at which science studies converges with all sorts of postmodernisms' (Pickering 1992, 22). Reviewing the impact of ANT some years later, Latour came to much the same conclusion but specified Pickering's diagnosis as follows: 'The difference between ANT and the masses of reflection on modernity and post-, hyper-, pre- and anti-modernity, was simply that it took to task all of the components of what could be called the modernist predicament simultaneously' (Latour 1999b, 21). We might add to Pickering's observation and Latour's confirmation that the fundamental *reboot* of ontology suggested by ANT applies not only to Western 'modernist' ontology, but to foundational ontological assumptions (e.g. subject/object distinctions) which are widespread across the world, presently as well as historically. The actor-network, when conceived as 'a semiotic machine for waging war on essential differences' (Law 1999, 7), indeed has many foes.[14] Not surprisingly, considering the scope of the undertaking, it seems difficult to escape the impression that this conceptual war on all fronts remains a daunting distance away from obtaining its strategic aims. But the strategy of all-encompassing rupture is not only extremely ambitious and analytically difficult, to say the least – it is also *easy*, in the sense that it has allowed its proponents to answer its most incisive critics (e.g. Bloor 1999a; Collins & Yearley 1992a) by continuous questioning of the fundamental building blocks of their arguments (Callon & Latour 1992; Latour 1999c). As several critics have complained (e.g. Bloor 1999b, 131-32; Collins & Yearley 1992b, 378-80), such infinite rejection of premises – or 'progressive regress' (Collins & Yearley 1992b, 379) – isolates theoretical combatants in epistemological safe-houses, between which no substantial discussion of ontology is possible. This practice, which the relationism and accompanying empirical fluidity of ANT does not dictate but certainly offers favourable conditions for, is perhaps particularly ironic for a school of thought that simultaneously questions precisely the value of 'classical' epistemological analysis (e.g. Latour 1999a).

Actor-network theory might be described as the best and the worst that could happen to social theory. The best because it has drawn general attention to how different human societies would be without the ubiquitous human reliance on technology (i.e. that they would hardly qualify as 'societies' in the sense assumed by most scholars studying them), and because it has attempted to provide an antidote to the largely immaterial conception of societal 'structures' which has pervaded many influential theories, for instance the dialectical sociologies of Berger & Luckmann (1967), Bourdieu (1977; 1990) and Giddens (1979; 1984). The worst because it has done so on a philosophical basis that challenges the causal importance of the very material substance to which it wants to draw attention. ANT's origin in and loyalty to post-structuralist semiotics (cf. Latour 1991; Law 1999) from the very beginning compelled its ontological project to continue a trajectory of giving such power to *relations* that the specific material properties of entities become causally epiphenomenal. While the intimate connection between the ideology underlying the semiotization of ontology that many proponents of a 'material turn' sought to redress, and that underlying ANT's particular contribution to the latter seems to have slipped general attention in some fields (e.g. archaeology), some advocates of ANT have in fact mapped it rather well (Olsen 2006b; 2007).[15] For now, however – despite ANT's commendable call for rematerialization – the feasibility of curing the ailments of a First Semiotization of ontology with a Second, arguably more omnivorous Semiotization remains to be demonstrated.

'Agency is (simply) causation': implications and problems

Gell's anthropology of art and agency and ANT's sociology of science and technology offer each their version of the proposition that *agency* (or actantiality) is something that is distributed across humans and inanimate objects, structures, substances etc. – rather than something restricted to humans. Traditionally, in the humanities and social sciences (in contrast to some other scientific pursuits, like chemistry), the notion of agency has been used to designate and emphasize the causal powers of humans. But, while two very different specifications are advocated by Gell and ANT, both of these perspectives suggest that *agency* should be used in a broader sense that includes and acknowledges the *causal significance* of inanimate, non-human entities and relations. Both are thus suggesting that the meaning of *agency* be extended in such a way that it becomes synonymous with the less idiomatic concept of *causation* (as it is, for instance, in chemistry).

It is possible to imagine an Inanimate Agency Proposition which had this semantic revision as its simple ambition, and which did *not* call into question the existence of inherent causal differences between inanimate and animate entities. But evidently, with one arguable exception (Robb 2004),[16] the IAPs examined above are not of this kind. Granted, it is precisely this tight-rope act attempted by Gell in parts of his argument, not least in his dual concept of agency (which inspired Robb and many others), but other parts bring him indistinguishably close to the fully-fledged relationism of ANT. For Gell, in the latter incarnation, and for ANT consistently, such categorical distinctions between different entities represent a serious obstacle for acknowledging the causal importance of inanimate entities. Clearly, both humans, inanimate entities and their relations are causally very significant in human life and culture and, in each their way, both ANT and (again, at times) Gell suggest that the best way to recognize this is to refrain from thinking and talking about their respective contributions as categorically (i.e. conceptually) distinct. This, then, is a general logic underlying the IAP: proper causal credit is best given to inanimate entities by showing that their causal contributions are not fundamentally different from those of humans (whose significance we never doubted). While Gell remained caught in the limbo of simultaneously embracing and rejecting this logic, ANT has shown no signs of hesitation. As demonstrated in the discussion above, it created profound analytical problems in the ontological frameworks of both Gell and ANT. Inanimate Agency Propositions in archaeology, to the significant extent that they are founded more or less directly upon these frameworks, have inherited these problems.

Paradoxically, the central logic of the IAP is profoundly anthropocentric: Since a) humans have been/are the model of highly significant causal entities in the (human) world, then b) toning down differences between the causal contributions of humans and inanimate entities allows the latter to be seen as causally highly significant. This raises an obvious question: By which standard does it follow that inanimate entities are (to be seen as) causally insignificant or negligible, if their inanimacy is accepted as making them radically different from humans and, by the way, other animate organisms? This would seem to be the very standard that proponents of the IAP wanted to break away from, but they have nonetheless founded their response solidly upon its prior acceptance. Rather than purging anthropocentrism from attempts to grapple with the causal significance of distinctly non-human entities, the IAP inadvertently serves to re-consolidate it in a less overt and thus more entrenched theoretical position. The question is, though, whether archaeologists (or scholars in other disciplines) should accept the implicit assumption that to treat inanimate entities – artefacts, substances, structures – as inherently, qualitatively different from humans, as *essential outsiders*, necessarily implies treating their causal significance as marginal? Is it really necessary to envelop inanimate entities in an aura of human-style significance in order to take them seriously? Or might it be that acknowledging inherent differences is in fact a prerequisite, rather than an obstacle, for understanding many aspects of their causal potential?

In human relations, the 'otherness' of inanimate objects and structures – the fact that they are *not* human, i.e. that they are *not* distinct animate agents with contestable agendas – seems to be one of their key qualities. Humans constantly exploit the 'factuality' of the objective world (not least those parts which they shape themselves) in attempts to naturalize relations, distributions and agendas in their social environments. The spectacular prow-boards which embellish Trobriand canoes work precisely because they are not like their makers. They work because their optical surrealness, their quality and splendour is, in a sense, indisputable. They constitute testimonies to the virtuosity, audacity and resourcefulness of their makers and owners, which are far less contestable and far more persuasive than would be, say, oral proclamations of such qualities. In the words of Gell (1992, 46), 'It is the fact that an impressive canoe-board is a physical token of magical prowess on the part of the owner of the canoe which is important, as is the fact that he has access to the services of a carver whose artistic prowess is also the result of his access to superior carving magic'. Producing, manipulating and displaying inanimate entities, it seems, allows humans to do social (and other) work that might otherwise be very difficult. To take a rather different (and rather overt) example, it is much more difficult to question the greatness of a dictator when facing his colossal statue in a city of boulevards, parks and palaces created in his glory than it would be in the unlikely scenario (zealously avoided by dictators) of facing, simply, the man himself, stripped of all pomp and circumstance. Does this attest to 'the agency of inanimate things' – or does it attest to the human ability to exploit precisely the fact that, contrary to human organisms, the crown jewels and the iPhone are *not* identifiable agents but factual things whose 'objective reality' it is very difficult to argue with or to meet with suspicion? Inanimate artefacts and structures not only allow humans to exert power and persuasion in their own absence (cf. Callon & Latour 1981; Strum & Latour 1987), as in their presence; they allow humans to exert them in ways which are *qualitatively different* from – and at times significantly more efficient than – those facilitated by their own bodily presence and activity. This point concerning the significance of inherent, material qualities for the different causal potentials of entities (whether artefacts or humans) might have emerged as a very clear lesson from many of the examples discussed above under the IAP heading but has remained theoretically subdued by the pervading anthropocentric conception of ontological significance. Contrary to suggestions that the 'otherness' of the artefactual world is something that archaeologists should (and can) overcome (Watts 2007), the simple examples just discussed indicate that it is exactly the inherent *non-humanness* of artefactual objects and structures that render them potent, not only as mundane tools of vital economic practicality but also as components in those distinctly human, socially ubiquitous *technologies of enchantment*.

While trivializing differences between the causal contributions of humans and inanimate, artefactual entities may seem to bring immediate gratification in the rush to do causal justice to the latter, in reality the logic of the Inanimate Agency Proposition does not serve to accentuate the peculiarities of particular artefacts or the possibilities they present; if anything it serves to obscure the character of their significance and indispensability in human societies. This may in itself seem a considerable price to pay for this perspective, but it constitutes only half of the expense that the IAP puts on archaeological ontology. A corresponding and equally burdensome problem is the inability to identify the distinct qualities of *animate agency* that this perspective promotes. As illustrated by the discussion and quotations above, most variants of the IAP in archaeology (e.g. Malafouris 2008; Robb 2004; Watts 2007; Webmoor 2007), like the frameworks of Gell and ANT inspiring them, have assumed that attempts to distinguish human agency from other causal factors would stand or fall with the identification of *intentionality*. Irrespective of the considerable difficulties in defining and delimiting what constitutes 'intentionality', this is in some respects surprising, since some of the most influential, classically anthropocentric theories of agency (which are problematized by the IAP) make no such assumption. For instance, Giddens' theory of structuration very explicitly argued that human agency quite often does *not* rest on (prior) intentionality (e.g. Giddens 1984, 8-12).[17] Nonetheless, staging the assumption of intentionality as a premise for distinguishing human (animate) agency from the causation of (inanimate) objects and structures, and then showing the problems often associated with this premise, has been one of the central strategies used to argue against the possibility or relevance of such distinctions. This is, for instance, the direction taken by Malafouris' 'extended mind' argument discussed above, which depends crucially on the suggestion that '... if intentionality is not an internal property, it cannot be used as the criterion for the attribution of agency to humans' (Malafouris 2008, 33).

Previous discussion here has already hinted that perhaps *intentionality* does not deserve the central theoretical role accorded to it by proponents of the IAP.

Recall that, despite Gell's focus on intentionality, the clearest explanation he was able to provide for maintaining distinction between the causal contributions of human agents and the inanimate entities manipulated by them turned not on 'intentionality' but on something much more basic, namely the fact that humans, as opposed to their 'secondary agents', have the ability to '*initiate actions on their own behalf*' (Gell's 1998, 36, emphasis added). This, of course, is not a capacity unique to humans but one that humans share with all forms of organic life. All living organisms 'initiate actions on their own behalf', i.e. *act*, in the world in order to fulfil (perceived) *needs*, i.e. with purpose. Trees extend their roots towards water, birds sing, carnivores kill and priests administer the Lord's Supper to their congregations. Beyond such general capacity for 'purposive action on their own behalf', of course, there are very substantial differences between the specific ways that different biotic organisms act purposively. But here it is sufficient to note that the capacity to '*initiate actions on their own behalf*' is a common denominator of organic life forms, a defining trait of their *animacy*, and something that distinguishes them from *inanimate* entities.

Such a categorical identification of different types of causal contribution is precisely the kind of distinction that proponents of the IAP in archaeology have argued against. One of these proponents clearly senses the centrality of this challenge, i.e. that a distinction between human and inanimate causal contributions might turn less on 'intentionality' or some other mental feature purportedly unique to humans than on the much more basic quality of *animacy*. Knappett (2005, 11-34) has responded by arguing that it is not so straightforward to define or delimit what does or does not constitute an animate organism, and attempts to illustrate this through a number of examples involving living organisms like mycelial fungi and hermatypic coral. While Knappett intends these examples to show the futility of trying to identify clear physical boundaries of animate organisms, and thus animacy (2005, 15-22), they rather seem to provide excellent illustrations of the impressive degree to which biologists, even in very complex cases of symbioses, have in fact been able to identify and distinguish the many different, discrete organisms involved.[18] However, Knappett extends his argument to consider the role of artificial implants and external devices like respirators that are sometimes involved in supporting the lives of human organisms in modern societies, arguing that it is impossible or meaningless to see such devices as completely detached from the *animacy* of these organisms: 'A life-support machine may be external... but nonetheless it is integrated within the organism's process. As such, it too can be said to partake of animacy' (Knappett 2005, 25). For Knappett, then, '...it is hard to answer anything but "yes" to the following question posed by J. Scott Turner: "If an organism modifies its environment for adaptive purposes, is it fair to say that in doing so it confers a degree of livingness to its apparently inanimate surroundings?" [2000, 6]' (Knappett 2005, 16).[19]

In style with Malafouris' argument on intentionality, Knappett's argument on *animacy* attempts to show that the latter quality is not exclusively something located in the *bodies* of organisms, but rather something *distributed* between organism and environment (Knappett 2005, 23). Given the close association of animacy with *agency* observed by Knappett (2005, 24), this attempt in turn is taken to support the logic underlying the IAP, i.e. that no clear-cut or fruitful distinction can be made between the causal contributions of animate organisms like humans – their *agency* – and those of inanimate entities. However, while Knappett draws attention to several fascinating aspects of human (bio-)technology, which in general say significantly more about modern societies than they do about those of the archaeological past, the degree to which these examples support his attempt to establish the distributed nature of *animacy*, and thus *agency*, seems very limited. Needless to say, as Knappett also notes (2005, 15), organic life, or animacy, is not a static property but one that is fundamentally *processual* (ontogenetically as well as phylogenetically). Individual organisms come into being, exist for a period of time during which they act in and exchange matter with the world, and then die. But, in general, humans (and most other organisms) and their animacy do not have very 'fuzzy boundaries': we have no difficulty in identifying that it is their *delimited bodies* – and not, say, their clothes – that are conceived and born, that may become ill or injured (and have the need for life support), and which die. During the period when the organism is alive, there really does seem to be something that sets it radically apart from inanimate entities. As already noted, biotic organisms, contrary to inanimate things, have *needs* of many different kinds, and they have physical powers to act towards the fulfilment of those needs – if they did not, they would not exist as life forms. Even the most advanced, human-made 'artificial organisms' are strikingly unlike biotic organisms in this respect.[20] Of course, the actions of organisms often have consequences other than the fulfilment striven for, and this aspect is immensely central for understanding their causal impact. But the central point here is that *all biotic organisms depend on the agency of their bodies to live.* To note that all biological organisms evolved and developed to live in specific environments, meaning that in some other environments they will be incapacitated, does not detract from this observation (cf. Ingold 2008).

The points just raised indicate that the 'problem of anthropocentrism' with traditional notions of *agency* in the humanities and social sciences is perhaps not so much that they posit a fundamental difference between the causal qualities of humans and those of the inanimate objects, structures and substances that we depend upon, as it is the fact that they posit a fundamental difference between the causal qualities of humans and those of all the other organic beings with which we co-construct many aspects of the world, and whose life processes and activities we are certainly no less dependent upon than our myriad of artefacts.

Coming back to life in the discipline of things?

This paper has reviewed the Inanimate Agency Proposition and has questioned its usefulness for archaeological ontology. While variants of the IAP constitute explicit attempts to do causal justice to non-human materiality, they are in general founded on theoretical premises which are antithetical to this very agenda – not least the central logic that causal significance is predicated on close causal kinship with *humans*. Further, the IAP is sustained by a more or less synchronic style of causal reckoning, which seems fundamentally inadequate from the temporally sensitive perspective open to archaeology. The discussion above has begun to outline the possibility of an alternative revision of *agency* in archaeology, which is more compatible with the empirical, methodological and epistemological resources of the discipline. Inspired by Alfred Gell's concise diagnosis, 'agency' may be defined as *the physical capacity to initiate actions on one's own behalf.* This makes agency a capacity of all living organisms – albeit one that has dramatically different prerequisites, purposes and consequences across species. All living organisms, not only humans, in some sense 'make history'. Since all actions have consequences extending in time and thus contribute to setting the stage for subsequent actions, all organisms take part in situating themselves and subsequent individuals historically. Though some actions, like sounds and gestures, only have fleeting environmental presence and while many others, such as the inconspicuous exchange of matter between microscopic organisms and their habitat, in general go unnoticed by humans, they all to some extent contribute to defining future environments. All organisms are, in their own way, modifiers of the world, or *niche constructers* (Odling-Smee *et al.* 2003). From this perspective, the difference between the particular causal contributions of humans and other biotic organisms lies not in the basic capacity of *agency* but in the distinct character and complexity of human mental and social life, in the diversity and material potency of human technological action and, crucially, in the way that human agency interacts with its own feedback and feedforward repercussions on the individual and collective levels. This comprises two elements: a) the extent to which humans not only inherit environments modified by previous agency but also culturally particular, socially shared ways of doing things (languages, rituals, technologies, etc.); and b) the unparalleled extent to which these two kinds of inheritance, the environmental inheritance and the inheritance of conventional forms of practice, have potential to change the specific, qualitative *character* of subsequent human agency in the world (Johannsen 2010).

Given that archaeology, in the end, has a legitimate main interest in *humans*, thinking of *agency* as a capacity of all living organisms may seem to some as drastically limiting this concept's relevance to the discipline. But I would put it differently: defining agency in such a manner drastically limits the analytical burden that we expect this one concept to carry. The IAP may be seen as a variant of a broader trend towards attempting to capture as many aspects as possible of the whole causal dynamic involved in the lives of humans – of their motivations, environments, practices and technologies, of their ecological and culture-historical situatedness – using one admired concept, *agency*. This strategy implies a continuous commitment to refining this concept, to adding new forms and aspects of agency, *ad infinitum*. What is suggested here is that, rather than engaging in a Sisyphus project of embedding in *agency* exhaustive understandings and definitions of highly complex phenomena like intentionality, consciousness, personhood, social identity, or the totality of ways in which material environments and practices condition and influence action and thought, i.e. rather than striving for a one-word theory of causation in human life and culture, archaeology may be much better off settling for a much simpler, more restricted and less ambitious concept of *agency* and allowing its attempts to capture the causal complexity of human cultural life to be structured not by the endless elaboration of one concept but by its interplay with many other important notions, like (in alphabetical order) activity, artefact, body, cognition, emotion, environment, history, inheritance, network, power, practice, sociality, structure, technology, and many more. Each of these notions, of course, presents its own theoretical and definitory challenges, but that is a different story.

Notes

1 Bracketed here because archaeologists have in general granted them little attention when discussing the concept of *agency* (a state which the final part of this paper takes initial measures to redress).

2 In this context, as in any other critique of Gell's main statement on agency (1998), it is appropriate to acknowledge that Gell had not finished editing this work when he died (cf. Thomas 1998). It is likely that Gell would have weeded out inconsistencies and internal contradictions if he had had the chance to do so. Nonetheless, the debate must, by necessity, refer to the published, highly influential version of Gell's intended work.

3 Gell (1998, 23) adds the qualifier that '... in the vicinity of art objects, struggles for control are played out in which "patients" intervene in the enchainment of intention, instrument, and result, as "passive agents", that is, intermediaries between ultimate agents and ultimate

patients... The concept of the "patient" is not, therefore a simple one, in that being a "patient" may be a form of (derivative) agency.'

4 Paradoxically, the more diachronically oriented aspects of Gell's theoretical work are perhaps those that have received least attention in archaeology (though see Gosden 2005, 195-96).

5 The fact that Gell scarcely mentions this perspective in *Art and Agency* (though, see 1998, 74) is perhaps indicative of the extent to which his previous conceptual strategy takes things in a different direction – arguably one that would have allowed Gell to develop the strengths of his *magnum opus* more fully. But, of course, in the intellectual market where Gell was trading, *technology* was probably a much harder commodity to sell than *agency*.

6 Once again, however, it is not difficult to find places where Gell strikes a rather different note, for instance: '[That is to say] "social agents" can be drawn from categories which are as different as chalk and cheese (in fact, rather more different) because "social agency" is not defined in terms of "basic" biological attributes (such as inanimate thing vs. incarnate person) but is relational – it does not matter, in ascribing "social agent" status, what a thing (or a person) "is" in itself; what matters is where it stands in a network of social relations' (Gell 1998, 123).

7 Some of the conclusions reached by ANT on this theme bear strong similarities to points emphasized by previous archaeological work on 'stylistic' aspects of artefactual form, not least the discussion by Wobst (1977).

8 In recent years, however, this rejection of the *agency/agent* vocabulary seems to have softened significantly (e.g. Callon & Law 1995; Latour 2005), probably in part for the pragmatic reason that ANT's alternative vocabulary has not achieved the intended currency.

9 For previous uses in archaeology, see for instance Knappett (2005, 30), Knappett & Malafouris (2008, xi-xii), Robb (2004, 131) and Webmoor (2007, 571).

10 So is the provenance of the human being, but this has implications which are of less interest here (since guns cannot produce humans in the way that humans can produce guns).

11 Paraphrasing Latour's own search warrant (1992), these are the 'masses' sent missing by ANT's synchronic perspective on causation.

12 Callon & Law (1997) and Latour (1996b) provide further examples of ANT's effort to render 'the individual', which has been so central to Western philosophy and science, problematic or, at the very least, uninteresting.

13 It is not difficult to see the ostensible compatibility between the temporal scales of ANT's causal analyses and its main interest in *power relations*, i.e. social relations involving the exercise of persuasion, coercion and permission *between people who co-exist* in an environment, who are contemporary (as social relations are normally construed), though not necessarily co-present at any point in time.

14 Apparently, no aspect of this war lacks in political relevance or priority. Proponents of ANT frequently, explicitly or more indirectly, cast the traditional causal emphasis on humans (at the expense of inanimate non-humans) as a kind of 'speciesism' parallel in its hegemonic oppressiveness to such stances as racism and gender chauvinism (for a couple of the more explicit instances, see Callon & Law 1995, 502-4; Law 1991, 16). This parallelization, and the casual play with the chameleonic, liberationist drive of post-modernity that underlies it, clearly raises massive ethical issues.

15 At least one previous critique of ANT in archaeology has also identified it clearly (Glørstad 2008).

16 This is the exception that underlies the profound difference between the overall conclusions invited by Robb's and Olsen's (2007) respective versions of the IAP, to which attention has been drawn above.

17 'Agency refers not to the intentions people have in doing things but to their capability of doing those things in the first place (which is why agency implies power: cf. the Oxford English Dictionary definition of an agent, as "one who exerts power or produces an effect")' (Giddens 1984, 9).

18 If biologists had not gone through the painstaking effort that made such distinctions possible, Knappett would not have been able to provide the information that he does, e.g. that 'mycelial fungi... in certain environmental conditions, form into tubes (hyphae) that branch out to create cellular networks' (2005, 14) or that the microorganism *Mixotricha paradoxa* 'that inhabits the hindgut of a South Australian termite' not only lives in symbiosis with the termite but 'itself carries thousands of spirochetes, spiral-shaped bacteria that actually allow the microbe to swim', that 'The symbiosis is in fact more complicated still, as there are two different species of spirochete involved, and three other kinds of symbiont' and, in summary, that 'each *Mixotricha* host supports and is supported by about one million of the five kinds of symbionts (all prokaryotes)' (2005, 20-21).

19 It might be argued that Knappett's argument here comes closer to the philosophical position of 'hylozoism' (the ascription of life to all matter) than does ANT, which has elsewhere been charged with this form of esotericism (Schaffer 1991).

20 Advocates of the IAP seem in general to ignore one of the core messages that has emerged from several decades of research on and development of artificially intelligent and robotic entities, i.e. that '...there are, for the time being, strong inductive reasons to couple agency with the kind of integrated/integrative adaptive self-maintenance so far solely found in living systems' (Sørensen & Ziemke 2007, 121). In other words, those human-made entities that would appear to be the strongest inanimate, artefactual candidates for 'animate qualities' may *mimic* or simulate the agency of organisms, but as long as they not have bodily *needs* and the associated organismal drive to satisfy them (and thus remain alive, reproduce, etc.), they do not act 'on their own behalf' but on behalf of their makers. Whether or not this state of things is likely to change in the future is an interesting question but, in any case, the outcome will not change the ways in which causal factors, including *agency*, operated in the past societies studied by most archaeologists.

References

Akrich, M. & B. Latour 1992. 'A Summary of a Convenient Vocabulary for the Semiotics of Human and Nonhuman Assemblies'. In: W.E. Bijker & J. Law (eds.), *Shaping Technology/Building Society: Studies in Sociotechnical Change*. Cambridge (MA): MIT Press, 259-64.

Barrett, J.C. 2000. 'A thesis on agency'. In: M.-A. Dobres & J.E. Robb (eds.), *Agency in Archaeology*. London: Routledge, 61-68.

Barrett, J.C. & K.J. Fewster 2000. 'Intimacy and Structural Transformation: Giddens and Archaeology'. In: C. Holtorf & H. Karlsson (eds.), *Philosophy and Archaeological Practice: Perspectives for the 21st Century*. Gothenburg: Bricoleur Press, 25-33.

Berger, P.L. & T. Luckmann 1967. *The Social Construction of Reality: A Treatise in the Sociology of Knowledge*. London: Penguin.

Bijker, W.E. 1995. *Of Bicycles, Bakelites, and Bulbs: Toward a Theory of Sociotechnical Change.* Cambridge (MA): MIT Press.

Bille, M. & T.F. Sørensen 2007. 'An Anthropology of Luminosity: The Agency of Light'. *Journal of Material Culture,* 12(3), 263-84.

Bloor, D. 1999a. 'Anti-Latour'. *Studies in History and Philosophy of Science,* 30(1), 81-112.

Bloor, D. 1999b. 'Reply to Bruno Latour'. *Studies in History and Philosophy of Science,* 30(1), 131-36.

Boast, R. 1997. 'A Small Company of Actors: A Critique of Style'. *Journal of Material Culture,* 2(2), 173-98.

Boivin, N. 2004. 'Mind over Matter? Collapsing the Mind-Matter Dichotomy in Material Culture Studies'. In: E. DeMarrais, C. Gosden, C. Renfrew (eds.), *Rethinking materiality: the engagement of mind with the material world.* Cambridge: McDonald Institute for Archaeological Research, 63-71.

Bourdieu, P. 1977 (1972). *Outline of a Theory of Practice.* Cambridge: Cambridge University Press.

Bourdieu, P. 1990 (1980). *The Logic of Practice.* Cambridge: Polity Press.

Brown, L.A. & W.H. Walker 2008. 'Prologue: Archaeology, Animism and Non-Human Agents'. *Journal of Archaeological Method and Theory,* 15(4), 297-99.

Buchli, V.A. 1995. 'Interpreting material culture: The trouble with text'. In: I. Hodder, M. Shanks, A. Alexandri, V. Buchli, J. Carman, J. Last, G. Lucas (eds.), *Interpreting Archaeology: Finding meaning in the past.* London: Routledge, 181-93.

Callon, M. 1986a. 'Some elements of a sociology of translation: domestication of the scallops and the fishermen of St Brieuc Bay'. In: J. Law (ed.), *Power, Action and Belief: A New Sociology of Knowledge?* London: Routledge & Kegan Paul, 196-233.

Callon, M. 1986b. 'The Sociology of an Actor-Network: The Case of the Electric Vehicle'. In: M. Callon, J. Law, A. Rip (eds.), *Mapping the Dynamics of Science and Technology: Sociology of Science in the Real World.* London: Macmillan, 19-34.

Callon, M. 1991. 'Techno-economic networks and irreversibility'. In: J. Law (ed.), *A Sociology of Monsters: Essays on Power, Technology and Domination.* London: Routledge, 132-61.

Callon, M. & B. Latour 1981. 'Unscrewing the big Leviathan: how actors macro-structure reality and how sociologists help them to do so'. In: K. Knorr-Cetina & A.V. Cicourel (eds.), *Advances in social theory and methodology: Toward an integration of micro- and macro-sociologies.* London: Routledge & Kegan Paul, 277-303.

Callon, M. & B. Latour 1992. 'Don't Throw the Baby Out With the Bath School! A Reply to Collins and Yearley'. In: A. Pickering (ed.), *Science as Practice and Culture.* Chicago: University of Chicago Press, 343-68.

Callon, M. & J. Law 1982. 'On Interests and their Transformation: Enrolment and Counter-Enrolment'. *Social Studies of Science,* 12, 615-25.

Callon, M. & J. Law 1995. 'Agency and the Hybrid *Collectif*. *South Atlantic Quarterly,* 94(2), 481-507.

Callon, M. & J. Law 1997. 'After the Individual in Society: Lessons on Collectivity from Science, Technology and Society'. *Canadian Journal of Sociology,* 22(2), 165-82.

Collins, H.M. & S. Yearley 1992a. 'Epistemological Chicken'. In: A. Pickering (ed.), *Science as Practice and Culture.* Chicago: University of Chicago Press, 301-26.

Collins, H.M. & S. Yearley 1992b. 'Journey Into Space'. In: A. Pickering (ed.), *Science as Practice and Culture.* Chicago: University of Chicago Press, 369-89.

Conkey, M.W. 1990. 'Experimenting with style in archaeology: some historical and theoretical issues'. In: M. Conkey & C. Hastorf (eds.), *The uses of style in archaeology*. Cambridge: Cambridge University Press, 5-17.

Dobres, M.-A. 2000. *Technology and Social Agency: Outlining a Practice Framework for Archaeology*. Oxford: Blackwell.

Dobres, M.-A. & C.R. Hoffman 1994. 'Social Agency and the Dynamics of Prehistoric Technology'. *Journal of Archaeological Method and Theory*, 1(3), 211-58.

Dobres, M.-A. & J.E. Robb 2000a. *Agency in Archaeology*. London: Routledge.

Dobres, M.A. & J.E. Robb 2000b. 'Agency in archaeology: paradigm or platitude?'. In: M.-A. Dobres & J.E. Robb (eds.), *Agency in Archaeology*. London: Routledge, 3-17.

Dobres, M.A. & J.E. Robb 2005. '"Doing" Agency: Introductory Remarks on Methodology'. *Journal of Archaeological Method and Theory*, 12(3), 159-66.

Dornan, J.L. 2002. 'Agency and Archaeology: Past, Present, and Future Directions'. *Journal of Archaeological Method and Theory*, 9(4), 303-29.

Gamble, C. 2007. *Origins and Revolutions: Human Identity in Earliest Prehistory*. Cambridge: Cambridge University Press.

Gell, A. 1992. 'The technology of enchantment and the enchantment of technology'. In: J. Coote & A. Shelton (eds.), *Anthropology, Art and Aesthetics*. Oxford: Clarendon Press, 40-63.

Gell, A. 1998. *Art and Agency: An Anthropological Theory*. Oxford: Clarendon Press.

Giddens, A. 1979. *Central Problems in Social Theory*. London: Macmillan.

Giddens, A. 1984. *The Constitution of Society: Outline of the Theory of Structuration*. Cambridge: Polity Press.

Glørstad, H. 2008. 'Celebrating Materiality: The Antarctic Lesson'. In: H. Glørstad & L. Hedeager (eds.), *Six Essays on the Materiality of Society and Culture*. Gothenburg: Bricoleur Press, 173-211.

Gosden, C. 2001. 'Making sense: archaeology and aesthetics'. *World Archaeology*, 33(2), 163-67.

Gosden, C. 2005. 'What Do Objects Want?' *Journal of Archaeological Method and Theory*, 12(3), 193-211.

Haraway, D.J. 1997. *Modest_Witness@Second_Millenium.FemaleMan©_Meets_OncoMouse™: Feminism and Technoscience*. London: Routledge.

Hegmon, M. & S. Kulow 2005. 'Painting as Agency, Style as Structure: Innovations in Mimbres Pottery Designs From Southwest New Mexico'. *Journal of Archaeological Method and Theory*, 12(4), 313-34.

Hodder, I. 1986. *Reading the past: Current approaches to interpretation in archaeology*. Cambridge: Cambridge University Press.

Ingold, T. 2008. 'When ANT meets SPIDER: Social theory for arthropods'. In: C. Knappett & L. Malafouris (eds.), *Material Agency: Towards a Non-Anthropocentric Approach*. New York: Springer, 209-15.

Joerges, B. 1988. 'Technology in everyday life: Conceptual queries'. *Journal for the Theory of Social Behaviour*, 18(2), 219-37.

Johannsen, N. 2010. 'Technological Conceptualization: Cognition on the Shoulders of History'. In: L. Malafouris & C. Renfrew (eds.), *The Cognitive Life of Things: Recasting the boundaries of the mind*. Cambridge: McDonald Institute for Archaeological Research, 59-69.

Johnson, M.H. 1989. 'Conceptions of Agency in Archaeological Interpretation'. *Journal of Anthropological Archaeology*, 8, 189-211.

Johnson, M.H. 2000. 'Self-made men and the staging of agency'. In: M.-A. Dobres & J.E. Robb (eds.), *Agency in Archaeology*. London: Routledge, 213-31.

Johnson, M.H. 2006. 'On the nature of theoretical archaeology and archaeological theory'. *Archaeological Dialogues*, 13(2), 117-32.

Jones, A. 2002. *Archaeological Theory and Scientific Practice*. Cambridge: Cambridge University Press.

Joyce, R.A. & J. Lopiparo 2005. 'PostScript: Doing Agency in Archaeology'. *Journal of Archaeological Method and Theory*, 12(4), 365-74.

Knappett, C. 2002. 'Photographs, Skeuomorphs and Marionettes: Some Thoughts on Mind, Agency and Object'. *Journal of Material Culture*, 7(1), 97-117.

Knappett, C. 2005. *Thinking Through Material Culture: An Interdisciplinary Perspective*. Philadelphia: University of Pennsylvania Press.

Knappett, C. 2008. 'The Neglected Networks of Material Agency: Artefacts, Pictures and Texts'. In: C. Knappett & L. Malafouris (eds.), *Material Agency: Towards a Non-Anthropocentric Approach*. New York: Springer, 139-56.

Knappett, C. & L. Malafouris 2008. 'Material and Nonhuman Agency: An Introduction'. In: C. Knappett & L. Malafouris (eds.), *Material Agency: Towards a Non-Anthropocentric Approach*. New York: Springer, ix-xix.

Kristiansen 2004. 'Genes versus agents. A discussion of the widening theoretical gap in archaeology'. *Archaeological Dialogues*, 11(2) 77-99.

Latour, B. 1983. 'Give me a laboratory and I will raise the world'. In: K.D. Knorr-Cetina & M. Mulkay (eds.), *Science Observed: Perspectives on the Social Study of Science*. London: Sage, 141-70.

Latour, B. 1987. *Science in Action: How to follow scientists and engineers through society*. Cambridge (MA): Harvard University Press.

Latour, B. 1988. *The Pasteurization of France*. Cambridge (MA): Harvard University Press.

Latour, B. 1991. 'Technology is society made durable'. In: J. Law (ed.), *A Sociology of Monsters: Essays on Power, Technology and Domination*. London: Routledge, 103-31.

Latour, B. 1992. 'Where Are the Missing Masses? The Sociology of a Few Mundane Artifacts'. In: W.E. Bijker & J. Law (eds.), *Shaping Technology/Building Society: Studies in Sociotechnical Change*. Cambridge (MA): MIT Press, 225-58.

Latour, B. 1993 (1991). *We Have Never Been Modern*. Cambridge (MA): Harvard University Press.

Latour, B. 1996a. *Aramis, or, The love of technology*. Cambridge (MA): Harvard University Press.

Latour, B. 1996b. 'Cogito ergo sumus! Or psychology swept inside out by the fresh air of the upper deck ...' *Mind, Culture, and Activity*, 3(1), 54-63.

Latour, B. 1999a. *Pandora's Hope: Essays on the Reality of Science Studies*. Cambridge (MA): Harvard University Press.

Latour, B. 1999b. 'On recalling ANT'. In: J. Law & J. Hassard (eds.), *Actor Network Theory and After*. Oxford: Blackwell, 15-25.

Latour, B. 1999c. 'For David Bloor... and Beyond: A Reply to David Bloor's 'Anti-Latour''. *Studies in History and Philosophy of Science*, 30(1), 113-29.

Latour, B. 2000. 'The Berlin key or how to do words with things'. In: P.M Graves-Brown (ed.), *Matter, Materiality and Modern Culture*. London: Routledge, 10-21.

Latour, B. 2005. *Reassembling the Social: An Introduction to Actor-Network-Theory*. Oxford: Oxford University Press.

Law, J. 1986. 'On the methods of long-distance control: vessels, navigation and the Portuguese route to India'. In: J. Law (ed.), *Power, Action and Belief: A New Sociology of Knowledge?* London: Routledge & Kegan Paul, 234-63.

Law, J. 1991. 'Introduction: monsters, machines and sociotechnical relations'. In: J. Law (ed.), *A Sociology of Monsters: Essays on Power, Technology and Domination*. London: Routledge, 1-23.

Law, J. 1999. 'After ANT: complexity, naming and topology'. In: J. Law & J. Hassard (eds.), *Actor Network Theory and After*. Oxford: Blackwell, 1-14.

Law, J. & M. Callon 1992. 'The Life and Death of an Aircraft: A Network Analysis of Technical Change'. In: W.E. Bijker & J. Law (eds.), *Shaping Technology/Building Society: Studies in Sociotechnical Change*. Cambridge (MA): MIT Press, 21-52.

Malafouris, L. 2008. 'At the Potter's Wheel: An Argument *for* Material Agency'. In: C. Knappett & L. Malafouris (eds.), *Material Agency: Towards a Non-Anthropocentric Approach*. New York: Springer, 19-36.

Martin, A. 2005. 'Agents in Inter-Action: Bruno Latour and Agency'. *Journal of Archaeological Method and Theory*, 12(4), 283-311.

Miller, D. 1982. 'Artefacts as products of human categorisation processes'. In: I. Hodder (ed.), *Symbolic and structural archaeology*. Cambridge: Cambridge University Press, 17-25.

Odling-Smee, F.J., K.N. Laland, M.W. Feldman 2003. *Niche Construction: The Neglected Process in Evolution*. Princeton: Princeton University Press.

Olsen, B. 1987. *Arkeologi, tekst, samfunn. Fragmenter til en post-prosessuell arkeologi*. Tromsø: University of Tromsø.

Olsen, B. 1990. 'Roland Barthes: From Sign to Text'. In: C. Tilley (ed.), *Reading Material Culture: Structuralism, Hermeneutics and Post-Structuralism*. Oxford: Blackwell, 163-205.

Olsen, B. 1997. *Fra ting til tekst: Teoretiske perspektiv i arkeologisk forskning*. Oslo: Universitetsforlaget.

Olsen, B. 2003. 'Material Culture after Text: Re-Membering Things'. *Norwegian Archaeological Review*, 36(2), 87-104.

Olsen, B. 2006a. 'Archaeology, hermeneutics of suspicion and phenomenological trivialization'. *Archaeological Dialogues*, 13(2), 144-50.

Olsen, B. 2006b. 'Scenes from a Troubled Engagement: Post-Structuralism and Material Culture Studies'. In: C. Tilley, W. Keane, S. Küchler, M. Rowlands, P. Spyer (eds.), *Handbook of Material Culture*. London: Sage, 85-103.

Olsen, B. 2007. 'Keeping things at arm's length: a genealogy of asymmetry'. *World Archaeology*, 39(4), 579-88.

Pickering, A. 1992. 'From Science as Knowledge to Science as Practice'. In: A. Pickering (ed.), *Science as Practice and Culture*. Chicago: University of Chicago Press, 1-26.

Pickering, A. 1995. *The Mangle of Practice: Time, Agency, and Science*. Chicago: University of Chicago Press.

Robb, J.E. 2004. 'The Extended Artefact and the Monumental Economy: a Methodology for Material Agency'. In: E. DeMarrais, C. Gosden, C. Renfrew (eds.), *Rethinking materiality: the engagement of mind with the material world*. Cambridge: McDonald Institute for Archaeological Research, 131-39.

Schaffer, S. 1991. 'The Eighteenth Brumaire of Bruno Latour'. *Studies in History and Philosophy of Science*, 22(1), 174-92.

Schiffer, M.B. 1999. *The Material Life of Human Beings: Artifacts, behavior, and communication*. London: Routledge.

Shanks, M. & C. Tilley 1982. 'Ideology, symbolic power and ritual communication: a reinterpretation of Neolithic mortuary practices'. In: I. Hodder (ed.), *Symbolic and structural archaeology*. Cambridge: Cambridge University Press, 129-54.

Silliman, S. 2001. 'Agency, practical politics and the archaeology of culture contact'. *Journal of Social Archaeology*, 1(2), 190-209.

Smith, A.T. 2001. 'The limitations of doxa: Agency and subjectivity from an archaeological point of view'. *Journal of Social Archaeology*, 1(2), 155-71.

Strum, S.S. & B. Latour 1987. 'Redefining the social link: from baboons to humans'. *Social Science Information*, 26, 783-802.

Sørensen, M.H. & T. Ziemke 2007. 'Agents without Agency?' *Cognitive Semiotics*, 0, 102-24.

Thomas, N. 1998. 'Foreword'. In: A. Gell, *Art and Agency: An Anthropological Theory*. Oxford: Clarendon Press, vii-xiii.

Tilley, C. (ed.) 1990. *Reading Material Culture: Structuralism, Hermeneutics and Post-Structuralism*. Oxford: Blackwell.

Tilley, C. 1991. *Material Culture and Text: The Art of Ambiguity*. London: Routledge.

Turner, J.S. 2000. *The Extended Organism: The Physiology of Animal-Built Structures*. Cambridge (MA): Harvard University Press.

Watts, C.M. 2007. 'From purification to mediation: overcoming artifactual 'otherness' with and in Actor-Network Theory'. *Journal of Iberian Archaeology*, 9/10, 39-54.

Watts, C.M. 2008. 'On Mediation and Material Agency in the Peircean Semeiotic'. In: C. Knappett & L. Malafouris (eds.), *Material Agency: Towards a Non-Anthropocentric Approach*. New York: Springer, 187-207.

Webmoor, T. 2007. 'What about 'one more turn after the social' in archaeological reasoning? Taking things seriously'. *World Archaeology*, 39(4), 563-78.

Webmoor, T. & C.L. Witmore 2008. 'Things Are Us! A Commentary on Human/Things Relations under the Banner of a 'Social' Archaeology'. *Norwegian Archaeological Review*, 41(1), 53-70.

Witmore, C.L. 2007. 'Symmetrical archaeology: excerpts of a manifesto'. *World Archaeology*, 39(4), 546-62.

Wobst, H.M. 1977. 'Stylistic Behavior and Information Exchange'. In: C.E. Cleland (ed.), *Papers for the Director: Research Essays in Honor of James B. Griffin*. Ann Arbor: Museum of Anthropology, University of Michigan, 317-42.